MW00603855

"Clifton Black has long been regarded as one of our most sensitive and insightful readers of Scripture. Now Professor Black joins Jesus in teaching us how to pray in the name of Jesus. This is a beautiful, encouraging book that pastors and congregations will find quite useful in deepening their prayer life."

—Will Willimon, United Methodist Bishop (retired), Professor
of the Practice of Christian Ministry, Duke Divinity School,
and author of *How Odd of God: Chosen for the Curious
Vocation of Preaching*

"Clifton Black spreads a feast of learning and thought in this splendid volume on the Lord's Prayer. In addition to a rich analysis of the Prayer itself in the context of the Gospels and ancient culture, he shows its theological depth and its ecumenical possibilities. As lagniappe, he provides a glimpse of the history of the interpretation of Jesus' prayer. A book valuable both to scholars and pastors."

—Luke Timothy Johnson, Robert W. Woodruff Professor
Emeritus of New Testament and Christian Origins,
Emory University

"The words are as familiar as any in the language, prayed every day for two thousand years, in gorgeous liturgy, uttered by frightened men and women facing danger, offered at weddings and funerals and by the bedsides of seriously ill patients, whispered before sleep, and commented on by biblical scholars and theologians in every age. Clifton Black has written a consummate and comprehensive, scholarly but accessible book, helpfully placing the Prayer in the context of the Greco-Roman world and the spiritual traditions of first-century Judaism. If you have only one book on the Lord's Prayer, this should be it—an invaluable resource for thoughtful readers, seekers, and preachers and teachers alike."

—John M. Buchanan, Fourth Presbyterian Church of Chicago
and former Editor/Publisher, *The Christian Century*

"The Lord's Prayer is Christ's precious gift to the church and world. Wisely, Clifton Black has been entrusted to guide us through it. The Prayer could not be in better hands. Faithful to its purpose, learned in its history of interpretation, and, most of all, pastoral in his exposition, Black leads us through the simple words many of us recite every day. This beautiful book will add a second blessing to the Prayer and help us hear it anew."

—Richard Lischer, James T. and Alice Mead Cleland Professor
Emeritus of Preaching at Duke Divinity School and author
of *Reading the Parables* and *Stations of the Heart*

"Faced with this book on the Lord's Prayer, I have three questions. Do I agree with all the interpretations? No, but the range of material discussed here is so rich that I can think about them afresh for myself. Did I go along with all the theology? No, but the larger context here, from the prayers of ancient Greece, Rome, and Israel to those of spiritual and theological giants of every age, has opened my eyes to unguessed treasures. Did it make me want to pray and give me fresh resources to do so? Yes. Abundantly. That's what matters."

—N. T. Wright, former Bishop of Durham and Professor
of New Testament and Early Christianity at
the University of St Andrews, Scotland

"Black provides a detailed exegetical commentary on the Lord's Prayer, with careful analysis of the difficulties of this beloved and well-known text. At the same time, he offers a rich theological commentary on the Prayer, sensitive to its lengthy history of interpretation and to the challenges facing contemporary Christians. This volume will be a welcome resource for pastors and for theologically engaged students of the New Testament."

—Harold W. Attridge, Sterling Professor of Divinity,
Yale Divinity School

The Lord's Prayer

INTERPRETATION

Resources for the Use of Scripture in the Church

INTERPRETATION

RESOURCES FOR THE USE OF SCRIPTURE IN THE CHURCH

Samuel E. Balentine, *Series Editor*
Ellen F. Davis, *Associate Editor*
Richard B. Hays, *Associate Editor*
Susan E. Hylen, *Associate Editor*
Brent A. Strawn, *Associate Editor*
Patrick D. Miller, *Consulting Editor*

OTHER AVAILABLE BOOKS IN THE SERIES

Markus Bockmuehl, *Ancient Apocryphal Gospels*
Walter Brueggemann, *Money and Possessions*
Ronald P. Byars, *The Sacraments in Biblical Perspective*
Jerome F. D. Creach, *Violence in Scripture*
Ellen F. Davis, *Biblical Prophecy: Perspectives for
Christian Theology, Discipleship, and Ministry*
Robert W. Jenson, *Canon and Creed*
Luke Timothy Johnson, *Miracles: God's Presence
and Power in Creation*
Richard Lischer, *Reading the Parables*
Patrick D. Miller, *The Ten Commandments*

C. CLIFTON BLACK

The Lord's Prayer

INTERPRETATION *Resources for the Use of
Scripture in the Church*

WESTMINSTER
JOHN KNOX PRESS
LOUISVILLE · KENTUCKY

© 2018 C. Clifton Black

First edition
Published by Westminster John Knox Press
Louisville, Kentucky

18 19 20 21 22 23 24 25 26 27—10 9 8 7 6 5 4 3 2 1

All rights reserved. No part of this book may be reproduced or transmitted in any form or by any means, electronic or mechanical, including photocopying, recording, or by any information storage or retrieval system, without permission in writing from the publisher. For information, address Westminster John Knox Press, 100 Witherspoon Street, Louisville, Kentucky 40202-1396. Or contact us online at www.wjkbooks.com.

Unless otherwise indicated, Scripture quotations are from the New Revised Standard Version of the Bible, copyright © 1989 by the Division of Christian Education of the National Council of the Churches of Christ in the U.S.A., and are used by permission.

Scripture quotations marked JB are from *The Jerusalem Bible*, copyright © 1966, 1967, 1968 by Darton, Longman & Todd, Ltd., and Doubleday & Co., Inc. Used by permission of the publishers.

Scripture quotations marked NIV are from *The Holy Bible, New International Version*. Copyright © 1973, 1978, 1984, 2011 by Biblica, Inc.® Used by permission. All rights reserved worldwide.

Scripture quotations marked NJB are from *The New Jerusalem Bible*, copyright © 1985 by Darton, Longman & Todd, Ltd., and Doubleday, a division of Bantam Doubleday Dell Publishing Group, Inc. Reprinted by permission of the publisher(s).

Scripture quotations marked NJPS are from *The TANAKH: The New JPS Translation according to the Traditional Hebrew Text*. Copyright 1985 by the Jewish Publication Society. Used by permission.

Scripture quotations marked REB are from *The Revised English Bible*, copyright © Oxford University Press and Cambridge University Press, 1989. Used by permission.

Scripture quotations marked RSV are from the Revised Standard Version of the Bible, copyright © 1946, 1952, 1971, and 1973 by the Division of Christian Education of the National Council of the Churches of Christ in the U.S.A., and are used by permission.

See page v, "Permissions," for other permissions information.

Book design by Drew Stevens
Cover design by designpointinc.com

Library of Congress Cataloging-in-Publication Data

Names: Black, C. Clifton (Carl Clifton), 1955– author.
Title: The Lord's Prayer / C. Clifton Black.
Description: First edition. I Louisville, KY : Westminster John Knox Press, 2018. I
Series: Interpretation: resources for the use of Scripture in the church I
Includes bibliographical references and index. I
Identifiers: LCCN 2018036065 (print) I LCCN 2018036574 (ebook) I ISBN
9781611648935 I ISBN 9780664234898 (hbk.)
Subjects: LCSH: Lord's prayer—Criticism, interpretation, etc.
Classification: LCC BV230 (ebook) I LCC BV230 .B57 2018 (print) I DDC
226.9/906—dc23
LC record available at https://lccn.loc.gov/2018036065

♾ The paper used in this publication meets the minimum requirements of the American National Standard for Information Sciences—Permanence of Paper for Printed Library Materials, ANSI Z39.48-1992.

Westminster John Knox Press advocates the responsible use of our natural resources. The text paper of this book is made from 30% post-consumer waste.

Most Westminster John Knox Press books are available at special quantity discounts when purchased in bulk by corporations, organizations, and special-interest groups. For more information, please e-mail SpecialSales@wjkbooks.com.

PERMISSIONS

This page constitutes a continuation of the copyright page. The author and publisher express sincere appreciation to the following agencies for their kind permission to reproduce excerpts from the following, previously published works:

C. Clifton Black. "The Education of Human Wanting: Formation by *Pater Noster*." Excerpts from *Character and Scripture: Moral Formation, Community, and Biblical Interpretation*, edited by William P. Brown, 248–63. Grand Rapids and Cambridge: Wm. B. Eerdmans Publishing Company, 2002. All rights reserved.

C. Clifton Black. "Sin in the Synoptic Gospels." Excerpts from *The T&T Clark Companion to the Doctrine of Sin*, edited by Keith L. Johnson and David Lauber, 61–78. London and Edinburgh: Bloomsbury Publishing / T&T Clark / Continuum, 2016. All rights reserved.

C. Clifton Black. "Whose Kingdom? Whose Power? Whose Glory?" In *Horizons in Biblical Theology* 36 (2014): 1–20. Copyright © 2014 by E. J. Brill Publishers. All rights reserved.

Edna St. Vincent Millay. Excerpt from "And must I then, indeed, Pain, live with you?" From *Collected Poems*. Copyright 1954, © 1982 by Norma Millay Ellis. Used with the permission of The Permissions Company, Inc., on behalf of Holly Peppe, Literary Executor, The Edna St. Vincent Millay Society, www.millay.org.

The author and publisher extend special thanks to Claire Weatherhead of Bloomsbury Publishing for her help with copyright status research.

AD HONOREM

Dale C. Allison Jr.

George L. Parsenios

CONTENTS

SERIES FOREWORD

This series of volumes supplements Interpretation: A Bible Commentary for Teaching and Preaching. The commentary series offers an exposition of the books of the Bible written for those who teach, preach, and study the Bible in the community of faith. This new series is addressed to the same audience and serves a similar purpose, providing additional resources for the interpretation of Scripture, but now dealing with features, themes, and issues significant for the whole rather than with individual books.

The Bible is composed of separate books. Its composition naturally has led its interpreters to address particular books. But there are other ways to approach the interpretation of the Bible that respond to other characteristics and features of the Scriptures. These other entries to the task of interpretation provide contexts, overviews, and perspectives that complement the book-by-book approach and discern dimensions of the Scriptures that the commentary design may not adequately explore.

The Bible as used in the Christian community is not only a collection of books but also itself a book that has a unity and coherence important to its meaning. Some volumes in this new series will deal with this canonical wholeness and seek to provide a wider context for the interpretation of individual books as well as a comprehensive theological perspective that reading single books does not provide.

Other volumes in the series will examine particular texts, like the Ten Commandments, the Lord's Prayer, and the Sermon on the Mount, texts that have played such an important role in the faith and life of the Christian community that they constitute orienting foci for the understanding and use of Scripture.

A further concern of the series will be to consider important and often difficult topics, addressed at many different places in the books of the canon, that are of recurrent interest and concern to the church in its dependence on Scripture for faith and life. So the series will include volumes dealing with such topics as eschatology, women, wealth, and violence.

The books of the Bible are constituted from a variety of kinds of literature such as narrative, laws, hymns and prayers, letters, parables, miracle stories. To recognize and discern the contribution and importance of all these different kinds of material enriches and enlightens the use of Scripture. Volumes in the series will provide help in the interpretation of Scripture's literary forms and genres.

The liturgy and practices of the gathered church are anchored in Scripture, as with the sacraments observed and the creeds recited. So another entry to the task of discerning the meaning and significance of biblical texts explored in this series is the relation between the liturgy of the church and the Scriptures.

Finally, there is certain ancient literature, such as the Apocrypha and the noncanonical gospels, that constitutes an important context to the interpretation of Scripture itself. Consequently, this series will provide volumes that offer guidance in understanding such writings and explore their significance for the interpretation of the Protestant canon.

The volumes in this second series of Interpretation deal with these important entries into the interpretation of the Bible. Together with the commentaries, they compose a library of resources for those who interpret Scripture as members of the community of faith. Each of them can be used independently for its own significant addition to the resources for the study of Scripture. But all of them intersect the commentaries in various ways and provide an important context for their use. The authors of these volumes are biblical scholars and theologians who are committed to the service of interpreting the Scriptures in and for the church. The editors and authors hope that the addition of this series to the commentaries will provide a major contribution to the vitality and richness of biblical interpretation in the church.

The Editors

ACKNOWLEDGMENTS

Since accepting the invitation in 2008 to write this commentary—can a full decade have slipped away?—I have accrued more than the usual number of debts in its preparation. Early drafts have been presented to Princeton Theological Seminarians in a regularly offered course, "Prayer in the New Testament," as well as to members of Virginia's Williamsburg Presbyterian Church (2000) and Doylestown Presbyterian Church in Pennsylvania (2013). I was also honored to offer portions of what follows to the College of Arts and Sciences at the University of South Carolina as the Nadine Beacham and Charlton F. Hall Sr. Visiting Lecturer in New Testament (2013) and to Saint Michael and All Angels Episcopal Church, Dallas, as the Robert E. Ratelle Distinguished Lecturer on Faith and Culture (2016). To all my listeners on these varied occasions, I tender appreciation for their gracious hospitality.

Because this volume is intended as a resource for Scripture's use in the church, I knew from the start that guidance from some clerical leaders was imperative. Accordingly I solicited the counsel of twoscore pastors and priests across the United States: What questions did they hope a book such as this might answer? Whether I have addressed all their queries is impossible for me to say, but each deserves thanks for answering my plea: Gregory Bezilla, Michael Cave, Oscar Dowdle, Nan Duerling, Gregory Gibson, Gayle Kerr, Michael Lindvall, Elisa Owen, Fleming Rutledge, Gretchen Sausville, Patrick Willson, and Claude Young. Melanie Howard, my former research assistant, now Assistant Professor of Biblical and Religious Studies at Fresno Pacific University, and Kate Skrebutenas, ace Reference Librarian, helped me to mine the rich veins of the Princeton Theological Seminary Library.

For the original summons to this journey, I am beholden to Patrick Miller, a founding editor of the Interpretation series. His successor, Samuel Balentine, gave me the periodic, kindly boosts I needed to complete it. Sam's associate editor, Susan Hylen, worked with care and efficiency through the entire manuscript, spurring me to make my points clearer, more accurate, and more helpful. In competence and good humor my editors and proofreaders at

Westminster John Knox have few peers and no superiors: Jon Berquist, Marianne Blickenstaff, Bridgett Green, S. David Garber, Tina E. Noll, and Daniel Braden. For their expert preparation of the indexes of ancient sources and subjects, I thank, respectively, S. David Garber and Kathleen Strattan. For their encouragement I am grateful to Harold Attridge, James Black, Charles Bachus, Maria Massi Dakake, Heath Dewrell, Peter Ochs, and †Moody Smith. Above all I thank Harriet Black, without whom nothing would get done or seem worth doing.

C. C. B.
The Epiphany of the Lord
January 6, 2018
Princeton, New Jersey

ABBREVIATIONS

General

=	equals, is parallel to, is similar to
¶(¶)	paragraph(s)
§(§)	section(s)
×	times
AD	anno Domini, "in the year of [our] Lord"
alt.	altered
ASV	Authorized Standard Version (1901)
AT	author's translation
b.	Babylonian Talmud (b. preceding the title of a tractate)
BC	before Christ
BDAG	Danker, Frederick W., Walter Bauer, William F. Arndt, and F. Wilbur Gingrich. *A Greek-English Lexicon of the New Testament and Other Early Christian Literature*. 3rd ed. University of Chicago Press, 2001
c.	century
ca.	circa, about
CASSIRER	Cassirer, Heinz W., trans. *God's New Covenant: A New Testament Translation*. Eerdmans, 1989
CD	Barth, Karl. *Church Dogmatics*. Translated by Geoffrey W. Bromiley and Thomas F. Torrance. 14 vols. T&T Clark, 1936–77
CEB	Common English Bible (2011)
cf.	*confer*, compare
chap.	chapter
CIL	*Corpus Inscriptionum Latinarum*. Editio altera. Reimerum, 1893
DSST	*The Dead Sea Scrolls Translated: The Qumran Tests in English*, trans. Florentino García Martínez and Wilfred G. E. Watson. E. J. Brill, 1994.
ed(s).	editor(s), edited by
esp.	especially

et al.	*et alii*, and others
frag.	fragment
Gk.	Greek
GNB	Good News Bible (1976)
GOODSPEED	Goodspeed, Edgar J., trans. *The New Testament: An American Translation*. University of Chicago Press, 1923
Heb.	Hebrew
j.	Jerusalem Talmud (*j.* preceding the title of a tractate)
JB	Jerusalem Bible (1955)
KJV	King James Version
LATTIMORE	Lattimore, Richmond, trans. *The New Testament*. Farrar, Straus & Giroux, 1996
LCL	Loeb Classical Library
LXX	Septuagint
m.	Mishnah (*m.* preceding the title of a tractate)
MOFFATT	Moffatt, James, trans. *The Holy Bible Containing the Old and New Testaments*. University of Chicago Press, 1922
NAB	New American Bible (1970)
NEB	New English Bible (1970)
NIV	New International Version (1978)
NJB	New Jerusalem Bible (1985)
NJPS	*Tanakh: The Holy Scriptures*. Jewish Publication Society, 1985
NRSV	New Revised Standard Version (1989)
OEBT	*The Oxford Encyclopedia of the Bible and Theology*. Edited by Samuel E. Balentine. 2 vols. Oxford University Press, 2015
OTP	*The Old Testament Pseudepigrapha*. Edited by James H. Charlesworth. 2 vols. Doubleday & Company, 1983, 1985
par(s).	and parallel(s)
REB	Revised English Bible (1989)
rev.	revised
RSV	Revised Standard Version (1952)
TDNT	*Theological Dictionary of the New Testament*. Edited by Gerhard Kittel and Gerhard Friedrich. 10 vols. Eerdmans, 1977

trans.	translator, translated by
vol(s).	volume(s)

Dead Sea Scrolls

1QH	*Thanksgiving Hymns (Hodayot)*
1QM	*War Scroll*
1QS	*Rule of the Community*
4Q280	*4QBlessings^f*
4Q286	*4QBlessings^a*
4Q508	*4QFestival Prayers^b*
11QPs^a	*11QPsalms^a*

Pseudepigrapha

As. Mos.	*Assumption of Moses*
2 Bar.	*2 Baruch*
1 En.	*1 Enoch*
Jub.	*Jubilees*
Pss. Sol.	*Psalms of Solomon*
Sib. Or.	*Sibylline Oracles*
T. Dan	*Testament of Dan*
T. Mos.	*Testament of Moses*
T. Sol.	*Testament of Solomon*

Apostolic Fathers

Barn.	*Barnabas*
2 Clem.	*2 Clement*
Did.	*Didache*
Herm.	*Shepherd of Hermas*
Mart. Pol.	*Martyrdom of Polycarp*
Pol. Phil.	Polycarp, *To the Philippians*

INTRODUCTION

Pray as you can, and do not try to pray as you can't. Take yourself as you find yourself, and start from that.

—Dom John Chapman

The purification of desire, the education of human wanting, is one of the principal ways in which God answers prayer. It is always a reduction, which reaches its culmination in the single desire for God himself and his kingdom.

—J. Neville Ward

If asked to write on the back of an envelope what I believed about the Lord's Prayer, its intent and efficacy, I would scribble "the education of human wanting." Neville Ward's apt phrase identifies two basic, intersecting dimensions of all prayer, crystallized in the Lord's Prayer. When praying as Jesus taught his disciples, we enroll ourselves in a twofold curriculum: one of *ēducere* (Latin, "to lead out") and of *ēducāre* ("to bring up"). The first of these cognate terms refers to the drawing out of our latent potentialities; the second refers to our habits, manners, and intellectual aptitudes. The Lord's Prayer explicates who we truly are: creatures made in God's image, warped by sin and under restoration by God's Holy Spirit. Simultaneously, the Prayer trains what we are becoming: God's obedient children, whose minds are renewed by God's merciful will (Rom. 12:2).

By that double-pronged education, the Prayer reforms our manifold "wanting" as human creatures. What we most profoundly *need* is evoked and exposed. What we most ardently *desire* is developed and disciplined. Each petition of the Lord's Prayer contributes to this complex, lifelong process. Perhaps that is why, notwithstanding the apostle Paul's frank admission that we do not know how to pray as we ought, the prayer Jesus gave his followers articulates something more than "sighs too deep for words" (Rom. 8:26). Jesus' model prayer meets us where we are and quickens us to pray as we can, not as we can't.

Viewed from that vantage, the Lord's Prayer—indeed, every prayer in conformity with Jesus' attitude and instruction, his life and death—is *always* answered, for the simple reason that we cannot make such petitions as he taught us without simultaneously receiving them.

> So I tell you, whatever you ask for in prayer, believe that you have received it, and it will be yours. (Mark 11:24; cf. Matt. 21:21)

> I write these things to you who believe in the name of the Son of God, so that you may know that you have eternal life. And this is the boldness we have in him, that if we ask anything according to his will, he hears us. And if we know that he hears us in whatever we ask, we know that we have obtained the requests made of him. (1 John 5:13–15)

Regrettably, too many Christians regard the God to whom they pray as a celestial slot machine. "Answered prayer" is believed to be getting what we want: if we're lucky or if God is paying attention, the spinning wheels will land on three cherries and we'll hit the jackpot. Nowhere in Scripture is prayer so presented. The biblical God is trusted to listen and to fulfill our *needs*, even when they do not jibe with our *wants*. If God granted our every wish, we would have serious reason to doubt the wisdom of God.

The key ingredient is prayer offered *in accordance with God's will*, which in one way or another preoccupies the Lord's Prayer in its entirety. It is impossible for us to ask that God's name be made holy and God's will be done—that the meaning of human existence be redefined by the authority of one God who is Father and King—without the breakthrough or amplification of that power in our own lives. To ask it is to receive it. For that reason most of what is dismissed as "unanswered prayer" is a misnomer: an unreflective description of something we have requested that falls short of God's glory, defies God's beneficent intent, or disappoints our foreshortened vision or unworthy aspirations. In a strict sense there's no such thing as unanswered Christian prayer. If the God to whom we appeal in the Lord's Prayer is what we want, then that, most assuredly, is what we shall get.

In writing this book for the church's preachers and teachers, my hope is to help them pray the prayer Jesus taught his disciples with better understanding and deeper appreciation. Despite its familiarity and apparent simplicity, the Prayer contains words and phrases hard to understand. As a whole it issues from a culture that, while at some points comparable to ours, is also very different. This is true of all Scripture. On many occasions I shall ask my readers to flex their exegetical muscles, in an honest attempt to recover what we need to know—linguistically, historically, socially, and religiously—about the Prayer, so that it may speak to us more intelligibly. The metaphor that seems to me most apt, which I suggest to my students and have elaborated elsewhere ("Trinity and Exegesis," 26), is one I have pilfered from the saints of the church. Scripture, wrote Bernard of Clairvaux (1090–1153), is a love letter addressed to us from the God who wants to marry us (*Sermons on the Song of Songs* 83.3; see Dumontier, *Saint Bernard et la Bible*, 86–97). "You are reading? No, your betrothed is talking to you. It is your betrothed, Christ, who is united with you [cf. 2 Cor. 11:2]. He tears you away from the solitude of the desert and brings you into his home, saying to you, 'Enter into the joy of your Lord'" (anonymous, but attributed to Jerome [ca. 342–430] by Špidlík, *Drinking from the Hidden Fountain*, 16). If this be so, then we who read these billets-doux should want to learn everything we can about our Lover: the messengers through whom that love is conveyed (prophets and psalmists, evangelists and apostles), the foreign languages they spoke (Hebrew, Aramaic, Greek, and Latin), and the strange worlds they inhabited (Mesopotamia and Caesar's empire). Historical inquiry of the sort undertaken in this volume is governed, finally, not by science (*scientia*) but by love (*caritas*).

In each of the following chapters I shall also tender theological reflections on the Prayer's several petitions. I neither ask nor expect my readers to agree with my assessments at every point or, for that matter, at any point. Every interpreter must come to terms with Scripture's claims for oneself. My aim is only to invite those using this book to engage some larger conversations that I consider important and pertinent to the concerns of the Prayer that Jesus taught his disciples. I hope that my comments in those veins will prompt readers to frame better questions than mine, as well as answers more congruent with Christian faith and theological reason.

Finally, this volume is offered with confidence in the power of our Lord's Prayer for the formation of Christian character. Inherently fertile, the Prayer accomplishes that which God purposes (cf. Isa. 55:11). It is impossible for us to pray it and remain unreconstructed by the mind of Christ (cf. 1 Cor. 2:16). By its praying, measure by measure, grace softens our self-centeredness, and love enlarges our noblest capacities: trust in our heavenly Father, desire that God's name and all creation be sanctified, regarding our fellow creatures with merciful eyes. The Lord's Prayer is nothing other than Christ's own curriculum in the education of human wanting.

Works Cited in the Introduction

Black, C. Clifton. "Trinity and Exegesis." In *Reading Scripture with the Saints*, 8–34. Cascade Books. Eugene, OR: Wipf & Stock, 2014.

Chapman, Dom John. *The Spiritual Letters of Dom John Chapman*. London: Sheed & Ward, 1935.

Dumontier, Pierre. *Saint Bernard et la Bible*. Bibliothèque de spiritualité médiévale. Paris: Desclée de Brouwer, 1953.

Špidlík, Tomáš, ed. *Drinking from the Hidden Fountain: A Patristic Breviary*. Kalamazoo, MI: Cistercian Publications, 1994.

Ward, J. Neville. *The Use of Praying*. Peterborough: Epworth Press, 1998.

PART ONE

Getting Our Bearings

The Religious World of the Lord's Prayer
Prayer in the Gospels

The Religious World
of the Lord's Prayer

You can safely assume that you've created God in your own image when it turns out that God hates all the same people you do.

—Anne Lamott

According to Luke (11:1), one of Jesus' disciples requested that he teach them how to pray. That was no silly question with an obvious answer. Many options were available to them. Doubtless his disciples truly wanted to know how Jesus prayed and thus how they should pray. That serious question sets the stage for this chapter.

Religious devotion is among humanity's oldest, most pervasive, and multifaceted activities. Where there is religion, there is prayer. Some anthropologists reckon prayer as old as any known cultural artifact and as universal, perhaps, as language itself. "Prayers have this diagnostic value: they present in microcosm the longings, beliefs, ideals, and assumptions that drive the inner life of individuals and the corporate life of human cultures. In prayer, the dreams of a civilization take lucid and articulate form" (Zaleski and Zaleski, *Prayer*, 15). Prayer is primary speech: a form of human discourse that reaches for the godly, coordinating tongue with head and heart and gut. Enough evidence from antiquity survives to support these assessments; however, those remains are somewhat spotty and uneven in quality. Again, no surprise: like us, most of our forebears prayed without committing their prayers to writing. They had no Book of Common Prayer: their religious beliefs were too diverse.

3

Prayers uttered in ritual were deliberately formalized; prayers inscribed upon buildings adopted ceremonial rhetoric; prayers uttered by dramatic characters were artistic fictions. We may assume enough verisimilitude that ancient audiences would have recognized all these as prayers. Possibly the wording of such public specimens molded that of informal prayers, much as a regular churchgoer today might reflexively confess, "We have left undone those things which we ought to have done, and we have done those things which we ought not to have done."

It is impossible to know with the precision we desire how most of Jesus' ancestors and contemporaries prayed. Nevertheless, the effort to reconstruct that is not wasted. Jesus himself was heir to a rich, multicultural tradition of prayer. It is important to recognize those points at which the prayer taught to his disciples intersects with that heritage. It is equally important to perceive where that prayer deviates from religious patterns of his own day. This chapter presents, not a clear photograph, but an impressionist painting of prayer in that world where Jesus was born. We shall be less concerned about what the ancients said about prayer, more interested in how they prayed—insofar as that may be recovered from literary remains.

Prayer in Greco-Roman Religions

Ancient Greece (ca. 850 BC–AD 50)

Although many aspects of prayer in classical Greece are controversial, Simon Pulleyn (*Prayer in Greek Religion*) has identified some constant elements. First, ancient Greeks believed in many gods, inscrutable though not necessarily omniscient, who desired *timē*: "honor" or "esteem in others' eyes" (Euripides, *Hippolytus* 1). Second, offering an appropriate gift (*charis*, "something pleasing"), mortals, whether kings or commoners, invoked the gods for specific benefits (Plato, *Timaeus* 27c). Third, those offerings were typically accompanied by cultic ritual (Plato, *Statesman* 290cd). Fourth, because the Greeks did not share Israel's sense of sin as disobedience of divine commandments, Greek prayers were not motivated to repair a broken relationship. They attempted, instead, to establish a quid pro quo between mortals and gods: "Give to me because I have given to you." Commonplace in ancient Greek prayers was the conditional, gently coercive construction *ei pote*: "if

4

ever" a god has bestowed favor to a generous petitioner in the past, such beneficence may again be counted upon.

> Hear me [Apollo], you of the silver bow, who protects Chryse and holy Cilla and rules with might over Tenedos: if ever I [Chyrses, the priest] have roofed over for you a pleasing temple or burnt up for you fat thighs of bulls or goats, fulfill for me this wish: may the Danaans pay for my tears by your arrows. (Homer, *Iliad* 1.37–42, trans. S. Pulleyn)

> Lady [Artemis], you who saved me before in the glades of Aulis from my father's terrible, murderous hand, save me again, and these people, too. (Euripides, *Iphigenia in Tauris* 1082–84, trans. Pulleyn)

As Pulleyn notes, the pattern for such prayer corresponds with the terms of hospitality assumed by ancient guests of their hosts: "I entreat you [Nestor], if ever my father, noble Odysseus, performed for you some word or deed that he had promised, remember these now, I [Telemachus] ask you" (Homer, *Odyssey* 3.98–101, trans. Pulleyn).

Petitioners sought the gods for all manner of reasons: advice in business affairs, magical incantations for self-improvement, and cries for rescue from beyond the grave.

> O Lord Sarapis Helios, beneficent one. [Say] whether it is fitting that my son Phanias and his wife should not agree now with his father, but oppose him and not make a contract. Tell me this truly. Farewell. (Question to an oracle, Oxyrhynchus Papyrus 1148 [1st c. AD], trans. Pulleyn)

> Everyone fears Your Great Might. Grant me the good things: the strength of AKRYSKYLOS, the speech of EUONOS, the eyes of Solomon, the voice of ABRASAX, the grace of ADONIOS the god. Come to me, Kypris, every day! The Hidden Name bestowed to You: THOATHOE'THATHO-OYTHAETHO'USTHOAITHITHE'–THOINTHO; grant me victory, repute, beauty toward all men and all women! (*Greek Magical Papyri Texts* 92.1–16)

5

> My dearest, if any voice of mortals is heard in Hades, I say this to you, Heracles. Your father and your children are dying, and I am perishing, too. . . . Help—come—appear to me, even as a

shadow. It would be enough if you came as a dream. For those who are killing your children are wicked. (Euripides, *Hercules* 490–96, trans. Pulleyn)

The Greeks realized that gods were not at their beck and call. Some prayers suggest a bargain, splitting the difference between favorable and unfavorable outcomes:

Grant victory to Ajax, and that he might win shining fame. But if you love Hector and care for him, give equal might and glory to both. (Homer, *Iliad* 7.203–5, trans. Pulleyn)

Occasionally, as in the *Homeric Hymn* 9, which praises Artemis for her military prowess, no explicit petition is made to a god or goddess. Euripides suggests that at times the one who offers thanks could still hold a grudge:

O Zeus, it took you a long time to heed my troubles,
But I am thankful to you nonetheless for what has been done.
    (*Children of Hercules* 869–70, trans. Pulleyn)

On the other hand, the ancient Greeks were capable of a self-critical attitude toward prayer:

Our poets, understanding prayers as requests made to the gods, should exercise utmost care that they not inadvertently ask for evil under the guise of good. To make such a prayer would surely be a most ridiculous blunder. (Plato, *Laws* 7.801b, AT)

That sentiment lacks the direct force of "Deliver us from evil" and "Thy will be done," but it's headed in the same direction.

Imperial Rome (27 BC–AD 476)

After beginning to undermine Greek hegemony over the Mediterranean world in the second century BC, the early Roman republic was coming unglued in a series of civil wars whose climax was the assassination of Julius Caesar in 44 BC. After Caesar's adopted son, Octavian, triumphed over his political adversaries, the Roman Senate conferred on him the title "Augustus" and unprecedented power of command over the entire empire (27 BC–AD 14). Augustus walked a tightrope between tradition and novelty. On one side,

6

he countenanced worship of proliferating local, municipal, and domestic deities, including the Greek gods under Latin names, such as Jupiter (Zeus), Minerva (Athena), and Diana (Artemis). On the other, Augustus gradually consolidated his new, one-man dominion by means of temple-building, veneration of his deceased predecessor as a deity, public prayers for the emperor's well-being, and identification of himself as *pontifex maximus*, "supreme bridge-builder" between all priests and their gods. Precedents for such beliefs and practices were as ancient as Egypt's pharaohs, as recent as Alexander the Great and his Seleucid and Ptolemaic successors in Egypt.

Rome ascribed its military conquests to its *pietas* (religious duty) and *pax deorum* (peace with the gods). In Cicero's words, "There is really no human activity in which human valor [*virtus*] approaches more closely the divine power [*numen*] of the gods than the founding of new states [*civitatis*] or the preservation of those already founded" (*Republic* 1.12, AT). Acts of prayer in imperial Rome, like religious practice in general, were bent toward social policy and adroit governance. This was no Augustan flimflam: "Ordinary inhabitants of the Roman empire *expected* that political power had a religious dimension" (Beard, North, and Price, *Religions of Rome*, 1:359).

Many Roman prayers perpetuated Greek beliefs in reciprocity between mortals and gods, now styled as *do ut des*: "I give [to you] that you may return [the favor]." One observes this principle at work in prayers offered by Romans in a variety of settings.

> Kindly Pales [patron deity of shepherds], please grant your favor to one who sings of shepherds' rites, if I show dutiful respect to your festival [namely, the Parilia, a livestock ritual associated with Rome's own foundation]. (Ovid, *Fasti* 4.721–22, trans. Mary Beard)

Often besought for cures was Asclepius, the god of healing whose serpent-entwined staff remains the symbol of modern medicine. The following prayer is typical:

> Asclepius, child of Apollo, these words come from your devoted servant. Blessed one, god whom I yearn for. How shall I enter your golden house unless your heart incline towards me and you will to heal me and restore me to your shrine again, so that I may look on my god, who is brighter than the earth in springtime? (Apuleius, *Apology* 55, trans. Beard)

7

Equally persistent were prayers for military conquest. Here a general, Decius Mus (340 BC), vows to sacrifice himself and his troops to Rome and to the gods:

> Janus, Jupiter, Mars Pater, Quirinus, Bellona, Lares, . . . gods whose power extends over us and our enemies, divine Manes [gods of the underworld]: I pray to you, I revere you, I beg your favor and beseech that you advance the strength and success of the Roman people . . . and afflict [their] enemies with terror, fear, and death. As I have pronounced in these words, so on behalf of the state, the Roman people, . . . the army, the legions, and auxiliaries of the Roman people, . . . I devote the legions and auxiliaries of the enemy, along with myself, to the divine Manes and to the earth. (Livy, *History of Rome* 8.9.1–8, trans. Beard)

Like the Greeks, Romans tendered beautiful prayers to Universal Reason or Law, personified as a deity. To Cleanthes, Zeno's successor as head of the Stoic school in Athens, is attributed this *Hymn to Zeus* (frag. 537.1–10, mid-3rd c. BC):

> Most glorious of the Immortals, many named,
> Almighty Zeus, ruler of Nature, that governest all things with law.
> Hail! For lawful it is that all mortals should address Thee.
> For we are Thy offspring, taking the image of only Thy voice,
> As many mortal things as live and move upon the earth.
> Therefore I shall hymn Thee, and sing Thy might forever.
> For Thee doth all this universe that circles round the earth obey,
> Moving whithersoever Thou leadest, and is gladly swayed by Thee.
> (Epictetus, *Teaching* 35, trans. Frederick E. Grant [alt.])

There was no single "imperial cult," a coinage appearing nowhere in ancient literature. Instead, there were as many cultic venerations of the emperor as there were provincial villages and cities. Still, in the Roman Empire during the first and second centuries AD, no other religion was as widespread, well organized, and centrally endorsed (by the emperor himself). Prayers to the emperor followed suit. Special priesthoods, staffed by provincial aristocrats, were created to offer sacrifices to deceased emperors in temples dedicated to them alone. About three years after the death of Augustus, an altar inscription at Narbo (present-day Narbonne, France) bound its residents "to worship his divine spirit in perpetuity" (*CIL* 12.4.333). The lyric poet Horace, Octavian's contemporary, affirmed: "We have always believed that the thundering Jupiter reigns in heaven; Augustus will be held as god present" (*Song of the Ages* 3.5.1–3, AT). By strict senatorial protocol an emperor was not fully divinized until his postmortem apotheosis. Nevertheless, as Horace gushes and as many common folk may have believed, Augustus seems to have been regarded in life as a sort of "honorary god" in a conceptual world where "godhood" enjoyed a flexible meaning. By conferring upon Octavian the title "Augustus," the Senate had opened a fateful door: a claim that the Roman emperor was not merely great or superior to all other sovereigns, but rather *the* recipient par excellence of divine power to engender life, nourish growth, and dispense blessings. In Horace's words (*Letter to Augustus* 2.1.15–16), he was *praesens deus*, "god present." This, as we shall see, became the crux of a dangerous stalemate between Hellenistic Jews and their Roman potentate.

Prayer in the Hebrew Bible and Emergent Judaism

Ancient Israel (1200–200 BC)

In some ways the prayers of ancient Israel parallel those of ancient Greece. Both exhibit rough similarities with modes of Egyptian, Hittite, and Akkadian prayers, particularly their association of prayer with sacrificial offerings (see Pritchard, *ANET*, 375, 394–95; Miller, *They Cried to the Lord*, 5–31). A personal deity is addressed and petitioned, with express motivation for the request. Greek prayers resembled guests' expectation of benefaction by their hosts; likewise, in Israelite prayers some scholars discern a replica of human petitions in everyday life (Aejmelaeus, *Traditional Prayer*, 88–89).

Yet, when reading Hebrew prayers, one moves into a different religious world, molded by and expressive of different theological assumptions. Most obviously, Greco-Romanism was riotously polytheistic. From among primitive Canaanite gods (Num. 25; Judg. 6; 1 Kgs. 18) the LORD of Israel had emerged as sole and sovereign; by the sixth century, despite occasional backslides into idolatry (Deut. 32:21; 1 Kgs. 16; 2 Chr. 24:18), a rigorous monotheism was built into the Deuteronomist's credo (Deut. 6:4, 13; cf. 1 Chr. 16:26). That belief remains a defining characteristic of Judaism to the present day.

9

The other distinguishing feature of Hebraic and later Jewish prayer was the milieu created by the Sinaitic covenant, for which no exact parallel exists in Greco-Romanism. Most ancient peoples seem to have assumed some "compact" between mortals and deities: as we have seen, "Give to me because I have given to you"; "I give that you may give in return." Critically different was Israel's belief that the LORD God had unilaterally instigated with that people the Sinai covenant and all subsequent codicils (Gen. 17:1–14; Num. 25:10–13; 2 Sam. 23:5; Ps. 89:3, 28–29)—owing not to the nation's magnitude or righteousness, but rather to the LORD's selection of this people over all others and a steadfast fidelity to those promises (Deut. 7:7; 9:5). We have seen that some Greek prayers refer to *charis*, a gift pleasing to the gods, proffered by humans to encourage a favorable disposition. The Septuagint uses the same Greek term to translate the Hebrew word *khēn*, but the framework for its use in the Bible diverges from that of Homer and the tragedians: God's gracious mercy to Israel is utterly self-motivated, in no way the discharge of any reciprocal debt owed to those who sacrifice to the LORD (Exod. 34:6; Num. 6:25; Neh. 9:17, 31; Ps. 86:15). Unlike Olympus's residents, Israel's God needs no mortal honor. The LORD accepts sacrifice, properly presented (Lev. 3–4, 7–9; Num. 7), but beyond all burnt offerings desires the nation's obedience (1 Sam. 15:22), steadfast love (Hos. 6:6), justice (Sir. 35:9), "a broken spirit, and a broken and contrite heart" (Ps. 51:17). Within this framework Israel's prayers are best understood.

Many of Israel's prayers were motivated by similar concerns in Greece and the Roman Empire. We witness such in the ancient hymn of praise ascribed to Moses, immediately followed by Miriam's closely related hymn, sung after Israel's rescue at the Red Sea:

I will sing to the LORD, for he has triumphed gloriously;
   horse and rider he has thrown into the sea.
The LORD is my strength and my might,
   and he has become my salvation;
this is my God, and I will praise him,
   my father's God, and I will exalt him.
The LORD is a warrior;
   the LORD is his name. . . .
Who is like you, O LORD, among the gods?
   Who is like you, majestic in holiness,
   awesome in splendor, doing wonders?

You stretched out your right hand,
   the earth swallowed them.
In your steadfast love [*khesed*] you led the people whom you
      redeemed;
   you guided them by your strength to your holy abode. . . .
You brought them in and planted them on the mountain of your
      own possession,
   the place, O LORD, that you made your abode,
   the sanctuary, O LORD, that your hands have established.
The LORD will reign forever and ever.
   (Exod. 15:1b–3, 11–13, 17–18)

This single hymn encapsulates many of Israel's fundamental claims about itself and God. First, it is a response of faithful praise from a people who have experienced rescue from foreign captivity. Second, it dilates on the LORD's sole responsibility for that gracious liberation: the Israelites did nothing to save themselves. Third, the occasion for praise is a discrete event in Israel's history: "*Then* Moses and the Israelites sang this song to the LORD" (Exod. 15:1a). Fourth, that critical event demonstrates the LORD's creative and redemptive power over all other divine claimants, both now and forever. Fifth, by the LORD's decisive action at the sea, the way is paved for Israel's entry into an abiding covenant: "You brought them in and planted them on the mountain of your own possession, the place, O LORD, that you made your abode" (15:17; cf. 19:1–20:21).

The more one mulls over this hymn, the more intelligible is the pattern into which fall so many of Israel's other prayers to its God. Psalm 117 expresses a succinct example:

Praise the LORD, all you nations! [the call to praise, issued
      universally]
Extol him, all you peoples! [the same call, reiterated]
For [*kî*] great is his steadfast love toward us, [the justification for
      praise: God's *khesed*]
   and the faithfulness of the LORD endures forever. [that *khesed*
      assured in perpetuity]
Praise the LORD! [the climactic call to praise]

Analyzing other hymns like the songs of Deborah (Judg. 5) and of Hannah (1 Sam. 2:1–10), as well as numerous blessings (*běrākôt*) of the LORD distributed throughout Scripture (e.g., Gen. 14:20), Samuel Balentine describes some interesting patterns (*Prayer in*

11

the Hebrew Bible, 199–224). While often originating as personal expressions of praise in historical narratives, these hymns unfold as proclamations to Israel at worship.

Equally interesting is Balentine's observation that, structurally and substantively, praise and lamentation are two sides of a single coin:

Imperative address	Motivation
Praise: Sing to the LORD,	for [*kî*] he has triumphed gloriously. (Exod. 15:21)
Lament: Deliver me, please,	for [*kî*] I am afraid of [my brother]. (Gen. 32:11)

As it was for ancient Israel, so it remains for many worshipers today: the life of prayer is a constantly reciprocating circuit between the poles of thanksgiving and lamentation (see also Westermann, *Praise and Lament in the Psalms*, esp. 154).

Complaints, pleas for help, and cris de coeur (cries from the heart) dominate Jeremiah's oracles (11:18–23; 12:1–6; 15:10–21; 17:14–18; 18:18–23; 20:7–18) and Job's responses (chaps. 3, 29–31); they absorb the book of Lamentations and by a considerable margin outnumber all other types of prayers in the Psalter. The linkage of lament with praise is evident in Jehoshaphat's cultic prayer, in Jerusalem's assembly, on the eve of terrifying invasion (2 Chr. 20:6–12):

O LORD, God of our ancestors, are you not God in heaven? Do you not rule over all the kingdoms of the nations? In your hand are power and might, so that no one is able to withstand you. Did you not, O our God, drive out the inhabitants of this land before your people Israel, and give it forever to the descendants of your friend Abraham? They have lived in it, and in it have built you a sanctuary for your name, saying, "If disaster comes upon us, the sword, judgment, or pestilence, or famine, we will stand before this house, and before you, for your name is in this house, and cry to you in our distress, and you will hear and save." See now, the people of Ammon, Moab, and Mount Seir, whom you would not let Israel invade when they came from the land of Egypt, and whom they avoided and did not destroy—they reward us by coming to drive us out of your possession that you have given us to inherit. O our God, will you not execute judgment upon them? For we are powerless against this great multitude that is coming against us. We do not know what to do, but our eyes are on you.

12

Jehoshaphat is impaled on the dilemma of faith. All the questions in this prayer are indirect thanksgivings. *Of course* the LORD is the same God in heaven whom our ancestors worshiped. *Without question* this God rules over all nations and kingdoms. *Certainly* the land given to Abraham is his descendants' inheritance forever. *Beyond doubt* the LORD will come to the defense of his holy temple. *So*—the enemies are at the gate. We cannot withstand them. We don't know what to do. We're looking to you, God. Where are you?

In the Psalter's classic laments, similar confessions and questions address personal rather than national distress, which came to be uttered in a cultic setting.

> My God, my God, why have you forsaken me?
> > Why are you so far from helping me,
> > > from the words of my groaning?
> O my God, I cry by day, but you do not answer;
> > and by night, but find no rest.
> Yet you are holy,
> > enthroned on the praises of Israel.
> In you our ancestors trusted;
> > they trusted, and you delivered them.
> To you they cried, and were saved;
> > in you they trusted, and were not put to shame.
> But I am a worm, and not human;
> > scorned by others, and despised by the people.
> All who see me mock at me;
> > they make mouths at me, they shake their heads;
> "Commit your cause to the LORD; let him deliver—
> > let him rescue the one in whom he delights!" (Ps. 22:1–8)

The psalmist hasn't the cold solace of an agnostic or atheist. There *is* a God, now and forever enthroned on Israel's praises. That God knows the sufferer's torments and shame. That God hears this prayer. Why doesn't God do something to remedy the circumstances? The last verse could be read as a desperate attempt to shame God into action: if you don't care about the mockery my attackers are making of me, why not do something to safeguard your own honor?

Verses 22–24 of the same psalm may be interpreted as the psalmist's vow: a bargaining promise that the Almighty shall be upheld in the congregation if only divine relief will come:

> I will tell of your name to my brothers and sisters;
> > in the midst of the congregation I will praise you:

13

You who fear the LORD, praise him!
 All you offspring of Jacob, glorify him;
 stand in awe of him, all you offspring of Israel!
For he did not despise or abhor
 the affliction of the afflicted;
he did not hide his face from me,
 but heard when I cried to him.

Some biblical cris de coeur express no petition at all, only anguished questions followed by something like a capitulation to misery:

O LORD, how long shall I cry for help,
 and you will not listen?
Or cry to you "Violence!"
 and you will not save?
Why do you make me see wrongdoing
 and look at trouble?
Destruction and violence are before me;
 strife and contention arise.
So the law becomes numbed
 and justice never prevails.
The wicked surround the righteous—
 therefore judgment comes forth perverted.
 (Hab. 1:2–4, slightly alt.)

Still, the inner-scriptural dialogue continues. In the teeth of suffering, the powerless, discerning a response from the absent God, seize words of trust that melt into doxology.

I waited patiently for the LORD;
 he inclined to me and heard my cry.
He drew me up from the desolate pit,
 out of the miry bog,
and set my feet upon a rock,
 making my steps secure.
He put a new song in my mouth,
 a song of praise to our God.
Many will see and fear,
 and put their trust in the LORD. (Ps. 40:1–3)

14

Sing praises to the LORD, O you his faithful ones,
 and give thanks to his holy name.

For his anger is but for a moment;
　his favor is for a lifetime.
Weeping may linger for the night,
　but joy comes with the morning. (Ps. 30:4–5)

Hebraic prayer defies simple synopsis. Let this much be said: Israel's Scripture reveals a perpetual conversation—frequently, a debate—between that people and their God over religious, social, and political matters of fundamental consequence. In a millennia-long process, continually renewed without reaching closure, Israel's basic beliefs about itself, the world as a whole, and the LORD God were articulated and evolved. Israel's emergent picture of humanity reveals vulnerable yet blessed creatures, subject to a range of conflictive passions and conduct: gratitude, violence, discouragement, persistence, miscarriage of justice, nobility, terror, and exuberance. The God to whom Israel prayed is One, personal yet transcendent, sovereign yet responsive, righteous yet merciful, present yet hidden, properly summoned by all yet answerable to none. No less than for any ancient Greek or Roman community, prayer was a primary means of cohesion and self-understanding among contemporaneous Hebrews. Here, too, prayer evinces the education of human wanting.

Second Temple Judaism (ca. 200 BC–AD 70)

More closely approaching the time of Jesus, we witness a flourishing of varied Jewish prayers. At this point the specimens are so numerous, the literature so vast, that taking their full measure becomes impossible. The best we may do is to consider some samples of Jewish piety in the centuries and decades immediately preceding the beginning of Jesus' movement.

The *Apocrypha* and *Pseudepigrapha* are conventional though clunky categories used to describe a large body of Jewish literature of multifarious genres. Because most of these texts originated in languages other than Hebrew, most rabbis did not regard them as canonical, on a level with that of Torah, Prophets, and Writings (Tanakh). Different Christian groups have variously assessed their authority: to this day Roman Catholic Bibles include works like Sirach and the Wisdom of Solomon, which appear in the

15

Septuagint; some African Orthodox Churches regard *1 Enoch* as scriptural. In any event this bountiful literature opens windows onto Jewish prayer in the shadow of Persian, Egyptian, then Roman political occupation.

Befitting its pious protagonists, the folktale of Tobit (ca. 200 BC) is deeply doxological. This book revisits many of Job's issues, transplanted into a Diaspora Jewish environment. The story is bifocal: it entwines the shifting fortunes of Tobit, whose loyalty to Torah gets him into trouble, and Sarah, a woman whose seven successive husbands have been demonically slain before any marriage could be consummated. Both Tobit and Sarah devoutly assert their innocence and plead for death. "With much grief and anguish of heart," Tobit prays:

> You are righteous, O Lord,
>   and all your deeds are just;
> all your ways are mercy and truth;
>   you judge the world. . . .
> Command, O Lord, that I be released from this distress;
>   release me to go to the eternal home,
>   and do not, O Lord, turn your face away from me.
> For it is better for me to die
>   than to see so much distress in my life. . . . (3:1–2, 6cd)

"At that same time, with hands outstretched toward the window," Sarah prays:

> Blessed are you, merciful God!
>   Blessed is your name forever;
>   let all your works praise you forever. . . .
> Already seven husbands of mine have died.
>   Why should I still live?
> But if it is not pleasing to you, O Lord, to take my life,
>   hear me in my disgrace. (3:11, 15de)

Their requests are fulfilled. God delivers both from their distress.

Yet this book moves a step beyond Job by aligning the laments of particular Jews with that of the nation as a whole. In its penultimate chapter (13:1–17) Tobit prays that a chastened Israel may be redeemed from exile.

16

> Blessed be God who lives forever,
>   because his kingdom lasts throughout all ages. . . .

O Jerusalem, the holy city,
> he afflicted you for the deeds of your hands,
> but will again have mercy on the children of the righteous.
Acknowledge the Lord, for he is good,
> and bless the King of the ages,
> so that his tent may be rebuilt in you in joy.
May he cheer all those within you who are captives,
> and love all those within you who are distressed,
> to all generations forever. (Tob. 13:1, 9–10)

Interwoven into a tale that is at once fantastical, humorous, and heartrending is a concerto of praise, lament, thanksgiving, and trust in God's dedication to a wayward, restored Israel.

Corporate concerns rise to the fore in the book of Judith (ca. 150 BC), set in the age of the Assyrian king Nebuchadnezzar and his relentless general Holofernes (606–562 BC). As nations are toppled right and left, a widow of Bethulia rises to confront a seemingly invincible force. Judith is the exemplary feminist avant la lettre: wise, courageous, wealthy, beautiful, cunning, and sexy. She's Miriam (Exod. 15:20–21), Deborah (Judg. 4:4–16), Jael (Judg. 4:17–22), and the women of Thebez (Judg. 9:53–54) and Abel-beth-maacah (2 Sam. 20:14–22) all rolled into one. After seducing Holofernes into a drunken stupor, she decapitates him. Shame upon Assyria; victory for Israel! Yet, throughout this tale, the prayers of Judith are eloquent and by no means extraneous to the plot. She warns her countrymen: "Do not try to bind the purposes of the Lord our God; for God is not like a human being, to be threatened, or like a mere mortal, to be won over by pleading. Therefore, while we wait for his deliverance, let us call upon him to help us, and he will hear our voice, if it pleases him" (Jdt. 8:16–17). Thus does Judith pray:

For your strength does not depend on numbers,
> nor your might on the powerful.
But you are the God of the lowly,
> helper of the oppressed,
> upholder of the weak,
> protector of the forsaken,
> savior of those without hope.
Please, please, God of my father,
> God of the heritage of Israel,
> Lord of heaven and earth,
> Creator of the waters,

17

King of all your creation,
hear my prayer! (Jdt. 9:11–12)

Judith concludes the festival honoring her triumph with a royal hymn (16:13, 17):

I will sing to my God a new song:
O Lord, you are great and glorious,
    wonderful in strength, invincible. . . .
Woe to the nations that rise up against my people!
    The Lord Almighty will take vengeance on them in the day
      of judgment;
he will send fire and worms into their flesh;
    they shall weep in pain forever.

References to Sarah, Judith, and other Hellenistic Jewish women at prayer prompts one to wonder if the occasion, forms, and contents of their prayers differed in substance from those of their male counterparts. In a copiously detailed study (*Prayers*), Markus McDowell concludes that the authors of Second Temple Jewish literature tended to portray prayerful women and men in much the same way, though the perspective adopted by the majority of these women's prayers employs female imagery and vocabulary (197–214). For example, in *Joseph and Aseneth*, an early first-century-AD exposition of Genesis 41:45–51 and 46:20, Aseneth, Potiphar's daughter and the story's main character, offers five of nine personal prayers (11:16–18; 12–13; 17:10; 21:10–21; 27:10). Aside from a few passing references ("I . . . was a boastful and arrogant virgin . . . who trusted in the richness of my glory and in my beauty," 21:12d, 16c, trans. Buchard [*OTP*]), the substance of her prayers could be offered by any model convert, male or female, from idol worship to loyal obedience to Israel's God (McDowell, 123–36).

The *Psalms of Solomon* (150 BC) collect eighteen poems blending lament, hymns of trust, praise, and thanksgiving. Some have the nation Israel in view, its recent circumstances or eschatological future (*Pss. Sol.* 1, 2, 7, 8, 11, 17, 18). Others concentrate on personal piety by contrasting sinners with the righteous (3, 4, 5, 6, 8, 9, 10, 13, 14, 15, 16). The tenth psalm catches the didactic flavor of the rest:

18

Happy is the man whom the Lord remembers with rebuking,
    And protects from the evil way with a whip
    (that he may) be cleansed from sin that it may not increase. . . .

And the devout shall give thanks in the assembly of the people,
And God will be merciful to the poor to the joy of Israel.
For God is good and merciful forever,
And the synagogues of Israel will glorify the Lord's name.
(vv. 1, 6–7, trans. R. B. Wright [*OTP*])

While interesting in its own right, the lengthy seventeenth psalm is a curtain-raiser for New Testament eschatology. This hymn is focused on God's royal sovereignty: "O Lord, Thou art our King for ever and ever" (v. 1; also vv. 2–4, 43–49). Removal of sinners' military occupation of Israel will demonstrate God's kingly power (vv. 6–22). God's chosen instrument for this deliverance will be a Davidic king (cf. 2 Sam. 7:13–14; Ps. 89:19–37) who embodies not only martial strength, but also wisdom, righteousness, and blessing (*Pss. Sol.* 17:25, 29, 40, 42, 44). This "Lord Messiah" (v. 32: *māshîakh* [Heb.]; *christos* [Gk.]) is a human rather than a divine figure, as idealized as the age over which he will preside as God's regent:

And [Israel's king] will gather a holy people
whom he will lead in righteousness;
and he will judge the tribes of the people
that have been made holy by the Lord their God.
He will not tolerate unrighteousness [even] to pause among them,
and any person who knows wickedness shall not live with them.
. . . .
[He] will bless the Lord's people with wisdom and happiness,
And he himself [will be] free from sin, [in order] to rule a great people.
He will expose officials and drive out sinners
by the strength of his word.
And he will not weaken in his days, [relying] upon his God,
for God made him
powerful in the holy spirit,
and wise in the counsel of understanding,
with strength and righteousness.
(*Pss. Sol.* 17:26–27a, 35b–37, trans. Wright)

Like Psalms 2 and 110, this is a royal psalm that acknowledges God's sovereignty through an appointed king on earth. Unlike those psalms, *Psalms of Solomon* aspires to a future age of perfect piety. 19

The *Dead Sea Scrolls* (200 BC–AD 70) open wide a treasure trove of Second Temple prayers, including three-quarters of the Psalter in the earliest Hebrew manuscripts known to us. Here we shall concentrate on excerpts from the fragmentary Thanksgiving Scroll (*Hodayot*), whose speaker may have been the Qumran community's venerated "Teacher of Righteousness." Much of what these hymns profess is epitomized in 1QH 5:2: "Only by your goodness is man acquitted, / [purified] by your abundant compa[ssion . . .] / You embellish him with your grandeur, / you install him in your abundant pleasures, / with everlasting peace and lengthy days" (trans. Martínez/Watson). The rest of the *Hodayot* are variations, light and dark, on this theme.

> What is flesh compared to this?
> What creature of clay can do wonders?
> He is in sin from his maternal womb,
> and in guilty iniquity right to old age. . . .
> The path of man is not secure
> except by the spirit that God creates for him,
> to perfect the path of the sons of man
> so that all his creatures come to know the strength of his power
> and the extent of his compassion
> with all the sons of his approval. (1QH 12:29b–30a, 31b–32, *DSSE*,
>   trans. Martínez/Watson)

Human creatures are utterly dependent upon their Creator, not only for life but also for the means of righteousness (the gift of Torah, "an everlasting possession": 1QS 11:5–8). Not only that: the *Hodayot* repeatedly insist on a divine, dualistic predeterminism:

> I know that every spirit is fashioned by your hand,
> [and all its travail] you have established
> even before creating him.
> How can anyone change your words?
> You, you alone, have created the just man. . . .
> Upon flesh you have raised his glory.
> But the wicked you have created for the time of wrath,
> from the womb you have predestined them for the day of
>   annihilation. (1QH 7:17b–18, 21, *DSSE*, trans. Martínez/Watson)

Such a view does not degrade into the hymnist's arrogance in being numbered among the elect. Rather, this sharp dualism is amplified in the stark contrast between mortals and God.

> I am dust and ashes,
> what can I plan if you do not wish it?

What can I devise without your agreement?
How can I be strong if you do not make me stand?
How can I be learned if you do not mold me?
What can I say if you do not open my mouth?
And how can I answer if you do not give me insight?
See, you are prince of gods and king of the glorious ones,
Lord of every spirit, owner of every creature.
Without your will nothing happens,
And nothing is known without your wish. . . .
Be blessed, Lord,
God of compassion and of abundant favor,
because you have made me know these things
So that I recount your marvels,
and I not keep silent day and night. (1QH 18:5–9b, 14–15a, *DSSE*,
     trans. Martínez/Watson)

In this light, one so blessed is responsible to God and to one's fellows. An appropriate response is thankful blessing:

For in the distress of my soul you heard my call,
you identified the outcry of my pain in my complaint
and saved the soul of the poor man in the lair of lions,
who sharpen their tongue like swords. . . .
But you, my God, have changed {my soul} the storm to a calm, . . .
Be blessed, Lord,
Because you did not abandon the orphan,
Nor have you have slighted the wretch.
For Your strength [is unfathomable]
and your glory measureless. (1QH 13:12b–13, 18a, 20–21a, *DSSE*,
     trans. Martínez/Watson)

Qumran's hymnbook piles on blessing, dedication, and pleas
for help:

Be blessed, Lord,
creator [of all things,]
[mighty] in acts
everything is your work.
You have resolved, in fact, to take pity [on your servant,]
to show me favor by the spirit of your compassion
and by the splendor of your glory. . . .
I know that no one besides you is just.
I have appeased your face by the spirit that you have given me,
to lavish your favor on your servant for [ever,]

21

to purify me with your holy spirit,
to approach your will according to the extent of your kindnesses.
(1QH 8:16–17b, 19–20, trans. Martínez/Watson)

Because God "discriminat[es] between the just and the wicked"
(4Q508 f1:1), an oath is taken to assure the community's righteous
integrity:

But I,
I have known, thanks to the wealth of your goodness,
and with an oath I have enjoined my soul
not to sin against you
and not to do anything that is evil in your eyes.
In this way I force all the men of my counsel
To make progress in the community.
According to his intelligence I promote him,
I love him in proportion to his abundant inheritance.
I do not lift my face to evil,
or consider a wicked gift.
I do not exchange your truth for wealth,
or for a gift all your judgments.
Quite the reverse, . . .
I will not admit into the council [of your truth]
someone distant from your covenant. (1QH 6:17–20c, 21b–22,
trans. Martínez/Watson)

Such fidelity God will reciprocate to the community for all
eternity. The hymnist, appointed "like a father for the sons of favor,
like a wet-nurse to men of portent" (1QH 15:20c–21a), again offers
gratitude:

I give you thanks, Lord,
Because you have sustained me with your strength,
you have spread your holy spirit over me so that I will not stumble,
you have fortified me against the wars of wickedness,
and in all their calamities you have not discouraged me from your
    covenant. . . .
Who is like you, Lord, among the gods?
Who is like your truth?
Who, before you, is just when judged? . . .
All the sons of your truth
You take to forgiveness in your presence,
You purify them from their sins

22

by the greatness of your goodness,
and in your bountiful mercy,
to make them stand in your presence
forever and ever.
For you are an eternal God,
and all your paths remain from eternity to eternity.
And there is no one apart from you. (1QH 15:6–8a, 28, 30–31,
    DSSE, trans. Martínez/Watson)

Qumran covenanters exiled themselves from a world, including fellow Jews, that they considered irredeemably corrupt. By
contrast, the Alexandrian Jew *Philo* (25 BC–AD 50) embraced and
interpreted Hellenistic thought for Diaspora Judaism. There's no
little mysticism in Philo; some of his writings, such as his *Life of
Moses*, verge on the ecstatic. While taking a very dim view of pagan
mystery religions and their heroes, Philo devoutly prays *to Moses* as
revealer, since on Sinai he most closely approached a vision of God's
divine essence:

> Now is it not fitting that even blind men should become sharp-
> sighted in their minds to these and similar things, being endowed
> with the power of sight by the most sacred oracles, so as to be
> able to contemplate the glories of nature, and not to be limited to
> the mere understanding of the words? But even if we voluntarily
> close the eye of our soul and take no care to understand such
> mysteries, or if we are unable to look up to them, the hierophant
> himself [i.e., Moses] stands by and prompts us. And do not thou
> ever cease through weariness to anoint thy eyes until you have
> introduced those who are duly initiated to the secret light of the
> sacred scriptures, and have displayed to them the hidden things
> therein contained, and their reality, which is invisible to those
> who are uninitiated. (*Dreams* 1.164–65, trans. F. H. Colson/G. H.
> Whitaker [LCL])

Indeed, Philo identifies Moses exactly as John the evangelist refers
to Jesus: the *Logos*, which Philo understands as God's self-emanation
of the divine reality that bridges creation and its redemption (*Cherubim* 27–28; *Migration of Abraham* 131; cf. John 1:1).

Philo's works reveal little of their author at prayer and virtually
nothing of prayer texts in his day. This should not surprise us. None   23
of his treatises is strictly devotional; they are exegetical, philosophical, or otherwise analytical (consult Leonhardt, *Jewish Worship in*

Philo of Alexandria). From comments en passant we can assemble a picture of prayer as Philo commends it. "Prayer is a request for good things" (*Agriculture* 99; also *Immutability* 87; *Sacrifice* 52); conversely, "I should pray, if ever I had a design to commit injustice, that I might fail in my iniquity" (*Posterity and Exile of Cain* 82). Positively: "For the undefiled high priest [= *logos*; cf. *Dreams* 1.215], conscience, has derived from nature this most especial honor, that no error of the mind can find any place within him; on which account it is worth our while to pray that [*logos*] may live in the soul [as a] judge who has received jurisdiction over the whole of our minds" (*Flight and Finding* 118). We pray, Philo suggests, that our moral center may be controlled by that wisdom by which God created and holds all things together. In a more general sense Philo considers a long, happy life and a good death "those things that are especially admired among us, of the things which are really goods, every one of which we pray to attain to at suitable seasons, and if we do attain to them, we are called the happiest of men" (*Sacrifices of Abel and Cain* 99; cf. 100–126). Encouraging prayers for moderation, he sounds perfectly Aristotelian (cf. *Nicomachean Ethics* 2.6.7): "But that we may not, through deviating from the right road, be compelled to yield to one of two rival faults, let us desire and pray to be able to proceed straight along the middle of the road. Now, the middle between temerity and cowardice, is courage; the mean between profuse extravagance and illiberal stinginess, is temperance; that between crafty unscrupulousness and folly, is prudence; and the proper path between superstition and impiety, is piety" (*Unchangeableness of God* 164).

Philo regards prayer as a virtue: "If anyone is a friend of virtue, let him pray that all good things may be implanted in him and may appear in his soul, like some symmetrical proportion conducing to beauty in a statue or a picture" (*Husbandry* 168). Virtue's highest object is God. "The beginning and the end of the greatness and numerousness of good things is the ceaseless and uninterrupted recollection of God, and an invocation of his assistance in the civil and domestic, confused and continual, warfare of life" (*Migration of Abraham* 56). For Philo, Jacob's prayer at Bethel (Gen. 28:20–22) is exemplary:

24

God is the name of the beneficent power, and Lord is the title of the royal power. What, then, can anyone call a more ancient and important good, than to be thought worthy to meet with unmixed and unalloyed beneficence? . . . And it appears to me that it was because the practitioner of virtue saw that he uttered that most admirable prayer that "the Lord might be to him as God" [Gen. 28:21], for he desired no longer to stand in awe of him as a governor, but to honor and love him as a benefactor. (*Dreams* 1.163, trans. Colson/Whitaker [LCL])

Prayer is properly situated in the temple, wedded to ritual sacrifice by irreproachable priests (*Life of Moses* 2.5). Roughly a third of Philo's lengthy tractate on *Special Laws* is devoted to careful exegesis of Numbers and Leviticus. Penitence and remission of sins by sacrifice are actually "virtues" (*Dreams* 2.299; *Moses* 1.146–51; *Special Laws* 3.121). Philo stresses the unifying power of pure worship: not only of all Jews in all times and places (*Embassy to Gaius* 280), but also of all nations, who are blessed by the merciful "Ruler and Governor of the universe, . . . who take[s] to himself [Israel] out of all other nations and to consecrate to the priesthood, that it might forever offer up prayers for the whole universal race of mankind, for the sake of averting evil from them and procuring them a participation in blessings" (*Life of Moses* 1.149).

Considered at greater depth, prayer, for Philo, is ultimately an expression of gratitude to God that transcends place or convention:

While each of the virtues is a holy matter, thanksgiving is supremely so. Buildings, offerings, and sacrifices, customary for most people, cannot genuinely express our gratitude to God. Not even the whole world would be a temple adequate to render the honor due to God. To the contrary, such must be expressed through hymns of praise—even then, not by a voice straining to be heard, but by music repeated through the intellect too pure for the ear to discern. (*Planting* 30.126 AT)

In AD 38, following a summer of riots between Jews and Greeks in Alexandria, Philo led a Jewish delegation to the emperor Gaius Germanicus (aka Caligula, AD 12–41), hopeful of securing Jewish exemption from edicts commanding imperial worship. Here follows an excerpt of Philo's report of that meeting:

25

And while [Gaius] was triumphing in these super-human appellations, the sycophant Isidorus, seeing the temper in which he was, said, "O master, you will hate with still more just vehemence these men whom you see before you and their fellow country-men, if you are made acquainted with their disaffection and dis-loyalty towards yourself; for when all other men were offering up sacrifices of thanksgiving for your safety, these men alone refused to offer any sacrifice at all; and when I say, 'these men,' I com-prehend all the rest of the Jews." And when we all cried out with one accord, "O Lord Gaius, we are falsely accused; for we *did* sacrifice, and we offered up entire hecatombs, the blood of which we poured in a libation upon the altar, and the flesh we did not carry to our homes to make a feast and banquet upon it, as it is the custom of some people to do, but we committed the victims entire to the sacred flame as a burnt offering: and we have done this three times already, and not once only; on the first occasion when you succeeded to the empire, and the second time when you recovered from that terrible disease with which all the habit-able world was afflicted at the same time, and the third time we sacrificed in hope of your victory over the Germans." "Grant," said [Gaius], "that all this is true, and that you did sacrifice; nev-ertheless you sacrificed to another god and not for my sake; and then what good did you do me? Moreover, you did not sacrifice *to me*." Immediately a profound shuddering came upon us the first moment that we heard this expression, similar to that which overwhelmed us when we first came into his presence. (*Embassy to Gaius* 355–57, trans. Colson [LCL], emphasis added)

In imperial Rome radical monotheism could cost its adherents very dearly, as John of Patmos was quick to remind others (Rev. 13–14).

Conclusion

Standing at the foot of the Acropolis, Paul declared (so Luke tells us), "Athenians, I see how extremely *deisidaimonesterous* you are in every way" (Acts 17:22). That Greek adjective is ambiguous; it can be translated as "religious" or "superstitious." However one assesses the evidence presented in this chapter, the record is clear that, in antiquity, human beings paid attention to matters divine. The examples of prayer we have witnessed were not fixed points on a single evolutionary line. Instead, they emerged as lively options amid complex, overlapping contexts.

Taken altogether, the heritage of prayer for Jesus and his dis- ✓
ciples was rich and wide-ranging. Whether uttered by Greeks or
Israelites, Romans or Hellenistic Jews, prayers were directed heav-
enward at moments of crisis, on occasions of everyday need, and in
outbursts of praise. For all their variety, ancient cultures accepted
a reciprocating loop between mortals and the divine. Their perception of relations with the gods or one God copied human inter-
actions with one another and their mortal sovereigns, even as a
sense of the transcendent exploded mundane models. In prayer the
boundaries between personal and national, between private and
communal, were recognized yet permeable. All such characteristics
will reappear in our study of the Lord's Prayer.

Works Cited in Chapter 1

Aejmelaeus, Anneli. *The Traditional Prayer in the Psalms.* Berlin
and New York: de Gruyter, 1986.
Balentine, Samuel E. *Prayer in the Hebrew Bible: The Drama of
Divine-Human Dialogue.* Overtures to Biblical Theology. Min-
neapolis: Fortress Press, 1993.
Beard, Mary, John North, and Simon Price. *Religions of Rome.* 2
vols. Cambridge: Cambridge University Press, 1998.
Epictetus. *The Teaching of Epictetus.* Translated, annotated, and
introduced by T. W. Rolleston. Chicago: Dunnohoe, Henne-
berry & Co., 1900.
Galinsky, Karl. *Augustan Culture.* Princeton, NJ: Princeton Univer-
sity Press, 1996.
Lamott, Anne. *Traveling Mercies: Some Thoughts on Faith.* New
York: Pantheon, 1999.
Leonhardt, Jutta. *Jewish Worship in Philo of Alexandria.* Texte und
Studien zum antiken Judentum 84. Tübingen: Mohr Siebeck,
2001.
Martínez, Florentino Garcia, ed. *The Dead Sea Scrolls Translated:
The Qumran Texts in English.* Trans. Wilfred G. E. Watson.
Leiden: E. J. Brill, 1994.
McDowell, Markus. *Prayers of Jewish Women: Studies of Pat-
terns of Prayer in the Second Temple Period.* Wissenschaftli-
che Untersuchungen zum Neuen Testament. 2nd series 211.
Tübingen: Mohr Siebeck, 2006.

27

Miller, Patrick D. *They Cried to the Lord: The Form and Theology of Biblical Prayer.* Minneapolis: Fortress Press, 1994.

Pritchard, James B., ed. *ANET = Ancient Near Eastern Texts Relating to the Old Testament.* 3rd ed. Princeton, NJ: Princeton University Press, 1969.

Pulleyn, Samuel. *Prayer in Greek Religion.* Oxford Classical Monographs. Oxford: Clarendon Press, 1997.

Westermann, Claus. *Praise and Lament in the Psalms.* Translated by Keith R. Crim and Richard N. Soulen. Atlanta: John Knox Press, 1981.

Zaleski, Philip, and Carol Zaleski. *Prayer: A History.* Boston: Houghton Mifflin, 2005.

CHAPTER 2

Prayer in the Gospels

*English was good enough for Jesus Christ and it's good enough for the
children of Texas.*
—Attributed to Texas Governor Miriam "Ma" Ferguson (1924)

Before proceeding to the prayer Jesus taught his disciples, we
should consider another contextual field with different dimensions:
the Gospels. This is important. Not everything pertaining to prayer
in the Gospels is reducible to the Lord's Prayer. Moreover, none
of Jesus' words has come to us directly: all have been mediated by
evangelistic presentations of its founder that the early church considered most reliable for faith and conduct. No stenographer took
down Jesus' remarks verbatim; all of the Gospels offer us Jesus [as]
remembered (Dunn). To acknowledge this is no counsel of despair:
despite bursts of hyperskepticism that have freckled the Gospels'
study since the Enlightenment, the majority of responsible scholars have always depended on the New Testament's Gospels as primary sources for the Jesus of history because, for all their particular
biases, they probably got the teaching of Jesus right more often than
not. To take only one example: the petition for God's kingdom to
come (Matt. 6:10 = Luke 11:2) dovetails with the dominant subject
of Jesus' discourse in the Synoptics, the kingdom of God, as we shall
see in chapter 5 and as almost all modern historians agree (Sanders,
Jesus and Judaism, 123–241; Meier, *A Marginal Jew,* 2:237–506;
Allison, *Constructing Jesus,* 31–204). As this commentary unfolds

29

we shall situate the elements of the Lord's Prayer within the Gospels' overlapping contexts. Here it is worth considering that framework on its own terms, if only in brief overview.

Mark (ca. AD 70)

The shortest and likely earliest of the Gospels has less to say about prayer than the others. The usual Greek term for praying, *proseuchomai* (a request of, or promise to, a deity), occurs only ten times in Mark (1:35; 6:46; 11:24, 25; 12:40; 13:18; 14:32, 35, 38, 39); *proseuchē*, "[place of] prayer," twice (9:29; 11:17); *eucharisteō*, "to render thanks [to God]," especially at mealtimes, twice (8:6; 14:23); *doxazō*, "to praise or glorify [God]," once (2:12). Nevertheless, prayer in Mark is a serious subject, arising at critical points in that narrative. The necessity of appropriate prayer is embedded in Jesus' critiques of a faithless generation (9:19, 29), of the temple's misappropriation by religious contemporaries (11:17), and of scribes who pray without integrity (12:38–40). On occasions of extraordinary need (1:32–37; 6:34–48; 8:6–9), Jesus prays. Viewing the prospect of the temple's destruction (11:15–18; 13:1–2), symbolized by a cursed fig tree (11:12–14, 20–21), Jesus urges his disciples to continue trusting God with confidence in the face of catastrophe (11:22–24). When the temple, the locus of sacrifice for Israel's sins and their atonement, no longer exists, communal forgiveness is incumbent on praying disciples, "so that your Father in heaven may also forgive you your trespasses" (11:25, cf. Matt. 6:12 = Luke 11:4).

Prayer, in Mark, is the elastic band that quivers in tension between power and suffering (Dowd, *Prayer*, 164). Disciples are admonished to pray when their everyday world has begun falling apart (13:14–19). At Gethsemane (14:32–42) Jesus models the prayer of a faithful follower when there is no way out, when one relies on friends whose loyalty dwindles, when the summit of divine will trumps the pit of human anguish. At Golgotha (15:34) Jesus' last words are drawn from the first lament of Psalm 22:1 (see Black, *Mark*, 292–97, 328–37). Mark's most important contribution to the Gospels' meditations on prayer may lie at the collision of desperate need and sheer begging for help. Such clashes "cannot be driven out by anything but prayer" (Mark 9:29 RSV).

30

John (ca. AD 100)

The Fourth Gospel employs some different terms for prayer than ✓
those in the Synoptics. The commonplace expression of thanksgiving to God at meals, *eucharisteō*, appears twice at supper (John
6:11, 23) and again in Jesus' prayer at Lazarus's tomb (11:41).
Instead of *proseuchomai* and *proseuchē*, which John never uses,
we find *erōtaō* (27×) and *aiteō* (11×), which in the New Testament
are essentially synonymous: "to ask for" or "request." John uses the
same wording for affairs both human (1:19, 21, 25; 4:9–10, 31, 40,
47; 5:12; 8:7; 9:2, 8, 15, 19, 21, 23; 12:21; 16:5, 19, 30; 18:7, 19, 21;
19:31, 38) and divine (11:22; 14:13–14, 16; 15:7, 16; 16:23–24, 26;
17:9, 15, 20). (In Mark the verbs *erōtaō* and *aiteō* appear a total of
38× but only once with reference to prayer: at 11:24, which may be
literally translated, "everything whatsoever that you pray and ask
for.") In John *erōtaō* and *aiteō* appear interchangeable: linguistically the Fourth Gospel makes no distinction between petitions to
God and everyday requests of humans.

As in many other respects John's presentation of prayer stands
apart from the Synoptics'. In the Fourth Gospel Jesus prays (11:41–
42; 12:28; 17:1–26), though usually for reasons dissimilar to those in
the other Gospels. John 12:27–28a could be interpreted as knowing yet rejecting Jesus' torment in the Gethsemane tradition: "Now
my soul is troubled. And what should I say—'Father, save me from
this hour'? No, it is for this reason that I have come to this hour.
Father, glorify your name." At the Last Supper in Luke (22:31–32),
Jesus assures Simon of his prayer that Peter's faith might withstand
satanic assault and that he might repent and strengthen his brothers; the Johannine Jesus prays that God may keep his disciples from
the evil one (John 17:15). Yet the rest of Jesus' prayers for those he
leaves behind, separated from the world, are without parallel in the
Synoptics:

> [Father,] I am asking on their behalf; I am not asking on behalf
> of the world, but on behalf of those whom you gave me, because
> they are yours. . . . Holy Father, protect them in your name that
> you have given me, so that they may be one, as we are one. . . .
> Sanctify them in the truth; your word is truth. As you have sent
> me into the world, so I have sent them into the world. . . . I ask
> not only on behalf of these, but also on behalf of those who will

31

believe in me through their word, that they may all be one. (John 17:9, 11b, 17–18, 20)

Gathered into these entreaties is a wealth of insight into Johannine ecclesiology: God's election, separation, and sustenance of the church in truth, which the world at large rejects; the Father's protection of Christ's followers after his departure; their role as emissaries into the world, commissioned by the Son who was himself sent by the Father (3:17; 3:34; 4:34; et al.); the extension of discipleship to those who entrust themselves to the earliest disciples' proclamation of Jesus; the unity of the church in Christ across time and space.

Nowhere in the Synoptic Gospels do we find repeated petitions for the Son's mutual glorification with the Father who sent him, which forms the basis of the church's unity with the Son and the Father:

Father, the hour has come; glorify your Son so that the Son may glorify you. . . . So now, Father, glorify me in your own presence with the glory that I had in your presence before the world existed. . . . The glory that you have given me I have given them, so that they may be one, as we are one, I in them and you in me, that they may become completely one, so that the world may know that you have sent me and have loved them even as you have loved me. Father, I desire that those also, whom you have given me, may be with me where I am, to see my glory, which you have given me because you loved me before the foundation of the world. (John 17:1, 5, 22–24; cf. Matt. 11:27 = Luke 10:22)

Time and again in John, God or God's name is "glorified" (*doxazō*: 11:4; 12:28; 13:32; 14:13; 15:8; 17:1, 4; 21:19). Because the incarnate Logos is the window onto divine glory (1:14), it is not unusual for Jesus to be glorified by God or by his disciples (7:39; 11:4; 13:31–32; 16:14; 17:5, 10)—though the Son never glorifies himself (8:54) and the unique opportunity for his glorification is, ironically, "the hour" of his crucifixion (12:23; 17:1; cf. 12:16). Reciprocally, the church is beneficiary of that glory and unity in love that binds the Son with the Father.

In John, there is a palpable sense of "overhearing" Jesus' prayers. Even though his disciples are presumably auditors of the

32

great prayer in 17:1–26, they fade out of the narrative: the reader of John 17 seems the true audience of the Son's pleas. That impression tallies with Jesus' assertion at Lazarus's tomb (11:41b–42): "Father, I thank you for having heard me. I knew that you always hear me, but I have said this for the sake of the crowd standing here, so that they may believe that you sent me." The unity of the Son with the Father is so deep that the Son needn't ask anything of the latter: "'Father, glorify your name.' Then a voice came from heaven, 'I have glorified it, and I will glorify it again.' . . . Jesus answered, 'This voice has come for [the crowd's] sake, not for mine'" (12:28, 30). In John, Jesus' repeated request of God is his disciples' unity in love with one another, with the Son, and with the Father (17:12, 17–18, 21–23; 13:34–35; 14:21, 31; 15:12–14).

Only in John does Jesus encourage disciples to pray in *his* name, after his departure (14:13; 16:24, 26; cf. 1:12; 2:23; 3:18; 20:31)—an astonishing admonition that is again predicated on Jesus' oneness with God: "The works that I do in my Father's name testify to me" (10:25; cf. 5:19–21). Prayer offered in Jesus' name will be granted (14:13–14; 15:16; 16:23–24). The suppressed premise of this assurance is that petitions commensurate with the Son's own words and deeds, which replicate those of the Father, define prayer offered in Jesus' name. This point is made explicit, not in the Fourth Gospel, but in the theologically cognate First Letter of John: "And this is the boldness we have in him, that if we ask anything *according to his will*, he hears us. And if we know that he hears us in whatever we ask, we know that we have obtained the requests made of him" (1 John 5:14–15, emphasis added; cf. Mark 11:24).

In the view of some commentators (Brown, *John (xiii–xxi)*, 747–48; Brooke, "Lord's Prayer Interpreted through John and Paul"; Walker, "Lord's Prayer in Matthew and John"), John 17 exhibits points of contact with the Lord's Prayer: glorification (or hallowing) of the Father's name (vv. 1, 4, 6, 11–12; cf. Matt. 6:9 = Luke 11:2), completion of the work begun by Jesus (John 17:4; cf. Matt. 6:10 = Luke 11:2), protection from the evil one (John 17:15; cf. Matt. 6:13 = Luke 11:4), and perhaps provision of bread (cf. Matt. 6:11 = Luke 11:3 with John's equation of "the bread of life" and "eternal life," as suggested in 6:32–58; 17:1–2). Jesus' prayer in John 17 is virtually the Lord's Prayer transposed into a Johannine key—with a difference: "[John 17] is as much declaration as petition, uttered under the conviction that Jesus did the will and work

33

of his Father and thus brought glory to the Father . . . [and] life to the world" (Thompson, *John*, 346–47).

Matthew (ca. AD 85)

The language of prayer in Matthew exceeds that in Mark though it is less frequent than in John. In Matthew the verb *proseuchomai* occurs fifteen times (5:44; 6:5 [2×], 6 [2×], 7, 9; 14:23; 19:13; 24:20; 26:36, 39, 41, 42, 44); the noun *proseuchē*, twice (21:13, 22). *Eucharisteō*, the mealtime thanksgiving, occurs twice (15:36; 26:27); *doxazō*, when used for praising God, twice (5:16; 9:8). John's preferred verbs for "asking," *erōtaō* and *aiteō*, appear in Matthew, respectively, twelve (also counting *eperōtaō*) and fourteen times. The first verb is never used in reference to prayer; the second, however, is thus employed several times, conspicuously in the Sermon on the Mount:

> Ask [*Aitete*], and it will be given you; search, and you will find; knock, and the door will be opened for you. For everyone who asks receives, and everyone who searches finds, and for everyone who knocks, the door will be opened. Is there anyone among you who, if your child asks for bread, will give a stone? Or if the child asks for a fish, will give a snake? If you then, who are evil, know how to give good gifts to your children, how much more will your Father in heaven give good things to those who ask him! (Matt. 7:7–11)

These exhortations correspond with other comments on prayer in Matthew: God knows what we need before we ask (6:8), "my Father in heaven" will ratify concurrent prayers in conformity with Jesus' teachings on mercy and judgment (18:19), and petitions faithfully offered will be granted (21:22). Beyond a version of the Lord's Prayer itself, Matthew offers precisely what the Gospel of John does not: Jesus' detailed instructions on *how* his disciples should pray—with unreserved love and magnanimity: "But I say to you, Love your enemies and pray for those who persecute you" (Matt. 5:44).

34

Matthew's version of the Lord's Prayer invites more precise location within that Gospel as a whole, attentive to this evangelist's literary style and theological concerns.

1. Without pushing the evidence beyond reasonable limits, the ✓✓ whole of Matthew and its Sermon on the Mount (5:1–7:29) may be considered commentaries on Jesus' prayer in Matthew 6:9–13 or at least developments of its constituent elements (see Dillon, "Obedience of Prayer"; Kiley, "Lord's Prayer"). The address to "Our Father in heaven" (6:9) chimes with Jesus' reference to God throughout this Gospel (5:16, 45, 48; 6:1, 14, 26, 32; 7:11, 21; 10:32–33; 11:25; 12:50; 15:13; 16:17; 18:10, 14, 19, 35; 23:9). Jesus' Great Commission mandates baptism "in the name of the Father and of the Son and of the Holy Spirit" (28:19). The heavenly kingdom's coming and fulfillment of divine will (6:10) loom large in the Matthean Jesus (3:2; 4:17; 6:33; 10:7; 12:28, 50; 18:14; 21:31). Jesus' own prayers for strength under human pressure and satanic assault (6:12–14) recur in this Gospel (4:1–11; 14:13–21; 15:32–39; 26:36–46); as in Mark, Matthew's Jesus is the model disciple of God's kingdom that none of his own disciples can be. Several restatements of the Prayer's petitions occur in material that is distinctive to Matthew, appearing in none of the other Gospels (3:2–3; 6:1–8, 14–18; 21:28–32; 28:16–20).

2. Especially with regard to Jesus' five great discourses in this Gospel, which constitute the narrative's spine (Matt. 5:1–29; 10:5–42; 13:1–52; 18:1–35; 24:1–25:46), commentators have long admired Matthew's careful organization. The Lord's Prayer in this Gospel displays comparable precision. It is strategically positioned (6:5–15) as the second of three examples of authentic, practical piety that Jesus' disciples should practice (alongside almsgiving, or just charity for the poor [6:1–4] and fasting, or spiritual disciplines [6:16–18]). Moreover, the Prayer is centrally located within the Sermon on the Mount (about 116 verses into that section, with 114 verses completing it) as "the powerhouse for living the Sermon's discipleship" (Bruner, *Matthew*, 292). The Prayer itself is symmetrically balanced, with two tables that correlate three invocations for that which is worthy of God—

Hallowed be your name; (6:9)
Your kingdom come; (6:10a)
Your will be done; (6:10b)

—with another three confessing human need:

Give us this day our daily bread; (6:11)
And forgive us our debts; (6:12a)
And do not bring us to the time of trial, but rescue us. (6:13)

A similar pattern is discernible in the Ten Commandments, whose first table acknowledges the LORD God (Exod. 20:1–11 = Deut. 5:6–15); its second, communal responsibilities that flow from that theological basis (Exod. 20:12–17 = Deut. 5:16–21).

3. The Prayer's first three petitions, concentrated on God, set the stage for the rest: as a whole, the Prayer is theocentric, addressed to God alone. For Matthew, as for Karl Barth (*CD* 3/4:88), "Prayer is not prayer if it is addressed to anyone else but God"—even if its words are misappropriated for demonstrations of human faith or covert sermonizing. For Matthew, prayer intends not to move God but rather to reform disciples' dispositions (Byrne, *Lifting the Burden*, 64). Praying in this way creates order and cohesion in the praying community (Carter, "The Lord's Prayer"). Nevertheless, the church's reformation and coherence are *by-products* of the Prayer, not its primary purpose: the honor of God.

4. God alone is the measure of true righteousness (*hē dikaiosynē*; cf. 5:17–20). "Be perfect [*teleios*], therefore, *as your heavenly Father is perfect*" (5:48, emphasis added). In context Matthew refers not to "impeccable sinlessness" but instead to an essential wholeness or integrity, derivative from the heavenly Father, that properly activates human conduct: "that you may be children of your Father in heaven; for he makes his sun rise on the evil and on the good, and sends rain on the righteous and on the unrighteous" (5:45a). Jesus' disciples follow his own lead in living as God lives: embracing the poor (5:3; 11:5; 19:21) and even the enemy (5:44; 26:50).

5. The anthropological correlate for prayer with integrity is an acknowledgment of humanity's utter dependence on God for everything, with no special petitions made at others' expense. Matthew underscores the *opposite* of such integrity in prayer:

> And whenever you pray, do not be like the hypocrites; for they love to stand and pray in the synagogues and at the street corners, so that they may be seen by others. Truly I tell you, they have received their reward. But whenever you pray, go into your room and shut the door and pray to your Father who is in secret; and your Father who sees in secret will reward you. When you are praying, do not heap up empty phrases as the Gentiles do; for they think that they will be heard because of their many words. (6:5–7)

Hypocrisy (*hē hypokrisis*) is the disparity between word and deed, appearance and reality (cf. Matt. 15:7–9; 22:18; 23:13, 15, 23, 25,

27–29; 24:48–51), exemplified by prayer babbled for public display. "Prayer is necessarily hidden. . . . When people pray, they no longer know themselves; they know only God, to whom they are calling. [Prayer] is the least demonstrative act there is" (Bonhoeffer, *Discipleship*, 153). Before God there is no self-conscious posturing; there is only the child's cry of need to an utterly loving Parent who meets us in secret. Another corruption of prayer is verbosity, as though God were ignorant of our needs and required briefing (Matt. 6:32; cf. Isa. 65:24; Eccl. 5:2) or would attend to us only if we kept yammering away (cf. Isa. 1:15). "God," mused Luther, "has no need of such everlasting twaddle. . . . Prayers ought to be brief, frequent, and intense" (*Sermon on the Mount*, 142–43). Of all the evangelists only Matthew uses the term *doxazō* in a negative sense: praise that should be accorded to God is bastardized by "hypocrites who [give alms] in the synagogues and in the streets, so that they may be praised [*doxasthōsin*] by others" (Matt. 6:2).

6. Matthew's Gospel shows evidence of a Jewish community, perhaps a synagogue in exile, claiming that in Jesus the Messiah has come, a claim placing it in conflict with its coreligionists (Matt. 10:17; 23:1–39). That, however, by no means eradicates its foundational Jewish attitudes and assumptions. Intertestamental as well as later rabbinic texts, likely based on traditions proximate to Jesus' day, echo many of Matthew's own claims (see Finkel, "The Prayer of Jesus in Matthew").

Do not babble in the assembly of the elders,
    and do not repeat yourself when you pray.
       (Sir. 7:14 [2nd c. BC])

Transpersonal matters will be forgiven to you but not interpersonal matters until you reconcile with your friend. (*Sifra* to Lev. 15:30)

R[abbi] Eleazar [prayed]: May it be Your will, O Lord our God, that there be in our midst love, and brotherhood and peace, and friendship, that many disciples may come to study under our auspices. . . . May You help us grow toward perfection in Your world through good companions and through good impulses. . . . Rabbi [Judah ha-Nasi] . . . added the following: May it be Your will, O Lord our God, to save us from arrogant men and guard me from showing arrogance toward others. . . . R[abbi] Safra . . . added the following: May it be Your will, O Lord our God, to establish

37

> peace in the heavenly order above and in the earthly order below
> and among disciples who study Your Torah. . . . And . . . may it
> be Your will that they study it for its own sake. . . . (b. Berakhot
> 16b–17a)

The correlations with Matthew are obvious: repudiation of pious showboating (6:1–8, 16–18); the imperative of communal reconciliation before praying (5:23–24; 6:14–16); the desire for peace that issues from the law's fulfillment (5:17–18; 7:12; 22:37–40). Matthew's congregation appears to have been moving away from others' synagogues (10:17; 23:1–26), but it never abandons Judaism. This Gospel is so fully Jewish that it is unintelligible apart from first-century Judaism, its ancient inheritance and rabbinic legacy.

Luke (ca. AD 85)

In the Third Gospel, Jesus' ministry is also rooted in Judaism, though with a different flourish. Luke appears to address a wider Gentile world needing reminder of the gospel's Jewish heart (1:1–4; 24:47). And no Gospel emphasizes prayer to a greater degree than does Luke. Of all the Evangelists, Luke's vocabulary of prayer is the richest: *proseuchomai*, "request of the Deity," occurs 18 times (1:10; 3:21; 5:16; 6:12, 28; 9:18, 28–29; 11:1–2; 18:1, 10–11; 20:47; 22:40–41, 44, 46); *proseuchē*, "prayer," thrice (6:12; 19:46; 22:45); *aiteō*, "ask in prayer," 5 times (11:9–13); *eucharisteō*, "thanks [to God]," 4 times (17:16; 18:11; 22:17, 19); *erōtaō*, "ask in prayer," once (16:27); *deēsis*, "urgent request," 3 times (1:13; 2:37; 5:33: a term appearing 15 times in the New Testament Epistles though never in Matthew, Mark, or John). A favorite Lukan verb for prayer is *doxazō*, occurring 9 times (2:20; 5:25, 26; 7:16; 13:13; 17:15; 18:43; 23:47), with such "praise" directed once toward Jesus (4:15). Save *deēsis*, all these synonyms frequently recur in the Acts of the Apostles, Luke's second volume.

The Third Gospel is bookended by prayer. "The whole assembly of the people was praying outside" the temple at the moment when Zechariah, while offering incense, was confronted by the angel Gabriel and assured that his prayers and those of Elizabeth had been heard (Luke 1:8–13). After having been blessed by the risen Jesus, his disciples "were continually in the temple blessing God" (24:51–53). Luke's entire narrative is thus situated within Judaism's liturgical life. This theme is repeated in Luke's characterization of the prophet Anna, who "never left the temple but worshiped there with fasting and prayer night and day" and "began to praise God and to speak about [Mary's] child to all who were looking for the redemption of Jerusalem" (2:37–38). Only Luke's infancy narrative contains the great Advent and Christmas canticles: the Annunciation to Mary (1:32–33, 35), Mary's Magnificat (1:46–56), Zechariah's Benedictus (1:68–79), the Gloria in Excelsis Deo of the heavenly host (2:14), Simeon's Nunc Dimittis (2:29–35). As free paraphrases of Old Testament material (see Brown, *Birth of the Messiah*, 346–92), all these are blessings (1:68; 2:28) or praises (1:46; 2:13) to God for his Messiah's coming.

Jesus, "a Savior, who is Christ the Lord" (2:11 RSV), executes a ministry that is distinguished by prayer. All of the evangelists mention that, as Luke puts it (5:16), Jesus "would withdraw to deserted places and pray" (cf. Matt. 14:23; Mark 1:35; 6:46; Luke 6:12). Often Luke reports events found in the other Synoptic Gospels but inserts a note that Jesus is praying when they occur: his baptism (3:21), his selection of the Twelve (6:12), Peter's confession at Caesarea Philippi and Jesus' first passion prediction (9:18), Jesus' transfiguration (9:28), and his special prayer for Simon at the Last Supper (22:32). Jesus is at prayer when a disciple asks that he teach them to pray, "as John taught his disciples" (11:1): details absent from the other Gospels. Prayer is built into the Lukan Jesus' dispatch of an advance guard of seventy (seventy-two, in some manuscripts): "The harvest is plentiful, but the laborers are few; therefore ask the Lord of the harvest to send out laborers into his harvest" (10:1–2; cf. Matt. 9:37–38). Emphasizing its inspired jubilation (cf. Matt. 11:25–27), Luke presents Jesus' thanksgiving to God: "I thank you, Father, Lord of heaven and earth, because you have hidden these things from the wise and the intelligent and have revealed them to infants; yes, Father, for such was your gracious will. All things have been handed over to me by my Father; and no one knows who the Son is except the Father, or who the Father is except the Son and anyone to whom the Son chooses to reveal him" (10:21–22; a prayer absent from Mark but theologically reminiscent of John). The third evangelist shares with the first evangelist Jesus' teaching

39

about prayer's efficacy (Luke 11:9–13 = Matt. 7:7–11; cf. Mark 11:25); only in Luke do we find parables about prayer (the friend at midnight, 11:5–8; the rich man and Lazarus, 16:19–31; the widow and the unrighteous judge, 18:1–8; the Pharisee and the tax collector, 18:9–14). In their accounts of Jesus at the Mount of Olives (Gethsemane), all the evangelists report that he went there to pray (Matt. 26:36 = Mark 14:32; Luke 22:41) and urged the same of his faltering disciples (Matt. 26:41 = Mark 14:38 = Luke 22:40); only Luke states that Jesus' act was customary (22:39; cf. 4:16). Some manuscripts of Luke memorably describe the appearance of an angel strengthening Jesus, who in anguish "prayed more earnestly, and his sweat became like great drops of blood falling down on the ground" (22:43–44). As in Matthew (27:46) and Mark (15:34), in Luke (23:46) the crucified Jesus' last words quote the Psalter, though in Luke it is Psalm 31:5 (not 22:1): "Father, into your hands I commend my spirit." Some Lukan manuscripts attribute to the dying Jesus yet another prayer: "Father, forgive them; for they do not know what they are doing" (23:34). The Lukan Jesus is himself the exemplar of prayer (Edmonds, "The Lucan Our Father").

Of all the evangelists, Luke's view of prayer is hardest to grasp—not because he makes the subject difficult, but because it has so many different facets. As we have seen, unadulterated prayer is a mandate for discipleship in Matthew, which highlights ways in which prayer may be perverted. Prayer is no less characteristic of discipleship in Luke, who is also bothered by hypocrisy (6:42; 12:1, 54–56; 13:15; 20:20); nevertheless, Luke's stress is less hortatory or corrective. Prayer is one aspect of "a sense of God" that pervades Luke and Acts (Beck, *Christian Character*, 55–70). "Amazement," even "fear," is a typical human response in Luke-Acts (1:12–13, 30, 63; 2:9–10, 18, 33, 47; 4:22, 36; 5:9; 7:9; 8:25; 9:43; 11:14, 38; 21:26; 24:5, 12; Acts 2:7; 3:10, 12; 4:13; 7:31; 8:9, 11, 13; 9:21; 12:16; 13:41): when God, mysterious and powerful, revisits Israel and the nations through Jesus and the Holy Spirit, the appropriate reaction is one of awe. As modeled by Jesus (Luke 3:21; 5:16; 6:12; 9:18, 28; 22:41), prayer is humanity's proper stance—better is bowing (22:41; Acts 7:60; 9:40; 20:36; 21:5)—before such a God.

Having awaited Israel's consolation, pious Simeon is empowered by the Spirit to take in his arms the infant Messiah and praise God (Luke 2:25–28):

40

Master [*Despota*], now you are dismissing your servant [*doulon*]
    in peace,
    according to your word;
for my eyes have seen your salvation,
    which you have prepared in the presence of all peoples,
a light for revelation to the Gentiles
    and for glory to your people Israel. (2:29–32)

Simeon's modes of address and self-identification strike, for Luke, the proper balance: the God who invades human history remains *Despota*, "the Most High" Lord over mortal slaves and handmaidens (cf. 1:35, 38).

Such recognition of God's authority evokes several responses. One is humility: seeing God for who God is reveals to us the truth about ourselves. "Do you thank the slave for doing what was commanded? So you also, when you have done all that you were ordered to do, say, 'We are worthless slaves; we have done only what we ought to have done!'" (17:9–10; cf. 14:7–11; 16:14–15; 22:24–27). Granted that sense of perspective, the refusal to trade on religious duty is depicted most poignantly in this parable of prayer, found only in Luke:

> Two men went up to the temple to pray, one a Pharisee and the other a tax collector. The Pharisee, standing by himself, was praying thus, "God, I thank you that I am not like other people: thieves, rogues, adulterers, or even like this tax collector. I fast twice a week; I give a tenth of all my income." But the tax collector, standing far off, would not even look up to heaven, but was beating his breast and saying, "God, be merciful to me, a sinner!" I tell you, this man went down to his home justified rather than the other; for all who exalt themselves will be humbled, but all who humble themselves will be exalted. (18:10–14)

Luke introduces that parable by saying that Jesus told it "to some who trusted in themselves that they were righteous and regarded others with contempt" (18:9). In the kingdom's scheme of values, righteousness cannot be self-generated (16:15); God bestows it only upon those who abase themselves before him. That, for Luke (as for the Old Testament), is what repentance means: the acknowledgment of God's just verdict upon us (7:29, 35; cf. 1 Kgs. 8:31–34;

41

Job 8:1–8; Isa. 2:12–17; Ezek. 28:1–26). When the prodigal child can own up to his sin, God's grace races to embrace and honor him (Luke 15:17–24).

✓   More than the other evangelists, Luke associates prayer with joy and praise of God. Forty-two times the third Gospel uses eleven verbs that ring changes on "rejoice" or "praise"; by comparison, John mentions this response 20 times; Matthew, 14; Mark, 5. Cognate nouns and adjectives appear 16 times in Luke, 10 in John, 8 in Matthew, and only twice in Mark. The sound of joy pervades the canticles of the Lukan infancy narrative (1:46–47, 68–69; 2:14, 29–30). Again Luke refers, neither to self-motivated feeling nor self-satisfaction with one's achievements, but rather to praise evoked by God's Holy Spirit for God's mighty acts (1:67–68, 78; 10:18, 21; 15:6, 9, 23–24; cf. Acts 2:11; 10:46; 13:52).

Because prayer strengthens Jesus at critical moments, it is natural for his followers to expect the same (Luke 22:40, 46). Yet the third evangelist expresses special concern that disciples may become disheartened, giving up on prayer and even on God's faithfulness:

> Then Jesus told them a parable about their need to pray always and not to lose heart. He said, "In a certain city there was a judge who neither feared God nor had respect for people. In that city there was a widow who kept coming to him and saying, 'Grant me justice against my opponent.' For a while he refused; but later he said to himself, 'Though I have no fear of God and no respect for anyone, yet because this widow keeps bothering me, I will grant her justice, so that she may not wear me out by continually coming.'" And the Lord said, "Listen to what the unjust judge says. And will not God grant justice to his chosen ones who cry to him day and night? Will he delay long in helping them? I tell you, he will quickly grant justice to them. And yet, when the Son of Man comes, will he find faith on earth?" (18:1–8)

In that context it is significant that one of Jesus' disciples asks him for specific instructions on how they should pray (11:1). After fulfilling that request, Jesus returns to the issue of persistence in praying, comparing the gifts of reluctant friends or incompetent parents with God's boundless grace (11:5–12): "If you then, who are evil, know how to give good gifts to your children, how much more will

42

the heavenly Father give the Holy Spirit to those who ask him!" (11:13; cf. Matt. 7:11).

The paradigmatic prayer Jesus offers in Luke (11:2–4) is much like that in Matthew (6:9–13), albeit simpler and crisper. One finds the same theocentricity, encompassing basic human need. Repeatedly in Luke, Jesus refers to God as his "Father" (2:49; 10:21–22; 22:29, 42; 23:46; 24:49), encouraging his disciples to regard God likewise (6:36; 11:2, 13; 12:30, 32). The intimacy of that address, linked with the assurance that God knows and will satisfy disciples' needs (11:3–13), quells anxiety about life's necessities (12:22–34) and frees Jesus' followers from misplaced confidence in mammon (6:24; 12:13–21, 33; 16:11–13, 19–31; 18:23–25). Every bit as much as Matthew and Mark, Luke presents Jesus as the vanguard of God's sovereign reign, in process of realization: "He will reign over the house of Jacob forever, and of his kingdom there will be no end" (1:33; cf. 4:43; 6:20; and 38 other references to the kingdom). No Gospel is more insistent than Luke on the responsibility of releasing sinners from their sin: "Forgive, and you will be forgiven. . . . If another disciple sins, you must rebuke the offender, and if there is repentance, you must forgive" (6:37; 17:3; see also 1:77; 3:3; 5:21, 24; 11:4; 17:4; 23:34; 24:47; Acts 5:31; 10:43; 13:38; 26:18). The importance of the petition to be spared "the time of trial" (Luke 11:4) is hammered home at the Mount of Olives immediately before Jesus' own arrest and trials (23:40, 46; cf. 22:47–23:25).

To summarize: Luke presents prayer both as a response invoked by God's presence and as a mandate for Jesus' followers. As in Matthew, so also in Luke: there's no separating a coherent understanding of God (theology) from moral responsibility that emanates from it (ethics). Prayer is the point of intersection for disciples' beliefs and actions. Luke's own belief is that, through prayer, the Holy Spirit replenishes faith and channels conduct becoming God's kingdom.

Various Versions of Jesus' Prayer: Which Shall the Interpreter Interpret?

Matthew and Luke offer alternative renderings of the Lord's Prayer, whose details we shall assess in the chapters that follow. A parallel

43

presentation clarifies their similarities and differences. In this table identical wording is underlined.

Table 1: The Lord's Prayer in the Canonical Gospels

Luke 11:2–4	Matthew 6:9–13
²Father,	⁹Our Father,
	who is in the heavens,
May your name be hallowed.	May your name be hallowed.
May your kingdom come.	¹⁰May your kingdom come,
	may your will come to pass
	as in heaven, so also on earth.
³Keep giving us each day	¹¹Give us today
the bread we need,	the bread we need,
⁴and cancel our sins,	¹²and cancel our debts,
for we also forgive everyone	as we also have forgiven those
indebted to us.	indebted to us.
And do not bring us into	¹³And do not bring us into
temptation." (AT)	temptation,
	but rescue us from the
	evil one." (AT)

The two different renditions immediately raise preliminary questions, none of which we may resolve with full assurance. These issues should be flagged as we prepare ourselves to ponder each of the Prayer's petitions.

How did Jesus himself articulate the prayer he taught his disciples? While Jesus could have been multilingual, most scholars assume that he originally taught his disciples in Aramaic. Because both Matthew and Luke present the Lord's Prayer in Greek, it follows that the evangelists were already interpreting it for their respective churches by their translations of a probably Aramaic original. Some specialists in ancient Aramaic have attempted to retroject Jesus' original prayer into his native tongue. That is not difficult for experts to do. When they do so, they come out with something very

44

close to the Greek versions preserved in both Matthew and Luke (see Lohmeyer, *Lord's Prayer*, 27–31; Moor, "Reconstruction of the Aramaic"). However, for the purpose of this commentary, we hold fast to the presentations in Greek, given us by the first and third evangelists. The reason for this is as simple as it is cautious: however much we might wish to pray the Lord's Prayer exactly as Jesus articulated it, that oral form is beyond recovery. Except in cases where the Greek makes little or no sense, we should not bind our understanding of the prayer, or of anything else Jesus taught, to even the most sophisticated scholarly conjectures, because they are just that: conjectures. Our footing is firmer with the Greek texts of the Prayer in Matthew and Luke, as (usually) rendered in the New Revised Standard Version (1989). By no means does this procedure imply that we are settling for second best. A healthy doctrine of Scripture reminds us of our indebtedness to all the evangelists for preserving, in writing, an oral tradition that would otherwise have been lost to us. Allowing for the grace of the Holy Spirit to guide its interpretations, the church of the first and twenty-first centuries meets its Lord through scriptural mediation: documents that the church, across many centuries, came to recognize as canonical and trustworthy for understanding Jesus, his life, and his teachings.

Which of the Gospels' presentations of the Lord's Prayer should we interpret: Matthew's or Luke's?
As one may see in table 1, the New Testament's two versions of the Prayer enjoy a considerable degree of material overlap. On the other hand, neither is exactly identical to the other. Which is earlier? How would we know? If we could know, what difference would it make for understanding the Prayer? Such questions remain lively and contentious among New Testament scholars.

For the better part of the past two centuries, it is fair to say that a majority of scholars have proceeded on the presuppositions that the Lord's Prayer, originating in Jesus' Aramaic instruction, was converted into a Greek tradition or written source upon which Matthew and Luke drew, with adaptations, independently of each other. Since about 1838 that common source has been referred to as Q (so named because the German term for "source" is *Quelle*). This Q is a hypothetical collection of Jesus' sayings shared by Matthew and Luke but probably unavailable to Mark. (For a recent development

45

of this hypothesis, consult Kloppenborg, *Excavating Q.*) In recent decades the hypothesis of Q has witnessed a renewed challenge: some scholars dispense with Q altogether, explaining the material shared by Matthew and Luke as evidence of one of those Gospels borrowing from and modifying the other (see, for instance, Goodacre, *The Case against Q*). This conjecture is not unreasonable; however, when one tests it in the Gospels case by case, it generates as many questions as it answers (Sanders and Davies, *Synoptic Gospels*, 112–19). To present and assess all the evidence for and against these competing hypotheses would carry us far afield, into another book altogether. It is fair to say that a majority of New Testament scholars still hold to the notion that Matthew and Luke derived their common material, apart from Mark, from a common source that we may as well call Q, whose precise contours and interaction with ongoing oral traditions cannot be ascertained with strict precision (see Rau, "Unser Vater im Himmel").

Whose version of the Prayer was closer to the version received in Q: Matthew's or Luke's? The obvious answer is that we cannot know with certainty: Q's very existence, while plausible, is itself conjectural. At this stage of our understanding, I think it fair to say that Luke's presentation of Q's material—in general, not simply with respect to the Lord's Prayer—may have been closer to Q than Matthew's. On what basis would we grant this possibility? It is an accepted principle of biblical textual criticism that scribes who transmitted biblical texts tended to expand the material they were copying rather than to contract it. If a text were brief and difficult, scribes tended to elaborate and try to explain what seemed to them truncated or inviting explanation (see K. Aland and B. Aland, *Text of the New Testament*, 280–82). One example demonstrates the principle: by a considerable margin, our earliest, most reliable, and most geographically diverse manuscripts of Luke 11:2c present the wording *elthetō hē basileia sou*, "May your kingdom come." Less than two hundred years after Jesus, a small number of manuscripts began to modify that petition: "May your Holy Spirit come upon us and cleanse us." That is a very different presentation of Luke 11:2c, perhaps created for the benefit of readers for whom Jesus' teaching about God's kingdom may have seemed remote, but whose theology of the Spirit (pneumatology) was sufficiently developed that it made its way into public or private recitation of the Lord's Prayer (cf. Delobel, "Textual Tradition").

46

For our purposes, it is more important to notice that the process of elaborating Luke's petition for the kingdom's coming had already begun *with Matthew*, who adds what is not found in Luke: "May your will come to pass, as in heaven, so also on earth" (Matt. 6:10bc AT). Matthew would have had excellent reason to append this petition: the same evangelist presents Jesus as teaching, "Not everyone who says to me, 'Lord, Lord,' will enter the kingdom of heaven, but only the one who does the will of my Father in heaven" (7:21; see also 12:50; 18:14; 21:31; 26:42). Although he does not include that saying in his Gospel, Luke, too, is interested in the fulfillment of God's will (22:42; cf. 12:47). Had Luke known some version of the Lord's Prayer—either Matthew's or Q's or another tradition's—that included a petition for the exercise of God's will on earth, why would the third evangelist have excised it from his version of the Lord's Prayer? It's as hard to imagine a good reason for Luke's omission of that petition as it is easy to understand Matthew's addition of it: a way of interpreting, by expansion, Jesus' prayer for the kingdom's coming. For this reason, among others, scholars who presuppose Q's existence tend to assume that, in general, Luke's rendering of it appears older and less developed than its parallel presentation in Matthew.

Even if one accepts such an argument, it is insufficient to account for all textual subtleties. Another pair of examples is noteworthy (cf. underlined terms):

> And forgive us our <u>debts,</u>
> as we also have forgiven <u>our debtors.</u> (Matt. 6:12)
> And forgive us our <u>sins,</u>
> for we ourselves forgive <u>everyone indebted</u> to us. (Luke 11:4ab)

Though not exact, these alternative wordings are very close. Which is more likely to have better approximated Jesus' own words? Conceivably Jesus could have said either; had he reminded his disciples to pray more than once—hardly a far-fetched possibility—he could have shifted the terms himself. Yet the term "debt" was a more common synonym for "sin" in Aramaic (*khôbā'*: see *j. Hagigah* 277d) than in Greek, even though Luke expects his Gentile readers to draw the metaphorical connection: "everyone indebted to us" clearly suggests "everyone who has sinned against us" (see Luke 7:41–48). For this and other reasons, Joachim Jeremias suggested,

47

"In *length* the shorter text of Luke is to be regarded as original, and in general *wording* the text of Matthew is to be preferred" (*New Testament Theology*, 196). Allowing for understandable exceptions (such as that in Matt. 6:10bc), many interpreters, myself included, would accept that position as reasonable.

Conclusions

As we turn to examination of the Prayer's petitions, where does all this leave us?

1. Although a few scholars claim that the Lord's Prayer originated indirectly from Mark's Gospel (Tilborg, "A Form-Criticism of the Lord's Prayer") or directly from Matthew (Goulder, "The Composition of the Lord's Prayer"), the vast majority trace its origin to Jesus himself. We are unable to recover his very words (*ipsissima verba*). Nevertheless, with due allowance for traditional modifications, the Lord's Prayer mostly likely captures Jesus' own voice (*ipsissima vox*). Most likely, both forms that we know from Matthew and Luke reflect the essence of the Prayer as Jesus taught his disciples (Bandstra, "The Original Form of the Lord's Prayer").

2. However one resolves the question of dependency—on what oral traditions or written sources Matthew and Luke were dependent—both the manuscript evidence for the Prayer and its earliest versions in patristic commentaries support the proposition that Luke's shorter text is probably its oldest recorded form. In the commentary that follows, I shall proceed on that basis, regarding Matthew's version as an important interpretive elaboration of Jesus' petitions—expansions that are compatible with Jesus' teaching overall. However, exceptions to this rule of thumb should be allowed: even among Q's most confident proponents, many questions concerning the textual transmission of Luke 11:2b–4 = Matt. 6:9b–13 remain controversial; some may be irresolvable (Carruth and Garsky, *Q 11:2b–4*).

3. We shall see that the forms of the Lord's Prayer in Luke and in Matthew correspond with the theological attitudes of their respective Gospels. From that we need not deduce that either evangelist played eccentrically with their inherited traditions of Jesus' teaching. Instead, the versions of the Prayer in each of these Gospels most likely reflect the slightly different modes of confession in the worshiping communities from which those Gospels emerged and

48

which, in turn, their evangelists attempted to mold (so also Brown, "The *Pater Noster*," 221–22).

4. *Neither* Luke's *nor* Matthew's presentation of the Lord's Prayer should be accorded pride of place in the interpretive task. Each version speaks in conversation with the other, and both bear witness, faithful to one Lord Jesus Christ, to the worshiping church of our day.

5. Although this chapter has dealt with particular issues that have preoccupied historical-critical scholarship since the Enlightenment, this commentary will not pretend that the only worthwhile insights into the Prayer's interpretation commenced in the nineteenth century (Black, *Reading Scripture*). In the pages that follow we shall attend to the grand history of the church's reflection from the patristic, medieval, and Reformation eras. For assistance in probing this sacred text, Origen and Luther and Jeremias, among many others, enjoy a place at the exegetical table. On the other hand, this volume is not intended to serve as a commentary on all other commentaries. Our focus throughout will be on the scriptural texts, with humble acknowledgment that we stand on the shoulders of interpreters more brilliant and more insightful than ourselves.

Works Cited in Chapter 2

Aland, Kurt, and Barbara Aland. *The Text of the New Testament: An Introduction to the Critical Editions and to the Theory and Practice of Modern Textual Criticism*. Grand Rapids: Wm. B. Eerdmans Publishing Co., 1989.

Allison, Dale C., Jr. *Constructing Jesus: Memory, Imagination, and History*. Grand Rapids: Baker Academic, 2010.

Bandstra, Andrew J. "The Original Form of the Lord's Prayer." *Calvin Theological Journal* 16 (1981): 15–37.

Barth, Karl. *Church Dogmatics*. Vol. 3, *The Doctrine of Creation*. Edinburgh: T&T Clark, 1977.

Beck, Brian E. *Christian Character in the Gospel of Luke*. London: Epworth, 1989.

Black, C. Clifton. *Mark*. Abingdon New Testament Commentaries. Nashville: Abingdon Press, 2011.

———. *Reading Scripture with the Saints*. Cascade Books. Eugene, OR: Wipf & Stock, 2014.

49

Bonhoeffer, Dietrich. *Discipleship*. Translated by Barbara Green and Reinhard Krauss. Minneapolis: Fortress Press, 2001.

Brooke, George J. "The Lord's Prayer Interpreted through John and Paul." *Downside Review* 98 (1980): 298–311.

Brown, Raymond E. *The Birth of the Messiah: A Commentary on the Infancy Narratives in the Gospels of Matthew and Luke.* New updated ed. Anchor Bible Reference Library. New York: Doubleday, 1993.

―――. *The Gospel according to John (xiii–xxi)*. Anchor Bible 29. Garden City, NY: Doubleday, 1966.

―――. "The Pater Noster as an Eschatological Prayer." In *New Testament Essays*, 217–53. New York: Paulist Press, 1965.

Bruner, Frederick. *Matthew: A Commentary*. Vol. 1. Grand Rapids: Wm. B. Eerdmans Publishing Co., 2004.

Byrne, Brendan. *Lifting the Burden: Reading Matthew's Gospel in the Church Today*. Collegeville, MN: Liturgical Press, 2004.

Carruth, Shawn, and Albrecht Garsky. *Q 11:2b–4*. Vol. 1 of *Documenta Q*. Leuven: Peeters, 1996.

Carter, Warren. "Recalling the Lord's Prayer: The Authorial Audience and Matthew's Prayer as Familiar Liturgical Experience." *Catholic Biblical Quarterly* 57 (1995): 514–30.

Delobel, Joel. "The Lord's Prayer in the Textual Tradition." In *The New Testament in Early Christianity: La réception des écrits néotestamentaires dans le christianisme primitif*, edited by Jean-Marie Sevrin, 291–309. Bibliotheca ephemeridum theologicarum lovaniensium 86. Leuven: Peeters, 1989.

Dillon, Richard J. "On the Christian Obedience of Prayer (Matthew 6:5–14)." *Worship* 59 (1985): 413–26.

Dowd, Sharyn Echols. *Prayer, Power, and the Problem of Suffering: Mark 11:22–25 in the Context of Markan Theology*. Society of Biblical Literature Dissertation Series 105. Atlanta: Scholars Press, 1988.

Dunn, James D. G. *Jesus Remembered*. Grand Rapids: Wm. B. Eerdmans Publishing Co., 2003.

Edmonds, Peter. "The Lucan Our Father: A Summary of Luke's Teaching on Prayer?" *Expository Times* 91 (1979–80): 140–43.

Finkel, Asher. "The Prayer of Jesus in Matthew." In *Standing before God: Studies on Prayer in Scriptures and in Tradition with Essays; In Honor of John M. Oesterreicher*, edited by Asher Finkel and Lawrence Frizzell, 131–69. New York: Ktav, 1981.

50

Goodacre, Mark. *The Case against Q: Studies in Markan Priority and the Synoptic Problem.* Harrisburg, PA: Trinity Press International, 2002.

Goulder, Michael. "The Composition of the Lord's Prayer." *Journal of Theological Studies* 14 (1964): 32–45.

Jeremias, Joachim. *New Testament Theology.* Vol. 1, *The Proclamation of Jesus.* New York: Scribner, 1971.

Kiley, Mark. "The Lord's Prayer and Matthean Theology." In *The Lord's Prayer and Other Prayer Texts from the Greco-Roman Era,* edited by James H. Charlesworth with Mark Harding and Mark Kiley, 15–27. Valley Forge, PA: Trinity Press International, 1994.

Kloppenborg, John S. *Excavating Q.* Minneapolis: Fortress Press, 2000.

Lohmeyer, Ernst. *"Our Father": An Introduction to the Lord's Prayer.* New York: Harper & Row, 1965.

Luther, Martin. *Luther's Works.* Vol. 21, *Sermon on the Mount and the Magnificat.* St. Louis: Concordia, 1968.

Meier, John P. *A Marginal Jew: Rethinking the Historical Jesus.* Vol. 2, *Mentor, Message, and Miracles.* Garden City, NY: Doubleday, 1994.

Moor, Johannes C. de. "The Reconstruction of the Aramaic Original of the Lord's Prayer." In *The Structural Analysis of Biblical and Canaanite Poetry,* edited by Willem van der Meer and Johannes C. de Moor, 397–422. Journal for the Study of the Old Testament Supplements 74. Sheffield: JSOT Press, 1988.

Rau, Eckhard. "Unser Vater im Himmel: Eine These zum Metaphorik der Rede von Gott in der Logienquelle." *Novum Testamentum* 53 (2011): 222–43.

Sanders, E. P. *Jesus and Judaism.* Philadelphia: Fortress Press, 1985.

Sanders, E. P., and Margaret Davies. *Studying the Synoptic Gospels.* Philadelphia: Trinity Press International, 1989.

Thompson, Marianne. *John: A Commentary.* New Testament Library. Louisville, KY: Westminster John Knox Press, 2015.

Tilborg, S. van. "A Form-Criticism of the Lord's Prayer." *Novum Testamentum* 14 (1972): 94–105.

Walker, William O., Jr. "The Lord's Prayer in Matthew and John." *New Testament Studies* 28 (1982): 237–56.

PART TWO

Interpreting the Prayer

The First Table

Our Father, who art in heaven,

hallowed be thy name.

Thy kingdom come,

thy will be done on earth as it is in heaven.

CHAPTER 3

Our Heavenly Father

Mama's relationship with God was different from Papa's. He taught us
to worship God formally, using prayers we had memorized. Mama's was
an intimate, personal kinship. God was her Father and our Grandfather.
She appealed to God directly: "Dear God, how long will this strike go on?
Have a little mercy. The children need shoes." Although she stood in awe
of the holy word, she said her prayers as she felt them. When the fourth
kid [of eight] went down with the measles, she began to lose patience.
"Enough already, dear God. How much do you think I can take?"
                                                          —Sam Levenson

Analysis of the Lord's Prayer, a phrase or clause at a time, is as necessary as it is convenient. Unfortunately that procedure may also
obscure. Take the Prayer's address and first two petitions in Luke
11:2bc:

> Father,
> Let your name hallowed.
> May your kingdom come.

God as "Father" requires an entire chapter of comment. However,
the moment that characterization is sheared away from its linkage
with God as king and the sanctity of the divine name, the text's
meaning is muffled—as though one had dialed a stereo's playback
to the left speaker only, muting the music in the right channel. For
that reason, in this and subsequent chapters, we shall consider
each of the Prayer's elements in interaction with what precedes

55

and follows. If Matthew's version was built upon Luke's foundation—"Our Father in heaven"—then already we see evidence of such interpenetrative interpretation. The prepositional phrase heightens the paternal image's congruence with "the kingdom of heaven" (Matt. 3:2; 4:17; 5:3, 10, 19–20; among others); the possessive pronoun "our" anticipates the community's cries for help in the Prayer's second half (6:11–13).

Fathers in Antiquity, Human and Otherwise

In Greek literature God's characterization as father was ancient and persistent. Homer's *Odyssey* (1.28; 8th c. BC) magnifies Zeus as "father of both mortals and gods"; Plato's *Timaeus* (28c; ca. 360 BC) speaks of God as "author and father of all things"; the Stoic *Hymn to Zeus* (mid-3rd c. BC) prays, "Scatter, O Father, the darkness from [your children's] souls; grant that they may find true understanding, which guides you in governing everything with justice" (AT). The comparison of worldly sovereigns with celestial counterparts is equally old and pervasive, from Xenophon's *Anabasis* (3.1.12: a "dream seemed to have come from Zeus in his character as the King" [AT, ca. 370 BC]) to Dio Chrysostom's reference to Zeus as "the great King of kings" (*Discourse* 2.75 [late 1st c. AD]; cf. Rev. 17:14; 19:16), the supreme coordinator of universal concord.

In ancient Mediterranean cultures the family was the fundamental social unit; its father was the family's head. The father's responsibility was to educate his children and to safeguard their inheritance, in return for which they were expected to revere their father. Roman civil law codified what had become customary: the paterfamilias—the father or the household's oldest male relative—exercised authority (patria potestas, "paternal power") over all family members (Treggiari, *Roman Marriage*, 15–36). In turn, "What does [the] character of a son imply? To esteem all that is his as his father's property; to obey him in every instance; never to blame him before anyone; not to say or do anything injurious to him; to give way and yield in everything; cooperating with him to the utmost of his power" (Epictetus [AD 55–135], *Discourses* 2.10.7).

Recent scholarship has challenged assumptions of the all-powerful paterfamilias in Hellenistic families. Whereas Roman law conferred on the father awesome powers over his offspring, in practice greater flexibility appears to have existed between them in such matters as economic allowances (*peculia*) and the selection of children's spouses (Treggiari, 83–124). Laws recognizing the power of bequests by deceased mothers qualified and occasionally abrogated patria potestas (Pliny the Younger [61–ca. 113], *Letters* 4.2; *Digest of Justinian* [6th c. AD] 5.3.58; 29.7.6). Even though Cicero (106–43 BC) repeatedly considers *pietas* (duty) obligatory among social inferiors to their superiors (*Composition of Arguments* 2.65–66), other evidence suggests that *pietas* was characterized by reciprocal affection and responsibilities shared by all family members (Renier, *Étude sur l'histoire*, 75). In an evil time "neither son nor father takes care for the other's well-being" (the Babylonian *Erra Epic*, tablet 2 [8th c. BC]). Richard Saller concludes, "The law set broad boundaries to behavior, but was very far from determining the Roman family experience, [which] was not perceived by the Romans as wholly asymmetrical with complete authority on one side matched by obedience on the other" ("*Pietas*, Obligation, and Authority," 410).

Fathers in the Old Testament and Second Temple Judaism

The Hebrew term *'abh* denotes the ancestor of a tribe: again, the primary social unit, conventionally denoted as "the father's house" (*bêth-'ābh*: thus, Gen. 12:1; Judg. 19:2–3; 1 Sam. 2:27–31 RSV). To encourage remembrance of its ancestry, Israel was directed to "look to Abraham your father and to Sarah who bore you; for he was but one when I called him, but I blessed him and made him many" (Isa. 51:2). Derivative kinship and authority resided in the clan's earthly father, who bequeathed to his children an inheritance (Gen. 31:14; Num. 27:11; 36:7, 9) and to whom were due his offspring's obedience, honor, and fear (Deut. 21:18; Mal. 1:6). To mock one's father invoked a curse on one's self (Gen. 27:12); in Deuteronomistic law flagrant violation of the fifth commandment (Deut. 5:16) was reckoned a capital crime (21:18–21). Israel's wisdom tradition stresses the mutual responsibilities of parents and children: the former, to instruct (Prov. 10:1; 22:6; 23:24); the latter, to be educated (15:20; 23:22, 25).

57

From that basic bond between generations many metaphorical applications of "fatherhood" flourished: among others, an occupation's founder (Jabal and Jubal, the fathers, respectively, of cattlemen and musicians: Gen. 4:20–21), priests (Judg. 17:10; 18:19) or prophets (2 Kgs. 2:12; 6:21), a counselor (Gen. 45:8; 1 Macc. 2:65), the servants' master (2 Kgs. 5:13), a protector of the poor or orphaned (Job 29:16; Isa. 22:21). The title of the Mishnaic tractate *Pirke Aboth*, "Sayings [or Precepts] of the Fathers" (ca. AD 200), epitomizes the term's application to Israel's esteemed teachers.

Reference to God as "father" is not as commonplace in the Old Testament as one might suppose. As Israelite Yahwism became more relentlessly monotheistic, that figure of speech may have seemed risky, opening the door to literal belief in humanity's kinship with the one God whose ways transcend those of all mortals (Isa. 55:7–9; Mal. 2:9–10). In any event two strands of thought can be traced in Second Temple Judaism. The first refers to God as "father of the world" (Wis. 10:1), which flirts with Plato's imagery of "the father and maker of all this universe" (*Timaeus* 28c). Reading the Septuagint through the lens of Greek philosophy, Philo of Alexandria (25 BC–AD 50) amalgamates God's fatherhood into cosmic generator (*Special Laws* 3.189; *The Creation* 84), spouse and father of the human soul (*Dreams* 2.273; *Change of Names* 205), author of virtue (*Flight and Finding* 62), and sovereign power (*The Cherubim* 27). Absolute reference to God as "the Father," commonplace in John's Gospel (e.g., 1:18; 3:35; 4:21, 23; 5:19–23; see table 2), is also typical of Philo (*The Creation* 46, 89, 156; *Special Laws* 2.59; *Migration of Abraham* 118). Josephus (AD 37–ca. 100) describes God as "father and source of the universe, maker of things both human and divine" (*Jewish Antiquities* 7.380), yet also particularizes God as "Lord and Father of the Hebrew race" (5.93).

The second aspect of God's paternity in Second Temple Judaism retains Israel's exclusive relationship to the Father. From this perspective, God is "our Lord and . . . our God, [who] is our Father and . . . God forever" (Tob. 13:4), "the first Father of all" (3 Macc. 2:21; cf. 6:2–3), "a Father to all the sons of Your truth" (Qumran's 1QH 9:35–36). As early as Exodus (4:22) the LORD God is acknowledged as the father of a people: "Thus says the LORD: Israel is my firstborn son."

58

The implication of Israel's sonship is made explicit in the Song of Moses, which links the paternal deity with mortal ancestors:

Do you thus requite the LORD, you foolish and senseless people?
Is not he your father, who created you, who made you and
    established you?
Remember the days of old, consider the years of many generations;
ask your father, and he will show you; your elders, and they will tell
    you. (Deut. 32:6–7 RSV)

In a Yahwistic thread of the book of Numbers, the parental metaphor is maternally tinted:

And Moses said to the LORD, "Why have You dealt ill with Your
servant, and why have I not enjoyed Your favor, that You have
laid the burden of all this people upon me? Did I conceive all this
people, did I bear them, that You should say to me, 'Carry them
in your bosom as a nurse carries an infant,' to the land that You
have promised on oath to their fathers?'" (Num. 11:11–12 NJPS;
cf. Isa. 49:15; 66:13)

God is the parent who births and nurtures Israel.

From the father to the firstborn son passes "birthright," the
family's legacy (Gen. 27:19; Deut. 21:15–17; 1 Chr. 5:1). "Thus said
the LORD: . . . I am ever a Father to Israel, Ephraim is My firstborn" (Jer. 31:7, 9 NJPS), "[My] very own tribe" (10:16 NJPS). To
Israel is bequeathed an inheritance, usually described as "a desirable land—the fairest heritage of all the nations" (Jer. 3:19 NJPS;
cf. Josh. 13:6–8; Ps. 105:11). Israel itself may be denoted as God's
bequest (1 Kgs. 8:53); conversely, the LORD is the Levites' inheritance (Num. 18:20–24; Deut. 10:9; 12:12). Much later, in the book
of *Jubilees* (2nd c. BC), this imagery is recaptured in Abraham's
blessing to Jacob: "May the LORD God be a father to you and you
the firstborn son, and to the people always" (19.29, trans. Winter-
mute [*OTP*]).

The LORD's claim upon his children is amplified in prophetic
oracles bewailing Israel's rebellion:

I thought how I would set you among my children, and give you a
    pleasant land,
    the most beautiful heritage of all the nations.
And I thought you would call me, My Father,
    and would not turn from following me. (Jer. 3:19; cf. Isa. 1:2;
    Hos. 11:12)

59

> A son should honor his father, and a slave his master. Now if I am a father, where is the honor due Me? And if I am a master, where is the reverence due Me?—said the LORD of Hosts to you, O priests who scorn My name. . . . Have we not all one Father? Did not one God create us? Why do we break faith with one another, profaning the covenant of our ancestors? (NJPS: Mal. 1:6; 2:10)

The prophets lament Israel's waywardness precisely because "[the] Lord, Father and Master of my life" (Sir. 23:1), is the source of the nation's creation and sustenance. "Father of the fatherless and protector of widows is God in his holy habitation" (Ps. 68:5). "As a father pities his children, so the LORD pities those who fear him" (Ps. 103:13 RSV). Trito-Isaiah, composed after Israel's return from Babylonian exile, reworks this theme of the divine disposition toward the people God has created:

> Surely You are our Father
> Though Abraham regard us not,
> And Israel recognize us not,
> You, O LORD, are our Father;
> From of old Your name is "Our Redeemer." (Isa. 63:16 NJPS;
>   cf. Isa. 45:9–11; 64:7)

The Hebrew Bible also characterizes God as the father of David and his line of kings. Like its West Semitic neighbors, Israel affiliated its monarchs with God, though less so than one might expect. The chief example is Nathan's promise to David: "Thus said the LORD: . . . When your days are done and you lie with your fathers, I will raise up your offspring after you, one of your own issue, and I will establish his kingship. . . . I will be a father to him, and he shall be a son to Me" (2 Sam. 7:5a, 12–14a NJPS). In the same vein are these coronation hymns from the Psalter:

> The LORD said to me,
>   "You are My son,
>   I have fathered you this day.
> Ask it of Me,
>   and I will make the nations your domain;
>   your estate, the limits of the earth." (2:7b–8 NJPS)

60

> [David, my servant,] shall say to Me,
> "You are my father, my God, the rock of my deliverance."

I will appoint him first-born,
highest of the kings of the earth.
I will maintain My steadfast love [*khesed*] for him always;
My covenant with him shall endure. (89:27–29 NJPS)

Nothing in these acclamations suggests the monarch's biological begetting by God, any more than "the rock of deliverance" invites geological dissection. The core issues are the LORD God's inviolable warrant for the authority of a sovereign of Davidic lineage and the expansive power, conferred by God, upon that adopted potentate.

Before leaving the Hebrew Bible, it is worth recalling its riot of metaphors and similes for God. Such images cascade in the Psalms: God as king (5:2; 10:16; 24:7–10), rock (18:2, 31, 46; 19:14; 28:1), fortress (18:2; 31:2, 3; 59:9, 16–17), shelter of refuge (14:6; 28:8; 31:4), hiding place (32:7; 119:114), shield (3:3; 18:2, 30; 28:7), rescuer (70:5; 140:7; 144:2), judge (7:11; 50:6; 94:2), shepherd (23:1; 28:9; 80:1), companion (55:13). In Deuteronomy's Song of Moses alone (32:1–43) God is primarily "the Rock" (vv. 4, 15, 18, 30–31) though also the Creator and fashioner (v. 6), "the Most High" (v. 8), a guard with a watchful eye (v. 10), a gliding and protective eagle (v. 11), a nursing mother (v. 13), a spurned mother (v. 18), an archer (vv. 23, 42), a planter (v. 34), an avenger (vv. 36, 41, 43), a shield (v. 38), a warrior (vv. 39, 41, 42), and a healer (v. 39). Transcending all personifications, Israel's God is intimate yet elusive, reliable yet mysterious—a paradox, as we shall see, that also pulses in the Lord's Prayer.

Who is this who obscures counsel without knowledge?
Indeed, I spoke without understanding
Of things beyond me, which I did not know. (Job 42:3 NJPS)

Jesus and the Father

Jesus appears to have used the paternal metaphor for God more frequently than many of his contemporaries in Second Temple Judaism. The numerical evidence is presented in table 2.

Compared with some 15 references to God as Father in the Old Testament and another 15 or so in the Apocrypha and Pseudepigrapha, that metaphor appears 173 times in the New Testament's Gospels. John accounts for 68 percent of the total; Mark, only 2

61

Table 2: Jesus' References to God as Father in the Gospels

	Matthew	Mark	Luke	John
	"The Father" (used absolutely): 4×	"The Father" (used absolutely): 1× (13:32)	"The Father" (used absolutely): 3× (9:26; 10:22 [twice]); also Acts: 2× (1:4, 7)	"The Father" (used absolutely): 80×
	"my Father": 15× (direct address: 26:39, 42)	"my Father": 0×	"my Father": 5×	"my Father": 26×
	"our Father": 1× (6:9, the Lord's Prayer)	"our Father": 0×	"our Father": 0×	"our Father": 0×
	"your Father": 13×	"your Father": 1× (11:25)	"your Father": 3× (6:36; 12:30, 32)	"your Father": 2×
	"his Father": 0×	"his Father": 1× (8:38)	"his Father": 0×	"his Father": 1×
	"her Father": 0×	"her Father": 0×	"her Father": 0×	"her Father": 0×
	"their Father": 0×	"their Father": 0×	"their Father": 0×	"their Father": 0×
	Direct address to God as "Father": 2×	Direct address to God as "Father": 1× (14:36)	Direct address to God "Father": 5× (10:21 [twice]; 11:2 (the Lord's Prayer); 22:42; 23:34)	Direct address to God as "Father": 9×
	Total: 35 occurrences	**Total: 4 occurrences**	**Total: 16 occurrences**	**Total: 118 occurrences**

percent. It occurs in Matthew more than twice as often as in Luke. The metaphor of God as Father is found in all the major traditional strata of which the Gospels are composed, in ascending frequency from L (Luke's special source), Mark, Q (the double tradition shared by Luke and Matthew), M (Matthew's special source), and John (whose references to God as Father appear in material almost entirely unique to the Fourth Gospel).

At least twenty years before any Gospel, Paul refers to God as Father with fair frequency (Rom. 6:4; 1 Cor. 8:6; 15:24; Gal. 1:1, 3; Phil. 2:11; 1 Thess. 1:1; as well as Eph. 1:3, 17; 2:18; 3:14; 5:20; 6:23; Col. 1:3, 12; 3:17; and 2 Thess. 1:2, which may or may not have been authored by Paul). In the Gospels, Jesus alone uses the metaphor. That fact corresponds with another: while Israel is now and then described in the Gospels as God's children (John 1:12; 11:52; cf. Matt. 7:11 = Luke 11:13) or "children" of the Deity (Matt. 5:9, 45; 8:12; 13:38; Luke 6:35; 16:8; 20:36; John 12:36), only Jesus refers to himself absolutely as *"the* Son" (Matt. 11:27 = Luke 10:22; Matt. 24:36 = Mark 13:32) or is acknowledged by others as God's Son (Matt. 2:15; 3:17 = Mark 1:11 = Luke 3:22; Matt. 4:3, 6 = Luke 4:3, 9; Matt. 8:29 = Mark 5:7 = Luke 8:28; Matt. 14:33; 16:16; 17:5 = Mark 9:7 = Luke 9:35; Matt. 27:43, 54 = Mark 15:39; Mark 1:1; 3:11 = Luke 4:41; Matt. 26:63; Mark 14:61; Luke 1:35). Johannine soteriology is grounded in the communion of Jesus the Son with God the Father (John 1:18; 3:16; 14:6, 13; 17:1), the former subordinated to the latter's authority (3:35; 5:19–23; 14:28): "For this is the will of my Father, that every one who sees the Son and believes in him should have eternal life; and I will raise him up at the last day" (6:40 RSV).

So much for the numerical data and their distribution throughout the New Testament's Gospels. We now turn to some thematic patterns that cut across the Synoptics.

The Kingdom Context

Extended consideration of Jesus' petition "Thy kingdom come" awaits us in chapter 5. Even so, that kingdom's bearing on Jesus' reference to God as Father merits mention here.

Jesus' model prayer is embedded in his proclamation of the kingdom of God (*hē basileia tou theou*), a heavenly kingdom, the hope for whose coming the prayer's second petition articulates

63

(Matt. 6:10a = Luke 11:2c). All the Synoptics identify this kingdom's approach as central in Jesus' preaching (Matt. 4:17; Mark 1:15; Luke 4:43). "The kingdom" is Jesus' primary metaphor for God's dynamic sovereignty, exerted throughout eternity, now impinging on this world (Luke 17:20b–21; cf. Matt. 13:18–23; Mark 4:26–32). The kingdom is not a human achievement; rather, it is God's gift to put right all things out of joint (Mark 10:23–27; Luke 12:32). Upending conventional expectations (Matt. 20:1–16; Luke 9:59–60), the kingdom requires repentance (*metanoia*, "turning the mind" toward God: Matt. 3:2; Luke 13:3, 5), forgiveness of others (Matt. 18:23–35), and childlike dependence (Mark 10:14–15). Those with faith anticipate its surprising future, embodied in Jesus, with joy and wonder (Luke 14:7–24); the faithless are hardened in their rejection (Mark 4:1–12, 25).

A fascinating cluster of Q sayings, associated by Matthew and Luke with Jesus' mighty works, epitomizes his role as mediator of his heavenly Father's kingdom. The passage begins as a prayer, then quickly turns into a soliloquy:

> At that time Jesus said, "I thank you, Father, Lord of heaven and earth, because you have hidden these things from the wise and the intelligent and have revealed them to infants; yes, Father, for such was your gracious will. All things have been handed over to me by my Father; and no one knows the Son except the Father, and no one knows the Father except the Son and anyone to whom the Son chooses to reveal him." (Matt. 11:25–27 = Luke 10:21–22)

Many scholars question the historicity of this "bolt from the Johannine blue," which attributes to Jesus a highly self-referential Christology redolent of the Fourth Gospel: "Everything that the Father gives me will come to me, and anyone who comes to me I will never drive away. . . . For this reason I have told you that no one can come to me unless it is granted by the Father" (John 6:37, 65; see also 5:21–23; 6:40–46; 16:12–15; 17:1–26). Nevertheless, Matt. 11:25–27 = Luke 10:21–22 corresponds to other elements of the Synoptic tradition, which identifies Jesus as the executor of judgment between God and mortals: "Everyone therefore who acknowledges me before others, I also will acknowledge before my Father in heaven; but whoever denies me before others, I also will deny before my Father in heaven" (Matt. 10:32–33 = Luke 12:8–9;

cf. Matt. 16:27 = Mark 8:38 = Luke 9:26). These pieces may be assembled into a roughly hierarchical pattern: the Father presides over all things in heaven and on earth, with knowledge superior to that of the angels and of the Son (Matt. 24:36 = Mark 13:32; cf. Matt. 26:53); the Son confers upon his disciples the kingdom and power that he has received from the Father (Matt. 19:28 = Luke 22:28–30; Matt. 25:34; cf. Luke 24:49; John 20:21; Acts 1:4; 2:33).

With respect to the Lord's Prayer, of particular importance in Jesus' thanksgiving in Matt. 11:25–27 = Luke 10:21–22 are (1) his expression of gratitude to the "Father," (2) "the Lord of heaven and earth," (3) who withholds his self-revelation from those whom this world considers competent ("the wise and the intelligent") (4) and endows that self-revelation and its attendant authority upon otherwise helpless mortals ("infants") (5) through the exclusive mediation of the Father's Son. In cumulative force these assertions are, as Paul Minear noted, "so bold as to be almost incredible" ("Two Secrets, Two Disclosures," 78). A unique, divine Father of unrecognized sovereignty is uniquely known and uniquely disclosed by a uniquely authorized Son, equally unrecognized. Those to whom the Son discloses this unique knowledge of the Father, who accept that revelation, are enabled to know themselves, their world, this Son, and this Father, who remains unseen yet whose sovereignty is no longer unknown.

While preaching and by his deeds enacting God's kingship, Jesus prayed and taught others to pray to God as "Father." Evidently he recognized no conflict between these royal and familial metaphors. They suggest complementary emphases: to acknowledge God's kingdom is to submit to its authority, prepared to receive its benefits; to address the heavenly King as Father is to express confidence in God's benevolence. Both accents converge in Jesus' assurance, reminiscent of Ezekiel's promise to a needy Israel: "Fear not, little flock, for it is your Father's good pleasure to give you the kingdom" (Luke 12:32 RSV; cf. Ezek. 34:31: "You are my sheep, the sheep of my pasture, and I am your God, says the Lord GOD").

"Our Father"

When most Christians pray the Lord's Prayer, their first word is a surprising anomaly: the *only* place in the Gospels where Jesus speaks of "our Father" and so directs his disciples to address God is Matthew's introduction to the prayer (6:9). By contrast Luke (11:2) preserves the simple vocative, "Father," absent the first-person plural pronoun (*hēmōn*). All the Gospels' other references to "our father," without exception, have as their subject or object one of Israel's noteworthy patriarchs: "our father Abraham" (RSV: Luke 1:73; cf. Matt. 3:9 = Luke 3:8; Luke 16:24, 27, 30; John 8:39, 53), "our father Jacob" (John 4:12), "our father David" (Mark 11:10). Although the locution ordinarily occurs in the salutations of Pauline Letters—"Grace to you and peace from God our Father and the Lord Jesus Christ" (Rom. 1:7; see also 1 Cor. 1:3; 2 Cor. 1:2; Eph. 1:2; Phil. 1:2; Col. 1:2; 2 Thess. 1:1; 2:16; Phlm. 3)—from the Gospels there is no evidence that Jesus haphazardly spoke of "our Father."

This point may be sharpened. In a Johannine saying lacking Synoptic counterpart, the risen Christ goes out of his way to draw a distinction: "Jesus said to [Mary Magdalene], 'Do not hold me, for I have not yet ascended to the Father; but go to my brethren and say to them, I am ascending *to my Father and your Father*, to my God and your God'" (John 20:17 RSV, emphasis added). Why not the simpler assertion: "I am ascending to our Father"? At issue, most likely, is not disjunction but priority, along the line of the Moabite Ruth's pledge of allegiance to Naomi and Israel's God: "Your people shall be my people, and your God my God" (Ruth 1:16). The Johannine tradition conveys a kind of adoptive progression that is at most tacit in the Synoptics. "But to all who received him, who believed in his name, [Jesus the Word] gave power to become children of God" (John 1:12). "Our fellowship is with the Father and with his Son Jesus Christ" (1 John 1:3b). "See what love the Father has given us, that we should be called children of God—and yet that is what we are" (1 John 3:1a AT).

A similar notion is developed in Romans (8:29), where Paul speaks of believers' predestined conformity "to the image of [God's] Son, in order that he might be the firstborn within a large family." The context is eschatological: disciples are children of God, not by human nature, but by a begetting "from above" (John 3:3). They are adopted into God's family through Jesus Christ: "in bringing many children to glory, . . . the one who sanctifies and those who are sanctified all have one Father," which is why "Jesus is not ashamed to call them brothers and sisters" (Heb. 2:10–11).

All this is a lot more than Matthew says; yet the mandate to pray to "our Father" tracks with such thinking, concentrated for the nurture of a community (*ekklēsia*: Matt. 16:18; 18:17) of siblings, called and disciplined by their Lord (Matt. 18:15–22; 23:8; 25:40). Eliezer, another late first-century rabbi, was remembered as saying, "On whom should we lean for support? On our Father who is in heaven" (*m. Sotah* 9.15).

Praying to "our" father also underscores the corporate nature of this prayer. Some historians believe that instruction on the Lord's Prayer was given to catechumens before baptism, to help them say the Lord's Prayer thoughtfully after emerging from the ritual waters (see chap. 10 below). If so, then Cyprian, a Carthaginian bishop (ca. 200–258) and one of our earliest commentators on the Prayer, picks up the Matthean thread for his own day:

> We do not say: "My father, who [is] in the heavens," nor "Give me my bread this day." . . . Our prayer is common and collective, and when we pray we pray not for one but for all people, because we are all one people together. The God of peace and master of concord, who taught that we should be united, wanted one to pray in this manner for all, as he himself bore all in one. (*The Lord's Prayer* 8, trans. Alistair Stewart-Sykes; see appendix C)

Like Matthew, Cyprian seems to have in mind "all one people together *in Christ*" (thus his immediate reference to Acts 1:14). As with Israel, so also the church: prayer begins within a community of concordant faith.

Even when solitary Christians pray the Lord's Prayer, their address to "Our Father" is a reminder that each prays as a member of a corporate entity: a single believer among a congregation, a local church within a worldwide fellowship. It is not I who am praying for me; it is we who are praying for us (cf. Jas. 5:16). One prays alongside one's sister and brother Christians—even when one is alone, even when that sibling is exceedingly hard to love. "Here my enemy prays by my side, since the world of prayer has no frontiers; and in so doing he ceases to be my enemy, because we meet in God" (Underhill, *Abba*, 15).

The testimonies of Deutero-Isaiah and Ephesians remind us that the church exists not for its cloistered edification. The family that God calls into existence is intended to model its Father's redemptive conduct and intent for the entire world, beyond religious walls.

67

> For [the LORD] has said:
> "It is too little that you should be My servant
> In that I raise up the tribes of Jacob
> And restore the survivors of Israel:
> I will also make you a light of nations,
> That My salvation may reach the ends of the earth." (Isa. 49:6 NJPS)

> For he has made known to us in all wisdom and insight the mystery of his will, according to his purpose which he set forth in Christ as a plan for the fullness of time, to unite all things in him, things in heaven and things on earth. (Eph. 1:9–10 RSV)

Luke's Gospel and the Acts of the Apostles balance the church's prayerful conformation to Christ with its evangelism to the world at large. Those present at Jesus' ascension become his witnesses (Luke 24:44–52), testifying to others (Acts 1:8) even as they devote themselves to prayer (Luke 24:53; Acts 1:14). This reciprocity is discernible in Matthew: "You are the light of the world. . . . Let your light shine before others, so that they may see your good works and give glory to your Father in heaven" (Matt. 5:14a, 16). Through Christ the church learns to pray to its Father and to offer testimony to a gospel that proclaims the Father's intent to restore all of creation.

The Heavenly Father versus Earthly Fathers

Unsurprisingly, Matthew's version of the Lord's Prayer (6:9b) is addressed to the Father "in heaven" (*en tois ouranois*). In the First Gospel Jesus characteristically refers to God as "your Father in heaven" or "your heavenly Father" (5:16, 45, 48; 6:14, 26, 32; 12:50; 15:13; 18:19, 35), a phrase appearing nowhere in the Old Testament and, outside of Matthew, only twice in the New Testament (Mark 11:25; Luke 11:13). For those listening with a scriptural ear, this description carries several interrelated connotations. (1) Israel prayed to the most high God, maker of both heaven and earth (Gen. 14:19, 22), who abides in a supernal realm of perfect justice beyond the sin-ridden world inhabited by mortals (2 Chr. 18:18; 20:6; Neh. 2:4; Pss. 11:4; 14:2; 33:13). "Behold, to the LORD your God belong heaven and the heaven of heavens, the earth with all that is in it" (Deut. 10:14 RSV). Precisely for that reason Jesus' preaching startles: God's heavenly kingdom has already begun redeeming his listeners' everyday life. (2) Prayer to the "heavenly Father" carries

68

an inbuilt paradox: the distant heavens wherein this God rides (Ps. 68:32–35) qualify the intimacy of fatherhood. To flip this idea positively: the transcendent God is as approachable as one's parent may be. (3) The difference between "our Father in heaven" and mortal fathers is not mathematically exponential but qualitatively infinite. "Upon all begotten beings, which do not participate [in the essence of divinity], there comes a certain glory and power from God, and, so to speak, an outflowing of divinity" (Origen, *Prayer* 23.5, trans. Stewart-Sykes).

Jesus' teachings about parents and earthly families are complicated. On the one hand, they are as religiously orthodox as one can imagine of a first-century Jew. Adherence to the Decalogue's Fifth Commandment remains inviolate (Matt. 19:19 = Mark 10:19 = Luke 18:20; Matt. 15:4 = Mark 7:10; cf. Exod. 20:12 = Deut. 5:16); those who use cultic flummery to fleece their parents of support are in big trouble (Matt. 15:5–9 = Mark 7:11–13). Separation from father and mother for marriage is legally warranted (Matt. 19:5 = Mark 10:7–8; cf. Gen. 2:24).

On the other hand, following Jesus' way sunders economic structures of the family unit (Matt. 4:21–22 = Mark 1:20). The kingdom's urgency overrides even the basic duty of burying one's father (RSV: Matt. 8:21–22 = Luke 9:59–60): "Leave the dead to bury their own dead"—a command of staggering repulsiveness. Commitment to the good news sets father against son, daughter against mother (Matt. 10:35 = Luke 12:53); whoever loves a parent or child more than Jesus is unworthy of him (Matt. 10:37 = Luke 14:26); for Jesus' sake parents and children will have each other killed (Matt. 10:21–22 = Mark 13:12–13). While impossible to know for sure, it may be that such admonitions to subordinate family ties to the gospel's demands were intended to encourage those whose following of Jesus as the Christ compelled them to abandon their families (Osiek, "Family," 339).

When natural families fall apart, new families are constituted around Jesus: "Truly, I say to you, there is no one who has left house or brothers or sisters or mother or father or children or lands, for my sake and for the gospel, who will not receive a hundredfold now in this time, houses and brothers and sisters and mothers and children and lands, with persecutions, and in the age to come eternal life" (Mark 10:29–30 RSV; cf. Matt. 19:29 = Luke 18:29b–30). Note: all that is lost will be restored a hundred times over—all save *a father*.

69

That stunning omission rhymes with another jolting aphorism in Matthew (23:9): "Call no one your father on earth, for you have one Father—the one in heaven." That sums up other teachings by Jesus: the benefactions of human fathers (and mothers) pale in importance beside those of the heavenly Father: "If you then, who are evil, know how to give good gifts to your children, how much more will your Father in heaven give good things to those who ask him!" (Matt. 7:11 = Luke 11:13, which specifies those "good things" as the Holy Spirit; cf. Matt. 10:20). Even those who do not solicit them receive that Father's gifts: "He makes his sun rise on the evil and on the good, and sends rain on the righteous and on the unrighteous" (Matt. 5:44–45), "for he is kind to the ungrateful and the wicked" (Luke 6:35). Nowhere in the Gospels does Jesus revere the house of his father Joseph as he does the house of his heavenly Father (Luke 2:41–42, 49; John 2:16), who is the touchstone of integrity (Matt. 5:48) and mercy (Luke 6:36). Those who invite Jesus to their churches to talk about patriarchal "family values" will get something other than what they bargained for.

The Abba Question

And going a little farther, [Jesus] threw himself on the ground and prayed that, if it were possible, the hour might pass from him. He said, "Abba, Father, for you all things are possible; remove this cup from me; yet, not what I want, but what you want." (Mark 14:35–36)

According to Mark, Jesus repeated this prayer in Gethsemane, "saying the same words" (14:39). Matthew (26:39) and Luke (22:42) offer approximations of this wording; in John, which contains nothing like the Synoptics' Gethsemane story, Jesus offers an altogether different prayer after declaring, "The hour has come for the Son of Man to be glorified" (that is, to die: John 12:23, 27–28a). In all these passages Jesus appeals to "[my] Father"; only in Mark 14:36 does the Aramaic term 'abbā occur, followed by its Greek translation (ho patēr). Outside the Gospels the term recurs twice in Paul's Letters:

When we cry, "Abba! Father!" it is that very Spirit bearing witness with our spirit that we are children of God, and if children, then heirs, heirs of God and joint heirs with Christ—if, in fact, we suffer with him so that we may also be glorified with him. (Rom. 8:15b–17)

Because you are children, God has sent the Spirit of his Son into our hearts, crying, "Abba! Father!" So you are no longer a slave but a child, and if a child then also an heir, through God. (Gal. 4:6–7)

Despite the facts that *'abbā* appears only thrice in the New Testament, only once in Mark, and never in Matthew or Luke's version of the Lord's Prayer, rivers of scholarly ink have flowed from and around this Aramaism. In twentieth-century scholarship the floodgates were opened by a German Lutheran theologian and student of ancient Near Eastern literature, Joachim Jeremias (1900–1979). Here is the pith of Jeremias's contention:

In the literature of Palestinian Judaism *no evidence has yet been found* of "my [dear] Father" [*'abbā*] being used by an individual as an address to God. It first appears in the Middle Ages, in Southern Italy [in *Seder Eliyahu Rabbah*, ca. AD 974]. It is quite unusual that Jesus should have addressed God as "my Father"; it is even more so that he should have used the Aramaic form *'Abbā*. . . . We *do not have a single example* of God being addressed as *'Abbā* in Judaism, but Jesus *always* addressed God in this way in his prayers. . . . The complete novelty and uniqueness of *'Abbā* as an address to God in the prayers of Jesus shows that it expresses the heart of Jesus' relationship to God. . . . *'Abbā* as a form of address to God expresses the ultimate mystery of the mission of Jesus. (*New Testament Theology*, 64, 66, 67, 68, with his emphases)

If this be the case, Jesus' use of the Aramaic *'abbā* in prayer might affect our understanding of "father" in the Lord's Prayer.

Jeremias's claims are an odd mixture of restraint and hyperbole. He circumscribes the evidence (first) to Palestinian Judaism, bracketing out Hellenistically tinged Jewish documents like Sirach ("O Lord, Father and Ruler [or God] of my life" [23:1, 4 RSV]), and (second) to an individual's address to God as Father. Jeremias retracted an earlier claim, which still bubbles up from Christian pulpits, that Jesus addressed God in a small child's babbling chatter (see Barr, "'*Abba* Isn't 'Daddy'"): "grown-up sons and daughters

71

addressed their fathers as *'abbā"* (Jeremias, *New Testament Theology*, 67). All that is on one side. On the other, Jeremias's deductions are largely fallacious arguments from silence. Pre-Christian Palestinian Jewish literature lacks extant parallels, not only to God as *'abbā*, but also to *human* fathers so addressed. Remember, too, that Mark 14:36 is the *only* New Testament instance of Jesus' address to God as deeply personal; to claim on the basis of a single occurrence that "Jesus always addressed God *in this way* in his prayers" (emphasis added) is to assert a lot more than anyone can know. Surely the same may be said of Jeremias's intent to correlate Jesus' use of *'abbā* with "the heart of Jesus' relationship to God" and "the ultimate mystery of the mission of Jesus." Only if he incessantly addressed God as *'abbā*, pausing to explain what that address signified for him, could we deduce Jesus' religious experience from his peculiar language. From the evidence available, he did neither.

There is a Romanticist flavor to all this: Jesus must be proved unique in order to be significant. When Jeremias states, "No Jew would have dared to address God [as *'abbā*]" (*Lord's Prayer*, 19–20), it's as though he has forgotten that Jesus was Jewish. Yet Jeremias well knew that Jesus' precursors associated divine fatherhood with compassion: in one Babylonian text the wrath of the god Ea "is like the deluge, yet his being is reconciled like a merciful father" (Falkenstein and von Soden, *Hymnen und Gebet*, 298). In the ancient Near East "the word 'Father,' as applied to God, thus encompasses, from earliest times, something of what the word 'Mother' signifies among us" (Jeremias, *Prayers of Jesus*, 11).

The Gospels' sole reference to God as *'abbā* has been asked to bear more weight than it can. In other respects, however, Jeremias's studies point us in positive directions. (1) While the word is rare, first-century Christians remembered that Jesus used *'abbā*, an affectionate appellation, in praying to God; a more plausible derivation of Paul's unusual use of that term, always in the context of prayer, is hard to imagine. That Mark imported *'abbā* into the Gethsemane story is unlikely: the locution in Mark 14:36, immediately followed by its translation, is consistent with that Gospel's handling of other inherited Aramaisms: thus 3:17 (*"Boanerges*, that is, 'Sons of Thunder'"); 5:41 RSV (*"Talitha cumi*, meaning, 'Little girl, I say to you, arise'"); 15:22 AT (*"Golgotha*, which means 'Skull-place'"). (2) Although he was not remembered as directing others to pray to God as *'abbā*, Jesus' use of that term jibes with the church's memory

72

that he prayed to God, not as king, but as father and in the Lord's Prayer taught his disciples to do likewise. (3) The occurrences of *'abbā* in the New Testament stand in cohesive alignment with one another: all constitute *direct address to God*; all are utterances of prayer in *eschatological contexts*, suggested by images of the "hour" (Mark 13:11, 32 RSV), the cup (Ps. 11:6; Isa. 51:17, 22), the Spirit (Joel 2:28–29), inheritance with Christ (Col. 3:24; Heb. 9:15; 1 Pet. 1:4), and glorification with Christ (1 Cor. 2:7; Eph. 1:18). Moreover, all are attached to *cries of rescue from distress*: a soul sorrowful unto death (Mark 14:34); suffering with Christ (Rom. 8:17); redemption from the law's enslavement (Gal. 4:5–7). Paul's use of *'abbā* consistently points up its association with "adoption" (*tēn huiothesian*) for "inheritance" (*hē klēronomia*): a conceptual cluster to which we shall return. *'Abbā* does not *define* God's fatherhood, but it colors that metaphor with particular, prominent hues.

God the Merciful Father

In several of Matthew's parables God's judgment corresponds to royal prerogative. Like a king settling his accounts, God takes pity on indebted slaves but can be pushed to punitive anger by beneficiaries who refuse such mercy's extension to their peers (Matt. 18:23–35). Like a king hosting a wedding banquet for his son, God angrily lays waste to those who abuse such hospitality (22:1–10) and expels those who presume upon it (22:11–14). Acting as God's viceroy, the Son of Man will come at the end of the age, gather and judge the nations, and separate sheep from goats based on acts of loving-kindness (Matt. 25:31–46).

When Jesus describes God's sustenance in Matthew and Luke, a paternal image is invariably invoked—even though spinning and weaving, like suckling, were female responsibilities in the Greco-Roman household (Knapp, *Invisible Romans*, 53–96).

> He said to his disciples, "Therefore I tell you, do not worry about your life, what you will eat, or about your body, what you will wear. . . . Consider the ravens: they neither sow nor reap, they have neither storehouse nor barn, and yet God feeds them. . . . Consider the lilies, how they grow: they neither toil nor spin; yet I tell you, even Solomon in all his glory was not clothed like one of these. But if God so clothes the grass of the field, which is alive

73

today and tomorrow is thrown into the oven, how much more will he clothe you—you of little faith!" (Luke 12:22, 24, 27–28 = Matt. 6:25a, 26a, 28b–30)

Put differently, Jesus speaks of God as "a motherly father" (O'Collins, *Lord's Prayer*, 29–33). Even though the Old Testament expressly describes God as father fewer than a dozen times, that maternal connotation is therein present: "As a mother comforts her child, so I will comfort you" (Isa. 66:13). During the Middle Ages, Anselm of Canterbury (1033–1109), Bernard of Clairvaux (1090–1153), and Julian of Norwich (ca. 1342–ca. 1416) expanded these maternal metaphors to Jesus (Bynum, *Jesus as Mother*, 110–69; cf. Matt. 23:37 = Luke 13:34).

God's parental benevolence—"sublime tenderness" (Calvin, *Institutes* 3.12.7)—defies measurement by any human standard, which is inescapably corrupted:

Is there anyone among you who, if your child asks for a fish, will give a snake instead of a fish? Or if the child asks for an egg, will give a scorpion? If you then, who are evil, know how to give good gifts to your children, how much more will the heavenly Father give the Holy Spirit to those who ask him! (Luke 11:11–13 = Matt. 7:9–11)

The life of discipleship is embraced by God's providence. Jesus' followers can keep their prayers simple, "for your Father knows what you need before you ask him" (Matt. 6:8b). They can rest assured that they've not been lost in the crowd: the shepherd God will leave a flock of ninety-nine to search for and rescue the one that has gone astray. "It is not the will of your Father in heaven that one of these little ones should be lost" (Matt. 18:14; cf. Luke 15:3–7). God's paternal beneficence extends beyond everyday protection to eschatological blessings, now and to come: "Do not be afraid, little flock, for it is your Father's good pleasure to give you the kingdom" (Luke 12:32).

At this juncture we may reflect on an unresolved controversy in the past five decades of Christian theology: the degree to which paternal imagery for God is complicit in abusive patriarchy. A few markers are noteworthy.

74

1. Christian Scripture is not fixated on God's gender: whether God is masculine, feminine, or asexual. Reacting to some patristic

and medieval confusion on this point, in 1973 Mary Daly rejoined, "If God is male, then male is God" (*Beyond God the Father*, 19). As hard as it may be for us to grasp in seasons when gendered identities preoccupy Western culture, Jesus' address to God as Father has nothing to do with gender as such, because the biblical God to whom Jesus prayed is beyond sexual difference. "The distinction of male and female does not exist in the Divine and blessed nature" (Gregory of Nyssa, *The Making of Humankind* 22.4). "Nothing in God is specifically feminine; nothing in God is specifically masculine; therefore nothing in our notions of God entails duties and prerogatives specific to one gender; all duties and prerogatives in our notions of God are duties and prerogatives of both genders" (Volf, *Exclusion and Embrace*, 173).

2. Exegetically and theologically, our footing is more secure when we regard Jesus' address to God as Father as the counterpart to his identity as the Son. In other words, the language of the Lord's Prayer is that of *relationship*, specifically intimate kinship (about which more will be said momentarily). The most penetrating recognition of this familial dimension lies within the New Testament: "No one has ever seen God. It is God the only Son, who is close to the Father's heart [lit., "breast" or "bosom"], who has made him known" (John 1:18). To be a child of God is to be loved by God (1 John 3:1). "Beloved, we are God's children now; it does not yet appear what we shall be, but we know that when he appears we shall be like him, for we shall see him as he is" (1 John 3:2 RSV). "[God,] who did not withhold his own Son, but gave him up for all of us, will he not with him also give us everything else?" (Rom. 8:32). What God prevented Abraham from doing with "[his] only son Isaac, whom [he] love[d]" (Gen. 22:1–14), God did with his own "beloved Son, with whom [the Father was] well pleased" (Mark 1:11 = Matt. 3:17 = Luke 3:22): God mercifully surrendered Jesus to death in order to destroy death, thereby reclaiming all of us in jeopardy of eternal separation from our Father.

3. Nowhere in the Gospels does Jesus speak of "the Father's rule," legitimating the authority of human fathers on the basis of God's fatherhood. As we have witnessed, the reverse is true: "Call no one your father on earth, for you have one Father—the one in heaven" (Matt. 23:9). "Remember that the revelation is not of the father manifested as God, but of God manifested as Father" (Hilary of Poitiers [310–367], *The Trinity* 3.22, AT). Where we place the

75

emphasis is critically important, as Kendall Soulen notes: "Whatever may be the case with other fathers or fatherhood in general, *this* Father is implacably opposed to every diminution of women for the sake of male privilege" ("Name of the Holy Trinity," 255).

The Child's Response to a Father So Gracious

No image of the church is more pervasive in the Gospels than that of a new family: "For whoever does the will of my Father in heaven is my brother and sister and mother" (Matt. 12:50 = Mark 3:35 = Luke 8:21). Jesus assures his followers of their embrace in a family, over which presides "my Father and your Father" (Mark 10:29–31; John 20:17). Surely that is a signal reason for the New Testament's portrait of the local Christian congregation as a "family of faith" (Gal. 6:10) or "household of God" (Eph. 2:19; 1 Tim. 3:15; 1 Pet. 4:17). Disciples practice secret piety (Matt. 6:1–6, 16–18), forgive one another (Matt. 6:14–15; 18:23–35; Mark 11:25), love their enemies and pray for their persecutors (Matt. 5:43–46; Luke 23:34), not because such things realize an innate human potential, but because in precisely these ways the heavenly Father interacts with mortal children (Matt. 5:45b). The essential principle is like Father, like son, or daughter: "Be merciful, just as your Father is merciful" (Luke 6:36), "so that you may be children of your Father in heaven" (Matt. 5:45a). The Fourth Gospel intensifies this idea christologically: "If you know me [the Son], you will know my Father also" (14:7; cf. 10:30). The Father's works are deducible from those of the Son (5:17, 19, 36; 8:16–38; 10:31–39; 12:49–50; 14:8–24); rejection of Jesus reveals the repudiator's diabolical patrimony (8:44–47; 15:18–25).

God's graciousness is not contingent on human deserts (cf. Matt. 21:28–32); unfathomable mercy is a function of God's consummate integrity. In this way, for this reason, God's children are expected to grow into adult integrity (*teleōsis*): "There must be no limit to your goodness [*teleioi*], as your heavenly Father's goodness [*teleios*] knows no bounds" (Matt. 5:48 REB). The author of Ephesians yearns for a comparable degree of sound maturity: "the unity of the faith and of the knowledge of the Son of God, to maturity [*teleion*], to the measure of the full stature of Christ" (4:13; cf. 1 Cor. 14:20).

76

The ultimate reach of human obedience is a fidelity to the heavenly Father unto death, which Jesus' disciples perceived in their master:

> And going a little farther, he threw himself on the ground and prayed, "My Father, if it is possible, let this cup pass from me; yet not what I want but what you want. . . . My Father, if this cannot pass unless I drink it, your will be done." (Matt. 26:39, 42 = Mark 14:36, 39 = Luke 22:42–44)

> Then Jesus, crying with a loud voice, said, "Father, into your hands I commend my spirit." Having said this, he breathed his last. (Luke 23:46)

The resurrection is faith's evidence that Jesus' cries were heard and his obedience was validated (Acts 2:32; 3:15). Even so, the New Testament's authors concur that the point of all human integrity is glorification of their heavenly Father:

> To our God and Father be glory forever and ever. Amen. (Phil. 4:20)

> To him who loves us and freed us from our sins by his blood, and made us to be a kingdom, priests serving his God and Father, to him be glory and dominion forever and ever. Amen. (Rev. 1:5b–6)

Ultimately that which Jesus' disciples desire is what he himself wanted and died for: the glorification of his Father in heaven (John 14:13; 15:8). To pray to "our Father" is an entrée into the education of human wanting.

Gathering the Threads

Though by no means unprecedented, Jesus' address to God as "Father" is distinctive in its connotations, consistency of use, and frequency of occurrence. Attribution of fatherhood to God acknowledges, in the first instance, God's gracious, comprehensive authority: the One who creates and sustains a people, to whom those elect are finally accountable. The Synoptics specify Jesus as

77

the "Beloved Son" on whom God has conferred faithful execution of divine authority—a belief sharpened in John (14:9): "Whoever has seen me has seen the Father."

Crucially important is the familial nuance. "The work that the Lord [Jesus] came to do was not to enable you to recognize the omnipotence of God as Creator of all things, but to enable you to know him as the Father of the Son who addresses you" (Hilary, The Trinity 3.22). In the New Testament "Father" identifies the one who thus prays to God as a sister or brother of Jesus, who appealed to his Father as the Son who does nothing of his own accord but only what he sees the Father doing (John 5:19; 11:41–42). To address God as Father implies the prayerful child's gracious share in Jesus' relationship with God, "heirs of God and joint heirs with Christ" (Rom. 8:17; Gal. 3:29; see Thompson, Promise of the Father, 116–32). Deepening that claim's poignancy is a painful acknowledgment of potential alienation from one's blood kin for the gospel's sake (Matt. 8:21–22; Mark 13:9–13; Luke 18:28; John 9:18–23).

Profoundly personal, the Lord's Prayer is never privatist. To appeal to God as Father is to confess our mutual accountability within a family that in every time and place appeals for *our* bread, release from *our* debts, and *our* direction away from temptation (Matt. 6:11–13; Luke 11:3–4). As we shall witness in coming chapters, these plural pronouns pull the Prayer's supplicants out of selfish individualism into a relationship of ever-expanding generosity.

Resonant as well in the Prayer's address to God as Father is a cry for help in time of need. Embedded in the New Testament's 'abbā texts (Mark 14:36; Rom. 8:15; Gal. 4:6) is a child's cry, in desperate straits and under eschatological pressure, to a parent of compassionate care. That rhymes with John's Gospel, in which Jesus' prayers to the Father increase as suffering suffuses the story (11:41–42; 12:27–33; 17:1–26). In none of these cases is God the tormentor. To the contrary: God is the Parent to whom agonized children flee for help. Yet the Father no more spares them suffering than he spared his own Son, giving up Jesus for all so that all may also receive everything with Christ (Rom. 8:32).

If Jesus the Son has sanctioned prayer to our Father, then nothing can strip us of membership in God's family. No longer are we slaves of fate, cynicism, or despair; we are adopted children of Infinite Love (cf. Gal. 4:7). Because that freely conferred dignity is fixed and irrevocable, because we *belong* to God, we can grow

78

into true freedom with confidence and a willingness to take healthy risks. "Jesus' own life is the measure of that; he's completely dependent on God, and yet he's as free as anybody could be imagined to be" (Williams and Beckett, *Living the Lord's Prayer*, 28).

The briefest and best commentary on "Our Father" may be the parable of the prodigal (Luke 15:11–32). When the younger of two sons requests his inheritance, prematurely and in full, he is worse than disobedient; he effectively tells his father to drop dead. Instead of cutting off the cur or even killing him—as in that culture the paterfamilias had legal right to do—the father grants the petition without reservation (vv. 11–12). Having wasted his entire bequest in wretched dissipation, dying in famine, the prodigal returns (vv. 13–20a). Before he has opportunity to grovel (v. 21), his Father, "filled with compassion, ran and put his arms around him and kissed him" (v. 20b). Let the family reunion commence (vv. 22–23)! The banquet is an Easter celebration: "We had to celebrate and rejoice, because this brother of yours was dead and has come to life" (vv. 24, 32). When the elder son complains that he has been shortchanged, in spite of having slaved in the household (vv. 25–30), his father corrects him with comparable mercy: "Son, you are always with me, and all that is mine is yours" (v. 31). Like his brother, the elder was and remains a son: he was never the hired hand that his woebegone brother was prepared to be (v. 19)—though, by characterizing himself as a slave, he reveals his own prodigality. The elder son also occupied "a distant country" (v. 13) though he never left home. *Neither* child was "worthy to be called [a] son" (v. 21), just as tax collectors, sinners, Pharisees, and scribes all huddle in the same sinking boat (Luke 15:1–2). Merit is irrelevant. The only thing that counts is the father's selfless, merciful pity. To riposte that no father could be so prodigally kind hits the nail on its head: God is the Father like none we have ever known.

Works Cited in Chapter 3

Barr, James. "*'Abba* Isn't 'Daddy.'" *Journal of Theological Studies* 39 (1988): 28–47.

Bynum, Caroline Walker. *Jesus as Mother: Studies in the Spirituality of the High Middle Ages*. Los Angeles: University of California Press, 1982.

79

Calvin, John. *Institutes of the Christian Religion*. Vol. 2. Edited by John T. McNeill. Translated by Ford Lewis Battles. Library of Christian Classics 21. Philadelphia: Westminster Press, 1960.

Daly, Mary. *Beyond God the Father: Toward a Philosophy of Women's Liberation*. Boston: Beacon Press, 1973.

Falkenstein, Adam, and Wolfram von Soden. *Sumerische und akkadische Hymnen und Gebet*. Zurich: Artemis, 1953.

Jeremias, Joachim. *The Lord's Prayer*. Facet Books. Philadelphia: Fortress Press, 1964.

————. *New Testament Theology: The Proclamation of Jesus*. New York: Charles Scribner's Sons, 1971.

————. *The Prayers of Jesus*. Philadelphia: Fortress Press, 1967.

Knapp, Robert. *Invisible Romans*. Cambridge, MA: Harvard University Press, 2011.

Levenson, Sam. *Everything but Money*. New York: Simon & Schuster, 1966.

Minear, Paul S. "Two Secrets, Two Disclosures." *Horizons in Biblical Theology* 29 (2007): 75–85.

O'Collins, Gerald. *The Lord's Prayer*. New York: Paulist Press, 2007.

Osiek, Carolyn. "Family." *OEBT* 1 (2015): 336–44.

Renier, E. *Étude sur l'histoire de la querela inofficiosi en droit roman*. Liège: Vaillant-Carmanne, 1942.

Saller, Richard P. "*Pietas*, Obligation, and Authority in the Roman Family." In *Alte Geschichte und Wissenschaftsgeschichte: Festschrift für Karl Christ zum 65. Geburtstag*, edited by Peter Kneissl and Volker Losemann, 393–410. Darmstadt: Wissenschaftliche Buchgesellschaft, 1988.

Schrenk, Gottlob. "*Patēr*." *TDNT* 5 (1967): 945–1022.

Soulen, R. Kendall. "The Name of the Holy Trinity: A Triune Name." *Theology Today* 59 (2002): 244–61.

Thompson, Marianne Meye. *The Promise of the Father: Jesus and God in the New Testament*. Louisville, KY: Westminster John Knox Press, 2000.

Treggiari, Susan. *Roman Marriage: Iusti Coniuges from the Time of Cicero to the Time of Ulpian*. Oxford: Oxford University Press, 1991.

Underhill, Evelyn. *Abba: Meditations Based on the Lord's Prayer*. London: Longmans, Green & Co., 1940.

Volf, Miroslav. *Exclusion and Embrace: A Theological Exploration of Identity, Otherness, and Reconciliation*. Nashville: Abingdon Press, 1996.

Williams, Rowan, and Wendy Beckett. *Living the Lord's Prayer*. Compiled by Su Box. London: Lion Hudson, 2007.

CHAPTER 4

The Consecrated Name

The Devil loves anonymity, but God has a name.
—Walter Lüthi

"Let your name be hallowed" (AT: Matt. 6:9c = Luke 11:2b) could be interpreted, not as a request per se, but rather as a blessing of God, to whom the entire prayer is addressed (Metzler, "Lord's Prayer"). If so, this clause would resemble a commonplace formulation in ancient Jewish prayers (as underlined):

Blessed be the LORD, the God of Israel,
    from everlasting to everlasting.
        Amen and Amen. (Ps. 41:13)

However much you bother Him,
the Holy One, blessed be He, will receive you. (*j. Berakhot* 9)

Yet the clause immediately following the address of God as "Father" in Matthew 6:9 = Luke 11:2 is grammatically constructed as a petition, the first of two (or three) in form:

Luke 11:2	*Matthew 6:9–10*	
Father,	Our Father in the heavens,	
(1) May your name be hallowed.	(1) May your name be hallowed.	83
(2) May your kingdom come.	(2) May your kingdom come.	
(AT)	(3) May your will be done,	
	as in heaven, so also on	
	earth. (AT)	

For Johann Albrecht Bengel (1687–1752), Lutheran pastor and New Testament textual critic, "The mood in 'hallowed be' has the same force as in 'come' and 'be done': therefore, petition, not praise is expressed" (quoted in Harner, *Understanding the Lord's Prayer*, 61). Bengel's lines were drawn too sharply. It is more accurate to say that the supplicant makes a petition to God that God be praised.

"Ask for the great things that the small shall be added unto you": so Clement of Alexandria (*Miscellanies* 1.24.58, AT) remembered Jesus as encouraging disciples in an aphorism unrecorded in our Gospels. In both Matthew and Luke the Prayer's first plea contains three components: a subject (God's "name"), a predicate ("hallowed"), and a verb conjugated in a particular voice and mood ("let it be"). Each of these items invites consideration.

Ancient Names

In antiquity names were more than mere labels; they expressed something essential about their bearers. "The man called his wife's name Eve, because she was the mother of all living" (Gen. 3:20 RSV; *khāy* [life] → *khawwâ* [Eve]). "For as his name is, so is he; Nabal [→ *nābāl*, "foolish"] is his name, and folly is with him" (1 Sam. 25:25). Melchizedek "is first, by translation of his name, king of righteousness, and then he is also king of Salem, that is, king of peace" (Heb. 7:2 RSV). "[The name] carries with it the mystery of the unique personality of its bearer" (Lochman, *Lord's Prayer*, 33).

Names carried power: invoking a name activated its carrier's character and potential energy (see Acts 4:7). The LORD God created every beast of the field and bird of the air, ceding to Adam the authority for conferring their names (Gen. 2:19–20); humankind was thus deputed contingent governance of creation. Naming a territory establishes its conqueror's right of possession (Ps. 49:11). Beseeching the LORD God's confirmation of Israel's providence in the wilderness, Moses receives this assurance: "This very thing that you have spoken I will do; for you have found favor in my sight, and I know you by name [*shēm*]" (Exod. 33:17 RSV). In Acts (15:14) James articulates Luke's sweeping conviction that "God first visited the Gentiles, to take out of them a people for his name" (RSV; cf. Matt. 12:21; Acts 9:15). "Your name shall be Abraham; for I have made you the father of a multitude of nations" (Gen. 17:5 RSV).

In ancient magical papyri, names have power to bless or to curse. "What is your divine name?" asks one conjurer. "Tell me the truth, that I may invoke him" (*Papyri Graecae Magicae* 1.10). Legend has it that Asmodeus, king of demons, was bound by a ring on which was inscribed a divine name (*b. Gittin* 68b). The names of Mary, John the Baptist, and the Trinity are invoked in fourth-century Christian magical papyri (*Papyri Graecae Magicae* 2.190–200). The Gospels' drama of the Gerasene demoniac (Mark 5:1–20 = Luke 8:26–39) turns on the attempt by an unclean spirit named "Legion," wielding the force of five thousand Roman soldiers (Mark 5:9 = Luke 8:30), to subdue Jesus: "I adjure you by God, do not torment me" (Mark 5:7). The demon fails and is spectacularly destroyed (Mark 5:10–13 = Luke 8:31–33).

Jesus' own name exemplifies such attitudes. In Matthew an angel commands Joseph to name his child "Jesus," a variant of "Joshua" (Yahweh is salvation), "for he will save his people from their sins" (1:21; cf. Luke 2:21). The First Evangelist further believes that Jesus' birth ratifies a prophecy in Isaiah 7:14 LXX: "'Behold, a virgin shall conceive and bear a son, and his name shall be called 'Emmanuel,' which means, 'God with us'" (Matt. 1:23 RSV). While Jesus is never again called "Emmanuel" in Matthew or elsewhere in the New Testament, that name's theological and ecclesiological importance is implicit in Jesus' promise, "For where two or three are gathered in my name, there am I in the midst of them" (Matt. 18:20 RSV; see also 28:19–20). The name of Jesus conveys authoritative power (Matt. 7:22; Acts 4:17–18). By his name Jesus' followers preach (Luke 24:47; Acts 8:12; 9:27, 29), teach (Acts 5:28, 40–41), exorcise (Mark 9:38 = Luke 9:49; Luke 10:17; Acts 16:18), perform other mighty works (Mark 9:39; Acts 4:30; 8:13), heal the sick (Acts 3:6, 16; 4:10; Jas. 5:14), baptize others for the forgiveness of sins (Acts 2:38; 8:16; 10:43, 48; 19:5; 22:16; 1 Cor. 6:11), receive the lowly (Matt. 18:5 = Mark 9:37 = Luke 9:48), and in turn may also be received by other benefactors (Mark 9:41). Apostles exhort in the name of the Lord Jesus (1 Cor. 1:2, 10; 5:4; Eph. 5:20; Col. 3:17; 2 Thess. 1:12; 3:6). Would-be deceivers misappropriate Jesus' name (Matt. 24:5 = Mark 13:6 = Luke 21:8; cf. Jas. 2:7); faithful witnesses suffer for its sake (Acts 9:14, 16, 21; 21:13; 26:9; 1 Pet. 4:14, 16). In the Johannine literature belief in the name of Jesus is both mandated and life-giving (John 1:12; 3:18; 20:31; 1 John 3:23; 5:13); petitions made in his name, consonant with the Holy Spirit

(John 14:26), are assured of fulfillment (14:13–14; 15:16; 16:23–24, 26). Peter's decisive claim to a Jerusalem audience—"And there is salvation in no one else, for there is no other name under heaven given among men by which we must be saved" (Acts 4:12 RSV; cf. 2:21)—chimes with the finale of the Christ hymn in Philippians 2:9–11: "Therefore God has highly exalted him and bestowed on him the name which is above every name, that at the name of Jesus every knee should bow, in heaven and on earth and under the earth, and every tongue confess that Jesus Christ is Lord, to the glory of God the Father" (RSV; cf. Rom. 10:13; Eph. 1:20–21; Heb. 1:4).

Acts 19:13–17 offers a provocative example of the power inherent in a name.

> Then some of the itinerant Jewish exorcists undertook to pronounce the name of the Lord Jesus over those who had evil spirits, saying, "I adjure you by the Jesus whom Paul preaches." Seven sons of a Jewish high priest named Sceva were doing this. But the evil spirit answered them, "Jesus I know, and Paul I know; but who are you?" And the man in whom the evil spirit was leaped on them, mastered all of them, and overpowered them, so that they fled out of that house naked and wounded. And this became known to all residents of Ephesus, both Jews and Greeks; and fear fell upon them all; and the name of the Lord Jesus was extolled. (RSV)

The message is clear. If you invoke the name of Jesus—or even that of Paul—you had better make sure you are worthy of summoning it. The name of the Lord Jesus is to be praised, not pilfered. The name carries power and is mishandled at one's peril.

The Divine Name

A *minore ad majus:* "from less to greater." If names in antiquity carried such weight, the names of angels were even heavier, and the name of Israel's God was heaviest of all. At the ford of the Jabbok, Jacob wrestled until daybreak with a stranger who dislocated Jacob's thigh (Gen. 32:22–25). Names are dropped right and left:

86

> Then [the stranger] said, "Let me go, for the day is breaking." But Jacob said, "I will not let you go, unless you bless me." And

he said to him, "What is your name?" And he said, "Jacob." Then
he said, "Your name shall no more be called Jacob, but Israel, for
you have striven with God and with men, and have prevailed."
Then Jacob asked him, "Tell me, I pray, your name." But he said,
"Why is it that you ask my name?" And there he blessed him. So
Jacob called the name of the place Peniel [= "the face of God"],
saying, "For I have seen God face to face, and yet my life is preserved." (Gen. 32:26–30 RSV)

After tussling with a divine intermediary, Jacob scores an equivocal
victory. He prevails: for that, he is blessed with the patriarchal name
"Israel" and can dub the place of the struggle to commemorate his
survival after a face-off with God (cf. Gen. 16:13). Yet Jacob hasn't
the power to wrest the angel's name, and from his encounter at the
Jabbok Jacob limps away.

A comparable outcome is narrated of Samson's father, Manoah,
unaware that news of his infertile wife's pregnancy had been relayed
by an angel of the LORD (Judg. 13:16):

> So Manoah said to the angel of the LORD, "What is your name? We
> should like to honor you when your words come true." The angel
> said to him, "You must not ask for my name; it is unknowable!"
> Manoah took the kid and the meal offering and offered them up
> on the rock to the LORD; and a marvelous thing happened while
> Manoah and his wife looked on. As the flames leaped up from the
> altar toward the sky, the angel of the LORD ascended in the flames
> of the altar, while Manoah and his wife looked on; and they flung
> themselves on their faces to the ground. . . . Manoah then real-
> ized that it had been an angel of the LORD. (Judg. 13:17–21 NJPS)

Even this angel's name is beyond human knowledge.

A crucial biblical text for understanding the power of God's
name is Exodus 3:13–15. At Horeb, the mountain of God, Moses
witnesses a bush, flaming yet unconsumed, and hears the LORD's
declaration to redeem Israel from Egyptian captivity.

> But Moses said to God, "If I come to the Israelites and say to
> them, 'The God of your ancestors has sent me to you,' and they
> ask me, 'What is his name?' what shall I say to them?" God said
> to Moses, "I AM WHO I AM [YHWH]." He said further, "Thus you
> shall say to the Israelites, 'I AM has sent me to you.'" God also said
> to Moses, "Thus you shall say to the Israelites, 'The LORD, the

87

God of your ancestors, the God of Abraham, the God of Isaac,
and the God of Jacob, has sent me to you':
This is my name forever,
and this my title for all generations."

This ancient text is remarkably subtle. The God who establishes
a covenant with soon-to-be liberated Israel is intimately engaged
with that nation's history: this is the God of its venerable patriarchs,
whose guidance stretches "for all generations." Even the cryptic
self-designation "I AM" impinges on worldly circumstances: this verbal form in four characters (YHWH, the Tetragrammaton) can be
variously translated, "I am who I am," "I shall be who I shall be,"
"I shall remain active in what I cause to happen." This is no deistic
God, who winds the cosmic clock and then, in absentia, allows it to
run itself down into fatalistic entropy. On the other hand God *on
God's own terms* is beyond comprehensible definition—and therefore beyond any human attempt to cajole, manipulate, or master.
Israel's God lives in human history, pays attention, and actively
intervenes—but does so by unilateral, self-revelatory initiatives of
grace and judgment, untouchable by magical incantation.

Abuse of the divine name is resolutely prohibited in the Decalogue's third commandment: "You shall not make wrongful use
[*tisâ'*] of the name of the LORD your God, for the LORD will not
acquit anyone who misuses his name" (Exod. 20:7 = Deut. 5:11). In
view here is not the use of God's name in cuss words. What is pro-
scribed is worship of any deity other than the LORD God (Lev. 18:21;
Ezek. 20:39; cf. the Decalogue's first and second commandments,
Exod. 20:3–6 = Deut. 5:7–10), recklessness with things dedicated
to the LORD's worship (Lev. 21:6; 22:2), and any endeavor—by sorcery, perjury, or greed—to empty the divine name's powerful purity,
thereby defying God's personal integrity for mischievous ends of
human self-aggrandizement (see Lev. 22:32; Prov. 30:9).

To be sure, the Old Testament testifies to occasions, often cultic in nature, when an Israelite calls upon the name of the LORD in
good faith, with assurance that God is reliably present, attentive,
and disposed to intervene (among others, Gen. 12:8; Deut. 18:5–7;
1 Kgs. 8:17–20; Job 1:21; Pss. 113:1–3; 148:5, 13; Joel 2:26, 32; as
well as the shouts of praise upon Jesus' entry into Jerusalem: Matt.
21:9 = Mark 11:9 = Luke 19:38, echoing Ps. 118:26; cf. Matt. 23:39
= Luke 13:35). Nevertheless, God is "The One Who Is" (*ho ōn*); as

88

Philo paraphrases God's assertion in Exod. 3:14, "No name at all may be properly used of me, in whom all existence subsists" (*Life of Moses* 1.75 AT). The One Who Is transcends verbal expression and lies beyond human ken (*On Dreams* 1.230–31; *Who Is the Heir?* 170). The name God offers Moses at Sinai veils the Namer in the very moment of self-revelation.

Elsewhere in Hebrew Scripture we observe a tendency to fill the name of the LORD with such authority that the Name itself becomes an effective proxy for God. "I am sending an angel before you to guard you on the way and to bring you to the place that I have made ready. Pay heed to him and obey him. Do not defy him, for he will not pardon your offenses, since My Name is in him" (Exod. 23:20–21 NJPS; cf. Mic. 5:4). The divine Name can be regarded as an instrument by which the LORD executes an action: "O God, deliver me by Your name; by Your power vindicate me" (Ps. 54:3 NJPS; cf. Ps. 20:1; Prov. 18:10). The Deuteronomistic tradition ventures an intriguing distinction: While the LORD is enthroned in heaven (Deut. 4:36; 26:15), he causes his Name to dwell in places of his choosing (12:11; 14:23), particularly wilderness sanctuaries (12:5–7; 2 Sam. 7:13, "a house for my name") and eventually Solomon's temple: "In this House . . . I will establish My name forever" (2 Kgs. 21:7 NJPS; cf. 1 Kgs. 9:3, 7).

In texts written after the temple's destruction and the Babylonian exile, the Name of the LORD seems interchangeable with the LORD himself:

> Every spirit of light that is capable of blessing, glorifying, extolling, and sanctifying your blessed name [shall bless him]; and all flesh shall glorify and bless your name with an exceedingly limitless power forever and ever. (*1 En.* 61:12, trans. E. Isaac [*OTP*]; cf. Pss. 9:11; 18:50; 68:5; Mic. 4:5)

To praise God's name is, therefore, tantamount to praising God.

Taking to heart this multifaceted yet coherent understanding, pious Jews have scrupulously avoided pronouncing the divine name, a tendency traceable to Hellenistic Judaism of the second and first centuries BC (Dalman, *Words of Jesus*, 179–83). For Josephus, the name of God inspires awe (*Jewish War* 5.438); he may have preferred to speak of God's Spirit, not of the divine name, as dwelling in the temple (*Jewish Antiquities* 8.114), though that locution may have been a concession to Roman readers unacquainted with biblical thought. In the same era Matthew's Gospel favors periphrastic mention of "the kingdom of heaven" (31× in all) over Mark and Luke's straightforward reference to "the kingdom of God" (cf., on the other hand, Matt. 12:28; 19:24; 21:31, 43). Only in the temple, in controlled conditions, was the divine name responsibly uttered. By custom, "Lord" is a reverent substitution for the Tetragrammaton, which in synagogues to this day is pronounced 'Adōnai ("My Lord").

Hallowing the Name

The English adjectives "sanctified" or "hallowed" stem from different feeder languages: sanctificare (Latin), "to render something sanctus" or "sacred"; and heiligen (German/Dutch), "something revered as 'holy.'" Their counterparts in ancient Hebrew and Greek, qadosh and hagios, carry similar connotations. Both terms' earliest associations are with sanctuaries (Latin, sanctuaria): shrines or any place "set apart" by cultic consecration. In the Yahwist legend of Sinai, in which the divine Name is at once disclosed and cloaked, God warns Moses to remove his sandals, "for the place on which you stand is holy ground ['admat-qōdesh]" (Exod. 3:5 NJPS; cf. Lev. 21:23; Josh. 5:15; 2 Chr. 30:8; as well as Herodotus, Histories 2.41, 44; 5.119; and Demosthenes, Orations 25.35; 59.77, both referring to pagan sanctuaries). Other places made sacred by God's presence are "holy": the heavens (Deut. 26:15; Jer. 25:30; Wis. 9:10), the tabernacle and its courts (Exod. 40:9; Num. 3:28), the temple and its precincts (2 Chr. 29:7; 36:14; Pss. 5:7; 63:2; 68:24; 138:2; Dan. 8:13; 1 Esd. 1:53), Jerusalem (Ezra 9:8; Neh. 11:1, 18; Zeph. 3:4; Tob. 13:9), Mount Zion (Obad. 17; Pss. 20:2; 24:3; Isa. 57:13; Zeph. 3:11), and the land of Israel (Ezek. 45:1; Zech. 2:12).

Beyond these sacred venues, various things and persons are distinguished as qōdesh: priests (Lev. 21:6; 2 Chr. 5:11; 23:6; 30:24; 31:18; Ezra 8:28) and Levites (1 Chr. 15:14; 2 Chr. 29:5, 34; 30:15, 17), altars (Exod. 29:37; 40:10; Sir. 50:11), sacrificial animals (Num. 18:17; Ezek. 36:38; Heb. 9:13), comestibles (Lev. 22:10–16), fasts and solemn assemblies (Joel 1:14; 2:15), books (1 Macc. 12:9), utensils (2 Chr. 29:19), swords (2 Macc. 15:16), ritual hours (Exod. 31:14–15), the Sabbath (Gen. 2:3; Exod. 16:23; 20:8, 11; 35:2; Ezek.

20:12, 20; 2 Macc. 5:25), the Year of Jubilee (Lev. 25:10), God's covenant with Israel (Dan. 11:28, 30), and occasionally Israel itself (Isa. 62:12; 63:18; Jer. 2:3; Joel 2:16). Anyone and anything set apart for God's worship falls within the purview of the holy. Beyond Hebrew Scripture, Philo (*Embassy to Gaius* 278; *Change of Names* 192; *Who Is the Heir?* 75) and rabbis of the Mishnaic period (ca. AD 20–220) demarcated sacred sectors: the city square (site of religious festivals), the synagogue, the ark of the Torah within the synagogue, veils of Scripture within the ark, scrolls of the prophets and the writings, and the Torah scroll, holiest of all artifacts, whose reading is the heart of worship (*m. Megillah* 3.1). "If two sit together and occupy themselves with Torah, God's presence [rests] among them" (*m. 'Abot* 3.2).

The root of holiness, nevertheless, is *God*, who in every respect stands apart from all else.

- God's *word* is resolutely holy: "The Lord GOD has sworn by his holiness" (Amos 4:2; cf. Ps. 89:35–36).
- God's *actions* are triumphantly holy: "His right hand, His holy arm, has won Him victory" (Ps. 98:1 NJPS; Isa. 52:10).
- God's *Spirit*, or abiding presence, is holy and grieved by Israel's rebellion (Isa. 63:10): "Then they remembered the ancient days, Him, who pulled His people out [of the water]: . . . 'Where is He who put in their midst His holy spirit, Who made His glorious arm march at the right hand of Moses?'" (Isa. 63:11–12a NJPS; cf. Ps. 51:11).

Above all God's *name*—God's personal presence in Israel's sanctuary and among his chosen people—is holy and under no circumstances may be profaned (Lev. 24:11). Consecrations of the Holy Name are embedded in Israelite liturgy:

> O you righteous, rejoice in the LORD
> and acclaim His holy name! (Ps. 97:12 NJPS; cf. 1 Chr. 16:10)

> Deliver us, O God, our deliverer,
> and gather us and save us from the nations,
> to acclaim Your holy name,
> to glory in Your praise. (1 Chr. 16:35 NJPS; cf. 29:16)

91

Conversely, trafficking in worship of foreign gods desecrates the LORD's sacred name:

> And I will set My face against that man and will cut him off from among his people, because he gave of his offspring to Molech [the Ammonite god: 1 Kgs. 11:4–8] and so defiled My sanctuary and profaned My holy name. (Lev. 20:3 NJPS; cf. Ezek. 22:26; 44:23)

Because the "name" conveys the essence of what is denominated, "hallowing the name" of God expresses God's holy otherness, acknowledging the qualitative difference of Israel's God from all creation and vouchsafing in the Name the same confidence one entrusts in its Bearer:

> We set our hope on the LORD,
>   He is our help and shield;
> in Him our hearts rejoice,
>   for in His holy name we trust. (Ps. 33:20–21 NJPS;
>   cf. Pss. 71:22; 89:18; 103:1)

No Hebrew prophet is more insistent in honoring the divine name and purging it from pagan defilement than Ezekiel (mid-6th c. BC). Repeatedly he indicts Israel for having desecrated the name of the Lord GOD through sorcery (13:19), idolatry (20:39; 36:20), apostasy (36:21), and other pagan abominations (43:7–8). Israel, however, is not competent to remedy its profanation of the Holy One.

> Thus said the Lord GOD: Not for your sake will I act, O House of Israel, but for My holy name, which you have caused to be profaned among the nations to which you have come. I will sanctify My great name which has been profaned among the nations— among whom you have caused it to be profaned. And the nations shall know that I am the LORD—declares the Lord GOD—when I manifest My holiness before their eyes through you. (Ezek. 36:22–23 NJPS)

Taking unilateral action to sanctify the divine name wherever it has been defiled (20:9, 14, 22; 39:7), God is passionate for the restoration of *both* his people *and* his name: "Assuredly, thus said the Lord GOD: I will now restore the fortunes of Jacob and take the whole House of Israel back in love; and I will be zealous for My holy name" (Ezek. 39:25 NJPS; cf. 37:28).

92

A Hallowed People

Holiness means the God-ness of God, and in Hebrew religion can be predicated of [the LORD] alone. To say that God is holy is to say that God is God. To say that things or persons are holy is to say that they have been separated by God to be his special possession, and have passed from the sphere of the worldly and familiar into the sphere of the sacred. (Evans, *Lord's Prayer*, 27–28)

Broadly speaking, two major developments issue from this understanding of the LORD's holiness: each branch is entwined with the other, and both are very old. First, Israel itself comes to acquire a secondary "holiness"—not divinity, but a sense of being set apart—from the Holy God who has called that people into existence. This awareness of precious separation apparently derived from the Sinaitic covenant that the LORD God cut out of sheer grace with the Hebrew people from among all of the earth's nations.

For *you* are a people holy [*'am-qādōsh*] to the LORD your God; the LORD your God has chosen *you* out of all the peoples on earth to be his people, his treasured possession. . . . It was because the LORD loved you and kept the oath that he swore to your ancestors, that the LORD has brought you out with a mighty hand, and redeemed you from the house of slavery, from the hand of Pharaoh king of Egypt. (Deut. 7:6, 8; cf. Gen. 15:18–20; Exod. 2:24; 6:4–5)

From this remembrance of Israel's salvation—its resurrection from death in an Egyptian tomb—a second major development in Israel's fundamental understanding of holiness immediately follows: the peculiar religious, social, and moral obligations binding upon that particular people to whom the LORD has elected to bind himself.

And the LORD has affirmed this day that you are, as He promised you, His treasured people who shall observe all His commandments, and that He will set you, in fame and renown and glory, high above all the nations that He has made; and that you shall be, as He promised, a holy people to the LORD your God. (Deut. 26:18–19 NJPS; cf. 4:23; Exod. 23:32; 34:15; Lev. 20:8)

93

In short: "[Israel] shall be holy; for I the LORD your God am holy" (Lev. 19:2; 20:26; 21:8, 15).

The barometer of Israel's holiness is its adherence to the commandments given at Sinai (Exod. 20:1–17), augmented in the Holiness Code of Leviticus 17–26. Ancient Israel held together two seemingly contradictory beliefs: God is holy, transcendent over the creaturely world, and that holiness weds God with Israel, ultimately all of creation, in deepest communion. "Holy, holy, holy is the LORD of hosts; the whole earth is full of his glory" (Isa. 6:3). "The only difference between God's holiness and man's holiness is that God *is* holy, whereas men and nations *become* holy" (Lohmeyer, *Lord's Prayer*, 71).

To a large degree the Deuteronomistic History, recounted in the books of Joshua, Judges, 1–2 Samuel, and 1–2 Kings, is a story of Israel's betrayal of the covenant (thus Ps. 78:41). In the mideighth century BC, Amos, the Judean prophet of Tekoa, takes Israel to task for rampant injustice, barbaric immorality, and hollow piety, all of which "profane [the LORD's] holy name" (2:7 NJPS). "My Lord GOD swears by His holiness," God's innermost essence, that thieves, swindlers, and swillers will receive their comeuppance (4:2 NJPS, in Hebrew details so obscure that their translation is uncertain). Isaiah's initial vision (ca. 740 BC) reclaims a trenchant sense of God's transcendent otherness:

In the year that King Uzziah died, I beheld my Lord seated on a high and lofty throne; and the skirts of His robe filled the Temple. Seraphs stood in attendance on Him. . . .

And one would call to the other,
"Holy, holy, holy!
  The LORD of Hosts!
His presence fills all the earth!"

The doorposts would shake at the sound of the one who called, and the House kept filling with smoke. I cried,
"Woe is me; I am lost!
  For I am a man of unclean lips
And I live among a people
    Of unclean lips;
Yet my own eyes have beheld
The King LORD of Hosts." (Isa. 6:1–5 NJPS)

In the late sixth century BC, Deutero-Isaiah maintains this transcendent vision of God—incomparable (Isa. 40:25), exclusive (45:5–6), inscrutable (45:9–11, 15; 55:8–9), creative from first to last (41:20; 45:7, 12)—with a stronger accent on rejuvenation than on judgment:

> For thus said He who high aloft
> Forever dwells, whose name is holy: . . .
> I who make spirits flag,
> Also create the breath of life. (Isa. 57:15, 16 NJPS)

Even more impassioned is Hosea (7th c. BC), for whom God's incomprehensible holiness is married with unfathomable love:

> How can I give you up, O Ephraim?
> How surrender you, O Israel? . . .
> For I am God, not man,
> The Holy One in your midst:
> I will not come in fury. (Hos. 11:8–9 NJPS)

The Holy One, who "fell in love with Israel when he was still a child" (11:1 NJPS), will not relax that maternal embrace, no matter how wild the child's disobedience.

Nine centuries later the authors of what became the New Testament borrowed the same metaphors of holy separation to characterize the peculiar origin and responsibilities of Christians. The church and its offerings have been sanctified by God (Acts 20:32; 1 Cor. 3:17; 1 Thess. 5:23) or God's word (John 17:17), Christ (Acts 26:18; Eph. 5:26), and the Holy Spirit (Rom. 15:16; 1 Cor. 6:11; 1 Pet. 1:2). For that reason Paul can address the faltering Christians in churches he founded and visited as "holy ones" (*hoi hagioi*: Rom. 8:27; 12:13; 15:25; 1 Cor. 1:2; 6:1–2; 2 Cor. 1:1; Phil. 1:1; 4:22; Col. 1:2). By no means are they impeccable; rather, God has declared their destiny by choosing to dwell among them, even as God consecrated Israel (Isa. 4:3; Dan. 7:18, 21; Tob. 8:15). Adopting the images of temple, priesthood, and atonement, the Epistle to the Hebrews repeatedly correlates God's sanctification of a people by Christ's self-sacrifice (2:11; 9:13; 10:10, 14, 29; 13:12).

God's intrinsic holiness exerts extrinsic impact on those who confess its reality. As George Foot Moore put it, "God 'hallows his name' (makes it holy) . . . by doing things that lead or constrain men

95

to acknowledge him as God. And as it is God's supreme end that all mankind shall ultimately serve him as the true God, so it is the chief end of Israel . . . to hallow his name by living so that men shall see and say that the God of Israel is the true God" (*Judaism*, 2:103). So, too, the church is made holy by acknowledging God's holiness: "the human being becomes holy because he . . . consecrates himself to the supreme Person and to the service of pure good, of the truth and justice willed by that Personal reality" (Stăniloae, *Experience of God*, 231).

"May It Be So"

By now it should be obvious: when Jesus instructed that his disciples pray for the hallowing of God's name, he drew from an Israelite spirituality that is deep, rich, and strange to most modern ears. Another element remains to be examined: the verbal conjugation *hagiasthētō*, "let it be sanctified." Who renders this sanctification, and in what manner?

At this point English-speaking readers benefit from a brief detour into the grammar of biblical languages. In ancient Greek verbs the passive voice (in which a subject is acted upon) evolved from the "middle" voice (in which an action is performed with reference to the subject). Vestiges of these connotations have been carried over into everyday English:

I spoke those words. (subject + active verb + direct object)
My words were spoken. (subject + passive verb)
I spoke up [for myself]. (subject + middle verb [+ *understood*: a reflexive prepositional phrase, referring back to the subject])

Ancient Hebrew and Aramaic, the Semitic tongues with which Jesus would have been most familiar, can also express this middle or reflexive mood (known as the *niphal*, underlined below). In Leviticus 10:3 Moses interprets for Aaron the meaning of a claim made by the LORD:

96

I show Myself to be holy among those near to Me,
And before all the people I am glorified. (AT)

Here and elsewhere in the Old Testament (Isa. 5:16; Ezek. 20:41), God is the subject of this sanctification, the effective agent of divine holiness or "set-apartness." That seems to be the most natural meaning of Matthew 6:9c = Luke 11:2b: to ask that God's name be hallowed is, in its most fundamental sense, to pray that *God*, first and foremost, will demonstrate the holiness of that name. Moreover, *hagiasthētō* is conjugated in the aorist tense and the imperative mood: in Greek, an exhortation with a sharp edge and a decisive tenor. One might paraphrase, "Almighty God: the divine majesty represented by your inexpressible Name—make that known now, comprehensively, once for all." God's primary agency of holiness is amplified in the petitions of Jesus' prayer immediately following: "Allow your kingdom to come" (Matt. 6:10a = Luke 11:2c); "May your will come to pass" (Matt. 6:10b).

Moralism is a trap into which it is so easy for us to tumble that we should be as precise as possible. Jesus was not pressuring us to do for God what only God can do. God's sanctity is not produced by even the most devout human effort. God's self-consecration kindles in us the yearning to revere the Almighty as God alone deserves.

Even though God is the primary agent of his own sanctity, we have noted evidence in the Old Testament for a qualified transference of holiness upon that people whom God has chosen. It is likely, then, that Matthew 6:9c = Luke 11:2b suggests a similar merging. When God honors his own divinity—"hallows the Name"—*God also consecrates those who offer this petition*, drawing supplicants into the sphere of a holiness intended to restore all creation to God's glory (see Rom. 5:2; 8:18, 21; 2 Cor. 3:18; 4:17; Phil. 3:21; 1 Thess. 2:12; 2 Tim. 2:10; Heb. 2:10; 1 Pet. 5:4, 10). By so praying, Jesus' disciples sing antiphonally with the synagogue, whose Kaddish opens and closes with a resonant blessing, an implicit thanksgiving of praise:

> Exalted and hallowed be His great Name
> in the world that He created. . . .
> May his great Name be praised forever
> and unto all eternity. (See appendix A)

"Those who speak on their own seek their own glory; but the one who seeks the glory of [the Father] who sent [the Son] is true, and there is nothing false in him" (John 7:18). Any holiness the church might claim is totally derivative, never to be sought for its own sake. It is, instead, transposed from God, whose essence is holiness and whose sanctity is always to be praised. "For from him and through him and to him are all things. To him be the glory forever. Amen" (Rom. 11:36; cf. Gal. 1:3–5; Eph. 3:20–21).

All Hallows' Eve

Ignorance seems bliss when in fact it is piss. Irrespective of our awareness, the first three petitions of the Lord's Prayer situate its supplicants in contradiction to a world that refuses to acknowledge its creator and sustainer, its judge and redeemer. To ask with sincerity that *God's* will be done, that earth be realigned with heaven, is to surrender every demand that *our* will be fulfilled. To hope for the coming of *God's* kingdom in its fullness is to abandon *our* aspirations of sovereignty. To pray that *God's* name be hallowed is to relinquish *our* claims for ultimate authority. (More on this in chap. 5.) Not a day passes that we, however faithful we might wish to be, are not tempted by idolatry or practical atheism: two roads that eventually converge into structural decadence. When we exercise our freedom to act with cruelty and injustice, to deform the earth created by God, to embezzle praise for ourselves, we defy God's consecration and deny how the world really is.

Even in twenty-first-century culture that has largely lost a Christian imagination, names still count for something. When I sign my name to a contract, a petition, or an affidavit, I am literally signifying that I stand behind that certificate's claims. When I write my name on the face of a check, I promise my debtor that I am trustworthy for payment. When I lay my name on a book's title page, I declare that its contents are my own (and at those points where I have drawn from other' accounts, I have admitted my debt). In a real sense my name *is* myself: in the public sphere, in my relationships with fellow human beings, it is the only self that matters. If I affix my signature to a rubber check, if I misrepresent another's words as my own, something more has occurred than default of payment or infringement of copyright. I have exposed myself as a fraud. No longer does a self stand behind the signature: the letters "Clifton Black" have become essentially meaningless. I have emptied my name of any standing to a degree that may prove impossible to refill.

98

So, too, with oaths: the invocation of my name in a sworn declaration. In court or in church I name myself as one who freely undertakes to fulfill a promise: to tell the whole truth, to be faithful in marriage, to raise a child in accordance with Christian faith. In Robert Bolt's play *A Man for All Seasons* (1960), Sir Thomas More tries to explain this to his daughter Margaret: "When a man takes an oath, Meg, he's holding his own self in his own hands. Like water. (*He cups his hands.*) And if he opens his fingers *then*—he needn't hope to find himself again. Some men aren't capable of this, but I'd be loath to think your father one of them" (81). Perjury is more than a lie. It rends the social fabric from throat to hem, and God's name is desecrated (Lev. 19:11–12) by one who lacks a self to dedicate.

It is critical, therefore, that the Lord's Prayer begins *both* by addressing God as Father *and* by beseeching the sanctity of God's holy Name: *God's own self*. Two things are said, at once and inextricably: the God who may be addressed with intimacy as Father is God in his transcendent God-ness. While permitted to address God as a parent, we concede that God is not our patron. God's name is holy (Ps. 111:9; Isa. 54:5; Luke 1:49), which means that God is living goodness and absolute purity: utterly other, mysterious, awesome, not "warm and cozy, but rather . . . a burning fire of love" (Bradshaw, *Praying as Believing*, 53). We are not God. God alone is God. God is already pure holiness; our prayers do not make it so. We pray that God's identity as Lord, God's true Self, may be recognized and honored by this world of God's own creation (thus, Augustine, *Sermon on the Mount* 2.19).

Scripture ticks to the metronome of Lord's extolment.

There is none like You among the gods, O Lord,
    and there are no deeds like Yours. . . .
Teach me Your way, O Lord;
    I will walk in Your truth;
    let my heart be undivided in reverence for Your name.
I will praise You, O Lord, my God, with all my heart
and pay honor to Your name forever. (Ps. 86:8, 11–12 NJPS;
    cf. Lev. 10:3; Pss. 22:23; 50:15)

So, too, young Mary, singing to Elizabeth, to the Lord, and to us who overhear:

And Mary said, "My soul magnifies the Lord,
    and my spirit rejoices in God my Savior, . . .

for he who is mighty has done great things for me,
and holy is his name." (Luke 1:46–47, 49 RSV)

The Magnificat expresses Jewish piety at its finest: personal but not privatist, girdling time and space. Those beyond Israel's borders who "attach themselves to the LORD," who "love the name of the LORD," will be gathered with dispersed Israel into a single "house of prayer for all peoples" (Isa. 56:6 AT; 56:7–8; cf. 25:3; 60:7).

Likewise is John's staggering vision of "a sea of glass mixed with fire," reverberating with a duet by Moses and the Lamb (Rev. 15:2, 3a):

Lord, who will not fear
and glorify your name?
For you alone are holy.
All nations will come
and worship before you,
for your judgments have been revealed. (15:4)

All these hymns chant the tripartition of the appeal, "Hallowed be your name": (1) God's Name, or Self, is set apart for reverence; (2) the LORD sanctifies the Name; (3) worshipers answer by honoring, or glorifying (Heb., *qādash*; Gk., *doxazō*), this God. "'Father, glorify thy name.' Then a voice came from heaven, 'I have glorified it, and I will glorify it again'" (John 12:28 RSV). The divine-human circuit is completed; the whole of the worshiping self is encompassed: the *word* of honor is braided by honorable *deeds*.

In the New Testament this consolidation's most transparent expression is the one who taught others to pray in this way. When Jesus acts in God's name to restore a ruptured world, his observers honor God (Matt. 9:8 = Mark 2:12 = Luke 5:26; Matt. 15:31; Luke 4:15; 7:16). One of the Fourth Gospel's persistent refrains is that Jesus does not honor himself; God honors Jesus precisely because he honors God in all he says and does (8:54; 13:31–32; 14:13; 15:8; 16:14; 17:1, 4–5, 10), especially by giving his life for the world (7:39; 12:16, 23; cf. 11:4; 21:19). For the evangelists, Jesus is the embodiment of Isaiah's hope for a redeemed and faithful Israel that glorifies the LORD (Isa. 29:13–14, 22–24; 44:23; 49:3; 55:5; 60:9, 21; cf. Acts 11:18; 13:48; 21:20).

Like teacher, like disciple: our adoration of God is manifested by adherence to Christ's norm (Rom. 15:6–9; 1 Cor. 6:20; 2 Cor. 9:13), notably in suffering:

100

If you are reviled for the name of Christ, you are blessed, because the spirit of glory, which is the Spirit of God, is resting on you. But let none of you suffer as a murderer, a thief, a criminal, or even as a mischief maker. Yet if any of you suffers as a Christian, do not consider it a disgrace, *but glorify God because you bear this name.* (1 Pet. 4:14–16, emphasis added; cf. 2:12; Rom. 8:17, 30; Eph. 3:13)

God asks of the Christian nothing other than what God did for us in Christ: evacuate Almighty Power into infant impotence (Matt. 1:18–2:23; Mark 10:15 = Luke 18:17; Luke 1:26–2:52; Gal. 4:4). First Peter extends Numbers 18:29 to its logical conclusion: "You shall set aside all gifts due to the LORD from everything that is donated to you, from each thing its best portion, the part thereof that is to be consecrated" (NJPS). In the end the best of all we have been given, to be returned to the Giver, is our life as a whole. The only honor befitting a Christian is the relinquishment of every honor whatsoever. The only name to be hallowed is that of God alone (cf. Rev. 2:13; 3:8, 12).

It is terribly simpleminded of humans to suppose that God's transcendence is a kind of religious glop, removed from everyday reality, when in scriptural perspective nothing is more real than God on God's own terms. All creatures have inbuilt cravings, some of which, left unchecked, can balloon into the selfish delusion that we are our own god. Such fantasy is more than cognitive error: eventually it leads to moral disaster. On false grounds we prey, exploit, abuse, and kill: in short, we desecrate what God intends to purify (Boff, *Lord's Prayer*, 48–52). To pray that God's sanctity may redeem everything profane, that God be proved true though every mortal be false (Rom. 3:4), that *God will be God* (Col. 1:15–20), is the Spirit's summons that God will reunite our equivocal self: "a lever to tear us from the imaginary into the real and from time into eternity, to lift us right out of the prison of self" (Weil, "The Our Father," 217). When we pray for the hallowing of God's name, we renounce our hedonism, our idolatries of nation and of market-place, any calculation of success or failure, all absorption in our own status, every debilitating fear, and render to God the glory that is God's sole property. As Bach inscribed at the end of all his church compositions: *S. D. G., Soli Deo gloria.*

Just here lies a deep paradox of faith. Like the builders of Babylon's tower who wrecked themselves by blowing the bubble

101

reputation (Gen. 11:1–9), we make hash of our lives by hallowing ourselves: our independence, our projects, the manifold manifestations of our self-interest. When we disown our dependence on the One "in [whom] we live and move and have our being" (Acts 17:28), we seek artificial stimulants that cannot satisfy: diet, drugs, sex, money, prestige, power ad infinitum, ad nauseam. As surely as we set ourselves up as our own goal, we shall never realize it, because such fulfillment is impossible. Thus Helmut Thielicke counseled his congregations in Stuttgart as it collapsed into ruin during World War II:

> A man cannot become a new person by deciding to become one. He can become a new person only when he allows himself to be incorporated in this process of fellowship with God. *This* is the real meaning of our life, and the "new person" is only a by-product of this process. . . . We should not begin with our own holiness, our own moral advance, but rather concentrate our whole prayer on this one thing, that *God* may become holy to us, that [*God*] may occupy the ruling place in our life. (*The Prayer*, 52–54)

Thielicke's qualification is critical. We do not pray "Hallowed be Thy Name" instrumentally: to the end of self-improvement, to wangle something out of the Almighty. Precisely the reverse: by surrendering ourselves to our Maker, by quitting one's hunger for preeminence and instead esteeming God, by thus praying *against* ourselves and *for* God, we end up being consecrated by the Holy One, living the life for which we were created. That is the point of the first, best-remembered question and answer in the Westminster Shorter Catechism (1646):

Q. 1. What is the chief end of man?
A. Man's chief end is to glorify God, and to enjoy him forever.

That destination is not simply yours or mine; it is humanity's in its universality. "When we say, 'Let your name be hallowed,' we ask that it be hallowed among us who are in him and, at the same time, in others whom the grace of God still awaits, so that we should be obedient to the command to pray for all, even for our enemies [Matt. 5:44]" (Tertullian, *Prayer*, 3, trans. Stewart-Sykes). "We make the petition for the whole human race, we make it for all the world, for all those people who daily sit down and argue that God is

102

not right-minded and does not judge in an upright way" (Augustine, *Exposition on Psalm 103* 1.3, AT). For all the differences we may see and stress among ourselves, finally all of us are knit together in our creation by the God whom we too often insult. Riffing on Matthew 5:16, Gregory of Nyssa (335–394) put to his listeners a question (*The Lord's Prayer*, 48–50): When others regard us, do they observe something of justice, truth, beauty, and goodness? Can they catch glimmers of a God whom they would be moved to glorify?
Soli Deo gloria.

Works Cited in Chapter 4

Augustine of Hippo. *Expositions of the Psalms 99–120*. Vol. 5. Book 3/19. *The Works of Saint Augustine: A Translation for the 21st Century*. Translated by Maria Boulding. Edited by Boniface Ramsey. Hyde Park, NY: New City Press, 2003.

Boff, Leonardo. *The Lord's Prayer: The Prayer of Integral Liberation*. Translated by Theodore Morrow. Melbourne: Dove; Maryknoll, NY: Orbis Books, 1983.

Bolt, Robert. *A Man for All Seasons: A Play in Two Acts*. New York: Vintage/Random House, 1962.

Bradshaw, Timothy. *Praying as Believing: The Lord's Prayer and the Christian Doctrine of God*. Regent's Study Guides 6. Oxford: Regent's Park College; Macon, GA: Smyth & Helwys, 1998.

Dalman, Gustaf. *The Words of Jesus Considered in the Light of Post-Biblical Jewish Writings and the Aramaic Language*. Translated by D. M. Kay. Edinburgh: T&T Clark, 1902.

Evans, C. F. *The Lord's Prayer*. London: SCM, 1963.

Gregory of Nyssa. *The Lord's Prayer, The Beatitudes*. Translated and annotated by Hilda C. Graef. Ancient Christian Writers 18. New York: Paulist Press, 1954.

Harner, Philip B. *Understanding the Lord's Prayer*. Philadelphia: Fortress Press, 1975.

Lochman, Jan Milač. *The Lord's Prayer*. Translated by Geoffrey W. Bromiley. Grand Rapids: Wm. B. Eerdmans Publishing Co., 1990.

Lohmeyer, Ernst. *"Our Father": An Introduction to the Lord's Prayer*. Translated by John Bowden. New York: Harper & Row, 1965.

Lüthi, Walter. *The Lord's Prayer: An Exposition*. Translated by Kurt Schoenenberger. Edinburgh: Oliver & Boyd, 1961.

Metzler, Norman. "The Lord's Prayer: Second Thoughts on the First Petition." In *Authenticating the Words of Jesus*, edited by Bruce Chilton and Craig A. Evans, 187–202. New Testament Tools and Studies. Leiden: E. J. Brill, 1999.

Moore, George Foot. *Judaism in the First Centuries of the Christian Era: The Age of the Tannaim*. 3 vols. Cambridge, MA: Harvard University Press, 1954.

Papyri Graecae Magicae [Die griechischen Zauberpapyri]. 3 vols. 2nd ed. Edited by Adam Abt and Albert Henrichs. Stuttgart: Teubner, 1973.

Stăniloae, Dumitru. *The Experience of God*. Translated and edited by Ioan Ioiță and Robert Barringer. Brookline, MA: Holy Cross Orthodox Press, 1994.

Tertullian, Cyprian, and Origen: On the Lord's Prayer. Translated and annotated by Alistair Stewart-Sykes. Popular Patristics Series. Crestwood, NY: St Vladimir's Seminary Press, 2004.

Thielicke, Helmut. *The Prayer That Spans the World: Sermons on the Lord's Prayer*. Translated by John W. Doberstein. London: James Clarke, 1960.

Weil, Simone. "Concerning the Our Father." In *Waiting for God*, translated by Emma Craufurd, 216–27. New York: G. P. Putnam's Sons, 1952.

CHAPTER 5

Kingdom and Will

Alexander III of Macedonia is known as Alexander the Great because he
killed more people of more different kinds than any other man of his time.
—Will Cuppy

While it is conceptually possible to separate petitions for the coming kingdom (Luke 11:2c = Matt. 6:10a) and the fulfillment of God's
will (Matt. 6:10b), that is theologically ill advised. As we shall see,
the notion of divine decree is built into the Greek term usually
translated "kingdom": God's will is supreme. Thus Matthew 7:21:
"Not everyone who says to me, 'Lord, Lord,' will enter the kingdom of heaven, but only the one who does the will of my Father
in heaven." Likewise, to pray that the divine will already governing heaven may also rule over earth (Matt. 6:10c) implies a supernal kingdom that impinges on this world as a whole. Whether one
traces it to Jesus himself or to the Matthean church, the prayer that
God's will be done on earth as in heaven is an apt paraphrase and
an emphatic reassertion of the supplicant's plea for God's coming
kingdom.

"Thy kingdom come" is among the most difficult of this Prayer's
petitions to grasp, in part because "the kingdom of God" (= "of
heaven") has proved to be among the most controversial features
of Jesus' teaching (see Chilton, *Kingdom of God*). In this chapter I
hope to show that, for all its complexity, the essence of what Jesus
probably meant by this term is within our reach: God's eternal

105

sovereignty, now invading human history. The fundamental difficulty does not lie in what the metaphor suggests, but in our readiness to appropriate and to ask for it. Embedded in this appeal is the collision of our kingdoms with that of God and our willingness to yield to an authority not our own.

God as King in the Old Testament and Ancient Judaism

In the Hebrew Bible the phrase "the kingdom of God" never appears, although something close to it occurs once, in 1 Chronicles 28:5: King David testifies before Israel's officers, "[The LORD God] chose my son Solomon to sit on the throne of the kingdom of the LORD [*malkûth yhwh*] over Israel" (NJPS). In the Greek Septuagint, Wisdom "showed [the righteous man] the kingdom of God [*basileian theou*], and gave him knowledge of holy things" (Wis. 10:10 [late 1st c. BC/early 1st c. AD]).

Acclamation that "the LORD is king" or "the LORD reigns" (*yhwh* [or *'ĕlōhîm*] *mālak*) is, however, commonplace in Old Testament hymns of praise (1 Chr. 16:31; Pss. 10:16; 47:8; 93:1; 96:10; 97:1; 99:1; 146:10). Israel did not invent this metaphor but adapted it from ancient Near Eastern religions (Hanson, *Dawn of Apocalyptic*, 299–324) to express wonder at the LORD's conquest of primordial chaos in the creation of heaven and earth (Pss. 29:10; 74:12–17; 93:3–4; 104:3, 6) and thanksgiving for the LORD's salvation of Israel as a special possession among the nations (Pss. 33:12; 47:2–4; Isa. 52:7).

As king, the LORD is both transcendent and immanent: Israel worships a cosmic monarch, beyond time and space (Pss. 11:4; 29:1–10), who chooses an attachment to Zion, or Jerusalem, the city of his foundation (87:1; 132:13; Isa. 24:23; Mic. 4:7). The LORD has endowed Israel with a special set of ordinances, the Torah, to guide the conduct of this people, selected from among all others (Pss. 78:1–8; 105:45; 147:12–20), and has anointed a lieutenant—prototypically, David—to execute divine justice among the earth's kingdoms (2:7–12; 45:6–7; 72:1–2; 78:56–72). There is no sphere over which the LORD is not regnant; to acclaim this God as king is to ascribe to him all dominion, without exception or remainder: "[God's] kingly sovereignty endures forever and ever"

(*Targum Onqelos* on Exod. 15:18 [2nd or 3rd c.]). James Luther Mays opined that the "declaration of *Yhwh malak* involves a vision of reality that is the theological center of the Psalter" (*The Lord Reigns*, 22). While other interpreters might disagree, one is hard pressed to identify a metaphor closer to the heart of Israel's praise and pedagogy.

Seeds for an eschatological expectation of God's kingdom are discernible but rare in the Old Testament. In Deutero-Isaiah (52:7), Obadiah (21), and Zephaniah (3:15), God's sovereignty is reasserted after the catastrophe of Judah's Babylonian exile. A few passages turn this figure of speech in an apocalyptic direction: the LORD's triumph over earthly kings (Isa. 24:21–23; 33:7–22; Dan. 2:1–49; 7:1–28; Zech. 14:9) and even death itself (Isa. 25:6–8).

The flowering of this trend is apparent toward the end of the first century BC, into the second century AD:

> Then [God's] kingdom will appear throughout his whole creation.
> Then the devil will have an end.
> Yea, sorrow will be led away with him. (*T. Mos.* 10:1, trans. Priest [*OTP*]; cf. *T. Dan* 5:10, 13; *As. Mos.* 10:1)
> And then, indeed [God] will raise up a kingdom for all
> ages among men, he who once gave the holy Law to the pious.
> (*Sib. Or.* 3:767, trans. Collins [*OTP*])

In such passages God's dominion is primarily an end-time aspiration for judgment of the wicked, as well as the reclamation of creation, Israel's faithful, and perhaps all humankind.

Paul's contemporaries Josephus (*Jewish Antiquities* 6.60) and Philo (*Change of Names* 135; *Special Laws* 4.164) rarely refer to the kingdom of God. Josephus suggests that Jerusalem has adopted a theocratic constitution (*theokratia*), congruous with imperial Rome, by which God rules through laws and a priestly aristocracy (*Apology* 2.164–66). Paul's own references to God's kingdom are sparse: six occurrences in the undisputed Paulines (Rom. 14:17; 1 Cor. 4:20; 6:9, 10; 15:50; Gal. 5:21), once in Colossians (4:11), and once in 2 Thessalonians (1:5).

This metaphor is scattered in rabbinic literature, vast as it is. "To accept the yoke of the kingdom of God" seems tantamount to recitation of the *Shema* (Deut. 6:4): to confess the one God as the King and to forswear all other gods (*b. Berakhot* 13b). The first petition of the Kaddish hopes for the "establish[ment of God's] kingdom . . . in your lifetime and in your days, and in the lifetime of the whole household of Israel, speedily and at a near time"; each of the twenty-seven petitions of the Abhinu Malkenu addresses God as "Our Father, Our King" (see appendix A). One of the loveliest utterances of God's sovereignty in the rabbinic prayer books follows the Psalter's lead, tinctured by an eschatological reverence:

> Therefore we bow in worship and thank the supreme King of kings, the Holy One, blessed be He, who extends the heavens and establishes the earth; . . . All the world's inhabitants will realise and know that to You every knee must bow down and every tongue swear loyalty. . . . They will accept the yoke of Your kingdom, and You will reign over them soon and for ever. For the kingdom is Yours, and to all eternity You will reign in glory. (Sacks, *Authorised Daily Prayer Book*, 141, 143)

Jesus, the Kingdom's Herald

A Numerical Orientation

The New Testament refers to "the kingdom" about 149 times. Some lack the modifying prepositional phrase ("of God") but contextually imply it (e.g., Matt. 4:23, 17; 8:12; Luke 12:31, 32). Most of these mentions occur in the same Gospels that preserve the Lord's Prayer: Matthew (51×, with 36 unique to that Gospel) and Luke (49×, with 31 only in Luke). Mark and John preserve the phrase, respectively, 18 times (with 6 peculiar to Mark) and 5 times (all unique to John). Over half of all Gospel references to the kingdom (63) appear in sayings of Jesus; the remainder appear in a narrator's comments (e.g., Matt. 9:35; Mark 15:43; Luke 8:1) or on the lips of others well-disposed to Jesus (e.g., Matt. 3:2; Luke 1:33).

These data direct us to an important point: in the Synoptics, the kingdom of God is the center and constant refrain of Jesus' message. No other subject approximates the core of his teaching and ministry than this. That it would recur in the Lord's Prayer is no surprise.

For most scholars this much is clear and indisputable. Beyond this point matters become murkier: while constantly referring or alluding to the kingdom, Jesus never *defines* it. Mindful of that fact, content with some irresolvable ambiguity, we may proceed by addressing a series of questions:

108

- What is the kingdom's *character*?
- What is the *timing* of God's kingdom? When did Jesus expect its coming?
- *How* did Jesus proclaim that kingdom? Are intimations of his understanding of his own role in the kingdom traceable?
- What does the kingdom reveal of God's *will*?
- How did the evangelists regard the kingdom, preached by Jesus, *in the light of their remembrance of his death by crucifixion and their conviction of his resurrection*?
- Grounded in that memory and confession, *what may today's Christians reasonably consider* when they pray as their Lord taught them: "May God's kingdom come" (AT)?

Though they move beyond Jesus' teaching, the last two questions are appropriate, indeed imperative. All that we know of Jesus' proclamation of the kingdom has been conveyed to us by early Christian witnesses who testified to his words and deeds in the unquenchable light of Good Friday and Easter Sunday.

What Is the Character of the Kingdom of God?

Why didn't Jesus develop a comprehensive explanation of the kingdom? Perhaps there was no need: the expression may already have been intelligible to his listeners. What sets Jesus apart from his Jewish ancestors, contemporaries, and descendants are the *dominance* and *degree of intensity* of God's *basileia* in his proclamation (Manson, *Teaching of Jesus*, 160). If not carefully harmonized, Jesus' teaching about the kingdom does strike four keynotes: (1) its origination by God; (2) its differentiation from human empires; (3) its intersection with, yet transcendence of, time and space; (4) justice and mercy as its reciprocal energies.

Theocentricity. The basic element in Jesus' claims about the kingdom lies in plain sight: its provenance and province in God alone. "Do not be afraid, little flock, for it is your Father's good pleasure to give you the kingdom" (Luke 12:32 = Matt. 25:34). Some of Jesus' sayings highlight the kingdom's theocentrism by contrasting it with this world's structures of authority or human attainments, all falling short of God's will: "Children, how hard it is to enter the kingdom of God!" (Mark 10:24; cf. Matt. 5:20) "Whoever becomes humble like this child is the greatest in the kingdom of heaven"

109

(Matt. 18:4 = Mark 10:15). These statements chime with the Old Testament's basic confession: God alone holds the reins and claims absolute obedience.

This aspect of the *basileia* preached by Jesus has long been obscured in the church's preaching, both liberal and conservative, whose implicit theologies are hangovers from the anthropocentricism of the Enlightenment, modernism, and postmodernism. Immanuel Kant (1724–1804) translated the kingdom into a philosophical principle "knowable through unassisted reason, . . . thanks to [its] natural affinity with the moral predisposition of rational beings generally" (*Reason Alone* [1793], 113, 127; cf. 85–138). Following Kant, Albrecht Ritschl (1822–89) argued that Christians *are* the kingdom of God insofar as they recognize their common humanity, act lovingly, and expand the community of moral conviction and moral goods (*Die christliche Lehre*, 3:271). Adolf Harnack (1851–1930) defined the kingdom as "the rule of the holy God in the hearts of individuals," establishing the human soul's infinite value (*What Is Christianity?*, 56). Walter Rauschenbusch (1861–1918) reckoned Jesus a social reformer and God's kingdom as "the Christian transfiguration of the social order" (*Social Gospel*, 145). Regarding theology as "transcendentalized politics," Shailer Mathews (1863–1941) attempted to peel away labels like "the kingdom of God" to reveal a "generic Christianity" congruent with ideologies of progressive humanism: realization of "the natural possibility for man's social capacities and powers" (*Social Teaching* [1897], 77). Since the 1960s liberation theologies both Catholic and Protestant have grappled with temptations to political messianism, attempting to distinguish the kingdom's outworking through humanitarian projects of social liberation from its definitive origin in God's unique action (Simonis, *Our Father*, 63–70). This Cook's tour of two centuries of Christian thought demonstrates with clarity that the more Christian theology is commandeered by contemporary secular manifestoes, the looser its tethering to a kingdom whose character is that of the God whom Jesus worshiped. "The LORD reigns: let the peoples tremble; . . . let the earth quake" (Ps. 99:1 RSV; cf. *Pss. Sol.* 17:3–4; 1QM 6:6).

A dominion unlike those of this world. Contrary to tendentious arguments that have been made across the centuries (Reimarus, *Fragments*; Brandon, *Jesus and the Zealots*; Aslan, *Zealot*), Jesus mounted no direct assault on the Roman Empire (Bammel

110

and Moule, *Jesus and the Politics*). When pressed to choose between Caesar and God, Jesus upheld the former's qualified authority under the latter's predominance (Mark 12:13–17 = Matt. 22:15–22 = Luke 20:20–26). Yet Jesus spoke of the kingdom in ways that subverted his listeners' social and political expectations, particularly those yearning for wholesale overthrow of Israel's overlords during the period stretching between the Maccabean uprising and Jerusalem's final destruction after the Bar Kokhba rebellion (167 BC–AD 135). "You know that among the Gentiles those whom they recognize as their rulers lord it over them, and their great ones are tyrants over them. But it is not so among you; but whoever wishes to become great among you must be your servant, and whoever wishes to be first among you must be slave of all" (Mark 10:42–44 = Matt. 20:25–27 = Luke 22:25–27). Jesus' life followed this dictum to its grisly conclusion: recalcitrant slaves were typically subjected to capital punishment by crucifixion (Hengel, *Crucifixion*, 51–63).

In John (18:36) Jesus tells Pilate, "My kingdom is not from this world." That, in Johannine lingo, corresponds with the tenor of Jesus' claims of God's kingdom in the Synoptics. When Reinhold Niebuhr asserted, "The only kingdom which can defy and conquer the world is one which is not of this world" (*Beyond Tragedy*, 284), he was paraphrasing the Gospels' testimony that, through Jesus, God's power was not manifestly assaulting those of this world but was subversively undermining them (John 16:33).

A reign transcending domain. In the Hebrew Bible the term *malkûth* is a flexible metaphor. With reference to worldly empires, it normally suggests a territorial domain (Esth. 5:3; 7:2; Dan. 9:1; 11:9). In the Psalms, God's dominion is not circumscribed: it is "an eternal kingship," "a dominion for all generations" (Ps. 145:13 NJPS; cf. 29:10; 103:19; 145:11–12). On the other hand, Solomon sits, in Jerusalem, "on the throne of the kingdom of the LORD over Israel" (1 Chr. 28:5 NJPS; cf. 17:14). Gustaf Dalman concluded that "both in the Old Testament and in Jewish literature *malkûth*, when applied to God, means always the 'kingly rule' [*Herrschaft*, "reign," "dominion"], never the 'kingdom' [*Reich*, "realm," "domain"] as if it were meant to suggest the territory governed by Him" (*Words of Jesus*, 93). That claim outruns the evidence, as Dale Allison has shown (*Constructing Jesus*, 170–74; see, e.g., 2 *Bar.* 40:2–4; 73:1, and *Songs of the Sabbath Sacrifice* among the Dead Sea Scrolls). Jesus likened God's *basileia* to a supper at which one may be seated

111

(Luke 13:28 = Matt. 8:11) and spoke of it as a realm into which one may enter (Matt. 5:20; 7:13; Luke 13:24; 18:24–25), "not [be] far" from (Mark 12:34), or be excluded from (Matt. 8:12; Luke 13:25 = Matt. 25:10). Matthew 5:33–37 suggests a triplex view of the cosmos: heaven, "the throne of God"; earth, the divine footstool; Jerusalem, "the city of the great King" (cf. Ps. 48:2). It seems fair to say that Jesus shared with his Jewish contemporaries a view of God's sovereignty that transcends geography but could be imagined spatially.

In one important respect, however, Jesus' teaching of the kingdom veers away from much Jewish eschatology (cf. Isa. 24:23; Mic. 4:7): he never localizes God's kingdom in Jerusalem (Zion) or anywhere else on Israel's map. The only verse in the Gospels that collocates Jerusalem with the kingdom is Luke 19:11: "As they were listening to this, he went on to tell a parable, because he was near Jerusalem, and because they supposed that the kingdom of God was to appear immediately." In the Gospels, Jerusalem is the locus, not of the kingdom's installation, but of the Son of Man's suffering (Matt. 16:21; 20:18 = Mark 10:33 = Luke 18:31), mourning for all of Israel's slain prophets (Matt. 23:37 = Luke 13:34; cf. Luke 23:28), and desolation by the Gentiles (Luke 21:20, 24). The devil tempted Jesus with offers of sovereignty over all the world's kingdoms, all their glory and authority, including Jerusalem with its temple's pinnacle. Jesus repudiated them all (Matt. 4:5–10 = Luke 4:6–9).

Images of a celestial Jerusalem, which could be interpreted as figuratively cognate with God's kingdom, appear elsewhere in the New Testament (Gal. 4:26; Phil. 3:20; Heb. 12:22; Rev. 3:12; 21:2, 10), the Old Testament Apocrypha (2 Esd. 13:36) and Pseudepigrapha (2 Bar. 4:33–34; T. Dan 5:12). The Kaddish and two of the Amidah's benedictions focus on Jerusalem as the center of God's worship (see appendix A). By contrast, the Lord's Prayer beseeches the kingdom's coming without reference to, much less circumscription within, Zion or any other site peculiar to Israel's devotional memory.

How, then, *does* Jesus speak of God's sovereignty?

1. God's *basileia* is the content of *a declaration of "glad tidings"* or *"gospel"* (*euangelizesthai*). Like servants of a king inviting others to a festal banquet (Matt. 22:3–4, 8–9, 14; cf. Luke 14:16–17, 24), "[Jesus] said to them, 'I must proclaim the good news of the kingdom of God to the other cities also; for I was sent for this purpose'" (Luke 4:43; 9:2; cf. Mark 1:14–15; Isa. 40:9; 41:27; 52:7). The

112

bequest of the kingdom is associated with "the joy of your master" (Matt. 25:21, 23).

2. Access to the kingdom is by *repentance*, a turning toward God (Matt. 4:17; Mark 1:15). One may disqualify oneself by reconsidering that decision, turning away (Matt. 11:20), or "looking back" (Luke 9:62).

3. God *prepares* (Matt. 20:23 = Mark 10:40; Matt. 25:34), *gives* (Matt. 21:43; Luke 12:32; Matt. 7:7 = Luke 11:9), or *bequeaths* (Matt. 5:3 = Luke 6:20; Matt. 19:14; Mark 10:14; Luke 18:16) the kingdom. For humans, it is something *to strive for, ask for* (Luke 12:31 = Matt. 6:33; Luke 11:9–10 = Matt. 7:7–8), *accept* (Mark 10:15 = Luke 18:17), or *inherit* (Matt. 25:34; cf. 1 Cor. 6:9–10; 15:50; Gal. 5:21) at the expense of their own resources (Matt. 19:29; Mark 10:29; Luke 18:29). Invitations are issued to all, but recipients must be ready to accept them (Luke 14:17 = Matt. 22:4, 8).

Justice and mercy.

> For God did not send the Son into the world to condemn the world, but rather to save the world through him. No one who believes is condemned; but those who do not believe have already been condemned, because they have not believed in the name of the only Son of God. This is the judgment: that the light has come into the world, but people loved darkness rather than light, for their deeds were evil. Those who do evil hate the light and do not come to the light so that their works may not be exposed. But all who do what is true come to the light, so that it may become manifest that their works have been worked by God. (John 3:17–21, trans. Marianne Thompson, *John*, 77)

This passage from the Fourth Gospel pinpoints a fundamental difference between John's presentation of Jesus and that of the Synoptics while epitomizing the latter's portrait of the kingdom of God. The difference: whereas Jesus of the Synoptics expatiates on the kingdom and speaks with reticence about himself, the Johannine Jesus exhibits just the reverse. The epitome: Jesus' preaching of the kingdom in the Synoptics confronts its listeners with a message of gracious salvation that judges those who refuse it.

Aligned with the preaching of John the Baptist (Matt. 3:1–2, 7–10 = Luke 3:7–10), Jesus' preaching of God's reign wields a cutting edge, portrayed in the social realia of his day. A king is

113

capable of jailing an execrable slave until he pays the last penny on an astronomical debt (Matt. 18:23–35). Another slave who has ruthlessly abused his master's stewardship will be hacked to pieces (*dichotomēsei*) when the householder unexpectedly returns (Luke 12:41–48). Still another servant who betrayed his trusteeship is deemed "useless, expelled into the outer darkness, to wail and grind his teeth" (Matt. 25:30 AT). Toxic vegetation—"children of the evil one"—will be scythed and incinerated (Matt. 13:36–43). Complacent self-satisfaction collides head-on with God's reckoning: "You fool! This very night your life is being demanded of you. And the things you have prepared, whose will they be?" (Luke 12:20). Individual men and women teeter on a precipice: "One will be taken and the other left" (Luke 17:34 = Matt. 24:40–41). All the nations will be gathered before God's deputy to be sorted for reward or punishment, as a shepherd separates sheep from goats (Matt. 25:31–46). Unlike much Jewish apocalypticism (e.g., 1QS 4:6b–14; *Pss. Sol.* 17; *Jub.* 23; *1 En.* 9:20a–27), none of Jesus' teachings presupposes that Israel is on the side of the angels and that Gentile sinners (Gal. 2:15) will be clobbered: as the Baptist warned, God can make children of Abraham out of rocks (Matt. 3:9 = Luke 3:8; see also Matt. 8:5–13 = Luke 7:1–10). As a whole "this generation" fails to notice the Damoclean sword suspended over its head (Luke 11:29–32 = Matt. 12:38–42; Luke 11:45–52 = Matt. 23:29–36), including Israel's leaders (Matt. 23:1–34; Luke 11:37–44) and Jesus' own disciples (Matt. 5:13, 21–48; Matt. 7:21–27; Luke 6:46–49). Again, the Fourth Gospel summarizes, in Johannine terms, a severity in Jesus' teaching that we prefer to ignore: "Whoever believes in the Son has eternal life; whoever disobeys the Son will not see life, but must endure God's wrath" (John 3:36; see Black, "Shouting at the Legally Deaf").

Built into God's supreme dominion is a pressure for righteousness (*dikaiosynē*): integrity, justice, a power to restore all that has been thrown out of joint beyond human capacity to repair. From this justice there is no escape. None of the evangelists intends to provoke despair: otherwise, their reassurance that God can save those incapable of saving themselves makes no sense (Matt. 19:26; Mark 10:27; Luke 18:26–27; John 3:16–17). Jesus' preaching of the kingdom harks back to that of Jonah while amplifying it: "The people of Nineveh will rise up at the judgment with this generation and condemn it, because they repented at the proclamation of

114

Jonah, and see, something greater than Jonah is here!" (Luke 11:32 = Matt. 12:41). God's kingdom bestows grace on a tired, burdened, stupid, and dying world by offering a yoke that is gentle, instructive, restful, and revitalizing (Matt. 11:29–30).

Taking up that yoke is an act of obedience, a willingness to trust Jesus, the kingdom's herald, without taking offense at him (Matt. 11:6 = Luke 7:23): the self-transcendence to recognize in ourselves, not masters, but servants who, having fulfilled all we have been commanded, can say, "We are worthless slaves; we have done only what we ought to have done!" (Luke 17:10). And what we have been ordered is nothing heroic but within our power to do: what the rabbis called *gĕmîlût khăsādîm*, "the giving of loving-kindness" (*m. 'Abot* 1.2; *b. Sukkah* 49b; cf. Isa. 58:7; Tob. 4:16; Sir. 7:33; 17:22; 35:2; 40:17).

Jesus' disciples tend the sick, feed the hungry, give drink to the thirsty, offer hospitality to strangers, clothe the naked, forgive debtors, and visit the imprisoned (Matt. 25:35–39, 42–43; Mark 11:25; Luke 17:3–4)—in short, we act as responsible slaves of God's kingdom—because Jesus has done the same for us (Mark 10:45; Luke 22:26–27). *Ultimately the gravamen on which we are judged is our failure to bestow on others the mercy conferred on us.* The first and last step, and all those in between, are those that Nineveh took: repentance (Jonah 3:5–10). The human agent turns 180 degrees away from self toward God: "The kingdom of God has come near; repent, and believe in the good news" (Mark 1:15).

Already we have anticipated the counterbalancing force in the kingdom preached by Jesus: a merciful God's salvation. Its quintessence is captured in Jesus' reply to emissaries of John the Baptist: "Go and tell John what you have seen and heard: the blind receive their sight, the lame walk, lepers are cleansed, and the deaf hear, the dead are raised up, the poor have good news preached to them" (Luke 7:22 RSV = Matt. 11:5; cf. Isa. 35:5–6; Matt. 4:23 = Luke 4:43; Matt. 9:35 = Luke 8:1; Matt. 10:7–8 = Luke 10:8–9). Matching that report is Jesus' activated interpretation of Isaiah 61:1–2: "The Spirit of the Lord is upon me, because he has anointed me to preach good news to the poor. He has sent me to proclaim release to the captives and recovering of sight to the blind, to set at liberty those who are oppressed, to proclaim the acceptable year of the Lord. . . . *Today* this scripture has been fulfilled in your hearing" (Luke 4:18–19, 21 RSV, emphasis added). Common to both of these synopses is special favor conferred on the socially stigmatized (Mark 10:14–15; Luke 6:20–23 = Matt. 5:3–12): the kingdom already belongs to the poor (Luke 6:20 = Matt. 5:3), while the rich squeeze in with the ease of a camel through a needle's eye (Matt. 19:24 = Mark 10:25 = Luke 18:25; cf. Luke 16:19–31). Those who have suffered physical mutilation are nearer the kingdom than the ostensibly whole and strong (Matt. 19:12; Mark 9:43–47); so, too, are children (Mark 10:14–15 = Luke 18:16–17) and widows (Mark 12:42–43 = Luke 21:2–3; Luke 7:11–17; 18:1–8), who tremble among society's powerless and most vulnerable. "Truly I tell you, among those born of women no one has arisen greater than John the Baptist; yet the least in the kingdom of heaven is greater than he" (Matt. 11:11 = Luke 7:28). "It is not the will of your Father in heaven that one of these little ones should be lost" (Matt. 18:14).

Those regarded as morally defective—toll collectors on the imperial payroll (Matt. 9:10–11 = Mark 2:15–16 = Luke 5:29–30; 7:34), indigent johnnies-come-lately (Matt. 20:1–16), lost sheep and lost children (Matt. 18:10–14; Luke 15:1–32), the flagrantly sinful (Matt. 9:10–11; Matt. 11:19 = Luke 7:34; Luke 15:1–2)—receive special attention from Jesus, to the predictable consternation of the pious. "Go and learn what this means, 'I desire mercy, and not sacrifice.' For I came not to call the righteous, but sinners" (Matt. 9:13 RSV = Luke 5:32). Why? "Those who are well have no need of a physician, but those who are sick" (Mark 2:17 = Matt. 9:12 = Luke 5:31). The currency of the kingdom is restoration, not retribution, because the kingdom's citizenry comprises forgiven sinners.

That inversion of penitent underdogs over top dogs still astonishes readers with a capacity to be shaken and affronted by the gospel. "[God my Savior] has brought down the powerful from their thrones, and lifted up the lowly; he has filled the hungry with good things, and sent the rich away empty" (Luke 1:52–53). "For all who exalt themselves will be humbled, but all who humble themselves will be exalted" (Luke 18:14). "Truly I tell you, the tax collectors and the prostitutes are going into the kingdom of God ahead of you" (Matt. 21:31). If these pronouncements do not induce squirming among the proud, the self-righteous, and the remorseless, then they haven't been paying attention.

116   To Jesus, the kingdom is aborning among those who turn to God as a child trusts a loving parent: for protection, guidance, and rescue from danger. Something radically new is bursting through

(Matt. 9:16–17 = Mark 2:21–22 = Luke 5:36–39), which unsettles beneficiaries of the status quo (Luke 5:30; 15:2, 28; 19:7) but for others awakens a contagious joy (Matt. 13:44; 25:23; Luke 6:23; 15:7, 10). Judgment and emancipation are a single act of God, which humans perceive from different angles. "God is not just without being merciful and is not merciful without being just" (Stăniloae, *Experience of God*, 21). As the psalmist promises: "Steadfast love and faithfulness will meet; righteousness and peace will kiss each other" (Ps. 85:10).

What Is the Timing of God's Kingdom?

Of all questions attached to Jesus' teaching of the kingdom, none has incited more debate than this. Gerd Theissen and Annette Merz (*Historical Jesus*, 242–45) have assembled over a century's trends in New Testament scholarship, whose summary here may benefit readers who will encounter one or more of them in other commentaries and want guidance in finding their way through a thicket of conflicting interpretations.

- *The kingdom de-eschatologized* (Ritschl, by way of Martin Luther): Jesus stripped the kingdom of its Jewish apocalyptic connotations, promulgating, instead, an ethic of love instituted by God's justification of sinners who collaborate in the kingdom's evolution within history.
- *The kingdom of a thoroughly futurist eschatology* (Johannes Weiss [1863–1914], *Jesus' Proclamation of the Kingdom*; and Albert Schweitzer [1875–1965], *Quest of the Historical Jesus*): Infused by prophetic elation, Jesus anticipated the irruption of a new world, inaugurated by God alone, following a series of cosmic catastrophes. With modifications, Allison (*Constructing Jesus*) has championed this interpretation.
- *The kingdom eschatologically realized in Jesus himself* (C. H. Dodd [1884–1973], *Parables of the Kingdom*): Through Jesus' message and person, God's sovereignty has already penetrated this world and is working itself out in the present.
- *The kingdom as a reality both present and future* (Werner Georg Kümmel [1905–95], *Promise and Fulfillment*): As the joint between present and future, Jesus has instantiated what the kingdom will bring. A variation on this theme is that of

117

Joachim Jeremias: Jesus announced a kingdom whose "eschatology . . . is in process of realization" (*Parables of Jesus*, 230).

- *The kingdom existentialized* (Rudolf Bultmann [1884–1976], *Jesus and the Word*): While Jesus proclaimed the kingdom apocalyptically, that myth requires translation into humanity's consciousness of its own "hour of decision," whether for one's self or for the world as a whole. Some of Bultmann's students ascribed this "demythologization" to Jesus himself (Ernst Fuchs [1903–83], *Studies of the Historical Jesus*, 104–66; Ernst Käsemann [1906–98], *Jesus Means Freedom*, 16–58). Others redirect attention away from temporality: God's royal power invades the sphere of human experience (Hans Weder [1946–], *Gegenwart und Gottesherrschaft* [1993]).

- *The kingdom symbolized:* Instead of eviscerating myth, Norman Perrin (1920–76) argued that the kingdom of God is a "tensive symbol": an evocative vision of reality that expressed Jesus' faith in God as creation's Sovereign and Israel's Defender, who would act decisively and soon to reassert governance over a rebellious creation (*Language of the Kingdom* [1976], 197–99). Perrin's approach has lately been appropriated by Eugene Boring (1935–, "Kingdom of God in Mark"); and Leander Keck (1928–, *Who Is Jesus?*, 69–70).

- *The kingdom unmasked* (John Gager [1937–], *Kingdom and Community* [1975]): Like other millenarian prophets, Jesus' expectation of the kingdom's overthrow of the Roman imperium was dashed, leaving his followers to intensify their missionary activity through cognitive dissonance.

- *The noneschatological kingdom* (John Dominic Crossan [1934–], *Historical Jesus*, 1991]; Marcus Borg [1942–2014], "A Temperate Case"): Jesus' teaching represents an atemporal wisdom tradition. The earliest Christians imported into their traditions most of the Gospels' claims for this world's future change.

From this survey one thing is unmistakable: in its study of the kingdom of God, New Testament scholarship has operated in accordance with Newton's third law of motion—for every action there is an equal and opposite reaction. Jeremias and Kümmel's embrace of both present and future in Jesus' understanding of the kingdom was a rapprochement of Dodd's reaction to the Schweitzer/Weiss

118

pushback against Ritschl's nonapocalyptic Jesus, lately reborn in the work of Crossan, Borg, and the Jesus Seminar (founded in 1985). Whereas myth was deemed an obstacle to modern faith (Bultmann) or a crutch by which faith persists contrary to facts (Gager), Perrin countered that religious symbols evoke myths that interpret historical experience. For us, the question remains: when Jesus prayed for the kingdom's coming, how may we best comprehend his intent?

Amid a tangle of opposing interpretations, the most secure ground to which we may repair is that in the Gospels themselves. In table 3 I have collected and categorized representative sayings of Jesus, remembered by the evangelists, which bear on the kingdom's temporality. From this array of evidence some conclusions may be drawn.

1. The preponderance of the evidence, gathered in §§1, 2, 5, 6, 7, supports the reading that Jesus regarded God's kingdom, certainly in its fullness, as *anticipated in the future*. That ingredient is detectable in all streams of the tradition that fed the New Testament's Gospels; moreover, that expectation has different colors. Those now suffering hunger, grief, deprivation, and persecution are promised reversal of their plight in God's kingdom (Matt. 5:4–10 = Luke 6:21). At his Last Supper with the disciples, Jesus himself denies drinking again "of the fruit of the vine until that day when I drink it new in the kingdom of God" (Mark 14:25 = Matt. 26:29). Most of his sayings about crisis and judgment, often associated with the coming of the Son of Man in an hour known only to God (Mark 13:24–32 = Matt. 24:29–36 = Luke 21:25–33), point to events to come:

> Someone asked him, "Lord, will only a few be saved?" He said to them, "Strive to enter through the narrow door; for many, I tell you, will try to enter and will not be able. When once the owner of the house has got up and shut the door, and you begin to stand outside and to knock at the door, saying, 'Lord, open to us,' then in reply he will say to you, 'I do not know where you come from.' . . . There will be weeping and gnashing of teeth when you see Abraham and Isaac and Jacob and all the prophets in the kingdom of God, and you yourselves thrown out. Then people will come from east and west, from north and south, and will eat in the kingdom of God. Indeed, some are last who will be first, and some are first who will be last." (Luke 13:23–25, 28–30 = Matt. 7:13–14; 8:11–12; 19:30; 20:16; 25:10b–12)

119

✓   Absent from Jesus' teaching are details of what that kingdom will look like, precisely how this world will be transformed. Unlike later rabbinic prayers (see appendix A), nothing is said of Israel's release from oppression, punishment of its oppressors, or restoration of Jerusalem and the temple's reconstruction. One outstanding image is that of a magnificent banquet: those who "sit at table in the kingdom of God" (Luke 13:29 RSV; cf. *m. 'Abot* 3.17; 4.16; *b. Baba Batra* 75a; *b. Pesakhim* 119b) will take their places not because of national privilege but owing to their acceptance of God's magnanimous invitation (Luke 14:15–24 = Matt. 22:1–10; cf. Luke 12:37–38; 16:19–31; 22:28–30). That Jesus expected the kingdom to change this world is clear from the Lord's Prayer itself: God's will is to be effected on earth as it is in heaven (Matt. 6:10; cf. 16:19; 18:18–19). One of those effects is the inheritance of this earth by "the meek" (Matt. 5:5), who have had no claims on it whatever. God's sovereign rule will transcend *both* earth *and* heaven (Luke 16:17 = Matt. 5:18; Matt. 24:35 = Mark 13:31 = Luke 21:33), a conviction consonant with the Psalms' depiction of the LORD God as both transcendent and immanent.

   2. "The time is fulfilled, and the kingdom of God has come near [or "is at hand": *ēngiken*]" (Mark 1:15; cf. Matt. 4:17). Jesus' opening proclamation in Mark points in another temporal direction: "the time"—*ho kairos*, the critical moment, the golden season—*has been* fulfilled. (The Greek verb *peplērōtai* is formed in the perfect tense, implying an accomplished event with enduring effect.) God's domain of righteous mercy is now breaking into this world's affairs. God *will* rule because God *already* rules. The clearest assertions of this belief are listed in table 3, §3:

> The kingdom of God is not coming with things that can be observed; nor will they say, "Look, here it is!" or "There it is!" For, in fact, the kingdom of God is among you. (Luke 17:20b–21)

> But if it is by the finger of God that I cast out the demons, then the kingdom of God has come to you. (Luke 11:20 = Matt. 12:28)

   Since these remarks are fewer than the many accenting the kingdom's futurity, some exegetes downplay them. That impulse should be resisted, because they tally with other elements in the church's traditions about Jesus. In different ways Jesus speaks of a triumph over Satan and his minions that has already occurred. After Jesus'

Table 3: The Timing of the Kingdom of God in the Jesus Tradition

Theme	Source	References in Gospels	Quotation or Paraphrase
1. The kingdom as coming	Mark	Mark 1:15 (cf. Matt. 3:2 [Baptist]; 4:17 [Jesus]; 10:7; [10:23 = Son of Man])	"The kingdom of God has come near."
	Mark	Mark 9:1 = Matt. 16:28 = Luke 9:27	"until they see the kingdom of God has come with power."
	Q	Luke 11:2, 4 = Matt. 6:10, 13	"Your kingdom come." "Do not bring us to the time of trial."
	L	Luke 21:31	Luke identifies an eschatological drama with coming kingdom.
2. The kingdom as future	Mark	Mark 14:25 = Matt. 26:29 = Luke 22:18	The Last Supper: Jesus' anticipated delay of another quaff.
	Mark	Mark 15:43 = Luke 23:51	Joseph of Arimathea, looking for the kingdom of God.
	Q	Luke 14:16–24 = Matt. 22:2–10	Parable of the wedding feast: likened to the kingdom, lying in the future.
	Q	Luke 13:28–29 = Matt. 8:11	"Then people will come from east and west, from north and south, and will eat in the kingdom of God.
	M	Matt. 7:21	"Not everyone who says to me 'Lord, Lord' will enter . . ."
	M	Matt. 18:23–25	The kingdom is designated as the time of reckoning.
3. The kingdom as present	Q	Luke 11:20 = Matt. 12:28	"But if it is by the finger [in Luke; likely more primitive than "Spirit," in Matt.] of God that I cast out demons, then the kingdom of God has come to you."
	L	Luke 17:20–21	". . . for, in fact, the kingdom of God is among you."

(continued on next page)

Theme	Source	References in Gospels	Quotation or Paraphrase
4. Ambiguous timing or no explicit temporal reference	Mark	Mark 4:26–29	"The seed growing secretly" likely refers to the kingdom's miraculous appearance.
	Mark	Mark 4:30–32 = Matt. 13:31–32 = Luke 13:18–19	The parable of the mustard seed: the contrast of a small beginning with a great consummation.
	Mark	Mark 10:14–15 = Matt. 19:14 = Luke 18:16–17	Children: "to such as these . . . the kingdom of God belongs."
	Mark	Mark 10:23 = Matt. 19:24 = Luke 18:25	"How hard it will be for [the wealthy] to enter God's kingdom."
	Q	Luke 13:20 = Matt. 13:33	Kingdom suggested by "leaven."
	M	Matt. 16:19	The keys of the kingdom. NB: Matthew's tendency to draw the church into the kingdom's ambit; cf. 13:24–30, 36–43.
	John	John 3:3, 5	"No one can enter God's kingdom without . . . water and Spirit."
	John	John 18:36	"My kingship is not of this world." (RSV)
5. Crisis sayings: Jesus' ministry indicates or foreshadows some turning point in time or history	Mark	Mark 3:25–28; cf. Luke 11:19–22 = Matt. 12:27–29	Accusation concerning demons; the parable of the strong man.
	Q	Luke 7:18–23 = Matt. 11:2–6	The answer to the Baptist.
	Q	Luke 16:16 = Matt. 11:12	The Baptist and the kingdom.
	Q	Luke 12:51–53 = Matt. 10:34–35	Division in households.
	L	Luke 12:49–50	"I came to bring fire to the earth, and how I wish it were already kindled! I have a baptism with which to be baptized, and what stress I am under until it is completed!"

Category	Source	Reference	Saying
6. Judgment sayings: Reference to a coming judgment, presumably preceding the kingdom's advent	Q	Luke 3:9 = Matt. 3:10	"Even now the ax is lying at the root of the trees."
	Q	Luke 10:13–15 = Matt. 11:20–24; Luke 10:16 = Matt. 10:40	Woes on Galilean cities.
	Q	Luke 11:31–32 = Matt. 12:36, 41–42	"The queen of the South will rise at the judgment with the people of this generation and condemn them, . . ."
	L	Luke 10:17; cf. 10:18	"Lord, in your name even the demons submit to us!" / "I watched Satan fall from heaven like a flash of lightning."
	John	John 12:31	Present judgment, pointing toward crucifixion: "Now is the judgment of this world; now the ruler of this world will be driven out."
7. Coming Son of Man sayings: The Son of Man's advent as part of the apocalyptic drama that concludes with establishment of the kingdom of God	Mark	Mark 8:38 = Matt. 16:27 = Luke 9:26	". . . of them the Son of Man will also be ashamed when he comes in the glory of his Father with the holy angels."
	Q	Luke 12:8–9 = Matt. 10:32	"Everyone who acknowledges me before others, the Son of Man [I] also will acknowledge before the angels of God [my Father in heaven]."
	Q	Luke 17:24 = Matt. 24:27	"For as the lightning flashes and lights up the sky from one side to the other, so will the Son of Man be in his day."
	M	Matt. 25:31	"When the Son of Man comes in his glory, and all the angels with him, then he will sit on the throne of his glory."
	L	Luke 21:36	"Be alert at all times, praying that you may have the strength . . . to stand before the Son of Man."
	John	John 5:27	"[The Father] has given him authority to execute judgment, because he is the Son of Man."

missionaries return to their Lord with exuberant news of the demons' subjection to his name, he replies, "I watched Satan fall from heaven like a flash of lightning" (Luke 10:17–18). Satan's kingdom is now being overthrown, "the strong man's house" already is being plundered by a superior force (Matt. 12:22–30 = Mark 3:22–27 = Luke 11:14–23). While the prince of demons still assaults Jesus' disciples (Mark 8:33 = Matt. 16:23; Luke 13:16; 22:3 = John 13:27; Luke 22:31), even as the devil tempted Jesus (Mark 1:12–13; Matt. 4:1–11 = Luke 4:1–13), Satan's power is dissipating: "He cannot stand, but his end has come" (Mark 3:26).

The positive counterpoint of these avowals is staggering: "All things have been handed over to me by my Father. . . . For I tell you that many prophets and kings desired to see what you see, but did not see it, and to hear what you hear, but did not hear it" (Luke 10:22a, 24 = Matt. 11:27a; 13:17). What is now visible and audible? The blind see, the lame walk, lepers are cleansed, the dead are raised, the poor are evangelized (Luke 7:22 = Matt. 11:5). By contrast, such happiness can only be awaited in the *Psalms of Solomon*:

> Blessed are those born in those days,
>> To see the good things of the Lord
>> which he will do for the coming generation;
> [which will be] under the rod of discipline of the Lord Messiah
>> in the fear of his God. . . . (18.6–7b, trans. Wright [OTP])

"The law and the prophets were in effect until John came; since then the good news of the kingdom of God is proclaimed, and everyone tries to enter it by force" (Luke 16:16; cf. Matt. 11:12). While no commentator is certain of this cryptic comment's meaning, one thing seems clear: John the Baptist marks the turning point toward a kingdom into which others are now attempting to barge their way, while hypocrites who "know how to interpret the appearance of earth and sky . . . do . . . not know how to interpret the present time" (Luke 12:56 = Matt. 16:3). The present is a time of festival, not fasting; of something fresh, not sour (Matt. 9:14–17; Mark 2:18–22; Luke 5:33–39).

For Jesus, God's kingdom overlaps both present and future. This may account for those traditions, remaining in table 3 (§4), whose temporality is obscure: they may point to what obtains now, later, or both. These sayings are not necessarily incoherent or contradictory; many commonplace analogies demonstrate their

124

reconciliation. Presidential administrations in the United States recognize a gap between the days of election and inauguration. Produce germinates before it is ready for harvest (Mark 4:26–29; Matt. 9:37–38 = Luke 10:2; Matt. 13:24–30, 36–44). Dawn breaks before night has given way to daylight (cf. Rom. 13:12; Eph. 5:14). Life in this age intersects—but is not yet coterminous—with eternal life (*'ôlām habā'* in rabbinic sources) in the age to come (Matt. 7:14; 18:8–9 = Mark 9:43, 45; Matt. 19:16–17 = Mark 10:17 = Luke 10:25; 18:18; Matt. 19:29 = Mark 10:30; Matt. 25:46). When we pray, "Thy kingdom come," we stand beside Jesus at the very edge of this world's end and from that peculiar vantage pray backward (see Evans, *Lord's Prayer*, 36).

What may we understand of the kingdom by the ways Jesus presented it? As glimpsed during Jesus' life, God's kingdom is revealed in three interlocking ways: mighty works, parabolic instruction, and Jesus himself as index of the kingdom.

Mighty works. Most modern readers of the Gospels have lost the social context in which the evangelists understood Jesus' many exorcisms, healings, and resuscitations. That he did such things can hardly be doubted: they are evident in every traditional stratum on which the Gospels were reliant; even Josephus reports that Jesus was "a doer of startling deeds" (*paradoxōn ergōn poiētēs*; *Jewish Antiquities* 18.3, AT). By no means was Jesus the only itinerant miracle worker in antiquity (see Cotter, *Christ of the Miracle Stories*). But at least four things distinguish Jesus' mighty deeds, and all jibe with his preaching of the kingdom.

1. The beneficiaries of his healing power were those on society's fringes: widows and children (Matt. 9:18–26 = Mark 5:21–43 = Luke 8:40–56; Luke 7:11–17; Matt. 17:14–21 = Mark 9:14–29 = Luke 9:37–43a), demoniacs and lepers and paralytics (Matt. 8:1–4 = Mark 1:40–45 = Luke 5:12–16; Matt. 9:1–8 = Mark 2:1–2 = Luke 5:17–26), the blind and the deaf and the hungry (Matt. 20:29–34 = Mark 10:46–52 = Luke 18:35–43; Matt. 15:29–31 = Mark 7:31–37; Matt. 14:13–21 = Mark 6:30–44 = Luke 9:10–17). Cures and evangelism converged: "Jesus went throughout Galilee, teaching in their synagogues and proclaiming the good news of the kingdom and curing every disease and every sickness among the people" (Matt. 4:23).

2. Jesus was remembered as linking his mighty works with the rout of the kingdom's enemies: those possessed by unclean spirits and demons (Mark 1:21–28 = Luke 4:31–37; Mark 3:11 = Luke

125

4:41a; Matt. 8:28–34 = Mark 5:1–20 = Luke 8:26–39; Mark 7:24–30 = Matt. 15:21–28). When scolded by a synagogue official for abrogating the Sabbath by healing a crippled woman, Jesus radically reframed the issue: "You hypocrites! . . . Ought not this woman, a daughter of Abraham whom Satan bound for eighteen long years, be set free from this bondage on the sabbath day?" (Luke 13:15a, 16).

3. Modesty ill became some ancient philosopher-healers. Here speaks Empedocles (ca. 490–ca. 430 BC): "Friends, . . . I, an immortal God, no longer mortal, wander among you, honored by all, adorned with holy diadems and blooming garlands. . . . I am praised by men and women, and accompanied by thousands, who thirst for deliverance, some ask for prophecies, and some entreat, for remedies against all kinds of disease" (Diogenes Laertius, *Lives* 8.61, trans. R. D. Hicks). By contrast, Jesus consistently deflected attention away from his curative power: "Many crowds followed him, and he cured all of them, and he ordered them not to make him known" (Matt. 12:15b–16; cf. Mark 7:36; 8:30; Matt. 9:30; 8:4 = Mark 1:44 = Luke 5:14; Mark 3:12; 5:43 = Luke 8:56). "Have faith in God" (Mark 11:22)—for it is by such trust that healing can occur (Matt. 8:13; Matt. 9:22 = Mark 5:34 = Luke 8:48; Matt. 9:29 = Mark 10:52 = Luke 18:42; Matt. 15:28; Luke 7:50; 17:19).

4. Faith in God's power makes astounding therapy both possible and intelligible. Jesus' mighty works were celebrated but also dismissed (Matt. 16:1–4 = Mark 8:11–13 = Luke 11:16; 12:54–56; 11:29), repudiated (Matt. 9:3 = Mark 2:6–7 = Luke 5:21) or misattributed to demonic authority (Matt. 12:24 = Mark 3:22 = Luke 11:15–16). Miracles were ambiguous acts, probative neither of God's kingdom nor of their agent's credibility.

Parabolic instruction. Throughout this chapter the kingdom's qualities have been extrapolated from Jesus' parables. No repetition of that is needed. Our primary concern here is Jesus' choice of a parabolic *form* to communicate his teaching about God's sovereignty.

Whether delivered in brief epigrams or narratives of variable length, most of Jesus' parables are akin to poetry. Words are windows into reality, "as imagination bodies forth / The forms of things unknown" (Shakespeare, *A Midsummer Night's Dream* 5.1). "The implicit invitation offered" by all poets, Helen Vendler suggests, is "that you will see things in a new light, the light of their construction of the world. We read imaginative works . . . in order to gain a wider sense of the real. . . . The words of the speaker become my own words. . . . Every word has to count. So does every gap. In fact, lyric depends on gaps, and depends even more on the reader to fill in the gaps" (*Poets, Poems, Poetry*, xxxix–xl, xli).

The parables do not explain religious precepts or allegorize doctrine, even though in later centuries the church exercised both gambits. Jesus' parables draw on everyday life in first-century Palestine—farming (Mark 4:3–9, 26–32), fishing (Matt. 13:47–50), herding (Luke 15:3–7), building (Matt. 7:24–27), commerce (Matt. 13:44–46; Luke 12:16–21), domestic relations (Luke 15:11–32), master-slave negotiations (Matt. 18:23–35; Luke 16:1–8), judicial or religious practice (Luke 18:1–14)—lulling listeners into familiarity before plunging them into a quirky reality that upsets their expectations in a manner either refreshing or disturbing.

One example may stand for all: Matthew 20:1–16. The kingdom is compared to a landowner who hires hands at different times during the day to cultivate his vineyard. Big deal: that's the world as we know it. At quitting time the boss publicly pays every laborer a full day's wage, whether they worked for twelve hours or sixty minutes. Unfair! Our comfortable framework of just labor relations has been blown apart, even though no one in the story was cheated of what he was promised. By this story the kingdom is not merely disclosed: in our mind and gut it has been *created*. A decision is required of us. Shall we continue to define our lives by conventional standards of performance, compensation, and equity? Or shall we accept our vocation as citizens of a different domain: the children of a heavenly Father, who, from a heart of incomprehensible graciousness, impartially sends sunshine and rainfall on the just and the unjust alike (Matt. 5:45; cf. Luke 6:32–36)?

Jesus' parables and mighty works coincide: the words match the deeds. In both, the kingdom explodes our ordinary world, rattles it in mysterious ways that startle or offend us, and begins the liberation of creation and society for their true destiny, as God intends.

Jesus as index of the kingdom. At least three statements attributed to Jesus crystallize all the evangelists' convictions that in Jesus himself the kingdom was at once both imminent and immanent. The first is a prayer:

127

I thank you, Father, Lord of heaven and earth, because you have hidden these things from the wise and the intelligent and have revealed them to infants; yes, Father, for such was your gracious will. (Luke 10:21 = Matt. 11:25–26)

The second is a claim:

But if it is by the finger of God that I cast out the demons, then the kingdom of God has come to you. (Luke 11:20 = Matt. 12:28; cf. Exod. 8:19)

The third, a cry:

I came to bring fire to the earth, and how I wish it were already kindled! I have a baptism with which to be baptized, and what stress I am under until it is completed! (Luke 12:49–50)

These sayings, as puzzling as Jesus' parables and mighty works, point to something basic in the Christian confession. Possibly— likely, I think—they indicate Jesus' understanding of his role in the kingdom. By the Father's decision and the Son's compliance, Jesus was already enacting the impact of a dominion yet to be fully realized on earth. Leander Keck expresses the point well: "If . . . Jesus regarded himself as God's 'finger,' translating the news of the kingdom into action, he also implied that it was his vocation *to embody the future by making it present as a sign of what is yet to come*" (*Who Is Jesus?*, 85, emphasis added).

In other words: to understand the character of the commonwealth for which Jesus taught his disciples to pray, one pays attention to the inner coherence of Jesus' deeds and words, through which God, who is and forever will be king, has already begun putting things right, ourselves included. Jesus dined with society's pariahs, just as he spun tales of contrite sinners, not because he romanticized their condition, but because they were most in need of realignment to God's norm, and Jesus claimed the authority to begin their rectification. Recovery of a single lost sheep excites greater jubilation than that for ninety-nine that never went astray: "So it is not the will of your Father in heaven that one of these little ones should be lost" (Matt. 18:14). In Matthew's context (18:1–35) "the little ones" probably refer to members of the church (16:18; 18:17); Luke's version of the same parable broadens its scope, contrasting one recovered sinner with the righteous ninety-nine needing no repentance (15:3–7). "*The kingdom of God is where Jesus Christ is*" (Thielicke, *The Prayer*, 60, emphasis original).

128

What Does the Kingdom Reveal of God's Will?

For Jesus' expression "the will of God" (*to thelēma tou theou*), the Hebrew Bible has no clear counterpart. The prophets and psalms speak of God's "delight" or "purpose" (*khāpēts*: Isa. 44:28; 46:10; 48:14; *rātsōn*: Ezra 10:11; Pss. 40:8; 103:21; 143:10), referring to the LORD's creation and sustenance of the natural world and the nation Israel, which responds by doing God's good pleasure. "Whom have I in heaven but you? And there is nothing on earth that I desire other than you" (Ps. 73:25).

Acknowledged is God's supreme authority, the spine of the metaphor "kingdom of God" (Matt. 7:21; see Hartman, "'Your Will Be Done'"). Matthew 6:10b is one of the few places where Jesus speaks of "the will [of God]." Most often the phrase appears in John as a christological assertion of the conformity of Jesus' actions with the intent of the Father, who has sent him (4:34; 6:39, 40; 7:17; 9:31). In Mark 3:35 the expression occurs only once and for its content depends on its context: "Whoever does the will of God is my brother and sister and mother" (cf. Matt. 12:50). The broad frame of reference is Mark's Gospel overall; the immediate situation is the split between Jesus' mother and brothers (outsiders who consider him a lunatic: Mark 3:21, 31) and the crowd, inside a house, gathered around him (3:19b–20, 32, 34). The same point is implied in Luke 11:27–28: a woman in the crowd who blessed the womb that bore Jesus and the breasts that nursed him. "But he said, 'Blessed rather are those who hear the word of God and obey it!'" (cf. Luke 7:23 = Matt. 11:6). (Understood either as scriptural precept or the good news associated with Jesus, "the word of God" is affiliated with "the will of God": Mark 7:13 = Matt. 15:6; Luke 8:11, 21). A compatible thread runs through Jesus' remaining references to God's will: the dissonance between those who know it, then default on their promise to uphold it, and those who may falter, reconsider, then carry out the master's command (Matt. 21:28–32; Luke 12:47).

The agony of surrendering one's will and embracing God's will is, once more, embodied in Jesus himself. "Anyone who wants to be a follower of mine must renounce self; he must take up his cross and follow me" (Mark 8:34 REB). Having trained his disciples to let go of anxiety (Luke 12:22–31 = Matt. 6:25–34), to hold fast to confession before murderous threat (Luke 12:2–12 = Matt. 10:26–33), and to entrust themselves to God in their hours of trial (Matt. 24:9–14 = Mark 13:11–13 = Luke 21:14–19), Jesus drops to his

129

knees, prays for the cup of self-sacrifice to be removed, yet places himself at the disposal of a heavenly purpose as down-to-hell as a gibbet: "yet, not my will but yours be done" (Luke 22:42; cf. Luke 22:40–46 = Mark 14:32–42 = Matt. 26:36–46). The Synoptic Jesus exemplifies what the Johannine Jesus professes: "I can do nothing on my own. . . . I seek to do not my own will but the will of him who sent me" (John 5:30; see also 6:38–39).

By yielding to his executioners, Jesus did what he had always done: drew from a future he could not see but of whose reality he was convinced, much as one clings to a table covered by a cloth (Barth, *Prayer*, 38). In extremis God's will in that coming kingdom was love. So it remains: "Hear, O Israel: the Lord our God, the Lord is one; you shall love the Lord your God with all your heart, and with all your soul, and with all your mind, and with all your strength.' The second is this, 'You shall love your neighbor as yourself'" (Mark 12:29–31a = Matt. 22:37–40 = Luke 10:27; also Matt. 19:19). The neighbor, then as now, embraces friend, enemy, and persecutor alike (Matt. 5:44 = Luke 6:27, 32, 35; John 3:16; 13:34–35; 15:9–17). We are told few of the words prayed by Jesus in Gethsemane, but by his decision the evangelists confirm that Jesus abandoned himself to the kingdom's advent, plaiting his will with that of his heavenly Father into "a single cord of love" (Underhill, *Abba*, 42).

God's Kingdom and Will: Good Friday and Easter Sunday

When Jesus taught his disciples how to pray, his crucifixion and resurrection were beyond the horizon of their vision. This, however, was no longer the case for the evangelists any more than it is for us, who have reviewed their Lord's ministry from the perspective of Golgotha and an empty tomb. Irrespective of the church's consciousness of it, Easter is embedded in Christians' prayer for the consummation of God's kingdom and will.

Every element of the kingdom we have examined is recapitulated in the Gospels' passion narratives. As the ending of a fine film stirs us to reevaluate all the scenes building to it, for the evangelists the nexus of Jesus' crucifixion-resurrection reclaimed, intensified, and reconfigured the meaning of God's kingdom, from bottom to top. First, *Jesus himself* came to be recognized as the kingdom's

130

signature: his life, death, and new life were now perceptible as intrinsically parabolic, exploding all religious categories ("Christ," "Son of God," "Son of Man," "Lord," wonder-worker, prophet, sage, revolutionary, social reformer, ad infinitum). Jesus is, as Eduard Schweizer put it (*Jesus Christ*, 13), "the man who fits no formula"— not even the schemata of Christian dogmatics.

Judgment and mercy must also be reassessed: Easter's vindication of Jesus, humiliated and accursed (Gal. 3:13; cf. Deut. 21:23), means that the demonic has been so toppled that those in its thrall may not be punished, but set free (Rom. 6:7, 22; 8:38–39; Eph. 6:12; Rev. 1:5). *Time and space* demand reconsideration: if death has been defeated in Jesus, then no realm is beyond the kingdom's coverage (Col. 1:16; 1 Pet. 3:22; Rev. 12:10), and eternity is now (John 10:28; 13:31; 17:3; 2 Cor. 6:2; Eph. 5:8; Col. 1:22; 1 John 5:11, 13).

Above all, *God* reasserts holy otherness both by his deafening silence at Golgotha (Mark 15:34 = Matt. 27:46) and by his powerful goodness by justifying the ungodly (Rom. 4:5). God is the one "who gives life to the dead and calls into existence the things that do not exist" (Rom. 4:17; cf. Matt. 28:5–6 = Mark 16:6 = Luke 24:5b–7). At Golgotha the trustworthy integrity of *both* Jesus *and* God were laid on the line. Easter Sunday delivered the Good. Death died. Those praying for the kingdom's complete reclamation of this earth may do so with costly confidence in the banishment of this world's chiaroscuro into the heavenly radiance where God's purposes are perfected (Matt. 18:10). "Where God's glory becomes the one will and work of every citizen, there perfect peace and fellowship will be consummated" (Minear, *Kingdom and the Power*, 150).

A Penitent Conclusion

Prayers for the coming of God's kingdom and the doing of God's will are daggers poised at the heart of all the world's nations. From its infancy the United States' myths have suckled—or suckered— its citizens into regarding America as the darling of divine providence. When commissioned by the Continental Congress (July 4, 1776) to propose a seal for the United States, Thomas Jefferson (1743–1826) suggested a tableau presenting "the children of Israel, led by a cloud by day and a pillar of fire by night" (*Papers*, 1:495),

131

in spite of owning more than one hundred slaves when he died. John Adams (1735–1826) was more circumspect: he wrote Jefferson (February 2, 1816), "Power always thinks it has a great Soul and vast Views beyond the Comprehension of the Weak; and that it is doing God's Service when it is violating all his Laws. Our Passions, Ambitions, Avarice, Love and Resentment, etc., possess so much metaphysical Subtlety and so much overpowering Eloquence, that they insinuate themselves into the Understanding and Conscience and convert both to their Party" (*Adams-Jefferson Letters*, 394).

Bereft of both eloquence and subtlety, political rhetoric in twenty-first-century America is blighted by the age-old, ugly mixture of religiosity and nationalistic power. With Irving Berlin's unwitting assistance, "God Bless America," sung by millions unable or unwilling to differentiate petition from patronage, has become the American president's equivalent of "Have a nice day." The gloves came off, the hubris bare-knuckled, in the comments of a senior adviser to the American president in 2004, twenty months after the U.S. invasion of Iraq:

> [Our critics live] in what we call the reality-based community, . . . [those who] believe that solutions emerge from your judicious study of discernible reality. . . . That's not the way the world really works anymore. We're an empire now, and when we act, we create our own reality. And while you're studying that reality—judiciously, as you will—we'll act again, creating other new realities, which you can study too, and that's how things will sort out. We're history's actors, . . . and you, all of you, will be left to just study what we do. (Suskind, "Without a Doubt," 51)

That is the voice, not of Jesus Christ, but of Caesar Augustus. From the standpoint of Christian faith, it is a lie: "an abomination unto the Lord, and a very present help in time of trouble," as Adlai Stevenson (1900–1965) mused on his fellow politicians (Green, *Political Quotes*, 212). The only ones helped by such a deception are self-interested cynics in search of reelection. Meanwhile, hundreds of thousands of volunteer soldiers and innocent civilians continue to die because we cannot bring ourselves to admit that "the earth is the LORD's and all that is in it, the world, and those who live in it" (Ps. 24:1), that "God is our salvation" (68:19b) and we creatures are not. God does not ram the kingdom down our throats. Anyone born after 1984 has, for half of their life, never known an

132

America not at war (Bump, "Here's How Much"). Refusal to accept the gospel has bloody consequences.

In a democratic country ultimate responsibility lies not merely with elected officials, who after all are but representatives of our own corruption. Finally, we are responsible for how we pray, how we conduct ourselves as citizens, how we live as disciples of Jesus. At Golgotha God unveiled the true Messiah and exposed his impostors, then and now. God also revealed that our principal adversary is not extraneous to us: another nation or ethnic group, our partisan opponents, or religious fanatics—be they our own or those of another faith. The prime enemy is a power inside ourselves, which covets the achievement of personal sovereignty—"*My* will be done"—and commits the blasphemy of expecting all others, especially those who are not "my kind of people," to submit to the kingdom's holy love while exempting ourselves by delusional self-confidence. "God, I thank you that I am not like other people" (Luke 18:11).

When we renounce our idols of mammon or Caesar and quit telling God what to do, we repent: not bewailing our failure to be sufficiently religious, but "turning Godward" (*shûv; metanoia*), regarding this world's realities from the vantage point of the heavenly kingdom, and staking our claim on God's future *now*. Christians have long awaited the kingdom, rarely asking if they need to turn around and face the opposite direction (2 Cor. 6:2). Those who grasp their salvation as the point at which their hope crisscrosses God's promise are beginning to experience their wants educated and desires purified. They have received the reward from their Father, who sees in secret (Matt. 6:4, 6, 18).

It is only the infinite mercy and love of God that has prevented us from tearing ourselves to pieces and destroying His entire creation long ago. People seem to think that it is in some way a proof that no merciful God exists, if we have so many wars. On the contrary, consider how in spite of centuries of sin and greed and lust and cruelty and hatred and avarice and oppression and injustice, spawned and bred by the free wills of men, the human race can still recover, each time, and can still produce men and women who overcome evil with good, hatred with love, greed with charity, lust and cruelty with sanctity. . . . There is not an act of kindness or generosity, not an act of sacrifice done, or a word of peace and gentleness spoken, not a child's prayer uttered, that

133

does not sing hymns to God before His throne, and in the eyes of men, and before their faces. (Merton, *Seven Storey Mountain*, 128–29)

Works Cited in Chapter 5

Adams, John. *The Adams-Jefferson Letters: The Complete Correspondence between Thomas Jefferson and Abigail and John Adams*. Edited by Lester J. Cappon. Omohundro Institute of Early American History and Culture. Chapel Hill: University of North Carolina Press, 1987.

Allison, Dale C., Jr. *Constructing Jesus: Memory, Imagination, and History*. Grand Rapids: Baker Academic, 2010.

Aslan, Reza. *Zealot: The Life and Times of Jesus of Nazareth*. New York: Random House, 2013.

Bammel, Ernst, and C. F. D. Moule, eds. *Jesus and the Politics of His Day*. Cambridge: Cambridge University Press, 1984.

Barth, Karl. *Prayer*. 50th anniversary ed. Edited by Don E. Saliers. Translated by Sara F. Terrien. Louisville, KY: Westminster John Knox Press, 2002.

Black, C. Clifton. "Shouting at the Legally Deaf: Sin's Punishment in the Gospels." *Interpretation* 69 (2015): 311–22.

Borg, Marcus J. "A Temperate Case for a Non-Eschatological Jesus." In *Jesus in Contemporary Scholarship*, 47–68. Valley Forge, PA: Trinity Press International, 1994.

Boring, M. Eugene. "The Kingdom of God in Mark." In *The Kingdom of God in 20th-Century Interpretation*, edited by Wendell Willis, 131–46. Peabody, MA: Hendrickson Publishers, 1987.

Brandon, S. G. F. *Jesus and the Zealots: A Study of the Political Factor in Primitive Christianity*. New York: Charles Scribner's Sons, 1967.

Bultmann, Rudolf. *Jesus and the Word*. Translated by Louise Pettibone Smith and Erminie Huntress. New York: Charles Scribner's Sons, 1934.

Bump, Philip. "Here's How Much of Your Life the United States Has Been at War." *Washington Post*, May 25, 2015.

Chilton, Bruce. *The Kingdom of God in the Teaching of Jesus*. Issues in Religion and Theology 5. London: SCM; Philadelphia: Fortress Press, 1984.

Cotter, Wendy J. *The Christ of the Miracle Stories: Portrait through Encounter.* Grand Rapids: Baker Academic, 2010.

Crossan, John Dominic. *The Historical Jesus: The Life of a Mediterranean Jewish Peasant.* San Francisco: HarperCollins, 1991.

Cuppy, Will. *The Decline and Fall of Practically Everybody: Great Figures of History Hilariously Humbled.* New York: Henry Holt, 1950.

Dalman, Gustaf. *The Words of Jesus Considered in the Light of Post-Biblical Jewish Writings and the Aramaic Language.* Translated by D. M. Kay. Edinburgh: T&T Clark, 1902.

Dodd, C. H. *The Parables of the Kingdom.* London: Nisbet & Co., 1935.

Evans, C. F. *The Lord's Prayer.* London: SCM, 1963.

Fuchs, Ernst. *Studies of the Historical Jesus.* Translated by Andrew Scobie. Studies in Biblical Theology 42. London: SCM, 1964.

Gager, John G. *Kingdom and Community: The Social World of Early Christianity.* Englewood Cliffs, NJ: Prentice-Hall, 1975.

Green, Jonathon, ed. *The Book of Political Quotes.* New York: McGraw-Hill, 1982.

Hanson, Paul D. *The Dawn of Apocalyptic: The Historical and Sociological Roots of Jewish Apocalyptic Eschatology.* Rev. ed. Philadelphia: Fortress Press, 1979.

Harnack, Adolf. *What Is Christianity?* Translated by Thomas Bailey Saunders. New York: Harper, 1957.

Hartman, Lars. "'Your Will Be Done on Earth as It Is in Heaven.'" *Africa Theological Journal* 11 (1982): 209–18.

Hengel, Martin. *Crucifixion in the Ancient World and the Folly of the Message of the Cross.* Translated by John Bowden. London: SCM, 1977.

Jefferson, Thomas. *The Papers of Thomas Jefferson.* Vol. 1. Edited by Julian P. Boyd, Lyman H. Butterfield, and Mina R. Bryan. Princeton, NJ: Princeton University Press, 1950.

Jeremias, Joachim. *The Parables of Jesus.* 2nd rev. ed. Translated by S. H. Hooke. London: SCM, 1972.

Kant, Immanuel. *Religion within the Limits of Reason Alone.* Translated by Theodore M. Greene and Hoyt H. Hudson. 1793. New York: Harper & Row, 1960.

Käsemann, Ernst. *Jesus Means Freedom.* Translated by Frank Clarke. London: SCM, 1969.

135

Keck, Leander E. *Who Is Jesus? History in Perfect Tense.* Studies on Personalities of the New Testament. Columbia: University of South Carolina Press, 2000.

Kümmel, Werner Georg. *Promise and Fulfillment: The Eschatological Message of Jesus.* Translated by Dorothea M. Barton. Studies in Biblical Theology 23. London: SCM, 1957.

Manson, Thomas Walter. *The Teaching of Jesus: Studies of Its Form and Content.* Cambridge: Cambridge University Press, 1959.

Mathews, Shailer. *The Social Teaching of Jesus: An Essay in Christian Sociology.* New York: Macmillan, 1897.

Mays, James Luther. *The Lord Reigns: A Theological Handbook to the Psalms.* Louisville, KY: Westminster John Knox Press, 1994.

Merton, Thomas. *The Seven Storey Mountain.* New York: Harcourt Brace Jovanovich, 1948.

Minear, Paul S. *The Kingdom and the Power: An Exposition of the New Testament Gospel.* 1950. Reprint, Louisville, KY: Westminster John Knox Press, 2004.

Niebuhr, Reinhold. *Beyond Tragedy: Essays on the Christian Interpretation of History.* New York: Charles Scribner's Sons, 1937.

Perrin, Norman. *Jesus and the Language of the Kingdom: Symbol and Metaphor in New Testament Interpretation.* Philadelphia: Fortress Press, 1976.

Rauschenbusch, Walter. *A Theology for the Social Gospel.* Nashville: Abingdon Press, 1945.

Reimarus, Hermann Samuel. *Fragments.* Edited by Charles H. Talbert. Translated by Ralph F. Fraser. Lives of Jesus Series. Philadelphia: Fortress Press, 1970.

Ritschl, Albrecht. *Die christliche Lehre von der Rechtfertigung und Versöhnung.* 4th ed. 3 vols. Bonn: Marcus, 1895–1903.

Sacks, Jonathan, ed. *The Authorised Daily Prayer Book of the United Hebrew Congregations of the Commonwealth.* Translated by Simeon Singer. 4th ed. London: Collins, 2007.

Schweitzer, Albert. *The Quest of the Historical Jesus.* Translated by John Bowden. London: SCM, 2000.

Schweizer, Eduard. *Jesus Christ: The Man from Nazareth and the Exalted Lord.* Edited by Hulitt Gloer. Macon, GA: Mercer University Press, 1987.

Simonis, A. J. Cardinal. *Our Father: Reflections on the Lord's Prayer.* Translated by Barbara Schultz-Verdon. Grand Rapids: Wm. B. Eerdmans Publishing Co., 1997.

Stăniloae, Dumitru. *The Experience of God*. Translated and edited by Ioan Ioiță and Robert Barringer. Brookline, MA: Holy Cross Orthodox Press, 1994.

Suskind, Ron. "Without a Doubt: Faith, Certainty, and the Presidency of George W. Bush." *New York Times Magazine*, October 17, 2004, 44–106.

Theissen, Gerd, and Annette Merz. *The Historical Jesus: A Comprehensive Guide*. Translated by John Bowden. Minneapolis: Fortress Press, 1998.

Thielicke, Helmut. *The Prayer That Spans the World: Sermons on the Lord's Prayer*. Translated by John W. Doberstein. London: James Clarke, 1960.

Thompson, Marianne Meye. *John: A Commentary*. New Testament Library. Louisville, KY: Westminster John Knox Press, 2015.

Underhill, Evelyn. *Abba: Meditations based on the Lord's Prayer*. London: Longmans, Green & Co., 1940.

Vendler, Helen. *Poems, Poets, Poetry: An Introduction and Anthology*. 3rd ed. Boston: Bedford, 2010.

Weder, Hans. *Gegenwart und Gottesherrschaft: Überlegungen zum Zeitverständnis bei Jesus und im frühen Christentum*. Biblisch-theologische Studien 20. Neukirchen-Vluyn: Neukirchener Verlag, 1993.

Weiss, Johannes. *Jesus' Proclamation of the Kingdom of God*. Translated and edited by Richard Hyde Hiers and David Larrimore Holland. Lives of Jesus Series. Philadelphia: Fortress Press, 1971.

PART THREE

Interpreting the Prayer

The Second Table

Give us this day our daily bread.

And forgive us our debts, as we forgive our debtors.

Lead us not into temptation, but deliver us from evil.

CHAPTER 6

Bread

There are people in the world so hungry that God cannot appear to them except in the form of bread.

—Mohandas Karamchand Gandhi

As in part 2, we open this study's third part with a word of orientation. In chapter 2 we reported that interpreters across the centuries have noticed a flow from the first three appeals of the Lord's Prayer to the last three (all AT):

a. May your name be made holy. (Matt. 6:9c = Luke 11:2b)
b. May your kingdom come. (Matt. 6:10a = Luke 11:2c)
c. May your will be done on earth, as in heaven. (Matt. 6:10bc)

All three of those petitions are clearly directed toward God as Father. An equally evident turn toward ourselves, the petitioners, is perceptible in the next three entreaties:

d. Give us this day our daily bread. (Matt. 6:11 = Luke 11:3)
e. And forgive us our debts, as we forgive our debtors. (Matt. 6:12ab = Luke 11:4ab)
f. And do not bring us to the time of trial, but rescue us from evil. (Matt. 6:13ab = Luke 11:4c)

141

While real, this adjustment in focus should not be exaggerated. Those who make the first three pleas are themselves implied. We address God as "[our] Father." While God is the primary agent of his name's holiness, we, too, are caught up in that sanctification. If heaven is the province in which the divine will is forever done, then we who pray this prayer are invested in the hope that God's will may prevail also on earth.

The same divine-human dynamic persists in the Prayer's next three entreaties. We want bread, but we look to God for its provision. Our sins require God's remission. We need rescue from danger that God alone can deliver. The shift occurring at the fourth petition is one, not of theme, but rather of perspective (Lochman, *Lord's Prayer*, 84).

In the Prayer's last three supplications yet another element is at work: our continued involvement, not only with God, but also with one another. This is most obvious in the fifth appeal—forgiveness of others' sins against us—but is tacit in the fourth and sixth. An important theological principle is revealed: we who pray in this manner are connected in a web of relationships, which this Prayer is positively drawing together. Western culture socializes us to think and act as autonomous individuals, so much so that this aspect of Jesus' prayer may be lost to us or, if recovered, off-putting. The fact remains, however, that we *are* bound to God and to one another. No matter how hard we might try, there's no escaping either. Even if such evasion were possible, the consequences would be disastrous.

> A man entirely unconcerned with his self is dead, [but] a man exclusively concerned with his self is a beast. . . . Human is he who is concerned with other selves. . . . [A] man cannot ever be in accord with his own self unless he serves something beyond himself. [He] can never be truly self-sufficient, not only by what he must take in, but also by what he must give out. . . . A vital requirement of human life is transitive concern, a regard for others, in addition to a reflexive concern, an intense regard for itself. (Heschel, *Man Is Not Alone*, 137–38)

The final petitions of the Lord's Prayer accent the reflexive and transitive concerns that run throughout the whole. As a variation on the classical doctrine of the Trinity—one God in three persons—this dynamic might be diagrammed as a triangle of interactive agents:

142

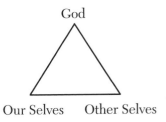

Our Selves   Other Selves

We now turn to the Prayer's fourth appeal. The simplest procedure is to examine its component parts.

The Verb

While not identical in form, the verbs in Matthew 6:11 and Luke
11:3 are the same: *didōmi*, "give" (cf. Matt. 4:9; 7:6, 11; Luke 17:18;
Acts 20:35). Luke's conjugation is a present imperative, *didou*,
which may be rendered either "give" or "keep giving." Matthew's
form is *dos*, an aorist imperative: "give." In Greek the aorist tense in
the indicative mood is often, though not always, a way of expressing
an action accomplished in the past. Conjugated in the imperative
mood, as we find here, the aorist can convey a "complexive" connotation: an action regarded as a single, unified event (thus 2 Cor.
11:24 NIV: "Five times I received . . . the forty lashes minus one").
If one prays the Prayer along Luke's line, one asks for a gift, with
the understanding that we keep asking for it. If one takes Matthew's
tack, one requests decisively, once and for all, a gift in its wholeness.
All the petitions in Matthew's version of the Lord's Prayer are cast
as aorist imperatives.

In both cases the important considerations are that (1) we
beseech as a gift what is not in our power to provide for ourselves,
and (2) the one of whom we make this entreaty is God (Matt. 6:9b =
Luke 11:2b), who is acknowledged as the sole benefactor. Two theological implications are entailed. First, this request acknowledges
the petitioners' essential neediness. Second, God, the exclusive
addressee in the Prayer's first three petitions, remains at the center.
Simply put: we are creatures, reliant on our Creator. Ultimately, of
our own volition, we do not create sustenance or anything else. We
are needy beings, dependent for everything on God. Teaching us to
pray, Jesus commands us to beg with open hands.

143

So to believe and so to pray may have been easier for Jesus' first disciples than for us. Ancient Israelites were not reluctant to confess their impotence (Wolff, *Anthropology*, 33–35):

> These all look to you[, O LORD,]
>> to give them their food in due season;
> when you give to them, they gather it up;
>> when you open your hand, they are filled with good things.
>> (Ps. 104:27–28)

> If [God Almighty] should take back his spirit to himself,
>> and gather to himself his breath,
> all flesh would perish together,
> and all mortals return to dust.
>> (Job 34:14–15)

If we are honest with ourselves, this biblical assumption is offensive, both theologically and anthropologically. If we are actual or virtual atheists, content with "a theology that presents God as a great unblinking cosmic stare" (Willard, *Divine Conspiracy*, 244–45), then we shall not appreciate reminders that our *next breath* is directly dependent on divine infusion.

Our understanding of our own humanity is also thrown radically into question. With its relentless mythology of self-reliance, its comparative wealth, and its almost pathological refusal to confront death, North American culture does not well equip its members to confess inadequacy. In reality we are no less impoverished than Jesus' first followers, nor any less indigent than the rest of our own world's population. The difference lies in our ability to disguise such need from ourselves. We may ruefully recognize ourselves in television's Bart Simpson: asked by his parents to return thanks at supper, the cartoon brat said, "God, we worked hard putting all this food on the table by ourselves, so thanks for nothing." Yet all our arrogance and possessions collapse when our reasons for getting up in the morning are stripped from us, when our families fall apart, when the lab tests come back positive. For that reason we pray, "Give"—but not as a means of last resort, when our backs are against the wall. Jesus' disciples approach their heavenly Father with open hands every morning.

144

If the Lord's Prayer did nothing other than confront us with the comprehensiveness of our need, in itself that would fill a gaping void in us all. George MacDonald strips the bark off our delusions: "The one principle of hell is—I am my own!" (Lewis, *George Mac-Donald*, 88). Escape from damnation is to entrust ourselves, our loved ones and neighbors and enemies, to God's safekeeping. Our wanting, our fundamental want as human beings, is disciplined by prayer that recognizes a God who loves us enough to provide what we cannot satisfy by ourselves.

Adverbs

Comparing Matthew and Luke's versions of the Prayer, we notice subtle variations in their verbs' modifications. In Matthew we ask God to give "today" (*sēmeron*, a noun declined in the accusative case that functions as an adverb). With a prepositional phrase that modifies the sentence's verb (*to kath' hēmeran*), Luke conveys the sense "give every day": this day and all other days. As scribes transmitted Luke's Gospel across the centuries, they tended to draw its wording of both verb and adverb in line with Matthew's expression. Our earliest, most diverse manuscripts preserve Luke's subtle distinctions.

Whether we follow Matthew ("today") or Luke ("day by day"), these simple adverbs bear theological import. We who ask God to supply us are not only needy: we are also *incessantly* needy. We need something from God, today and every day we pray this Prayer. Broadway's Little Orphan Annie is too self-assured: "The sun'll come up tomorrow"—but we may not. Human beings are contingent creatures, lacking within themselves the resources necessary for survival. The Lord's Prayer exposes those needs, pulls to the surface primary human desires, and trains supplicants' gaze upon the only One capable of fulfilling them.

"Today" or "each day" also restrains unhealthy anxieties about the future, the folly of insatiable fear. "Look at the birds of the air; they neither sow nor reap nor gather into barns, and yet your heavenly Father feeds them. Are you not of more value than they? And can any of you by worrying add a single hour to your span of life?" (Matt. 6:26–27 = Luke 12:24–25). When sparrows finally fall to the ground, their deaths do not occur "apart from your Father" (Matt. 10:29). "Yet not one of them is forgotten in God's sight" (Luke 12:6b).

145

Marvelous dexterity! To be able to take hold of all one's sorrow at once, and then to be able to cast it away from oneself so dexterously and hit the mark with such certainty! Yet this is what the lily and the bird do, and therefore they are unconditionally joyful at that very instant. And of course this is entirely in order, for God the Almighty bears the whole world and all the world's sorrow— including the lily's and the bird's—with infinite lightness. What indescribable joy! Joy, namely, over God the Almighty. (Kierkegaard, *Lily of the Field*, 83–84)

The Object

"Give us bread [*ton arton*]." Nothing could be more elementary (or alimentary): "The stomach demands its daily rights" (Ebeling, *On Prayer*, 89). As Jesus taught his disciples, that basic connotation was surely in view. The Twelve called by Jesus dropped everything to follow him: consider the Zebedee & Sons Fishing Company, which James and John abandoned to their father and his hired hands (*tōn misthōtōn*, Mark 1:19–20). When Jesus dispatched his small band for mission to surrounding areas, he charged them to go without bread, bag, or money in their belts (6:7–13): they, like Jesus himself, relied entirely on God and the kindness of strangers. Most of the latter were in no position to offer wayfaring disciples anything more than the basics for survival. Small farmers, tenants, slaves, and day laborers eked out a hand-to-mouth existence, with no prospects for upward social mobility. Then, as now, power and wealth were concentrated in 1 percent of the population: those who happened to have been born to wealth, privilege, and power. Unlike their modern counterparts, ancient cities didn't produce: they consumed. Outside of modest urban agora, no markets existed in the modern sense: few had buying power; fewer enjoyed a surplus to sell. Artisan classes existed to fabricate bricks and tiles and pottery, tools and weapons, but no workshops were rigged for mass production. The vast majority—perhaps as high as 70 percent—at best lived on a denarius a day, at a level of bare subsistence, thus teetering between stable and starving. At worst, they were utterly poor (E. Stegemann and W. Stegemann, *The Jesus Movement*, 88–95).

146

We should beware, therefore, of too quickly spiritualizing the Lord's Prayer's fourth petition: when Jesus instructed his followers to pray for enough bread to get them through the day, every day, most likely he meant just that. That injunction rhymes with Jewish prayers of blessing in the eras before and after Jesus:

> Let them thank the LORD for his steadfast love,
> for his wonderful works to humankind.
> For he satisfies the thirsty,
> and the hungry he fills with good things. (Ps. 107:8–9)

> Bless, O Lord our God, this year for us,
> and let it be good in all the varieties of its produce. (*m. Berakhot* 4.3; see appendix A)

> Blessed are You, O Lord our God, king of the universe, who feeds
> the whole world
> with Your goodness, with grace, with loving-kindness, and
> tender mercy:
> You give food to all flesh, for Your loving-kindness endures forever.
> (*m. Berakhot* 7.11)

The rabbis took such thanksgivings for nourishment at face value: "You nourish and sustain all beings and do good to all, and provide food for all Your creatures whom You have created" (*m. Berakhot* 7.11).

Even so, "bread" (Heb., *lekhem*) in the Old Testament and other ancient writings accrued a broad variety of metaphorical senses. Egyptian and Greek iconography often depicted deities holding clusters of grain, suggestive of everyday or immortal life (Burkert, *Ancient Mystery Cults*, 80–81). Sheaves, symbolizing either fertility or imperial beneficence, appeared on Roman coins. (Owing to a classical carryover, some American readers may recall the backs of "wheat pennies" [1909–58], onto which were stamped wreaths of wheat heads). According to an old Sumerian proverb, "Whosoever has gold, or silver, or cattle, or sheep, shall ever wait at the door of him who has grain" ("Disputation between Ewe and Wheat" 1.189–90, in Hallo and Younger, *Context*, 1:578).

Hospitality, offering a seat at mealtime to strangers, had long been recognized as fundamental benefaction (Gen. 18:5; 19:3; Exod. 2:20; Ruth 2:14), into which a moral imperative was imported: "share your bread with the hungry, and bring the homeless poor into your house" (Isa. 58:7; Ezek. 18:7). The Epistle of James (2:1–7) upbraids those who dishonor the poor; the Epistle to the Hebrews speaks poignantly of oppression suffered by the wretched poor who depend on *philadelphia*, "brotherly love" (13:1–2 RSV).

Nevertheless, the weaving of bread's literal and spiritual senses is as old as the story of God's feeding the Israelites with manna in the wilderness, aptly described in the Wisdom of Solomon (1st c. BC) as "food of angels" (Wis. 16:20–21).

> Then the LORD said to Moses, "I am going to rain bread from heaven for you, and each day the people shall go out and gather enough for that day. In that way I will test them, whether they will follow my instruction or not. On the sixth day, when they prepare what they bring in, it will be twice as much as they gather on other days." . . . Morning by morning they gathered it, as much as each needed; but when the sun grew hot, it melted. On the sixth day they gathered twice as much food, two omers apiece. When all the leaders of the congregation came and told Moses, he said to them, "This is what the LORD has commanded: 'Tomorrow is a day of solemn rest, a holy sabbath to the LORD; bake what you want to bake and boil what you want to boil, and all that is left over put aside to be kept until morning.'" (Exod. 16:4–5, 21–23)

Commemorating that heavenly gift, priests offered to God a special sacrifice, the bread of the Presence (Exod. 25:30; 40:23; 1 Kgs. 7:48; 2 Chr. 4:19; Mark 2:26; Heb. 9:2). At his Last Supper with the Twelve, Jesus identified a loaf of bread with his own body (Matt. 26:26 = Mark 14:22 = Luke 22:19; cf. 1 Cor. 10:16–17): a nuance amplified in John's Gospel (6:51) by way of Exodus 16: "I am the living bread that came down from heaven."

To dine at the Almighty's own banquet developed eschatological overtones:

> On this mountain [Zion] the LORD of hosts will make for all peoples
>   a feast of rich food, a feast of well-aged wines,
>   of rich food filled with marrow, of well-aged wines strained clear.
>   . . .
> Then the Lord GOD will wipe away the tears from all faces,
>   and the disgrace of his people he will take away from all the earth,
>   for the LORD has spoken. (Isa. 25:6, 8)

> Then people will come from east and west, from north and south,
>   and will eat in the kingdom of God. (Luke 13:29)

Some rabbis differentiated "a [mortal] meal, [of which] there is an end, [from] the meal of our God, which he will prepare in the future for the righteous, [of which] there is no end" (*Midrash Esther* 1.4.86b, in Strack and Billerbeck, *Kommentar,* 4:1155).

Given these multiple connotations, historical critics have perhaps been precipitate in criticizing patristic and medieval interpretations of the fourth petition in the Lord's Prayer, especially those that identify bread with the Eucharist (see appendixes B and C; also Wainwright, *Eucharist and Eschatology,* 30–34, 162–68; Wright, *The Lord,* 46–48). While sacramental bread was probably not the primary referent of that petition as it originated with Jesus, the seeds for an interpretive development blending everyday and everlasting bread had long been planted and had flourished in biblical literature. Jesus' response to the devil's first temptation quotes Deuteronomy (8:3), a reminder of God's forty-year provision of manna for Israel, to emphasize nourishment from "every word that comes from the mouth of God" (Matt. 4:4).

In the preaching of Thomas Aquinas, we witness an expert interpreter's sensitivity to manifold implications of "bread," our entreaty for its provision in the Lord's Prayer, and the many ways that petition might be perverted:

> The first [vice to which we are tempted] is that inordinate desire whereby we seek for things that are beyond our state and condition of life. . . . [The Lord] did not teach us to ask for ourselves delicacies, nor for many kinds of things, nor for what is over-refined, but for bread that is common to all, and without which human life cannot be sustained. . . . [Second,] we are taught here to shun [the] vice [of fraudulent acquisition], by asking for our own and not others' bread. . . . The third vice is excessive solitude. . . . What [the Lord] forbids is that we should not anticipate things by presuming to worry before it is time. Concern [yourself] with what is laid upon you now, . . . not something that may become your responsibility in the future. . . . The fourth vice is immoderate voraciousness: . . . [to] devour in one day what should be sufficient for several days. . . . The fifth vice is ingratitude. A person grows proud in his riches and does not recognize that what he has comes from God. This is a grave fault, for all the things we have, whether spiritual or temporal, come from God. Hence, in order to remove this vice, the prayer, *Give us* even *our daily bread,* reminds us that all we have comes from God. (*Lord's Prayer* §§1072–76; in Murray, *Praying with Confidence,* 66–68)

149

An Adjective: The Prayer's Most Vexing Word

Every day millions of Christians offer the Lord's Prayer while unaware that its fourth petition contains, in Greek, a word so obscure that its meaning has eluded two millennia of educated interpreters. That term, declined in the accusative case, is an appositive modifying *ton arton hēmōn*, "our bread": *ton epiousion*. Most English-speaking worshipers routinely translate this adjective "daily," but if precision is our aim, we cannot be certain of this rendering. Origen, one of the early church's most learned scholars, reported that he could not find *ho epiousios* in any Greek literature known to him and was unsure of its sense (*Prayer* 27.7; see appendix C). Eighteen centuries later, with vast computer banks of ancient texts available to us, we remain in roughly the same position as Alexandria's erudite commentator. To what kind of bread did Jesus refer? Complicating the problem is that Jesus likely taught his disciples in Aramaic: we cannot recover the term that Matthew and Luke (and, for all we know, their common source, Q) translated for their Greek-speaking listeners (see chap. 2). Our farthest reach backward ends with the baffling *epiousios*. It appears to be a verbal compound, consisting of a preposition, *epi* (which, in this context, invites the translation "for"), and a participial form of some Greek verb—of which verb, we cannot be confident.

Most of the alternative translations that have been proposed resolve themselves into six, each of which invites consideration. (Readers who know French will find an exhaustive review in Carmignac, *Recherches*, 118–221.) A word to the wary: the following remarks take us more deeply into the weeds of biblical languages than any other area of this commentary. Some readers may find this fascinating; others, as irredeemably dreary. But there's nothing to be gained in concealing from pastors and teachers who care about Scripture's interpretation the most difficult problem of translation presented by this Prayer.

Alternative 1: "Necessary for Existence"

Etymologically analyzed, *epiousios* might be a compound of *epi* and *ousia*: *epi-ousios*, literally, "for being" (using the participle of the verb *einai*, "to be" or "to live"). A free rendering: "Give us the bread we need to survive." The Peshitta, a fifth-century translation of the

150

Greek New Testament for Syriac churches, moves in this direction: "bread for our need." Such an interpretation has deep biblical roots with rabbinic outcroppings:

> Two things I ask of you [O LORD];
>   do not deny them to me before I die:
> Remove far from me falsehood and lying;
>   give me neither poverty nor riches;
>   feed me with the food that I need. (Prov. 30:7–8)

> In every hour the Shekinah [*kābōd*, God's radiance] provides sustenance for all the world's inhabitants, according to their need, and satisfies every living thing, and not only the pious and the righteous, but also the wicked and the idolaters. (*Mekilta Amalek*, quoted in Montefiore and Loewe, *Rabbinic Anthology*, 48)

It has been argued that this idea is fundamental in Jewish prayer. As one rabbi put it, "The needs of your people are many, but they are impatient; may it be Your will, O Lord, that You fulfill everyone's needs and supply each person's lack" (Tosefta *Berakhot* 3.11; see Lachs, *Rabbinic Commentary*, 120; Foerster, "*epiousios*," 598–99; Young, *Jewish Background*, 23–27). If we follow this lead, *epiousios* would indicate measure, not temporality.

Well and good. *Epiousios*, however, presents a linguistic problem: when *epi* and *ousios* are scrunched together, one would normally expect a compound with different lettering—*epousios*, with the "i" (Greek iota) elided (Lightfoot, *Fresh Revision*, 201–2). Another difficulty: in ancient Greek *ousia* usually refers to something like "means" or "possessions," which does not naturally fit the sentence's context. Moreover, other Greek words existed to express the idea of "necessary" or "needful." Why make up this one?

Alternative 2: "For Today"

This translation may be created from the same Greek terms, *epi* (for) and another participial form of *einai* (to be) while supplying an implied word: *epi tēn ousan* [*hēmeran*], "for the present [day]." Old Latin manuscripts of the early fourth century adopted this rendering (*cotidianum* or *quotidianum*), as well as Gregory of Nyssa (*The Lord's Prayer*) and John Chrysostom (*Homily on Matthew* 6:11). In ancient Greek *hē ousa* is an unusual locution for "the existing

151

day"; for this possibility to work, one imports the single word, "day," that makes sense of the expression. That mental jump may not have been excessive. When Proverbs 27:1 was translated into Greek from Hebrew, such a sense is suggested: *hē epiousa* (referring to "this day," *yōm*) is contrasted with *aurion* for *yōm mākhār* (tomorrow).

Other scholars remain unconvinced. Why would the second-century *Didache* (see appendix B) have prescribed the Lord's Prayer to be prayed thrice a day if one of its petitions were rendered obsolete—a prayer for today's bread—by afternoon and evening (Day, "In Search of the Meaning," 103)? Nevertheless, "daily" bread was the favored translation of Martin Luther (*täglich*), John Calvin, and the majority of Protestant Reformers (Wright, "What Kind of 'Bread'?"). Its adoption, spelled "dayly," by William Tyndale (ca. 1494–1536) in his English translation of the New Testament (1525) set the template for most English versions that followed and the liturgies based on them.

Alternative 3: "For the Day to Come"

How is this translation possible? By assuming a compound of *epi* with a different Greek verb: *hienai*, "to go" or "to come"; thus, *epiousion* (literally, "for that which is coming"; see Black, "Aramaic"). Other Syriac translations of the Lord's Prayer favored this option: "our upcoming," "continuing," or "constant" bread.

Saint Jerome, another superlative commentator of the early church, was inclined toward this possibility:

> In the *Gospel according to the Nazarenes* [ca. AD 200] for "daily bread" I found [the Aramaic word] *māchār*, which means "of tomorrow." Accordingly, the meaning [of *epiousios*] is "Our bread of tomorrow": that is to say, "Our future bread, give us today." (*Commentary on Matthew* 1.6.10, AT)

In this reading some interpreters see an analogy with the Latin word *diaria*, which referred to a soldier's daily ration (BDAG 376b). This possibility has been linked with an obscure item of odd provenance: a fifth-century Greek papyrus fragment of a householder's account book, recording "an expenditure of ½ obol for *epious*...." The text is broken off at a crucial point, whether by accident or as an abbreviation. Inconveniently, this shopping list went missing in the mid-twentieth century and has yet to be recovered (Metzger, "How Many Times?," 53). Even if it resurfaces, how much light would a grocery list throw on the shadowy wording of the Lord's Prayer four centuries earlier?

Commentators have fretted over an exegetical hitch in translating *epiousios* as "the next day" or tomorrow." That idea seems to fly in the face of Matthew 6:34: "So do not worry about tomorrow, for tomorrow will bring worries of its own. Today's trouble is enough for today." This contradiction is more apparent than actual. The expression *hē epiousa* is flexible in Koine Greek; its instances in ancient texts may be translated either "the next day," or "tomorrow" (from the standpoint of "today"), or even "today" (from the vantage of the night preceding or early morning). Invariably *hē epiousa nux* (the coming night) refers to "tonight," not "tomorrow night." "The accent is upon immediate sequence rather than on chronological date" (Hemer, "*epiousios*," 90). In our own day if one prayed the Lord's Prayer three hours before or after midnight, one could intelligibly ask for "bread for the coming day."

The linguistic snag with translating *epiousios* as "the next day" is that Koine Greek has commonplace ways to express "the day following" or "the day after this one": *hē epiousa hēmera* (Acts 7:26) or *tē epiousē* (Acts 16:11; 20:15; 21:18; also LXX: Prov. 3:28; 27:1) and the simple adverb *aurion*, "tomorrow" (Acts 23:20; Jas. 4:13; cf. *hē aurion* [*hēmera*], "the next day" [Matt. 6:34b; Luke 10:35] or "soon" [Luke 12:28; 1 Cor. 15:32]). Once again, why would Matthew and Luke settle on an obscure term when perfectly clear ones were available?

Alternative 4: "Heavenly"

As we have seen, a venerable interpretation of "bread" in the Lord's Prayer is that of the Eucharist. It is as old as the *Didache*'s reference to that rite's "spiritual food" (10.3) and the commentaries of Tertullian (*Prayer* 6) and Cyprian (*The Lord's Prayer* 18; see appendix C). With Origen we witness an attempt to construe the meaning of *epiousios* as "supersubstantial" bread. Unable to discover the Greek term among philosophers or in everyday usage, Origen supposed that the evangelists themselves may have coined *epiousios*, amplifying a basic meaning of *ousia* as "essence," "substance," or "reality" (*Prayer* 27.7).

153

> Just as corporeal bread received into the body of the person who is being nourished is accepted by his essence, so the living bread which has come down from heaven is received into the mind and the soul of whoever allows himself to receive nourishment from it, and imparts its own power to him. . . . The "supersubstantial" bread, therefore, [brings] about health and well-being to the soul and, since the word of God is immortal, [communicates] its own immortality to anyone who eats it. (*Prayer* 27.9)

This is a philosophical, not an etymological, argument. Origen proposes that the bread for which we should ask is that which nourishes the mind.

Jerome ties this interpretation to his discovery of *māchār* in the *Gospel according to the Nazarenes* (ca. AD 200), which he mistook for a version of the Gospel of Matthew written in Hebrew: "Give us today our bread for the following day; that is, the bread which will be given in your kingdom, give us today" (*Tractate on Psalm 135*; see Grumett, "Give Us This Day"). Cyril of Jerusalem (*Mystagogic Catecheses* 23.15) and Ambrose of Milan (337–397; *Sacraments* 5.24–26; *Faith* 3.15.127) endorsed this mystical interpretation, as did Erasmus of Rotterdam (1466–1536; *Annotations* on Matt. 6:11; Titus 2:14).

As mentioned earlier, an interpretation of "bread" encompassing that of the Lord's Supper is a reasonable overtone for those who pray the Lord's Prayer—all the more when that prayer precedes or follows observance of the sacrament. It seems less than satisfying as an interpretation of *epiousios*. Nothing in the Prayer or in the etymology of *epiousios* naturally suggests that connotation. The most literal Greek equivalent of the Latin term *supersubstantialis* is *hyperousios*, "hypersubstance." One may contend that the evangelists coined a unique adjective to distinguish a meal of special significance (LaVerdiere, "Give Us Each Day"), but such an argument assumes a predetermined conclusion.

Alternative 5: "End-Time"

With the twentieth century's recovery of the eschatological quality of Jesus' teaching, it was predictable that scholars would suggest that *epiousios* bears an apocalyptic tenor. So runs the reasoning: if, in Judaism of Jesus' day, *māchār* literally refers to "the next day,"

154

and if *epiousios* is somehow related to that Semitic term, then conceivably Jesus exhorted his followers to pray for the sustenance of "God's tomorrow": eschatological bread. This interpretation was championed by Ernst Lohmeyer (see appendix C), who argued that "all Jesus' sayings about eating and drinking [e.g., Luke 22:30; Matt. 25:34–35], being hungry [Luke 6:21], and giving feasts [Luke 14:16–24; Matt. 8:11], have a sense of eschatological fulfillment" (*Lord's Prayer*, 150). Similarly, Joachim Jeremias: "The disciples are to ask for their share in the glory of the consummation now. They may reach for the bread of life with both hands and pray: Now, here and now, today, give us the bread of life" (*New Testament Theology*, 201).

This interpretive option is a blend, with a twist, of the third and fourth just discussed: *epiousios* is understood to refer to the Day to Come. Here the stress falls on the eschatological future, portrayed as a banquet: "Blessed is anyone who will eat bread in the kingdom of God!" (Luke 14:15), a nuance we have witnessed in some Old Testament and rabbinic texts. Whereas Origen and Jerome arrived at their understanding of *epiousios* by way of liturgical practice at which Jesus, the Bread of Life, is consumed by communicants to seal them for eternity (John 6:35, 48, 51, 58), Lohmeyer and Jeremias stress the kingdom context of the Lord's Prayer and all its petitions as a way of historically explaining a hapax legomenon, a verbal one-off. Certainly the Lord's Prayer is colored by belief in the kingdom's coming; however, its next petition for forgiveness applies, not only to the end time, but also in the present. Special terms for something like "the Great Tomorrow" are absent from Jesus' teaching. A modern, eschatological rendition seems no less being read onto *epiousios* than the patristic commentators' sacramental bias.

Alternative 6: "Coming Bread"

Arland Hultgren ("Bread Petition") has ventured an interpretation of *epiousios* that has attracted comparatively less attention. He argues that the third alternative, mentioned above, needlessly complicates matters by importing the idea of bread for "*the day* to come." Instead, Hultgren suggests, we should take *ton epiousion* as a simple adjective, modifying "our bread": "Give us today our coming bread," the bread that comes to us (from God). He notes

155

a comment by Ambrose: while Latin-speaking Christians spoke of "daily [*quotidianum*] bread," those who spoke Greek said *epiousios*, with reference to "coming [*advenientem*] bread" (*The Sacraments* 5.24). Such a sense recalls the biblical idiom of bread that comes to Israel from the LORD God (Exod. 16:4; Ps. 105:40; Neh. 9:15) and the Johannine locution of bread come (down) from heaven (John 6:32–33, 41).

While Hultgren believes that his explanation is the simplest and best able to account for some others, he concedes that it does not solve a basic puzzle: if that is what the evangelists meant, why didn't they say it with everyday Greek participles (*ton eperchomenon*; *ton epionta*) that would have clarified their intent? Hultgren's hypothesis seems also to yield a rather tautologous petition: "Give us what is coming to us."

Assessment

In current scholarship the last three alternatives have fewer advocates than the first three, and among that trio I can discern no irrefutable favorite. The plain facts are two: not only do we remain unsure of what *ton epiousion* in Matthew 6:11a = Luke 11:3a means; we also lack the resources to solve the riddle. Others are better capable than I of constructing a more sophisticated linguistic argument for one alternative or another, but I am morally certain that they are less adept at the nuances, both strictures and flexibility, of Koine Greek than Origen, his predecessors, and his contemporaries. If the conundrum was beyond their ability to unravel, it is a safe bet that we shall be no more successful. Rightly or wrongly, Matthew and Luke assumed that their audiences could make clear sense of that adjective. We no longer can.

For argument's sake, let us suppose that scholars *could* formulate knockdown proof of, say, the first or third alternatives we have mentioned: "needful bread" or "bread for the day coming." Would that constitute a compelling reason to train everyday Christians to pray the petition in that way, requiring them to give up "daily bread"? I think not. Tyndale may have hit upon a rendering that was the best compromise among competing ambiguities: unless we construe it as needlessly redundant of the adverbial constructions in Matthew 6:11 ("this day") and Luke 11:3 ("each day"), "daily" implies, in English, something needed right away. That implication

156

embraces most of the linguistic nuances of *epiousios* that we have parsed in Greek. One may pray for "daily bread" with greater sensitivity to the adjective's subtleties. One needn't pretzel one's brains to satisfy modern linguists unable to arrive at consensus.

The Pronouns

The remaining words of this petition appear in both Matthew and Luke's version of the Prayer, are among the easiest to translate, and are all the more significant for hiding in plain sight: "Give to us [*hēmin*] our [*hēmōn*] bread." Not "me" and "mine," but "us" and "our." Those forms match all of the Prayer's other first-person pronouns: they are always presented in the plural, not in the singular.

Simple grammar can communicate intricate ideas: we are connected with one another, and all are bound to God. Indeed, the priority should be reversed: "only if [God] 'gives' *can* the people give, and only if [God] motivates their hearts *will* they give" (Betz, *Sermon on the Mount*, 379). Twenty-first-century Western culture both obscures and spotlights that interdependency. According to one estimate (Smith, *Lord's Prayer*, 78), 90 percent of American laborers made their living by farming in 1800; even city dwellers like teachers, clergy, and lawyers owned farms. In a 2000 census only 0.5 percent of respondents listed farming as their occupation. Still, before making its way to bakers, the bread that rests on our tables has been touched by the hands of farmers who plant and harvest the grain, millers who grind it into flour, miners who quarry salt, plumbers who conduct water to kitchens, and electricians who power modern ovens. If purchased from a grocery, bread has also been inspected, sliced, wrapped, and shipped by way of vehicles on roadways we ourselves haven't built. Viewed within that network of cooperative generosity, "Gimme a slice of bread" lands on the ear with the thud of thoughtless, selfish, and obscene ingratitude. (For patristic reflections in this vein, see Brown, *"Panem Nostrum."*)

In biblical perspective agriculture, economy, and spirituality are inseparable: all are mixed together, because everything finally comes from God, who "makes his sun rise on the evil and on the good, and sends rain on the righteous and on the unrighteous" (Matt. 5:45). Without sun and rain and grain, the farmer can do

157

nothing. All go back to God, whose benevolence to all invites thanks and elicits responsibility: "If you then, who are evil, know how to give good gifts to your children, how much more will your Father in heaven give good things to those who ask him!" (Matt. 7:11 = Luke 11:13). (In Latin a "companion" is, literally, someone with whom you share bread.) Nowhere in the Gospels is Jesus depicted as eating alone. Repeatedly he dines in the company of others, many of whom are unsavory (Matt. 9:10–13 = Mark 2:15–17 = Luke 5:29–32; Matt. 26:6–13 = Mark 14:3–9 = Luke 7:36–50; Luke 11:37–44). Jesus does not feed himself, not even after forty days of fasting (Matt. 4:1–4 = Luke 4:1–4); he feeds others (Matt. 26:17–19 = Mark 14:12–16 = Luke 22:7–13), sometimes by the thousands (Matt. 14:15–21 = Mark 6:35–44 = Luke 9:12–17; Matt. 15:32–39 = Mark 8:1–10).

> Happy are those whose help is the God of Jacob,
>   whose hope is in the LORD their God,
> who made heaven and earth,
>   the sea, and all that is in them;
> who keeps faith forever;
>   who executes justice for the oppressed;
>   who gives food to the hungry. (Ps. 146:5–7)

The LORD God models for us nourishment indivisible from justice. Thus runs a Latin American prayer before meals: "O God, to those who have hunger give bread; and to those who have bread give the hunger for justice" (Stendahl, "Your Kingdom Come," 263).

The plural pronouns in the Prayer's fourth petition point us toward thanking God and sharing bread with those who pray alongside us. Meister Eckhart (1260–1328) observed, "They who do not give to another what belongs to the other are not eating their own bread, but are eating both their bread and the other's" (*Sermon* 35.14, AT). That point is underscored by an old tale told to me by a Korean student: A person, recently deceased, was shown visions of hell and of heaven. Hell's occupants were seated at an endless table, groaning with food but supplied with six-foot chopsticks. All were starving in misery because the implements were too long to manipulate. Heaven's residents reclined at an infinite table, topped with the same food and utensils, but all were satisfied and joyous. What made the difference? "In heaven," said an angel, "we feed one another."

158

Lunch with Miss Burgess

M. F. K. Fisher (1908–92) was asked why she wrote twenty-seven books and hundreds of articles on cooking instead of important subjects, like power or love.

> The easiest answer is to say that, like most humans, I am hungry. But there is more than that. It seems to me that our three basic needs, for food and security and love, are so mixed and mingled and entwined that we cannot straightly think of one without the others. So it happens that when I write of hunger, I am really writing about love and the hunger for it, and warmth and the love of it and the hunger for it, . . . and then the warmth and richness and fine reality of hunger satisfied, . . . and it is all one. (*Art of Eating*, 363)

When we think straightly about the Lord's Prayer, we think of bread, yes, but also of love and warmth and generosity. Jesus' parable of Lazarus and the rich man hammers the point painfully: to ignore those starving at our feet is a ticket to torment in Hades, with a wide view of unreachable blessedness (Luke 16:19–31). The story of Agatha Burgess flips that parable.

In the latter decades of the twentieth century, Charles Kuralt (1934–97), a correspondent for CBS News, introduced Americans to ordinary people who lived at peace with their neighbors, helping one another along with a good deal of fairness and human decency. One of the most memorable was Agatha Burgess (1902–92), a widow who lived on a hill above Buffalo, South Carolina (population, 1,266 [2010]). At the age of eighty she was up every morning at five o'clock, cooking. After her corn muffins were in the oven, she checked the dressing for the turkey, then started on the biscuits. Then came the turkey, gravy, rice, fresh corn, green beans, and peach cobbler. By eleven o'clock volunteers arrived to load up Meals on Wheels for distribution to shut-ins she didn't know. By noon cars and trucks began pulling up. All sorts of people crowded into Miss Burgess's kitchen and dining room: mill workers, truck drivers, judges, and the owner of the Ford dealership. She welcomed everyone who came to her door, invited them to fill their plates, to go back for seconds if they wished, and asked them to put $2.75 in a box. If that was more than they could afford, she fed them free of charge. Afterward she washed the dishes, started

159

baking for the next day, and didn't go to bed until ten o'clock that night.

Agatha Burgess did this every day, five days a week, for over fifteen years. She told Kuralt, "I'm not out to make money. I don't have any money, but I'm not making any money." "Well, then," he asked her, "why do you keep doing it?" Here's what she said:

> I love it. This guy asked me the other day, he said, "Miss Burgess, why don't you stop and rest?" I said, "What would I have to live for?" Wouldn't have anything to live for. Because these people coming every day, they mean so much to me. I just fall in love with people. . . . I always wanted to be a person that lived by the side of the road, and be a friend to man. I have always wanted that. I've never wanted a big, fine home, I'm just satisfied like I am. I know you probably have a big, fine home—I don't want your big, fine home—I'm glad you got it. And I can enjoy and just be happy that you have it. But me, I'm fine. Got what I want. I always get everything I want—but I know *what* to want. (Kuralt, *On the Road*, 26, 28)

It all depends on whom you love, what you want, and how your wants have been educated.

Works Cited in Chapter 6

Betz, Hans Dieter. *The Sermon on the Mount: A Commentary on the Sermon on the Mount, including the Sermon on the Plain (Matthew 5:3–7:27 and Luke 6:29–49)*. Edited by Adela Yarbro Collins. Hermeneia. Minneapolis: Fortress Press, 1995.

Black, Matthew. "The Aramaic of *ton arton hēmōn ton epiousion* (Matt. vi.11 = Luke xi.3)." *Journal of Theological Studies* 42 (1941): 186–89.

Brown, Michael Joseph. "*Panem Nostrum*: The Problem of Petition and the Lord's Prayer." *Journal of Religion* 80 (2000): 595–614.

Burkert, Walter. *Ancient Mystery Cults*. Cambridge, MA: Harvard University Press, 1987.

Carmignac, Jean. *Recherches sur le "Notre Père."* Paris: Letouzey & Ané, 1969.

Day, C. "In Search of the Meaning of *epiousios* in the Lord's Prayer: Rounding Up the Usual Suspects." *Acta Patristica et Byzantina* 14 (2003): 97–111.

Ebeling, Gerhard. *On Prayer: Nine Sermons*. Translated by James W. Leitch. Philadelphia: Fortress Press, 1966.

Fisher, M. F. K. *The Art of Eating*. 50th Anniversary Edition. Hoboken, NJ: Wiley Pub., 2004.

Foerster, Werner. *"epiousios." TDNT* 2 (1964): 590–99.

Grumett, David. "Give Us This Day Our Supersubstantial Bread." *Studia Liturgica* 36 (2006): 201–11.

Hallo, William H., and K. Lawson Younger Jr., eds. *The Context of Scripture*. 3 vols. New York: E. J. Brill, 1997.

Hemer, Colin J. *"epiousios." Journal for the Study of the New Testament* 22 (1984): 81–94.

Heschel, Abraham J. *Man Is Not Alone: A Philosophy of Religion*. New York: Farrar, Straus & Young, 1951.

Hultgren, Arland J. "The Bread Petition of the Lord's Prayer." *Anglican Theological Review* 11 (1990): 41–54.

Jeremias, Joachim. *New Testament Theology: The Proclamation of Jesus*. New York: Charles Scribner's Sons, 1971.

Kierkegaard, Søren. *The Lily of the Field and the Bird of the Air: Three Godly Discourses*. Translated by Bruce H. Kirmmse. Princeton, NJ: Princeton University Press, 2016.

Kuralt, Charles. *On the Road with Charles Kuralt*. New York: G. P. Putnam's Sons, 1985.

Lachs, Samuel Tobias. *A Rabbinic Commentary on the New Testament: The Gospels of Matthew, Mark, and Luke*. Hoboken, NJ: Ktav; New York: Anti-Defamation League of B'nai B'rith, 1987.

LaVerdiere, Eugene A. "Give Us Each Day Our Daily Bread." In *Bread from Heaven*, edited by Paul Bernier, 19–33. New York: Paulist Press, 1977.

Lewis, C. S., ed. *George MacDonald: An Anthology*. New York: Simon & Schuster, 1996.

Lightfoot, Joseph Barber. *On a Fresh Revision of the English New Testament*. 2nd ed. New York: Macmillan, 1872.

Lochman, Jan Milič. *The Lord's Prayer*. Translated by Geoffrey W. Bromiley. Grand Rapids: Wm. B. Eerdmans Publishing Co., 1990.

Lohmeyer, Ernst. *"Our Father": An Introduction to the Lord's Prayer*. Translated by John Bowden. London: William Collins & Sons, 1965.

Metzger, Bruce M. "How Many Times Does 'Epiousios' Occur outside the Lord's Prayer?" *Expository Times* 69 (1957–58): 52–54.

Montefiore, Claude G., and Herbert Loewe. *A Rabbinic Anthology*. New York: Schocken Books, 1974.

Murray, Paul. *Praying with Confidence: Aquinas on the Lord's Prayer*. London: Continuum, 2010.

Smith, J. Warren. *The Lord's Prayer: Confessing the New Covenant*. Cascade Books. Eugene, OR: Wipf & Stock, 2015.

Stegemann, Ekkehard T., and Wolfgang Stegemann. *The Jesus Movement: A First Century of Its Social History*. Minneapolis: Fortress Press, 2001.

Stendahl, Krister. "Your Kingdom Come." *Cross Currents* 32 (1982): 257–66.

Strack, Hermann L., and Paul Billerbeck. *Kommentar zum Neuen Testament aus Talmud und Midrasch*. 4 vols. Munich: Beck, 1978.

Wainwright, Geoffrey. *Eucharist and Eschatology*. New York: Oxford University Press, 1981.

Willard, Dallas. *The Divine Conspiracy: Rediscovering Our Hidden Life in God*. San Francisco: Harper, 1998.

Wolff, Hans Walter. *Anthropology of the Old Testament*. Translated by Margaret Kohl. Philadelphia: Fortress Press, 1974.

Wright, David F. "What Kind of 'Bread'? The Fourth Petition of the Lord's Prayer from the Fathers to the Reformers." In *Oratio: Das Gebet in patristischer und reformatorischer Sicht*, edited by Emidio Campi, Leif Grane, and Adolf Martin Ritter, 151–61. Göttingen: Vandenhoeck & Ruprecht, 1999.

Wright, N. T. *The Lord and His Prayer*. Grand Rapids and Cincinnati: Wm. B. Eerdmans / Forward Movement, 1997.

Young, Brad. *The Jewish Background to the Lord's Prayer*. Austin, TX: Center for Judaic-Christian Studies, 1984.

CHAPTER 7

Debts and Forgiveness

Ah, if we could view with angelic sight these maimed human beings!
—Georges Bernanos

And forgive unto us our <u>debts</u>,
    <u>As</u> we, too, have forgiven those indebted to us. (Matt. 6:12 AT)
And forgive unto us our <u>sins</u>,
    <u>For</u> we, too, forgive everyone indebted to us. (Luke 11:4ab AT)

For the first time in the Prayer, a petition begins with a conjunction (*kai*, "and"), which returns in the final petition (Matt. 6:13 = Luke 11:4c). Thus links are forged between the three "we-petitions" for daily nourishment, release, and rescue.

Translating the Texts

The wording of the Lord's Prayer's fifth petition differs in Matthew and in Luke. In both clauses the main Greek verb is the same: *aphiēmi*, "to let go" (Matt. 27:50), "release" (John 11:48), "remit," "cancel," or "pardon" (Matt. 18:27; Luke 12:10; Rom. 4:7; 1 John 2:12). The verb is differently cast in the Prayer's two forms. In both Matthew and Luke an aorist imperative (*aphes*) controls the first clause, indicating a plea that the release be firm and whole. This request is balanced by the same verb, presented in the perfect

163

indicative in Matthew (*aphēkamen*, "we have forgiven") and in the present indicative in Luke (*aphiomen*, "we forgive" or "we are forgiving"). The difference in meaning is subtle. In Matthew, disciples claim already to have pardoned others, and that pardon remains in force. In Luke, Jesus' followers assert that, in the moment of appealing for their own pardon, they are releasing all others from what is due to them. In Aramaic the form *shebaqnan*, which could have underlain both Greek translations, is indeterminate in tense and may be rendered in either the Greek present or aorist tense.

Matthew refers to those debtors with a present participle of the basic verb: *tois opheiletais*, "the ones indebted [to us]." Luke also uses a substantive participle, differently cast: *panti opheilonti*, "everyone indebted [to us]." This difference lacks meaningful distinction. Matthew's terminology implies all debtors; Luke's wording is cast in a singular number, specifying "each." Depending on context the adjective *pas* may be translated as "every" (Matt. 3:10) or "all" (Matt. 3:5). Luke's phrasing clarifies what Matthew's suggests: we cancel the debts of all who are in our debt. In the petition's second clause both evangelists present a second *kai*, here used as an adverb qualifying the subject: "we also" or "likewise" (Matt. 5:39–40) or "even we" (Matt. 5:46–47) have forgiven/forgive.

Major variations between Matthew's and Luke's versions of this petition have been underlined in my translations above. The first is fairly easy to explain; the second is more difficult. Because the metaphor of indebtedness appears in the second clause of both versions, it may be that Matthew's reference to "debts" in the first clause recalls Jesus' own mode of expression. In Aramaic *khōbā'* carries a double meaning, "debt" and "sin," a spin-off from Hebrew phrasing: "For I will forgive their iniquities, and remember their sins no more" (Jer. 31:34b NJPS; cf. Isa. 40:2). In some Dead Sea Scrolls, *khōbā'* is a common synonym for "sin" (Fitzmyer, *Luke*, 906). In Greek, however, *to opheilēma* does not naturally suggest "sin"; it is a term operative in the world of economic contracts. "Wages are not reckoned as a gift but as something due [*kata opheilēma*]" (Rom. 4:4; see also Luke 7:41; 16:5, 7; Phlm. 18). A modern analogy is that of a loan or mortgage issued on an automobile or house: until the payoff, we are in debt to the bank without "sinning" against it. In general Luke appears to have been writing for an audience acquainted with Jewish Scripture and synagogue but not steeped in that culture to the degree of Matthew's readers. Accordingly, Luke

164

may have introduced the term "sins" (*tas hamartias*, "missing the mark," "errors," "faults," "failures") in 11:4a, then paraphrased it as "that which is forgiven" in 11:4b. This exemplifies a contradiction exhibited by the New Testament's different versions of the Lord's Prayer, which we noted in chapter 2 (above): while Matthew's longer presentation appears to be a secondary elaboration of Luke's simpler form, Matthew's phraseology may have been closer to Jesus' Aramaic antecedent than Luke's.

Many readers may wonder about a familiar, alternative English version of this petition: "Forgive us our *trespasses*, as we forgive those who *trespass* against us." Why the shift in metaphor, from loans to territorial encroachment? The introduction of "trespasses" is traceable to William Tyndale's influential translation of 1525. Until then early English versions variously conveyed the idea of *debita nostra* ("our debts" in the Latin Vulgate): "scylda" (Anglo-Saxon, of unknown etymology), "all that we haue don" (early Middle English), "misdedis" (= "misdeeds"; late 12th c.), "dettouris" ("detours": Wycliffe's version, 1380), "dettes" (Cranmer's Great Bible of 1539). With Tyndale, "trespasses" (spelled "treaspases": literally, "treasonous paces") enters the tradition, probably by way of Matthew 6:14–15, which in that Gospel immediately follows the Lord's Prayer: "For if you forgive others their trespasses [*ta paraptōmata*: "false steps" or "wrongdoings"], your heavenly Father will also forgive you; but if you do not forgive others, neither will your Father forgive your trespasses." Once inserted, Tyndale's interpretive decision influenced successive translations, especially in England: the primer of Henry VIII (1545: "trespaces") and the first Prayer Book of Edward VI (1549: "trespaces"). Reverting to the precedent set by the Great Bible, which adheres more closely to the Greek in Matthew 6:12a, the King James Version (1611) translated the petition, "And forgive us our debts, as we forgive our debtors," which was reiterated in the Revised (1952) and New Revised (1989) Standard Versions. Liturgical use of "trespasses" in modern, English-speaking congregations is a throwback to the Church of England's Book of Common Prayer (1559), which to the present day has perpetuated the version of the Prayer established in the Prayer Book of Edward VI. (For further discussion see Ayo, *Lord's Prayer*, 221–39.)

165

The most difficult exegetical problem raised by Matthew 6:12b = Luke 11:4b lies in their tiny conjunctive particles: *hōs*, "as" (Matthew), and *gar*, "for" (Luke). Some kind of comparison or qualitative correlation is being established between this petition's first clause (referring to God's forgiveness) and its second (pertaining to our own forgiving). The exact nature of that correspondence is hard to determine. To this question we shall return momentarily. Before doing so, we need to locate the Prayer's fifth plea in the larger context of Jesus' teaching.

Sin and the Synoptic Jesus

Those who pray the Lord's Prayer may offer its plea for forgiveness without considering its peculiarities in their Gospel contexts. Jesus' teaching in Matthew and Luke exercises a wide vocabulary of sin: *hē hamartia* (missing the mark, failure), *hē opheilē* (indebtedness), *hē adikia* (injustice, crookedness), *hē ponēria* (wickedness), *to paraptōma* (transgression), *hē anomia* (lawless disposition), or *hē kakia* (evil). Of all the Synoptics, Mark mentions sin the least (*hē hamartia* or its cognates: 1:4, 5; 2:5, 7, 9, 10, 15, 16, 17; 3:28; 8:38; 14:41; *ponēros* or *ponēria*: 7:22 [twice], 23; *ta paraptōmata*: 11:25). The Synoptics advert to disobedience without employing these terms (Matt. 3:7–10 = Luke 3:7–9; Matt. 4:1–11 = Luke 4:1–13) or by using more attenuated synonyms, like "stumbling" (*skandalizein*; see below). All in all, it is surprising just how little the Synoptic Gospels, comprising over one-third of the New Testament, refer to sin by one term or another: by my reckoning, 136 times. By no means do they neglect the subject; neither, however, do they belabor it. That Jesus drew attention to sin in the prayer he taught his disciples is noteworthy.

This contextual analysis may be fine-tuned. In many ways Jesus' teaching about sin in the Synoptics deviates from or downplays important aspects of its presentation in the Old Testament. Apart from warning his disciples away from mammon (Matt. 6:24 = Luke 16:13) he never castigates idolatry, Israel's worship of false gods (cf. 1 Sam. 15:23; 2 Chr. 33:7; Isa. 40:19; Jer. 18:15; Ezek. 23:49; Hos. 10:6). Unlike the prophets, Jesus never accuses Israel of violating its covenant with the LORD God (Isa. 24:5; Jer. 11:10; 22:9; Ezek. 17:18–19; Hos. 8:1; Mal. 2:5–10; cf. Ps. 78:10, 37). Luke (3:38) notes Adam among Jesus' ancestry, but Adam's primordial sin (Gen. 3:1–21) is never mentioned (cf. Rom. 5:14; 1 Cor. 15:22).

No distinction is suggested between willful and unwitting sins (cf. Lev. 4–5; Num. 15). Jesus neither accuses his listeners of forsaking God (Deut. 31:16; 2 Chr. 7:19; Ps. 119:53; Isa. 1:28; Jonah 2:8) nor warns them away from rebellion against the Almighty (cf. Exod. 23:21; Josh. 22:18–19; 1 Sam. 12:14–15; Isa. 1:20; Jer. 28:16; 48:8; Hos. 7:14). Nowhere in Jesus' teaching do we find anything like the harrowing diagnosis of Israel's chronic sins in Psalm 106:6–47. The nearest intersections between Jesus' allusions and Old Testament metaphors lie in his address of his generation as "adulterous," or unfaithful (Matt. 12:39; 16:4; Mark 8:38; cf. Exod. 34:15–16; Isa. 1:21; Ezek. 16:32; Hos. 4:10–15), and his warnings against "tripping up" others (Matt. 18:1–10 = Mark 9:42–50 = Luke 17:1–4; cf. Prov. 4:19; Jer. 18:15; Mal. 2:8). As Elijah reborn (Mark 6:14–29; cf. 1 Kgs. 18–21), blasting Israel's arrogance and summoning its repentance (Matt. 3:1–10; Luke 3:3–14), John the Baptist is more obviously reminiscent of the Old Testament prophets than is Jesus (cf. Matt. 16:13–16 = Mark 8:27–29 = Luke 9:18–20).

The simplest explanation for what we see is aligned with the Lord's Prayer itself—Jesus' concentration on *hē basileia tou theou*: God's kingdom, reign, and sovereign governance. God's sovereignty, instantiated by Jesus, is God's merciful power to rectify a corrupted creation, to put in right relationship with God all that has been fractured and divorced from its Creator. (See chap. 5 above.) Although Torah is concordant with the kingdom's demands (Matt. 22:35–40; Luke 16:17), the kingdom, as interpreted by Jesus, also explodes some commandments (Matt. 5:38–39, 43–44) or drives more deeply to the heart of their intent (Matt. 19:3–9 = Mark 10:2–12 = Luke 16:18). In the Synoptics "the kingdom of God" occupies the centrality of "covenant" in the Old Testament's prophetic and Deuteronomic traditions. For that reason the dynamic of human response is reoriented: instead of looking *backward* toward Mount Sinai, repenting of failure or refusal to maintain covenant fidelity, the believer is called by Jesus to live *forward* into God's new, invasive claim upon a creation whose divine reclamation is in progress. "The law and the prophets were in effect until John came; since then the good news of the kingdom of God is proclaimed, and everyone is pressed into it" (Luke 16:16 AT). In simple terms the prophets and John preached: Repent of your sins, and God will save you. Jesus affirmed God's preexisting mercy, *prior to* repentance, as the motive power for living in accordance with God's righteous kingdom. The punch line of a pronouncement story in John's Gospel epitomizes the position of the Synoptic Jesus: "Neither do I condemn thee: go, and sin no more" (John 8:11 KJV).

Jesus extends the hospitality of God's kingdom to all, pious Simon (Luke 7:36–50) and double-dealing Zacchaeus alike (19:1–10). Yet sinners who recognize themselves as such possess an odd advantage: *the Christ of the Synoptics fraternizes with sinners and welcomes them into the kingdom.*

> And as he sat at dinner in the house, many tax collectors and sinners came and were sitting with him and his disciples. When the Pharisees saw this, they said to his disciples, "Why does your teacher eat with tax collectors and sinners?" But when he heard this, he said, "Those who are well have no need of a physician, but those who are sick. Go and learn what this means, 'I desire mercy, not sacrifice.'" (Matt. 9:10–13a = Mark 2:16–17a = Luke 5:29–31)

Jesus could not have stated the gist more plainly: "I have come to call not the righteous but sinners" (Mark 2:17b = Matt. 9:13b = Luke 5:32).

The converse also applies: sin's deepest infestation is among self-righteous hypocrites who parade their religiosity or superior discernment (Matt. 6:16–18; 7:1–5 = Luke 6:41–42; Matt. 23:27–36). They do not avail themselves of God's mercy because they cannot recognize in themselves the failure (*hamartia*) or malice (*ponēria*) that they readily ascribe to others. "You are those who justify yourselves in the sight of others; but God knows your hearts; for what is prized by human beings is an abomination in the sight of God" (Luke 16:15). "Truly I tell you, the tax collectors and the prostitutes are going into the kingdom of God ahead of you" (Matt. 21:31b). No group or class is insulated from self-delusion about its sin. It besets Jesus' disciples (Matt. 25:14–30 = Luke 19:11–27; Matt. 25:31–46) and also his adversaries (Matt. 9:1–8 = Mark 2:1–12 = Luke 5:17–26; Matt. 12:1–15 = Mark 2:23–3:6 = Luke 6:1–11). Jesus' fellow Jews are not inherently superior to Gentiles: Jewish cities may be less repentant than their pagan neighbors (Matt. 11:20–24 = Luke 10:13–15).

No pattern pertaining to sin and salvation is more recurrent in the Synoptics than this: mercy for sinners, judgment of the self-satisfied. Jesus' welcome of those considered flagrantly wicked appears to have been a genuine, understandable bone of contention between him and his more conventionally pious Jewish contemporaries. For those in the first or twenty-first century, conditioned by Scripture to separate themselves from contamination by the wicked until they have mended their ways (Num. 16:26; 2 Chr. 7:14; Prov. 15:29; Isa. 26:10; Ezek. 33:8; 1 Cor. 5:13; 2 Tim. 3:13, among hundreds of examples), Jesus' attitude and actions remain scandalous (see Black, "Sin in the Synoptic Gospels").

Viewed in this context, the wording of the fifth petition of the Lord's Prayer is astonishingly simple: please release us from our sins. By comparison, consider the high-strung prayers of the synagogue, some contemporaneous with Jesus (see appendix A):

> Turn us back to you, O Lord, and we shall return. . . .
> Forgive us, our Father, for we have sinned against You.
> Blot out and remove our transgressions from before Your sight. . . .
>   (the Amidah's 5th and 6th benedictions)

> Our Father, Our King, we have sinned before You. . . .
> Our Father, Our King, rend from us the evil judgment decreed
>   against us.
> Our Father, Our King, erase the records of our guilt.
> Our Father, Our King, pardon and forgive our iniquities.
> Our Father, Our King, blot out our transgressions,
>   and make them pass away from Your sight.
> Our Father, Our King, let us return in perfect repentance
>   before You.
>   (Abhinu Malkenu, petitions 1, 13–17)

Alternatively, consider the prolonged wailing over human iniquity, the relentless breast-beatings, found in the 1559 Elizabethan Prayer Book (Book of Common Prayer), in a confession preparatory for approaching the Lord's Table for Holy Communion:

> Almighty God, Father of our Lord Jesus Christ, maker of all things, judge of all men, we [ac]knowledge and bewail our manifold sins and wickedness, which we from time to time most grievously have committed, by thought, word, and deed, against thy divine majesty, provoking most justly thy wrath and indignation against us. We do earnestly repent, and be heartily sorry for these our misdoings. The remembrance of them is grievous unto us,

169

the burden of them is intolerable. Have mercy upon us, have mercy upon us most merciful Father, for thy Son our Lord Jesus Christ's sake; forgive us all that is past, and grant that we may ever hereafter serve and please thee, in newness of life, to the honor and glory of thy name, through Jesus Christ our Lord. Amen. (*Book of Common Prayer 1559*, 259–60)

In the prayer that Jesus taught his disciples, the matter is far more cut and dried. We sin. We need for our sins to be canceled. We ask to be released. In this simplicity is marvelous comfort. It is not as though we must somehow attain a depth of religiosity before we are worthy to pray. When confessing our sins to God, we are not informing the Almighty of something God does not already know about us. *God is already with us when we make our confession.* In the very act of confessing our sin, in offering the prayer itself, God is educating our desire that we know ourselves and be known by God as we really are, warts and all, and to be released from all futile strategies of self-concealment.

Debt in Antiquity

The Prayer's description of sin *as debt* is curious. That figure of speech is rare in the Synoptics: from among their nineteen references to indebtedness only ten refer or allude to sin in Matthew (6:12 [twice]; 18:24, 28 [twice], 32) and Luke (7:41 [twice]; 11:4b; 13:4). This phenomenon is especially surprising in Luke, whose dominant metaphor for salvation is the complementary metaphor, "forgiveness" (1:77; 3:3; 5:20, 21, 23, 24; 6:37; 7:47, 48; 11:4; 12:10; 17:3, 4; 23:34; 24:47; Acts 5:31; 10:43; 13:38; 26:18). What special connotation of sin is conveyed by "debt"? To answer that question, a detour into the world of ancient economy is necessary.

Debt in the Greco-Roman World

While our sources on the subject are not plentiful, we know that debt was as much a concern in antiquity as in our own day. Its characteristics were differently tinted. During the centuries immediately before Christ, some Greek cities borrowed money for municipal projects, but such loans appear to have been occasional

170

(Migeotte, *L'Emprunt public*, 357–401). In the realm of public policy, the Roman Empire and its constituent cities avoided indebtedness as much as possible. A major exception occurred during Rome's wars against Carthage (264–146 BC), which were heavily funded by obligatory but purportedly refundable taxes of Roman citizens. During 91–81 BC a concentrated series of foreign and civil wars plunged Rome into social chaos, which in the year 86 led to a massive program of debt restructure and, for the first and evidently final time, a cancellation of a high percentage of imperial debt (Appian, *Civil Wars* 1.102).

Other causes of debt in Roman society were private. Issuing, receiving, and repaying loans greased the imperial economy: for their survival both aristocrats and those of lesser means depended on the risky beneficence of patrons, friends, and even children (Tacitus, *Annals* 11.21; Suetonius, *Life of Augustus* 39; see Saller, *Personal Patronage*, 119–22; Rowlandson, *Women and Society*, 116–17, 131–32). On the other hand, indebtedness generated economic turbulence within or between different social classes. Outstanding loans and unpaid taxes accounted for most personal debts. Though it sometimes canceled tax arrears, the Roman government was loath to erase debts between individuals, opting instead to adjudicate redistribution of a debtor's assets or the sale of estates (Tacitus, *Annals* 1.76.4; 2.42.8; Dio Cassius, *Roman History* 72.32). Privileged members of Roman society—senators, equestrians, local nobles, or other dignitaries who owned land, livestock, houses, and objets d'art—precipitated the harshest debt crises. Some had built their fortunes by borrowing, others by lending, still others by doing both. Owing to trade deficits, poor harvests, military destruction of property, and contractions in money supply created by anxious creditors or debtors, the indebted elite defaulted on their loans (Dio Cassius, *Roman History* 41.38.1–2). When that happened, economic consequences trickled up and down. Selling off assets or breaking up estates impugned their owners' rank and reputation (Sallust, *Catiline Conspiracy* 35.3–4). By trying to sell their land, the indebted wealthy immediately drove down its price (Valerius Maximus, *Memorable Deeds* 4.8.3).

Another cause of default was high interest on loans, which Tacitus (ca. 58–ca. 120) criticized as "an ingrained evil in the city of Rome, a frequent cause of sedition and discord, strongly disapproved" (*Annals* 6.16.1). All the same, lending with interest,

171

whether in cash or in kind, appears to have been widely practiced among those with the resources to support its practice.

If indebtedness among the upper class was an occupational hazard, it was a continual way of life for the vast majority of the Roman Empire's populace: farmers and sharecroppers, laborers, artisans, and small marketers. Most of them lived only one ruined harvest away from peasant insolvency. In that event the consequence could be *nexum*, "debt bondage," by which the bankrupt debtor was convicted and awarded to his creditor as a serf. If he was a Roman citizen, he could not be sold as chattel and removed from his own territory, but his freedom was sacrificed. By 326 BC debt bondage had aggravated a degree of social turmoil so high that it was legally abolished for Roman citizens, though not for those lacking that status (Josephus, *Jewish War* 7.60–61). The threat of forced servitude lingered over Roman military veterans, some of whose pensions were modest gifts of conquered territory. If they were driven into bankruptcy, a cruel creditor could, in theory at least, force former legion commanders to work his land until compensation was realized (Sallust, *Catiline Conspiracy* 33).

Debt among Israelites and Jews

Regulations of debt and repayment differed in ancient Israel and early Judaism. The general principle was the same: the lender expected repayment of a loan (Deut. 23:21). Whereas Greco-Roman legislation was skewed in the creditor's favor, Jewish law was biased toward the debtor's protection. "You shall not subvert the rights of the stranger or the fatherless. . . . Remember that you were a slave in Egypt and that the LORD your God redeemed you from there; therefore do I enjoin you to observe this commandment" (Deut. 24:17–18 NJPS; cf. Lev. 19:34). A conspicuous example of favor toward the vulnerable was the legally mandated Sabbatical Year: after every seven years all debts were canceled (Deut. 15:1–18; also Exod. 21:2–16; 23:10–11; Lev. 25:2–7), freeing the poor from interminable indebtedness (see Reimer, "Forgiveness of Debts").

The Torah, especially Leviticus (25:35–54), encourages loans of food or of money in support of the needy, with the aim of enabling them to escape perpetual poverty and helpless dependence on those more economically stable. Evidently the practice of a secured loan, with collateral, was recognized, because some biblical texts prohibit the acceptance as security of particular items, such as a protective garment (Deut. 24:12–13, 17) or a millstone (24:6), whose relinquishment could endanger the debtor's life or livelihood. Debt bondage of one Jew to another is expressly forbidden on theological grounds:

> If your kinsman under you continues in straits and must give himself over to you, do not subject him to the treatment of a slave. He shall remain with you as a hired or bound laborer; he shall serve with you only until the jubilee year. Then he and his children with him shall be free of your authority; he shall go back to his family and return to his ancestral holding.—For they are My servants, whom I freed from the land of Egypt; they may not give themselves over into servitude.—You shall not rule over him ruthlessly; you shall fear your God. (Lev. 25:39–43 NJPS)

Israelites could hold as transferrable property foreigners, slaves "from the nations round about you," since they stood outside the bounds of the covenant community (Lev. 25:44–46 NJPS). Nevertheless, a story told about Elisha is premised on a creditor's threat to seize the children of an Israelite widow as slaves, in default of a loan's repayment (2 Kgs. 4:1–7).

The question of interest charged on a loan is complicated in Scripture and became even more so in the Mishnah and Talmud. A cardinal principle was proscription of interest on a loan made by one Jew to another (Exod. 22:25–27; Lev. 25:35–37; Deut. 23:20). Ezekiel is adamant that exacting accrued interest on a loan is a capital crime (Ezek. 18:5–18; cf. *b. Baba Metzi'a* 61b). An assertion so extreme suggests that, at some times and in some places, usury was a serious problem, as corroborated by Nehemiah's attempt to eradicate it (5:1–13).

The ideal of lending without interest appears to have been anomalous among other ancient Near Eastern cultures. Among Mesopotamians, Hittites, Phoenicians, and Egyptians, interest rates appear to have been legally fixed, ranging from 10 to 15 percent on loans of silver, 20 to 35 percent for grains. The Babylonian Talmud (*Baba Batra* 60a) refers to ancient Babylonian loans issued at an annual interest rate of 20 percent. The justification for charging interest on so-called food money—seeds, olives, animals—was that, because animate matter was capable of reproducing itself, the

173

creditor was entitled to commensurate garnishment. Over time that entitlement was extended to monetary loans. The Mishnah, however, expressly prohibits interest and dividends drawn on such investments: income should be drawn from land and livestock, not from money itself. Jewish prohibition of interest charges was associated with the nature of loaning, which was intended, not as a business transaction, but as an act of kindness (Ps. 37:21; *m. 'Abot* 2.9).

Jewish law also recognized exceptions to the preceding, and some evasions can be documented. Interest-free loans were applied only to fellow Israelites, not to Gentiles: "You will extend loans to many nations, but require none yourself" (Deut. 15:6 NJPS). In later Mishnaic interpretation a Jewish lender could sidestep the prohibition against charging interest and realize a profit (*marbit* or *tarbit*) by upping the price (*neshekh*) of the loan before its delivery to the buyer. Another stratagem, which amounted to the same thing, was to lend someone an amount but to buy it back at a lower price (the secondary purchase being an independent transaction from the original loan). Two Jews could also use a Gentile as a third-party go-between: Aaron could float a loan to Alexander, with interest, which the Gentile then lent to Levi at the very same rate (*m. Baba Metzi'a* 5.6).

One of the most famous loopholes may be found in *m. Shebi'it* 10.3, attributed to Rabbi Hillel (ca. 110 BC–AD 10). The problem: creditors refused, or at least were reluctant, to lend money to the disadvantaged during the waning years of a seven-year sabbatical cycle (cf. Deut. 15:1–2). Because the lender knew that repayment of the loan was practically impossible within so brief a period, the loan was not issued at all. Hillel's solution was the *prozbul* (Heb., *parozvul*; Gk., *pros* + *boulē* = *prosbulē*, loosely translated as "referred to court"): allow the creditor to lend money interest-free to the needy with a writ transferring the loan to public courts, which were unconstrained by the law of automatic remission. So went the application: "I declare before you, judges in this place, that I shall collect my debt that I have outstanding with [X] whenever I desire" (*m. Shevi'it* 10.2; cf. *m. Gittin* 4.3). The happy result was win-win: satisfied that their loan was secure from sabbatical remission and, therefore, more likely to be repaid, creditors were encouraged to offer greater help to the needy before the Sabbatical Year. The less-than-happy outcome: subsequent rabbis disagreed whether Hillel had abrogated Torah's original intent. The *prozbul* is considered one of the earliest documented examples of a legal fiction (Lachs, "On Matthew VI.12").

Recently published papyri offer another angle of vision relevant to our study. Debt forgiveness and offers of amnesty appear to have been a prerogative, exercised by eastern Mediterranean rulers, to assure conquered peoples of their welfare and the new sovereign's philanthropy (Bazzana, "*Basileia* and Debt Relief").

> King Ptolemy and Queen Cleopatra the sister
> and Queen Cleopatra the wife proclaim an amnesty for
> all the subjects to their *basileia* for errors, crimes,
> accusations, condemnations, and charges of all kinds
>   up to the 9th of [the month of] Pharmouthi of the 52nd year,
> excepting the persons guilty of willful murder or sacrilege. . . .
> And they release everyone from debts for the period
> up to the 50th year in respect to the farming of the grain tax and the
>   money taxes, except for
> hereditary lessees who have given a surety. (trans. Bazzana, 517)

Closer to biblical home is an offer to conquered Israelites by the Seleucid king Demetrius:

> We have received the gold crown and the palm branch that you sent, and we are ready to make a general peace with you and to write to our officials to grant you release from tribute. All the grants that we have made to you remain valid, and let the strongholds that you have built be your possession. We pardon any errors and offenses committed to this day, and cancel the crown tax that you owe; and whatever other tax has been collected in Jerusalem shall be collected no longer. (1 Macc. 13:37–39)

Such diplomacy was strategic. In AD 66 Jewish revolutionaries torched the houses of Ananias the high priest and King Agrippa II in Jerusalem, which agitated a mob to "carry the fire to the archives, zealous to destroy the contracts of those who loaned money and to cancel the collection of debts" (Josephus, *Jewish War* 2.427–28, trans. Thackery, alt.). While the degree of debt in Galilee and Judea during the time of Jesus is contested (cf. Oakman, "Jesus and Agrarian Palestine"; Pastor, *Land and Economy*, 147–49; Fiensy, "Jesus and Debts"), indebtedness in the first century AD was serious for many, incendiary for a few. Within that harsh context the plea for debt forgiveness in the Lord's Prayer was an unusually evocative metaphor.

Structures of Indebtedness

Thinking Clearly about Forgiveness

Our excursion into social economics should help us straighten out the ways we have come to speak of forgiveness. Some are deeply confused and potentially quite harmful.

"Forget about it." Such dismissiveness may suit everyday pinpricks, but it is altogether inappropriate for serious violations. In economic terms this old saw makes no sense: one *cannot* forgive what has been forgotten, because the debt's cancellation depends on its remembrance. Psychologically regarded, some meanness or malice we have suffered or inflicted may be unforgettable: physical abuse, oppressive constraint, or unrepentant injustice. In extreme cases canceling such brutality from memory is ill advised, lest it be perpetuated or return in a different guise. The Holocaust and other heinous acts of ethnic genocide are prime examples. It is beyond human capacity to forget that which has crushed body or soul. As we shall see, it is possible to forgive it (Elizondo, "I Forgive but I Do Not Forget").

"It no longer hurts." One may deny the pain of injury, but psychologically and theologically that dodge is deceitful. Suppressed pain never dissipates; if anything, it grows in covert intensity. The lamenters of the Psalter may not be quick to forgive (12:3–4), but they are not hesitant to express their complainers' suffering (e.g., 3:1–2; 5:9–10; 22:1–2, 6–8, 12–21; 31:9–13; 38:1–17; 55:1–21; 69:1–3, 19–21; 88:1–18).

> How long, O LORD; will You ignore me forever?
> How long will You hide Your face from me?
> How long will I have cares on my mind, grief in my heart all day?
> How long will my enemy have the upper hand? (Ps. 13:2–3 NJPS)

Even the LORD God cries in anguish over Israel's betrayals before confessing that reprisal is not the last word (Hos. 2:1–13; 4:1–19; 6:4–6; 11:8–9). If voicing such agony is true of the Almighty, then how much truer for us? Absent a candid confession of trauma or grief, forgiveness is meaningless.

176

"We'll let it go this time." This, too, is a crummy denial of genuine harm. Often we concoct excuses for the inexcusable because of our naïveté or discomfort with confrontation. Jesus did not wink at

"evil thoughts, fornication, theft, murder, adultery, avarice, wickedness, deceit, licentiousness, envy, slander, pride, [and] folly" (Mark
7:21–23 AT, to which Matthew adds "false witness": 15:19). For
such rips in the social fabric there is no excuse: "All these evil things
come from within, and they defile a person" (Mark 7:23).

"I gave you a chance to make good." Placing an offender on
probation is a flimsy gambit; ultimately it does not qualify as forgiveness. We postpone our indignation until a later offense is committed or until our unresolved fury over its predecessor can no
longer be contained; then, after being disappointed, we withdraw
our clemency. "To grant forgiveness at a moment of softening of
the heart, in an emotional crisis, is comparatively easy; not to take
it back is something that hardly anyone knows how to do" (Bloom,
Living Prayer, 31).

Inevitably all such strategies fail. In spirituality as in economics,
forgiveness is a deliberate decision to release someone indebted
to us from compensation, however just that restitution may be. In
its deepest expression, forgiveness also releases our offenders from
the punitive consequences of their conduct, however much they
deserve to suffer. Forgiveness is finally a matter of mercy, sheer
generosity that originates from a God who is ready to pardon abundantly (Isa. 55:6–7). Shakespeare's Jessica was wrong (*The Mer-
chant of Venice* 2.6): love is not blind. Genuine love sees the whole
problem very clearly and forgives the debt in spite of its emotional
and spiritual cost, which in some cases may be enormous. Sin stinks.
"Take a good look at the cross of Jesus Christ if you want to know
what sin is, if you want to know the raw material of forgiveness. It is
not a comfortable sight" (Tugwell, *Prayer*, 82).

The Exceptional Couplet

A notable imbalance. "Forgive us our debts, as we also have forgiven
our debtors" (Matt. 6:12) is the only petition of the Lord's Prayer in
which human testimony is conjoined with divine action. That pairing is significant but in three respects theologically asymmetrical.

First: regarded within the context of Jesus' preaching of the
kingdom, most immediately in this Prayer's address (Matt. 6:9b =
Luke 11:2b) and second petition (Matt. 6:10a = Luke 11:2c), the
supplicant is already assured that God may be addressed as a loving
parent, of whom a petition so profound may be made (Matt. 7:7 =

177

Luke 11:9; Matt. 7:11 = Luke 11:13; cf. Mark 11:24). This elemental concept did not originate with Jesus; the goodness of the LORD, God's compassion to release Israel from its iniquity, runs like a scarlet thread throughout the Old Testament (Exod. 32:32; 34:6–7; Pss. 19:12; 23:6; 25:7, 18; 31:19; 51:17; 90:8; Jer. 31:12; Hos. 6:6; Zech. 9:17; Wis. 12:12; 2 Esd. 7:138).

> For you, O Lord, are good and forgiving,
>> abounding in steadfast love to all who call on you. (Ps. 86:5; cf. 130:7)

By comparison: "If you then, who are *evil*, know how to give good gifts to your children, how much more will your Father in heaven give good things to those who ask him!" (Matt. 7:11, emphasis added = Luke 11:13).

Divine and human forgiveness are disproportionate in a second respect: God the Creator is the source of forgiving love, indeed *is* love itself (1 John 4:7–8). Human beings are not: "What are mortals, that they can be clean? Or those born of woman, that they can be righteous?" (Job 15:14). In the moment we turn to God for release from our debts, we confess our incapability of paying them. For this reason well-meaning counsels to "forgive oneself" are theologically misguided. In biblical perspective we cannot wipe clean our own chalky slates, pull ourselves out of sin's quicksand, or free ourselves from ourselves (Ps. 51:1–17; Isa. 46:1–13; John 8:31–36; Rom. 3:19–26).

> Left to our own resources, we remain incapable of healing the harm our sins cause. In the Lord's Prayer Jesus is not proposing a self-help spirituality, as if self-acceptance would fix everything up. He does not say, "forgive others and then you will be at peace" or "forget about how others have offended you and your mind will become serene again." Rather, we are to ask our gracious God to forgive our sins and to do so in view of the fact that we are ready to forgive the sins others may have committed against us. . . . The Lord's Prayer implies a solidarity in seeking, accepting, and expressing forgiveness. (O'Collins, *Lord's Prayer*, 92–93)

178   Only the one whom we have offended—be it God or another human being—has the power to release us from the debts we owe.

A third point of asymmetry in the Prayer's fifth petition: while it focuses on debt as a way of speaking about sin, in a larger sense it reminds the petitioners that *their life in its entirety* is on loan from God, the Creator who feeds and clothes them (Matt. 6:25–33 = Luke 12:22–31), even numbering the hairs on the head (Matt. 10:30–31 = Luke 12:7). As we have witnessed throughout the Lord's Prayer, so also here: "What do you have that you did not receive?" (1 Cor. 4:7b). The answer to Paul's rhetorical question: Nothing whatsoever. The forgiving God is the God who has given us everything and keeps on giving (hence the fourth petition, considered in chap. 6 above). Human life in its totality is a loan from God: a point made in one of Augustine's sermons, when he argues how the gospel levels the field on which stand masters and slaves, rich and poor, generals and "buck-privates" alike (*Sermon* 56.11; see appendix C).

In all these respects the forgiveness of God, the true and only Sovereign, surpasses any amnesty a mortal monarch can offer. When the political winds blow south, Ptolemy and a couple of Cleopatras will renege on promises as fast as they were made. Demetrius can be bribed by as little as a headpiece and a tree branch. No potentates appreciate reminders that their power depends on lackeys who prop them up, until their own loans of life run out at the grave.

A perplexing conjunction. Earlier in this chapter I referred to two small but puzzling words in the fifth petition's subordinate clause:

As [*hōs*] we, too, have forgiven those indebted to us. (Matt. 6:12b AT)
For [*gar*] we, too, forgive everyone indebted to us. (Luke 11:4ab AT)

An educated guess: using different words, Matthew and Luke have rendered in Greek the comparative particle *ke* in Aramaic (Heb., *kî*). This little word and its Greek equivalents can be translated in different ways. The sense might be causal or conditional: If (or because) we forgive our debtors, (then, God,) forgive our debts (cf. Acts 28:19 [*hōs*]; Matt. 2:2 [*gar*]). These conjunctions might be rendered consequentially: As a result of our forgiving others, we ask you, God, to forgive us (cf. Heb. 3:11 [*hōs*]; 12:3 [*gar*]). A matter of degree could be implied: To the extent that we have forgiven, forgive us (cf. Luke 12:58 [*hōs*]; Rom. 5:7 [*gar*]). *Gar* can also suggest an explanation (Matt. 12:40)—"You see, we forgive"—or an

179

inference (Jas. 1:7): "By all means we forgive." All three particles— *ke*, *hōs*, and *gar*—may also suggest a remote comparison between two things, loosely attached yet lacking any subtle linkage. The question before us is this: how are we to understand Matthew and Luke's intent in these secondary clauses of the Prayer's petition? In my view, no conclusion can be decided on a strictly linguistic basis. These terms are too elastic to permit exactitude, and any interpretation depends on the Prayer's larger context.

I am inclined to think that, while Matthew and Luke ultimately agree on interrelating our treatment of debtors with God's treatment of us, the two evangelists interpret the Prayer's fifth petition with modest differences in emphasis. The correlation itself is hardly controversial: the two clauses in Matthew 6:12 = Luke 11:4ab display parallel constructions, with many of the same words positioned in the same place.

Do the prayers of the rabbis help us to construe the intent of the evangelists' subordinate clauses? Up to a point. Rabbinic prayers did not formulate simple connections between divine and human forgiveness (Abrahams, *Studies in Pharisaism*, 95–98).

> Rabbi Gamaliel said: "Let this be a sign to you, that whenever you are compassionate, the Compassionate One will have compassion upon you. . . . So long as you are merciful, God will have mercy upon you; and if you are not merciful, He will not be merciful unto you." (*j. Baba Qamma* 8.10)

> Even though a man pays another whom he has insulted, he is not forgiven by God till he seeks forgiveness from the man he has insulted. That man, if he does not forgive the other, is called merciless. (*b. Baba Qamma* 8.7)

Common to these maxims is the notion that a person must forgive the neighbor before expecting forgiveness by God (Montefiore, *Rabbinic Literature*, 268; Montefiore and Loewe, *Rabbinic Anthology*, 460–69). The rationale for this conviction is as old as the Wisdom of Jesus ben Sirach (ca. 150 BC):

> Forgive your neighbor the wrong he has done,
>   and then your sins will be pardoned when you pray.
> Does anyone harbor anger against another,
>   and expect healing from the Lord?

> If one has no mercy toward another like himself,
> can he then seek pardon for his own sins? (Sir. 28:2–4)

Here there is no quid pro quo, of the sort we observed in Greco-Roman prayers (chap. 1 above); instead, this is a healthy dilution of the sinner's gall. How dare I look to the Lord for restoration when I have refused to terminate an estrangement between my neighbor and myself? So, too, 1 John 4:20: "Those who say, 'I love God,' and hate their brothers or sisters, are liars; for those who do not love a brother or sister whom they have seen, cannot love God whom they have not seen." "By the angry man even the Shekinah [God's holiness] is not esteemed. . . . The angry man forgets what he has learned, and becomes more stupid" (*b. Nedarim* 22b).

Similar to Sirach 28:2–4 are the Matthean Jesus' teachings without parallel in Luke or Mark. The first of these two immediately follows the Lord's Prayer in Matthew:

> For if you forgive others their trespasses, your heavenly Father will also forgive you; but if you do not forgive others, neither will your Father forgive your trespasses. (Matt. 6:14–15)

> You have heard that it was said to those of ancient times, "You shall not murder"; and "whoever murders shall be liable to judgment." But I say to you that if you are angry with a brother or sister, you will be liable to judgment; and if you insult a brother or sister, you will be liable to the council; and if you say, "You fool," you will be liable to the hell of fire. So when you are offering your gift at the altar, if you remember that your brother or sister has something against you, leave your gift there before the altar and go; first be reconciled to your brother or sister, and then come and offer your gift. Come to terms quickly with your accuser while you are on the way to court with him, or your accuser may hand you over to the judge, and the judge to the guard, and you will be thrown into prison. Truly I tell you, you will never get out until you have paid the last penny. (Matt. 5:21–26)

God's forgiveness is not contingent on human forgiveness. "I, I am He who blots out your transgressions *for my own sake*, and I will not remember your sins" (Isa. 43:25, emphasis added). Rather, God "points sinners in the way that they should repent" (*j. Makkot* 31d). As Evelyn Underhill paraphrased the idea, "Every soul that appeals

181

for God's forgiveness is required to move over to His side, and share the compassionate understanding, the unmeasured pity, with which he looks on human frailty and sin" (*Abba*, 65). In this sense we may interpret Matthew's "Forgive, . . . as we also have forgiven."

As we have seen (Matt. 5:43–48; 20:1–16) and will be reminded below, Matthew concurs with Luke and the biblical witness overall in recognizing what later theologians describe as prevenient grace: divine mercy that precedes and elicits human compassion. If Luke's version of this portion of the Prayer differs from Matthew's in accent, it may be on a quality of human perception of God's graciousness.

> [Jesus said,] "A certain creditor had two debtors; one owed five hundred denarii, and the other fifty. When they could not pay, he canceled the debts for both of them. Now which of them will love him more?" Simon [the Pharisee] answered, "I suppose the one for whom he canceled the greater debt."

Jesus salutes Simon's conclusion but adds a warning: "You have judged rightly. . . . But the one to whom little is forgiven, loves little" (Luke 7:41–43, 47b).

> "Be on your guard! If another disciple sins, you must rebuke the offender, and if there is repentance, you must forgive. And if the same person sins against you seven times a day, and turns back to you seven times and says, 'I repent,' you must forgive." (Luke 17:3–4; cf. Matt. 18:21–22)

From this instruction Jesus draws the conclusion his disciples are expected to recognize: such clemency is not to be commended; it is commanded (Luke 17:9). "So you also, when you have done all that you were ordered to do, say, 'We are worthless slaves; we have done only what we ought to have done!'" (17:10). On the same wavelength are some rabbinic maxims, documented in the ninth century AD but likely much older in origin:

> If you have done much good, let it be in your own eyes as little. Do not say: "I have given from my own," but rather, "I have given from what others have given me," and for which you owe thanks to God. But let a small benefit from others to you seem in your eyes great. . . . Let a small wrong that you have done seem great to

you, but if much wrong has been done to you, let it seem little to you, and say, "I have been punished less than I deserved: a bigger punishment would have been fitting." (*Derekh Eretz Zuta* 2.8)

To summarize: the conjoined clauses in Matthew 6:12 = Luke 11:4ab do not argue that God's mercy depends in quality and degree on our own. Were that the case, we all would be wrecked by our wretchedness. "There is no man, who is not God's debtor, but God is gracious and pitiful and forgives previous sins" (*Exodus Rabbah* 31). To release others of the wrongs they have done us is a realization and extension of freedom, bestowed on us by God, from vicious reaction to action: a love that exterminates animosity. "To be a Christian means to forgive the inexcusable, because God has forgiven the inexcusable in you" (Lewis, "Forgiveness," 135).

The Communal Context of Forgiveness

However one chooses to translate the conjunction linking the fifth petition's two clauses, there's no mistaking the interrelationship of God's forgiveness of us and our forgiving one another. Debts are *intrinsically* relational in a way that other metaphors for sin may obscure. One may be personally cleansed of sin's filthiness (Ps. 51:7; Sir. 38:10; 1 John 1:9) while forgetting that a nation's stain before the Almighty must also be purged (Deut. 13:5; 17:7, 12; 19:19b; 21:21; 22:21–24).

In this connection it is striking how little the temple, Israel's religious center, and its cultic protocols (Lev. 1–7) figure in Jesus' teachings. In the Synoptics, Jesus never exhorts anyone to offer sacrifice through priestly mediation: his directives in Matthew 8:4 = Mark 1:44 = Luke 5:14 and Luke 17:14 are concerned, not with sin, but with *reintegration into society* of those whose disease had previously isolated them. In fact, Jesus redirects attention away from "all whole burnt offerings and sacrifices" toward unreserved love of God and neighbor (Mark 12:28–35 = Matt. 22:34–40 = Luke 10:25–28; cf. Deut. 6:4–5; Lev. 19:18–34; 1 Sam. 15:22). Jesus insists that his disciples' liberation from debt service by God's goodness is replicated in their release of one another from mutual burdens: "Whenever you stand praying, forgive, if you have anything against anyone; so that your Father in heaven may also forgive you your trespasses" (Mark 11:25).

183

Two of Jesus' most vivid parables underscore the communal dimension of forgiveness and its susceptibility to fracture.

He also told this parable to some who trusted in themselves that they were righteous and regarded others with contempt: "Two men went up to the temple to pray, one a Pharisee and the other a tax collector [likely a Jew hired by Roman overlords to collect severe taxes from their fellows: Josephus, *Antiquities* 17.204, 307]. The Pharisee, standing by himself, was praying thus, 'God, I thank you that I am not like other people: thieves, rogues, adulterers, or even like this tax collector. I fast twice a week; I give a tenth of all my income.' But the tax collector, standing far off, would not even look up to heaven, but was beating his breast and saying, 'God, be merciful to me, a sinner!' I tell you, this man went down to his home justified rather than the other; for all who exalt themselves will be humbled, but all who humble themselves will be exalted." (Luke 18:9–14)

[Jesus said,] "For this reason the kingdom of heaven may be compared to a king who wished to settle accounts with his slaves. When he began the reckoning, one who owed him ten thousand talents was brought to him; and, as he could not pay, his lord ordered him to be sold, together with his wife and children and all his possessions, and payment to be made. So the slave fell on his knees before him, saying, 'Have patience with me, and I will pay you everything.' And out of pity for him, the lord of that slave released him and forgave him the debt. But that same slave, as he went out, came upon one of his fellow slaves who owed him a hundred denarii; and seizing him by the throat, he said, 'Pay what you owe.' Then his fellow slave fell down and pleaded with him, 'Have patience with me, and I will pay you.' But he refused; then he went and threw him into prison until he would pay the debt. When his fellow slaves saw what had happened, they were greatly distressed, and they went and reported to their lord all that had taken place. Then his lord summoned him and said to him, 'You wicked slave! I forgave you all that debt because you pleaded with me. Should you not have had mercy on your fellow slave, as I had mercy on you?' And in anger his lord handed him over to be tortured until he would pay his entire debt. So my heavenly Father will also do to every one of you, if you do not forgive your brother or sister from your heart." (Matt. 18:23–35)

184

In these different stories four common features coalesce with the Lord's Prayer's fifth petition. (1) Both parables begin by presenting a magisterial God (in temple, in court) who receives sinners and compassionately releases them from their debts. (2) Both contrast two beneficiaries of their Master's graciousness. One, incapable of recognizing himself in his fellow debtor, ruptures all relationship with him: having been forgiven an unpayable debt, the once ruined slave instantly throws his own measly debtor into the slammer. The other is a pious Pharisee, confident in his own righteousness, who divorces himself from all whom he holds in contempt, which is just about everyone: thieves, rogues, cheats, and quislings. He can no more see himself as a scoundrel, standing by another, than the king's slave who is financially and morally bankrupt. "[A] real forgiveness really received by true repentance means that the offender conceives a burning desire to make reparation and to share the burdens of the one who forgave him" (Moule, "Theology of Forgiveness," 254). (3) And so the reversal: the humble penitent returns home, put right with God; the merciless slave receives punishment fitting his crime. (4) Both parables conclude with compatible warnings to Jesus' disciples: see yourselves for who you really are in relation to your peers, and treat them as you hope God may treat you.

Forgiveness runs in a re-creative cycle: "Love is to be no longer a centripetal but a centrifugal force" (Manson, *Teaching of Jesus*, 309). Through the kingdom, God is restoring not only us but also all of creation to himself, and in that process our own acts of rebuilding community are involved. In her typically gentle way Sister Wendy Beckett wondered:

> I sometimes think people don't quite realize what they're begging for. You're saying to God, "Look at the way I treat other people and treat me like that." It's a very powerful incitement to being loving and forgiving. What Jesus is saying is that your heart can't turn to God your father for forgiveness if you're not forgiving other people. It makes God's forgiveness impossible. God can't forgive a hard heart. He wants to but he can't, because you can't receive it. Your heart is closed to him. Open your heart to other people and you let him in. (Williams and Beckett, *Living the Lord's Prayer*, 58–59)

The caution of John Calvin (see appendix C) is more pointed: "If we retain feelings of hatred in our hearts, if we plot revenge and ponder any occasion to cause harm, and even if we do not try to get back into our enemies' good graces, by every sort of good office deserve well of them, and commend ourselves to them, [then] by this prayer we entreat God *not* to forgive our sins" ("Exposition of the Lord's Prayer," 206, trans. Elsie McKee, emphasis added). The wording of the Prayer's fifth petition runs along the same line as Jesus' teaching on "the unforgiveable sin" (Matt. 12:31–32 = Mark 3:28–29 = Luke 12:8–10): by the "devout schizophrenia" of refusing forgiveness to others, we drive ourselves away from Jesus' life-giving power to cancel our own debts (Lochman, *Lord's Prayer*, 122). "If we do not fully forgive our neighbor, then it is a sign that we have not fully requested the Father's forgiveness and we have thus made ourselves incapable of receiving the unrestricted forgiveness of God" (Boff, *Lord's Prayer*, 95). We cannot enter the kingdom for whose coming we pray if we cling to a bitterness that short-circuits the mystery of God's love.

The Restructured Self

At bottom, debt forgiveness amounts to self-renunciation. Unless we are on the receiving end of its benefit, who wants that? How is such a thing even possible?

Just here the position of the "we-petitions" (for bread, forgiveness, and rescue) after the "thou-petitions" (for God's sanctity, kingdom, and will) become intelligible, and the last three are patently indispensable. Those who offer the Lord's Prayer do not begin by paying compliments to God before getting down to brass tacks (what we need). Our most essential need, of which everyday necessities are by-products, is the radical restructuring of our selves that only God's holy kingdom, activated by Jesus, can realize. The culture we inhabit has so blinded us to this reality that we must ponder it, if only momentarily.

The popular attitude toward human existence hasn't evolved much beyond Rousseau's picture of innate human goodness, warped by civilization (*Origin of Inequality* [1754]). In this view the individual is a free, perfectible victim of the oppressive structures of a coercive society. At this writing (2018), one manifestation of this persuasion has been dubbed "intersectionality": a fluid, neo-Marxist theory that regards discrimination against race, class, sex, gender mapping, and handicapping conditions as "a matrix of oppression," exploited for the most part by affluent, white, heterosexual males

186

who determine what counts as knowledge and even truth (Collins, *Black Feminist Thought*). To be liberated from multiple, confluent vectors of abusive power, disadvantaged groups can achieve a greater degree of social justice by accessing authentic reality though the complexity of their "lived experience," by which they may find their voice and promote "knowledge potent for constructing worlds less organized by axes of dominion" (Haraway, "Situated Knowledge," 585; see also Grzanka, *Intersectionality*, 227–57). Like law, sociology, and philosophy, theology is being reshaped to acclimatize this position.

Make no mistake: structural inequalities and social injustice are real, global, and pernicious. The proper question is whether those victimized, as individuals or as groups, are as powerful and socially perfectible as is sometimes assumed. If so, then salvation will be achieved when the tightly knotted structures of oppression are slashed and defeated. If not—if none of us is as free or perfectible as we may think ourselves (Jibrin and Salem, "Revisiting Intersectionality")—then liberation will fail, because the liberated self can fulfill only what it truly is: a naive accomplice in its own bondage. "Lived experience" is inevitably selective (cf. Wylie, "Feminist Philosophy"): it is loath to render judgment on our aspirations, which are presumed to be legitimate just as they stand, as virtuous as our enemies' are vicious. Forgiveness, then, becomes at best a moot point, at worst a stratagem manipulated by hegemonic structures to deceive and further tyrannize. The deeper deception is a form of self-delusion: our tendency to veil from ourselves our own motives, our propensity to rationalize the most furious deeds under the cloak of our noblest ends. When promised freedom by corrupted insight, our enslavement is transferred from one master of harassment to another (Rom. 6:15–23; 2 Pet. 2:19). Looking back on his release after twenty-seven years of imprisonment in several South African jails, Nelson Mandela (1918–2013) said, "As I walked out the door toward the gate that would lead to my freedom, I knew if I didn't leave my bitterness and hatred behind, I'd still be in prison" (*Long Walk to Freedom*, 544).

That's why, in the preaching of Jesus and the New Testament generally, the kingdom of God breaks into this world *from outside*. Only a power not of this world can liberate those enslaved to it— which includes all of us, without exception. The prayer of forgiveness, like the Lord's Prayer of which it is a component, like the

187

gospel in which they are embedded, like the Messiah who lived and died for it, exposes us to our understanding of God.

> Does that reality we call God function as a support mechanism for who we now are? Who God really is for us is determined by whose will we obey and to whom we consider ourselves accountable. In other words, the issue is whether or not the fundamental thing to be said about God turns out to be an ideology, a rationale for the status quo, which insulates us from the truth. (Keck, "Evangelism," 59)

The truth in the Prayer's fifth petition is that God's realm does not underwrite the economy of debt and repayment under which our world lives. Forgiveness restructures the reality by which we live from top to bottom, since God is at work, not to improve us but to annihilate the vengeance we have suffered and have called down on others (see Sobrino, "Latin America," 52–56). The Messiah who called Matthew, the Roman toady (Matt. 10:3), and Simon the Zealot (Luke 6:15) was not forming a church of the like-minded, bound by common grievances. The nexus of discipleship to Jesus is a subversive bondage: not to debt, but to its release (Matt. 10:24–25a; 20:27 = Mark 10:44; Luke 22:26–27). Our acts of forgiveness—without limit (Matt. 18:21–22)—issue a down payment on the kingdom's advent in this world (see chap. 5 above), a declaration of independence from sin both for those oppressed and for their oppressors.

The Costs of Forgiveness

> Every time you take a human soul with you into your prayer, you accept from God a piece of spiritual work with all its implications and with all its cost—a cost which may mean for you spiritual exhaustion and darkness, and may even include vicarious suffering, the Cross. In offering yourselves on such levels of prayer for the sake of others, you are offering to take your part in the mysterious activities of the spiritual world; to share the saving work of Christ. (Underhill, *Life as Prayer*, 57)

188

What does forgiveness, such costly self-surrender to God, look like in this flawed, tormented world? I submit for your consideration three testimonies—not one of which forgets, excuses, denies, or dismisses abominable injustice.

A Letter from Hell

A Jewish prisoner in a German concentration camp left the following manifesto.

> Peace to all men of evil will! Let there be an end to all vengeance, to all demands for punishment and retribution. . . . Crimes have surpassed all measure, they can no longer be grasped by human understanding. There are too many martyrs. . . . And so, weigh not their sufferings on the scales of thy justice, Lord, and lay not these sufferings to the torturers' charge to exact a terrible reckoning from them. Pay them back in a different way! Put down in favor of the executioners, the informers, the traitors and all men of evil will, the courage, the spiritual strength of others, their humility, their lofty dignity, their constant inner striving and invincible hope, the smile that staunched their tears, their love, their ravaged broken hearts that remained steadfast and confident in the face of death itself, yes, even at moments of the utmost weakness. . . . Let all this, O Lord, be laid before thee for the forgiveness of sins, as a ransom for the triumph of righteousness; let the good and not the evil be taken into account! And may we remain in our enemies' memory not as their victims, not as a nightmare, not as haunting specters, but as helpers in their striving to destroy the fury of their criminal passions. There is nothing more that we want of them. And when it is all over, grant us to live among men as men, and may peace come again to our poor earth—peace for men of goodwill and for all the others. (Quoted by Bloom, *Living Prayer*, 17–18)

Embracing Your Mother's Murderer

On June 18, 2015, around nine in the evening, a young white man visited a black church in Charleston, South Carolina. He spent an hour listening to a Bible study with nine people before gunning them down in cold blood, one after another. At his bond hearing, the daughter of Ethel Lance, a 70-year-old employee of the church who was murdered, said to 21-year-old Dylann Storm Roof, "You took something precious from me. I will never talk to [my mother] ever again. I will never be able to hold her again. But I forgive you" (Graham, "Powerful Witness"). The teenaged son of Sharonda Coleman-Singleton, a 45-year-old part-time minister of Mother Emanuel AME Church, told a BBC reporter, "We already forgive him for what he's done, and there's nothing but love from our side

189

of the family. Love is stronger than hate" (BBC News, "Charleston Church Shooting").

"They Don't Know What They're Doing"

The final testimony stands somewhat apart from the others. Not only does it express forgiveness in extremis; it also offers a reasoned theological justification from a six-year-old child. In the 1954 Supreme Court decision *Brown v. the Board of Education of Topeka*, nine old white justices desegregated America's schools, but it was left to the children and parents of those schools to carry out that order. At that time Robert Coles, in training at Harvard as a child psychiatrist, visited New Orleans schools to study the effects of stress on young students, who were daily subjected to abusive mobs. While interviewing a first-grader, Ruby Bridges, Coles was astonished to learn that the youngster was praying for her antagonists:

> *You pray for the people there?*
> Yes.
> *Really? Why do you do that?*
> Because they need praying for.
> *Well, Ruby, why do you think they need you to pray for them?*
> Because I should.
> *Why?*
> Because I should.
> *Ruby, you know, I'm still puzzled by this. I'm trying to figure out why you think you have to pray for such people, given what they try to do to you twice a day for five days a week.*
> Well, especially it should be me.
> *Why you, especially?*
> Because if you're going through what they're doing to you, you're the one who should be praying for them.
>
> And then she quoted to me what she had heard in church that Sunday from the minister. He said that Jesus went through a lot of trouble and he said about the people who were causing this trouble, "Forgive them, because they don't know what they're doing." And now little Ruby was saying this in 1961, about the people in the streets of New Orleans.
>
> How is someone like me supposed to account for that, psychologically or any other way? (Coles, "Immanence and Transcendence," 212)

190

On this world's terms there's no accounting for this or for any of these testimonies. In a corrupted world that requires of us much forgiveness, a lot of consecrating, the acquittal of those irreparably bankrupt and utterly lost is nothing less than a miracle of grace. When we offer to others creative goodness and forgiving love, we become echoes of Christ's own miraculous healing and liberating power.

Works Cited in Chapter 7

Abrahams, Isaac. *Studies in Pharisaism and the Gospels.* 2nd series. Cambridge: Cambridge University Press, 1924.

Ayo, Nicholas. *The Lord's Prayer: A Survey Theological and Literary.* Notre Dame, IN: University of Notre Dame Press; Lanham, MD: Rowman & Littlefield, 1992.

Bazzana, Giovanni Battista. "*Basileia* and Debt Relief: The Forgiveness of Debts in the Lord's Prayer in the Light of Documentary Papyri." *Catholic Biblical Quarterly* 73 (2011): 511–25.

BBC News. "Charleston Church Shooting: Governor Calls for Death Penalty." June 19, 2015. http://www.bbc.com/news/world-us-canada-33195768.

Bernanos, Georges. *The Diary of a Country Priest.* Translated by Pamela Morris. New York: Macmillan, 1937.

Black, C. Clifton. "Sin in the Synoptic Gospels." In *The T&T Clark Companion to the Doctrine of Sin*, edited by Keith L. Johnson and David Lauber, 61–78. Bloomsbury Companions. London: Bloomsbury; Edinburgh: T&T Clark, 2016.

Bloom, Anthony (Metropolitan Anthony of Sourozh). *Living Prayer.* Springfield, IL: Templegate, 1966.

Boff, Leonardo. *The Lord's Prayer: The Prayer of Integral Liberation.* Translated by Theodore Morrow. Melbourne: Dove; Maryknoll, NY: Orbis Books, 1983.

The Book of Common Prayer 1559: The Elizabethan Prayer Book. Edited by John E. Booty. Charlottesville: University of Virginia Press; London: Folger Shakespeare Library, 2005.

Calvin, John. "Exposition of the Lord's Prayer." In *John Calvin: Writings on Pastoral Piety*, edited by Elsie Anne McKee, 197–209. Classics of Western Spirituality. New York: Paulist Press, 2001.

Coles, Robert. "Immanence and Transcendence." *Princeton Seminary Bulletin* 3 (1984): 203–15.

Collins, Patricia Hill. *Black Feminist Thought: Knowledge, Consciousness, and the Politics of Empowerment.* 2nd ed. New York: Routledge, 2000.

Elizondo, Virgil. "I Forgive but I Do Not Forget." In *Forgiveness*, edited by Casiano Floristán and Christian Duquoc, 69–79. Concilium: Religion in the Eighties. Edinburgh: T&T Clark, 1986.

Fiensy, David A. "Jesus and Debts: Did He Pray about Them?" *Restoration Quarterly* 44 (2002): 233–39.

Fitzmyer, Joseph A. *The Gospel according to Luke (X–XXIV).* Anchor Bible 28A. Garden City, NY: Doubleday, 1985.

Graham, Efrem. "Powerful Witness: Forgiveness in Charleston." CBN News. July 24, 2015. http://www.cbn.com/cbnnews/us /2015/June/Powerful-Witness-Forgiveness-in-Charleston.

Grzanka, Patrick R., ed. *Intersectionality: A Foundations and Frontiers Reader.* Boulder, CO: Westview; Philadelphia: Perseus Books, 2014.

Haraway, Donna. "Situated Knowledge: The Science Question in Feminism and the Privilege of Partial Perspective." *Feminist Studies* 14 (1988): 579–99.

Jibrin, Rekia, and Sara Salem. "Revisiting Intersectionality: Reflections on Theory and Praxis." *Trans-Scripts* 5 (2015): 1–24.

Keck, Leander E. "Evangelism in Theological Perspective." In *Evangelism: Mandates for Action*, edited by James T. Laney, 33–68. New York: Hawthorne, 1975.

Lachs, Samuel Tobias. "On Matthew VI.12." *Novum Testamentum* 16 (1975): 6–8.

Lewis, C. S. "On Forgiveness." In *The Weight of Glory and Other Essays*, 132–36. New York: Simon & Schuster, 1996.

Lochman, Jan Milič. *The Lord's Prayer.* Translated by Geoffrey W. Bromiley. Grand Rapids: Wm. B. Eerdmans Publishing Co., 1990.

Mandela, Nelson. *Long Walk to Freedom: The Autobiography of Nelson Mandela.* Boston: Little, Brown, 1994.

Manson, Thomas Walter. *The Teaching of Jesus: Studies of Its Form and Content.* Cambridge: Cambridge University Press, 1959.

Migeotte, Léopold. *L'Emprunt public dans les cités grecques: Recueil des documents et analyse critique.* Collection d'Études anciennes. Quebec: Les Éditions du Sphinx; Paris: Les Belles Lettres, 1984.

Montefiore, Claude G. *Rabbinic Literature and Gospel Teachings.* Library of Biblical Studies. New York: Ktav, 1970.

Montefiore, Claude G., and Herbert Loewe. *A Rabbinic Anthology: Selected and Arranged with Comments and Introductions.* New York: Schocken Books, 1974.

Moule, C. F. D. "The Theology of Forgiveness." In *Essays in New Testament Interpretation*, 250–60. Cambridge: Cambridge University Press, 1982.

Oakman, Douglas E. "Jesus and Agrarian Palestine: The Factor of Debt." *SBL 1985 Seminar Papers* 34 (1985): 57–73.

O'Collins, Gerald. *The Lord's Prayer.* New York: Paulist Press, 2007.

Pastor, Jack. *Land and Economy in Ancient Palestine.* London: Routledge, 1997.

Reimer, Ivoni Richter. "The Forgiveness of Debts in Matthew and Luke: For an Economy without Exclusions." In *God's Economy: Biblical Studies from Latin America*, edited by Ross Kinsler and Gloria Kinsler, 152–68. Maryknoll, NY: Orbis Books, 2005.

Rousseau, Jean-Jacques. *Discourse on the Origin of Inequality.* Translated by Donald A. Cress. Indianapolis: Hackett Publishing Co., 1992.

Rowlandson, Jane, ed. *Women and Society in Greek and Roman Egypt: A Sourcebook.* Cambridge: Cambridge University Press, 1998.

Saller, Richard. *Personal Patronage under the Roman Empire.* Cambridge: Cambridge University Press, 1982.

Sobrino, Jon. "Latin America: Place of Sin and Place of Forgiveness." In *Forgiveness*, translated by Dinah Livingstone, edited by Casiano Floristán and Christian Duquoc, 45–56. Concilium: Religion in the Eighties. Edinburgh: T&T Clark, 1986.

Tugwell, Simon. *Prayer: Living with God.* Springfield, IL: Templegate, 1975.

Underhill, Evelyn. *Abba: Meditations Based on the Lord's Prayer.* London: Longmans, Green & Co., 1940.

———. *Life as Prayer: Collected Papers of Evelyn Underhill.* Edited by Lucy Menzies. London: Longmans, Green & Co., 1946.

Williams, Rowan, and Wendy Beckett. *Living the Lord's Prayer.* Compiled by Su Box. Oxford: Lion Hudson, 2007.

Wylie, Allison. "Feminist Philosophy of Science: Standpoint Matters." *Proceedings and Addresses of the American Philosophical Society* 86 (2012): 47–76.

CHAPTER 8

Rescue from Ultimate Danger and Evil

A halo has to fall just a few inches to become a noose.
—Father Guido Sarducci (Don Novello)

In their best textual attestations, the final clauses of the Lord's Prayer are unusual and difficult to interpret (see Carmignac, *Recherches*, 236–319). The atypical aspect lies in the first clause: this is the Prayer's only petition that carries a negation (*mē*), a plea that God may *not* do something. The difficulties arise from two nouns whose translations are debatable and theologically problematic. To an appreciable degree the theological issues arise from the translations on which one decides. Although experts in Semitic languages are not of one mind on the matter, attempts to reconstruct the Aramaic underlying our Greek versions fail us in this case (Fitzmyer, "Lead Us Not"). To avoid predetermining the problems' resolutions, I render the sentence here as literally as possible, without translating its obscurities:

And do not bring us into *peirasmon*, (Luke 11:4c = Matt. 6:13a)
But save us from *tou ponērou.* (Matt. 6:13b)

Our primary task is to puzzle out, as best we can, what these petitions intend. The safest procedure is from the less controversial to the more heavily disputed.

195

Text-Critical Issues

Our earliest and most reliable manuscripts of Luke 11:4 do not include Matthew's second clause: among others, $\mathfrak{P}^{75}$ (Papyrus 75, early 2nd c.), Codices Sinaiticus and Vaticanus (both 4th c.). Most of the Prayer's earliest interpreters—Tertullian (ca. 160–ca. 240), Origen (ca. 185–ca. 254), Cyril of Jerusalem (313–386), Augustine (354–430)—do not comment on this clause in Luke. However, a wide variety of ancient Greek manuscripts, including Sinaiticus and Vaticanus—as well as Tertullian, Origen, Cyprian of Carthage (ca. 200–258), Gregory of Nyssa (ca. 335–ca. 394), Augustine, and Maximus the Confessor (ca. 580–662), among others—include or refer to the second clause that is found only in Matthew. In other words: our best manuscript evidence of Luke includes only the first clause, while Matthew's two-clause formula appears in our finest witnesses. Medieval scribes added Matthew's second clause to Luke 11:4, apparently to harmonize that petition in both Gospels (an expedient preserved in the KJV). The Prayer may well have ended as it does in Luke 11:4. Matthew may have appended the second clause to the first, perhaps to explain the latter by the former. In the following comments I shall operate on that assumption: while true to Matthean theology, Matthew 6:13b was likely an addition to Luke's simpler expression.

The Petition's First Clause

The Verb

In both Matthew and in Luke, the petition(s) for rescue are joined with the preceding prayers for bread and forgiveness by the simple conjunction *kai* (and). In both Gospels we find the same verb, identically conjugated and negated, with the same pronominal object, "us": *mē eisenenkēs hēmas*. The verb is *eispherein*, a simple compound of *eis* (into) and *pherein* (to bear, carry, move, bring, lead, drag [Luke 12:11]): thus, "to bring into" or "to lead into." The Greek verb's basic meaning is conveyed, twice, in the set-up for Luke's rendition of Jesus' healing of a paralytic: "They were trying to <u>bring</u> him <u>in</u> and lay him before Jesus; but finding no way to <u>bring</u> him <u>in</u> because of the crowd, they went up on the roof and let him down with his bed through the tiles into the middle of the

196

crowd in front of Jesus" (5:18b–19, underlines added). The verb in Luke 11:4c = Matthew 6:13a is an aorist subjunctive, expressing something unreal but possible. Therefore: "Do not bring [or "lead"] us" into something. Into what?

The Object

Ambiguities in translation. Here the wicket gets sticky and has been so regarded since the second century (Willis, "Lead Us Not"). English versions render this clause in diverse ways.

> And lead us not into temptation. (KJV [1611], ASV [1901], MOFFATT [1913], RSV [1946], NIV [1978])
> And do not bring us into temptation/the time of trial. (LATTIMORE [1996]; NRSV [1989])
> And do not subject us to temptation. (GOODSPEED [1948])
> Subject us not to the trial. (NAB [1990])
> And do not bring/put us to the test. (NEB [1961]/REB [1989], JB [1966], GNB [1976], NJB [1990])
> And do not bring us to the point of being put to the final test. (CASSIRER [1989])

Underlying these different objects in English is the word *ho peirasmos*, which also suggests different things in Greek. Cognate with the verbs *peiraomai* (to try, test, endeavor) and *peirazein* (to try, put to the test, tempt), *ho peirasmos* usually refers in the New Testament to "a trial" or "a temptation":

> Beloved, do not be surprised at the fiery ordeal that is taking place among you to test you [*pros peirasmon hymin*], as though something strange were happening to you. But rejoice insofar as you are sharing Christ's sufferings, so that you may also be glad and shout for joy when his glory is revealed. (1 Pet. 4:12–13)

> But those who want to be rich fall into temptation [*eis peirasmon*] and are trapped by many senseless and harmful desires that plunge people into ruin and destruction. (1 Tim. 6:9)

One might judge these alternative senses of *peirasmon* virtually interchangeable: the word "temptation" comes to us from Latin (*temptatio*) by way of Old French (*temptacion*): "handling," "testing," or "trying." Depending on context, a test or a trial can connote something neutral (a chemical experiment or clinical trial), positive (a discovery of something's strength or effectiveness), or negative (an academic examination or legal action in court, which only teachers or lawyers may enjoy). "Temptation" may carry a more sinister nuance: a desire or inducement to do something unwise, illegal, or wrong. In everyday English that to which one may be enticed covers a wide spectrum: criminal malfeasance, sexual abuse, a risky yet lawful endeavor, or another slice of pie.

Ambiguities of interpretation. Clearly, the Lord's Prayer suggests an allurement more serious than Apple Brown Betty, or Betty herself. The difficulty is twofold. First, lacking a specific frame of reference, we cannot securely identify the kind of test, trial, or temptation from which we are to pray for diversion. Second—and here the matter becomes quite tricky—not every trial or test (Heb., *nissah*) in the Bible is necessarily bad. In fact, some carry positive value and are administered by God.

> Remember the long way that the LORD your God has led you these forty years in the wilderness, in order to humble you, testing you [*lənassōtəkā*] to know what was in your heart, whether or not you would keep his commandments. . . . Know then in your heart that as a parent disciplines a child so the LORD your God disciplines you. (Deut. 8:2, 5)

> Test me [*bəḥānēnî*], LORD, and try me [*wənassēnî*],
> examine my heart and my mind;
> for your love is ever before me,
> and I walk continually in your truth. (Ps. 26:2–3 NIV)

In 26:2 the RSV/NRSV translates the Hebrew verb *bəḥānēnî* as "prove," NJPS as "probe."

> My child, when you come to serve the Lord,
> prepare yourself for testing [*eis peirasmon*]. (Sir. 2:1)

In none of these cases is "temptation" viewed as inducement to evil. *Nissah* or *peirasmos* refers to God's trial or probing of a person's character, to determine one's affection or loyalty. The same connotation is evident in the New Testament. While *peirasmoi* are generally regarded as hardships one might rather avoid (Luke 8:13; 22:28; Acts 20:19), they can also be considered as a positive purification of faith.

My brothers and sisters, whenever you face trials of any kind, consider it nothing but joy, because you know that the testing of your faith produces endurance; and let endurance have its full effect, so that you may be mature and complete, lacking in nothing. (Jas. 1:2–4)

In this you rejoice, even if now for a little while you have had to suffer various trials, so that the genuineness of your faith—being more precious than gold that, though perishable, is tested by fire—may be found to result in praise and glory and honor when Jesus Christ is revealed. (1 Pet. 1:6–7)

Turnabout, however, is illegitimate. Owing to the asymmetry of the covenant between God and Israel, mortals usurp power when *they* test the LORD. Massah and Meribah (literally, "Testing" and "Strife") are names for a place of Israelite revolt during its wilderness wandering (Exod. 17:7; cf. Ps. 95:8–9; Heb. 3:7–12). The earth's rulers are counseled not to put the Lord to the test, which amounts to distrusting him (Wis. 1:1–2). Similarly, in the New Testament, Jesus is subjected to hostile tests by religious leaders (Matt. 16:1 = Mark 8:11; Matt. 19:3 = Mark 10:2; Matt. 22:18 = Mark 12:15; Luke 10:25; John 8:4–6), and Peter asks Jerusalem's elders, "Why are you putting God to the test by placing on the neck of the [Gentile] disciples a yoke that neither our ancestors nor we have been able to bear?" (Acts 15:10). Little wonder that Ernst Lohmeyer referred to the Bible as "the Book of Temptations" (*Lord's Prayer*, 198).

What of the renderings "Do not bring us to the time of trial" (NRSV), "Subject us not to the trial" (NAB), and "Do not bring us to the point of being put to the final test" (CASSIRER)? In the Greek of both Matthew 6:12 and Luke 11:4, no definite article precedes *peirasmon*, and there is no word that would be translated as "time." As the NAB suggests and Cassirer spells out, "the trial" reflects some translators' hunch that, by *peirasmos*, Jesus referred to The Great Trial, an apocalyptic testing soon to come that would create terrible travails for his followers. As New Testament scholars in the twentieth century became increasingly sensitive to the apocalyptic tenor of Jesus' preaching of the kingdom of God (Kuhn, "New Light") many interpreters have assumed that this is the trial implied in the Lord's Prayer (e.g., Barth, *Prayer*, 59–61; Brown, "Pater Noster"; Vokes, "Lord's Prayer"). After all, the Prayer's second petition is for that kingdom's coming.

199

Nevertheless, that interpretation carries some snags. First, its acceptance entails coloring everything in the Lord's Prayer in a uniformly apocalyptic hue. That may be warranted—to be sure, many commentators think so—but it begs the question why other petitions of the Prayer—sanctification of God's name, beseeching bread, forgiveness of our sins—are not necessarily dependent on such eschatological urgency (Davies and Allison, *Saint Matthew*, 593–94).

Second, the word *peirasmos* does not appear in Jesus' discourse on the Mount of Olives (Matt. 24:4–44 = Mark 13:5–37 = Luke 21:8–36), which overflows with predictions of wars, persecutions, betrayals, and such suffering "as has not been from the beginning of the world until now, no, and never will be" (Matt. 24:21).

Third, reference to *peirasmos* as something like The Final Trial is rarer in the New Testament and other early Christian literature than one might suppose. Its clearest expression is in the letter of John of Patmos to the Philadelphians, a church with "little power" that has "not denied [the holy] name" (Rev. 3:8b): "Because you have kept my word of patient endurance, I will keep you from the hour of trial [*tēs hōras tou peirasmou*] that is coming on the whole world to test [*peirasai*] the inhabitants of the earth" (3:10). After reminding them of torments to which the angels, Noah, and Lot were subjected, 2 Peter assures its readers that "the Lord knows how to rescue the godly from trial [*peirasmou*], and to keep the unrighteous under punishment until the day of judgment" (2:9). In the Apostolic Fathers, a Christian corpus that overlaps the youngest New Testament writings, there are four occurrences of *peirasmos*. Two (Pol. *Phil.* 7.2; *Did.* 8.2) are quotations of the Lord's Prayer. Of the remaining pair, only one is set in an eschatological context; neither refers to a "time of trial":

> For I myself am utterly sinful and have not yet escaped from temptation [*ton peirasmon*]; but even though I am surrounded by the tools of the devil, I make every effort to pursue righteousness, that I may succeed in at least getting close to it, because I fear the coming judgment. (2 *Clem.* 18.2)

> And whenever you ask for something from the Lord, . . . do not become double-minded just because you did not receive your soul's request quickly, for assuredly it is because of some tempta-

tion [*peirasmon*] or some transgression, of which you are ignorant, that you are receiving your request rather slowly. (*Herm.* 39.7)

As far as I can see, Ulrich Luz's conclusion is sound: "Neither in Jewish apocalyptic nor in the New Testament is *peirasmos* an apocalyptic technical term" (*Matthew 1–7*, 384).

Joining Object, Action, and Agent

So mesmerized have we become by translating the pesky *peirasmos* that we have not yet linked it with the main verb in Matthew 6:13a = Luke 11:4c: "Do not lead [*eisenenkēs*] us." Lohmeyer, an exponent of the petition's eschatological interpretation, asserts that "temptation here is the attempt of the ungodly powers to obtain a final decision in the battle with God over the persons of the praying community who use the word 'we' to describe themselves" (*Lord's Prayer*, 207). At best that finesses the principal question; at worst it is evasive. The Prayer does not ask that "the ungodly powers" be prevented from gaining the upper hand over us in "a final decision"; rather, it beseeches *God* not to lead us somewhere horrible. John of Patmos promises (Rev. 3:10), not that God will bring us "into the hour of trial that is coming," but rather, that God shall "keep" [*tērēsō*]—"guard," "hold," "preserve"—us from it. John does not suggest that we are strong enough to follow the General's push into The Final Battle. Neither does the Lord's Prayer. In that respect it anticipates a well-known Talmudic prayer:

> Bring me not into the power of sin
> And not into the power of debt
> And not into the power of temptation
> And not into the power of contempt.
> May the good shoot prevail in me
> And may not the evil shoot prevail in me. (*b. Berakhot* 60b)

Consistent with the Lord's Prayer, the New Testament appears hesitant to claim that God subjects mortals to inordinate trials. When made, such statements are offered with reserve or qualification. "By faith Abraham, when put to the test, offered up Isaac. He who had received the promises was ready to offer up his only son" (Heb. 11:17). Notice that the author of Hebrews does not identify

201

God as the tester, even though that is manifestly the case in Genesis 22:1–19; Hebrews shifts the emphasis to Abraham's supreme fidelity. In Luke 22:28 Jesus acknowledges that his disciples "are those who have stood by me in my trials," without attributing to God culpability for those tests. Where agency is indicated, it is identified, expressly or by implication, with Satan or the devil.

> In fact, when we were with you, we told you beforehand that we were to suffer persecution; so it turned out, as you know. For this reason, when I could bear it no longer, I sent to find out about your faith; I was afraid that somehow the tempter [*ho peirazōn*] had tempted [*epeirasen*] you and that our labor had been in vain. But Timothy has just now come to us from you, and has brought us the good news of your faith and love. (1 Thess. 3:4–6a; cf. 1 Cor. 7:5; Rev. 2:10)

"The tempter," designating the devil, is rare in ancient Jewish and Christian literature. It does not appear in the Septuagint (the Greek translation of Hebrew Scriptures) or the apocalyptically tinged *Psalms of Solomon* and *Testaments of the Twelve Patriarchs*. If it occurs in the Dead Sea Scrolls, the Mishnah, or the Targums (Aramaic expositions of the Hebrew Bible), I have overlooked it. The only other occurrence of *ho peirazōn* in the New Testament is in Matthew 4:3, in the legend of Jesus' wilderness temptations, to which we shall return.

For all its approbation of trials as milestones on the rugged path toward maturity (1:2–4), the Epistle of James insists on something else, which merits quotation in full:

> Blessed is anyone who perseveres when trials [*peirasmon*] come. Such a person is of proven worth and will win the prize of life, the crown that the Lord has promised to those who love him. Never, when you are being put to the test [*peirazomenos*], say, "God is tempting [*peirazomai*] me"; God cannot be tempted [*apeirastos*] by evil, and he does not put anybody to the test [*peirazei*]. Everyone is put to the test [*peirazetai*] by being attracted and seduced by that person's own wrong desire. Then the desire conceives and gives birth to sin, and when sin reaches full growth, it gives birth to death. Make no mistake about this, my dear brothers: all that is good, all that is perfect, is given us from above; it comes down from the Father of all light; with him there is no such thing as

202

alteration, no shadow caused by change. (Jas. 1:12–17 NJB; see also Sir. 15:11–20)

In this passage three different English words—"trials," "test," "tempt"—are used to translate a single Greek term and its cognates: *peirasmos*. While *peirasmos* can suggest all these nuances, there's no reason to assume that James is altering its senses within the space of three adjacent sentences. The shift in some translations to forms of "tempt" in James 1:13 (RSV, GNB, NIV) lacks obvious justification. Beyond Paul Minear's wry observation that "Theological qualms rule out linguistic honesty" ("But Whose Prayer?," 332), we can only speculate on the reason for the translators' change. Is it to separate, as widely as possible, ascription to God as "the tempter" (cf. 1 Thess. 3:5)? Is it an attempt to differentiate a claim of God's "temptation" (Jas. 1:13a) from God's "testing" (1:13b)? If the latter, then James flouts instances in Hebrew Scripture that God, indeed, does test mortals for positive reasons. Apparently James's reason for so doing is to insulate divine majesty ("all that is [unalterably] good, all that is perfect") from human cravings (*epithymia*), which can be gratuitous (2 Pet. 2:10) or evil (1 Cor. 10:6). A distinction made by John Calvin (1509–64) follows this line of thought: "God tries in one way; Satan, in another. Satan tempts that he may destroy, condemn, confound, [and] cast down; but God [proves] His own children . . . and establish[es] their strength and courage by exercising it" (*Institutes* 3.46, trans. John McNeill).

Controversy over the Prayer's sixth petition continues. On December 8, 2017, Pope Francis made international headlines by having declared on Italian television the previous evening, "'Lead us not into temptation' is not a good translation. . . . It is not [God] that pushes me into temptation and then sees how I fall. A father does not do this. A father quickly helps those who are provoked into Satan's temptation" (Wamsley, "Pope Francis"). The pontiff suggested the substitute wording, "Do not let us fall into temptation" and commended its worldwide use (BBC News, "Lord's Prayer"). Beginning on the first Sunday in Advent, the Catholic Church of France adopted the wording, "Do not let us fall into temptation" (Conférence des évêques, "Notre Père"). The *National Catholic Reporter* (USA) reported a Parisian priest's concurrence with this decision. "[The new translation is] less ambiguous. The [earlier] version, 'Do not submit us to temptation' made some people think

God threw banana peels in front of people to see if they would slip and fall, but that is absolutely not the biblical view of God" (Heneghan, "Does God Lead Us into Sin?"). Apart from its flippancy this cleric's comment obscures a problem with which any thoughtful Christian must wrestle: in its scriptural context the wording of the Greek text is ambiguous, not simply its translation into French or English.

A Satisfying Translation?

If we could identify, in English, a word or phrase for *peirasmos* that gathered up its subtleties, we might be in better position to understand the sixth petition of the Lord's Prayer. Kenneth Grayston has suggested a possibility worth considering: "the exercise of provocation." Thus he paraphrases: "Lead us not into a situation where we exercise provocation, where we find the hardships so intolerable that we are forced into [provoking you] and trying your patience" (Grayston, "Decline of Temptation," 294). In its defense Grayston cites a Syriac Psalm found at Qumran:

> Remember me and forget me not,
>   And bring me not to unbearable hardships. (11QPs[a] 24:2, trans. Grayston)

In its favor this suggestion acknowledges biblical instances in which mortals have, out of weakness or folly, "provoked" or "tried God's patience" (Exod. 17:2–7; Ps. 95:8–9; Wis. 1:1–2; Matt. 16:1; Mark 10:2; Luke 10:25; Acts 15:10; John 8:4–6; Heb. 3:7–12). Consistent with this idea is Paul's lengthy exposition of Israel's rebellion in Exodus (13:21; 14:22; 16:4–35; 17:6; 32:4, 6) and Numbers (14:29–30; 21:5–6; 25:1–18) for the cautionary edification of the Corinthian church. Here we must condense:

> Do not become idolaters as some of [our ancestors] did. . . . We must not indulge in sexual immorality as some of them did. . . . We must not put Christ to the test, as some of them did. . . . These things happened to them to serve as an example, and they were written down to instruct us, on whom the ends of the ages have come. So if you think you are standing, watch out that you do not fall. No testing has overtaken you that is not common to everyone. God is faithful, and he will not let you be tested beyond

your strength, but with the testing he will also provide the way out so that you may be able to endure it. Therefore, my dear friends, flee from the worship of idols. . . . Or are we provoking the Lord to jealousy? Are we stronger than he? (1 Cor. 10:7a, 8a, 9a, 11–14, 22)

In other words: having deluded themselves that they are stronger than they are, some Christians may not take their own testing with sufficient seriousness, thereby setting themselves up for a fall. On the other hand, those fearful of tottering in distress may rely on God to steady them. Paul's warning the church away from idolatry resonates in every trial (*peirasmon*) of Jesus by the devil (*ho peirazō*), narrated in Matthew 4:1–11 = Luke 4:1–13. In all these diabolical tests a compromise or outright denial of God's providential sovereignty is put forth. "You are famished; God does not care." "Let's see just how far God will go to save you." "This world's kingdoms answer to Satan, not to God." Jesus refutes each of these lies.

Gethsemane (Matt. 26:36–46 = Mark 14:32–42 = Luke 22:39–46) distills all tests to their paradoxical essence, bringing faithful disciples to their knees beside their Lord. Jesus prays for the cup to pass from him, the chalice that he has known all along he must drink (Matt. 20:22 = Mark 10:38). *Still* he prays for its diversion— but *only if* that would jibe with his Father's will. It does not. So he drinks it. Meanwhile the companions whom he has urged to watch and pray that *they* not enter *peirasmon* snore away (Matt. 26:37–46 = Mark 14:32–42 = Luke 22:39–46; cf. Luke 8:13). No matter: they will awaken soon enough. "The cup that I drink you will drink" (Mark 10:39a = Matt. 20:23a).

Preliminary Conclusions

After a circuitous journey we return to the Lord's Prayer's sixth petition. Of it I believe we may draw some cautious deductions.

• One of its critical terms, *peirasmos*, may better be understood as a particular kind of testing, proving, or trial. "Temptation" may not always be the central issue.

• The simplest—albeit theologically problematic—translation of the negated verb *mē eisenenkēs* is "Do not bring [or "lead" us]" (cf. Luke 5:18b–19; 1 Tim. 6:7; Heb. 13:11).

205

• To petition God's prevention from entering every mortal trial or test defies both scriptural witness and common sense. What servant of the LORD has enjoyed a life free of tribulation? Even if that were possible, would it actually be desirable? As Origen observed, "We should pray not that we should not be tested, for this is impossible, but that we should not be engulfed by testing, for those who are in its midst are so overcome" (*Prayer* 29.11, trans. Stewart-Sykes).

• The test to which the Prayer refers *may* be the Decisive Trial at the close of this age. That interpretation is defensible. However, it is neither well attested in our primary sources nor logically necessary. On the other hand: if one's theology leans toward the Johannine—if "*Now* is the judgment of this world; *now* the ruler of this world will be driven out" (John 12:31, emphasis added)—then the sixth petition's double cry for rescue from evil and its defeat may be considered "the moment of crisis [viewed] within its ultimate context" (Minear, "Home of the *Our Father*," 222). Every genuine trial we confront in this life is a sip from the cup we must finally drink to the dregs, handed to us from the Son who himself received it from his Father (John 18:11).

• If we consider early Jewish and Christian thought as a whole, it is highly unlikely that the Prayer's sixth petition aims to place God in the role of "wicked tempter." God tests us but does not pitch us headlong into evil. Such a belief is remote from the character of the biblical God, whose works are the antithesis of evil, who may be addressed as heavenly Father, and who knows much more than earthly parents how to give good things to those who ask him (Matt. 7:11 = Luke 11:13). Even Deutero-Isaiah's radically monotheistic ascription to God of both weal and woe (Isa. 45:7) does not erase the same author's conviction that, in the end, the LORD intends goodness and steadfast love for redeemed Israel (48:17; 54:10; 55:3).

• The immediate causes of some hardships we suffer lie inside (Jas. 1:12–16) or outside ourselves. Some biblical authors identify that external force with a satanic tempter, whether foe (1 Thess. 3:5) or friend (Matt. 16:23 = Mark 8:33). "Far be it that the Lord should seem to tempt, as though he were either ignorant of the faith of each of us, or sought to dethrone it, for weakness and malice are of the devil" (Tertullian, *Prayer* 8, trans. Stewart-Sykes).

206

• Various New Testament traditions recall that God tested Jesus himself, who did not capitulate (Matt. 4:1–11 = Luke 4:1–13; Mark 8:33 = Matt. 16:23; Mark 14:32–42 = Luke 22:39–46). "Because he himself was tested by what he suffered, he is able to help those who are being tested. . . . For we do not have a high priest who is unable to sympathize with our weaknesses, but we have one who in every respect has been tested as we are, yet without sin" (Heb. 2:18; 4:15).

• The peril against which Jesus' disciples are instructed to pray is that which might either strain God's patience with us to the breaking point or induce us to renounce God altogether. We ask that we not be drawn into circumstances whose intensity is sure to defy our power to withstand them (Moule, "Unresolved Problem," 75). Why? Because, confessing our weakness, we are certain to fail (Knowles, "Once More"). As we have witnessed throughout this prayer, most immediately in its fourth and fifth petitions (chaps. 6–7 above), so also here: "The spirit indeed is willing, but the flesh is weak" (Matt. 26:41b = Mark 14:38b). We must eat to live: God, fill that need. We are bankrupt: forgive us, LORD, as we forgive others. We are weak and in danger of collapsing: Father, bolster us and lead us away from forsaking you. The same Lord who has guaranteed the prayers for bread and forgiveness stands behind this one. "Christ has stopped the mouth of the accuser. [This] petition has been heard: no devil can ever change that. The help from above is stronger than the attack from below" (Lüthi, *Lord's Prayer*, 62).

The Petition's Second Clause

The petition, "But save us from *tou ponērou*," may have originated with Jesus. That clause, however, does not appear in our earliest manuscripts of Luke 11:4c.

Matthew's tradition favors the prayer for salvation from *to ponēros*. That term and its cognates appear in Matthew 23 times: 30 percent of its 78 occurrences in the New Testament.

The adversative particle "but" (*alla*) suggests a strong contrast with the petition immediately preceding. The effect of that distinction seems twofold. First, in positive terms it paraphrases the clause just negated: "Do not bring us, but lead us away." Second, it clarifies that the trial mentioned in the preceding clause could eventuate in a catastrophe that should not be attributed to God, who is in no way *ponēros*: worthless, base, or evil. Matthew's additional clause opens another dimension onto the Prayer's sixth and final petition, ending

207

the Prayer on a hard, almost dissonant, note. That discord should not be exaggerated. Because the plea is for "rescue" (Matt. 27:43; 2 Tim. 4:18), "deliverance" (Rom. 7:24; 2 Cor. 1:10), "preservation" (Ps. 2:12; Isa. 25:4), even being "snatched away" (Ps. 91:3)—all connoted by the verb *ryomai*—it is consistent with the Prayer's repeated positioning of supplicants as destitute before God's majestic power and beneficence. We cannot escape evil under our own steam; we can only be saved by Another.

A basic exegetical question raised by this clause is the translation of *tou ponērou*: what or who is the *ponērou*, from which we pray to be protected? That singular Greek adjective is preceded by the definite article and can refer to a neuter principle (evil things; wickedness) *or* to a masculine personification (a wicked person; the evil one) if construed as a substantive. Because either is grammatically possible, English versions move in alternative directions: "evil" (KJV, LATTIMORE, MOFFATT, RSV); "the Evil One" or "the evil one" (CASSIRER, CEB, GNB, GOODSPEED, JB, NAB, NEB, NIV, NJB, NRSV, REB). Most of these versions refer their readers to the alternative possibility in a marginal note.

This uncertainty has long puzzled Christians. In general the Western church has favored the abstract connotation, "evil," frequently referring to acts of human wickedness (Augustine of Hippo, Thomas Aquinas, Margaret Ebner, Nicholas of Cusa); however, Tertullian (*Prayer* 30), Chrysostom (*Homily on Matthew* 19.10), Luther (in multiple commentaries), and Teresa of Avila (*Way of Perfection* 39.3–4) refer to the devil as *ho ponēros*. "The Evil One" has been the preferred translation by commentators in the Eastern church (Cyprian, Origen, Cyril); again, however, one notes exceptions (Maximus the Confessor, *Commentary on the Our Father* 5). Gregory of Nyssa accepts both (*Lord's Prayer* 5.18). In his commentary on Matthew (1.1; see also *Institutes* 2.914), Calvin left the question open, allowing either possibility. While concerned for the Christian's preservation from sin's blandishments, Calvin was not timid in speaking of Satan's temptations. If this problem of translation is soluble, context must supply it.

The Old Testament lays a foundation for understanding that extends only so far. Before God, the arbiter of good and evil (Isa. 5:20; Amos 5:14, 15; Mic. 3:2; Mal. 2:17), human impulses (Gen. 6:5; 8:21) and acts (Gen. 38:7; 2 Sam. 11:27; 1 Kgs. 14:22) can be evil (Heb., *raʿ*). "The wicked man," by definition, transgresses what the LORD has commanded in Torah (Deut. 17:7, 12; 22:21–24; 24:7; Isa. 9:16; Jer. 15:21; Ezra 7:24; Sir. 17:31). Neither women (Sir. 25:16, 23; 42:6) nor children (Wis. 3:12) nor society at large (Num. 14:27; 1 Esd. 1:24) are exempt from such a tendency. In an absolute sense, evil is contrasted with good (Gen. 2:9, 17; 2 Sam. 13:22; Isa. 5:20; Amos 5:15; Eccl. 12:14). The Hebrew Bible has not yet moved to identifying "the evil one" with a devilish figure: Satan (literally, "the Adversary") functions as a prosecutor in the heavenly court (1 Chr. 21:1; Job 1–2; Zech. 3:1–2). Instead, evil is contrary to God, and "the evil one" is anyone who acts in that manner. These basic ideas are perpetuated in the Dead Sea Scrolls, Philo and Josephus, and the Pseudepigrapha, although some documents in the latter corpus refer to restless spirits that assail humanity (*1 En.* 5:11; *T. Sol.* 4.4; see Harder, *"ponēros, ponēria,"* 551–54). The figure of Satan appears rarely in the Scrolls (4Q280; 4Q286 frag. 7; see Black, "Doxology," 333–36).

Although Satan and the Angel of Death are personified in later rabbinic sources (*b. Qiddushin* 81a; *b. Sukkah* 52b; *b. Baba Batra* 16a; *Exodus Rabbah* 30.18; Targum on Zech. 3), the rabbis usually associate evil with the *yetzer haraʿ*: an evil imagination, attitude, or inclination that stirs mortals to rebel against God (cf. Gen. 6:5; 8:21; Deut. 31:21; Schechter, *Aspects*, 242–63). "The evil *yetzer* of a man waxes strong against him day by day, and seeks to kill him, and if God did not help him, man could not prevail against it" (*b. Qiddushin* 30b). Some rabbinic traditions present contesting wills within human beings: the evil *yetzer*, prone to idolatry or adultery, and the good *yetzer*, which inclines toward obedience and wisdom (*Zohar* on Exodus 107a; Midrash on Prov. 12). The "sovereign remedy" against the evil *yetzer* is study and satisfaction of the law (Montefiore and Loewe, *Rabbinic Anthology*, 302); still, the righteous remain seducible by evil. "God never unites His name with the righteous during their lifetime, only after their death" (*Tanhuma*, Toledot 7). Even study of Torah is no infallible prophylactic against sin: "The evil *yetzer* attacks the scholars most of all" (*b. Sukkah* 52a). Neither do the New Testament's writings move in a uniform, consistent direction. Depending on its context, *ho ponēros* (masculine) or *to ponēron* (neuter), either of which could lead to the genitive *tou ponērou* in Matt. 6:13b, may refer to: 209

- Something useless (Matt. 7:18; 18:32; Luke 19:22) or despicable (Rev. 16:2).
- An evil person (Matt. 7:11 = Luke 11:13; Matt. 13:49; 22:10; 2 Tim. 3:13) or an adulterous generation (Matt. 12:39, 45; Luke 11:29 = Matt. 16:4).
- A wicked propensity (1 Tim. 6:4; Heb. 3:12; 10:22; Jas. 2:4) or deed (Matt. 5:11, 45; 12:35; Mark 7:22–23; John 3:19; 7:7; Acts 18:14; 25:18; 28:21; 1 Cor. 5:13; Col. 1:21; 1 Thess. 5:22; 2 Tim. 4:18; Jas. 4:16; 1 John 3:12; 2 John 11; 3 John 10).
- This age, probably owing to its sufferings and seductions (Gal. 1:4; Eph. 5:16; 6:13).
- A demon (Acts 19:12–13, 15–16).
- The devil (Matt. 13:19, 38; John 17:15; 1 John 2:13–14; 5:18–19; 2 Thess. 3:3 [?]). This use of *ponēros/ponēron* is picked up though not elaborated in the Apostolic Fathers (*Mart. Pol.* 17.1; *Did.* 8.2; *Barn.* 2.10; 19.11; 21.3).

If we narrow the scope only to the cognate adjective's occurrences in Matthew, we find a broad range of connotations: that which is "worthless" (5:37; 25:26), "rotten" (7:17–18; 12:34–35), "base" (5:11; 22:10), "evil" (6:23; 12:45; 15:19; 16:4; 20:15), "wicked" (5:45; 7:11; 12:39; 13:49), or "vicious" (9:4; 18:32).

Given this breadth of evidence within and beyond Matthew's Gospel, I consider the decisions by Gregory of Nyssa and Calvin well founded: the supplication in Matthew 6:13b may be legitimately interpreted as preservation from evil things, protection from the Evil One, or both. The concept of evil, which is no empty abstraction but has "a definite physiognomy" (Boff, *Lord's Prayer*, 115), coheres with Matthean usage generally; the personification of evil as a satanic or diabolical figure is clearly attested in Matthew 13:19, 38–39, coherent with other passages in that Gospel (12:26; 16:23; 25:41) and corroborated in the eschatologically tinctured Johannine literature. Matthew 4:1–11 exemplifies these ideas' conflation and provides a key for their mutual understanding: all of the devil's incentives are designed to turn Jesus toward the devil and away from God. That is what makes the bait evil: by it the Evil One reveals himself as God's nemesis.

210   If Matthew 6:13b was intended as an interpretation of 6:13a, then it serves that purpose admirably. The two clauses are complementary: reference to evil in 6:13b confirms that *peirasmos,*

mentioned in 6:13a, is potentially overwhelming. So we might para-phrase: "Heavenly Father, *do not take us into* an insuperable trial that would separate us from you. *Do take us away from* that which hatefully flouts what you intend for us and for the world." A similar pair of appeals is more eloquently enunciated in the ninth-century synagogue prayer Abhinu Malkenu (see appendix A):

> Our Father, Our King, nullify evil decrees from us.
> Our Father, Our King, renew for us good decrees.

The Evil That Would Divorce Us from God

I have suggested that the elemental concern of these final petitions boils down to heinous trials that, left unchecked, would divorce us from the LORD to whom we pray. To concentrate our deliberation on this terrible yet crucial subject, I offer three test cases. As my scriptural touchstone I take the legend of Jesus' temptations, nar-rated in Matthew 4:1–11 = Luke 4:1–13, which summarizes and clarifies the same trials to which Jesus' disciples are still subject. Following the lead of the evangelists, who shuffled the order of their presentation, I shall do the same here, for in fact all of these trials are interrelated.

Denial

Satan's second temptation in Luke 4:5–8 (the third in Matt. 4:8–10) was to offer Jesus the universal glory of all kingdoms—save God's—if only he would repudiate his Father and kneel before the devil. The allure of rejecting God and embracing Satan is full-frontal evil. The most important thing to be said of Luke 11:4c = Matthew 6:13ab may be that it appears in the prayer at all. Evil exists. Christian faith cannot deny that. To pretend otherwise not only turns a blind eye to the world as we know it; it also evacuates the necessity of the gos-pel. If Jesus was crucified for no reason other than a misjudgment by Caesar's minions, then it was merely a commonplace tragedy inflicted upon a single, eccentric Jew. Deny evil, and you deny the imperative for its eradication. If this world does not suffer assault by incomprehensible wickedness and death, if there is no need for this world's redemption, then "Christ died for nothing" (Gal. 2:21).

211

Fleming Rutledge's reflections on evil, "The Descent into Hell," are exemplary in their painstaking plain-spokenness (*The Crucifixion*, 395–461).

> At stake . . . is a concept of hell that is adequate to the horrors of the twentieth century and the looming terrors of the twenty-first. . . . It is necessary to posit the existence of a metaphorical hell in order to acknowledge the reality and power of radical evil—evil that does not yield to education, reason, or good intentions. Evil has an existence independent of the sum total of human misdeeds. The concept of hell takes seriously the nature and scale of evil. Without a concept of hell, Christian faith is sentimental and evasive, unable to stand up to reality in this world. Without an unflinching grasp of the radical nature of evil, Christian faith would be little more than wishful thinking. (Rutledge, *The Crucifixion*, 458)

Conversant with the whole of biblical and historical theology, Rutledge argues that evil is neither rationally nor morally intelligible. It lies beyond human explanation. Its horrendous reality, mysteriously permitted yet combated by God, cannot be contradicted. It can only be despised and resisted.

Satan frolics in our intellectual quagmires to explain the inexplicable, because they distract us from recognizing and confronting the demonic among us. He is also a master of disguise, adept at concealing himself in positive values and ideals while corrupting them from within (see Niebuhr, *Children of Light*). "The beginning of resistance is not to *explain*, but *to see*. Seeing is itself a form of action—seeing evil for what it is, not a part of God's plan, but a colossal *x* factor in creation, a monstrous contradiction, a prodigious negation that must be identified, denounced, and opposed wherever it occurs" (Rutledge, *The Crucifixion*, 434).

When we pray to be redirected from a trial that would break us, to be rescued from evil so abominable that it could sever us from God and one another, we *see* evil, recognize it for what it is, and beg for the strength to oppose it to the limit of human power. Our inability to explain evil cannot be allowed to mask its reality or to justify compromise with it. No matter how seductive his bogus baubles (Matt. 4:8–10 = Luke 4:5–8), we refuse to bow before the devil, which includes fatalistic concessions to the degradation of God's children. The first step of resistance is taken every time we pray this petition of the Lord's Prayer.

212

Displacement

To acknowledge the truth about evil is one thing. It is quite another to identify its source and the resources for its defeat. When the devil poised Jesus on the temple's pinnacle and egged him on for a magical display for the ages, underwritten by an inexhaustible fund of Providence, it was a temptation worthy of Madison Avenue and Washington, DC—both of which now capitalize and push their products with such ruthless skill that they are interchangeable.

Two of Satan's most potent, time-tested techniques are masterly sleights of hand: (1) diverting our attention away from deep devilry onto secondary or tertiary subjects and (2) confusion of genuine remedies for our sufferings. The key to their successful application is mongering fear. Thus senior demon Screwtape wrote to his nephew Wormwood, an apprentice tempter:

> The main point is . . . to increase fear. . . . What you must do is to keep running in [your patient's] mind (side by side with the conscious intention of doing his duty) the vague idea of all sorts of things he can do or not do, *inside* the framework of duty, which seem to make him a little safer. . . . The point is to keep him feeling that he has *something*, other than the Enemy [i.e., God] and courage the Enemy supplies, *to fall back on*, so that what was intended to be a total commitment to duty becomes honeycombed all through with little unconscious reservations. By building up a series of imaginary expedients to prevent "the worst coming to the worst," you may produce, at that level of will which he is not aware of, a determination that the worst *shall not* come to the worst. Then, at the moment of real terror, rush it out into his nerves and muscles and you may get the final act done before he knows what you're about. (Lewis, *Screwtape Letters*, 138–39)

That's the devil's therapy: reroute human beings away from dependence on God onto vain self-reliance, bedazzled by a misplaced sense of duty, and keep mainlining fear, like heroin, into the bloodstream.

One obvious exhibition of devilish displacement is nationalism (following Minear, *Kingdom and the Power*, 96–97). Choose a nation—any will do, though the wealthiest offer prime subjects for analysis—and observe how evil or the Evil One (take your pick, as long as you take it seriously) corrupts its citizens' compliance. For its leaders to shore up authority and the power to wield it, Satan pounds the timpani (more delicately, brushes the snare drum) of

213

nationalistic pride to escalate the citizenry's imagined aspirations, which naturally must be regarded as preeminent and superior in virtue to those of all other nations. The rights of *this* nation must be exalted as inalienable, lest its sovereignty be threatened, even qualified. The maintenance of *this* nation's security, wealth, and prestige must be lodged in every citizen's mind as the unquestionable criterion by which every act is justified or denounced. Sensitive instruments of propaganda rig public opinion to prevent deviation from a lockstep. Invisible censors monitor and regulate the citizenry's feelings, thoughts, and actions. In this nation's name extravagant pledges are made that can never be fulfilled. Any encroachment on this nation's fortunes, particularly those of its governing body, is branded and broadcast as a major crisis, a disaster that must be repelled. Dissent, which cannot be tolerated, is quashed by means of shame, slander, defamation, dishonoring of motive, or legal action. At all costs allegiance to *this* nation, its ends and the means for their attainment, must engulf and overrule the citizen's responsibility to conscience or to God. Any distinction between man and mammon, between God and Caesar, must be erased. To the emperor and the plutocrat belongs total fealty. And what holds for nations applies to all other earthly authorities. In maximizing strife, confusion, and fear, no society, including the church, is too small for Satan's interest.

A second conspicuous and diabolical displacement, peculiar to the United States, has become the gun. As Screwtape counseled Wormwood, "Keep [your client] feeling that he has *something*, other than [God] and courage [that] Enemy supplies, *to fall back on.*" "The right to bear arms," a military expression, has become a creedal affirmation beyond question, a fundamentalist claim of civil religion. In North American culture (excluding Canada) the gun has become a sacred object that can do no wrong, capable of reducing even the toughest politician or jurist to a gelatinous invertebrate. "Guns don't kill people; people kill people": a defiance of logic that trashes the indisputable fact that the highest number of deaths by gunfire corresponds precisely with the percentage of private ownership of guns.

A week after the mass murder of twenty children and six adults at Sandy Hook Elementary School in Newtown, Connecticut (December 14, 2012), Wayne LaPierre (1948–), executive vice president of the National Rifle Association of America, issued a formal statement (December 21, 2012): "The truth is that our society

214

is populated by an unknown number of genuine monsters—people so deranged, so evil, so possessed by voices and driven by demons that no sane person can possibly *ever* comprehend them. . . . How can we possibly even *guess* how many, given our nation's refusal to create an active national database of the mentally ill?" ("NRA Press Conference," 2, 3, with original emphasis). Mr. LaPierre's answer: "We need to have *every single school in America* immediately deploy a protection program proven to work—and by that I mean *armed security*" (8). His reason: "The *only* thing that stops a *bad* guy with a gun is a *good* guy with a gun" (5). In the Church of the Gun the only possible solution to America's devastation by firearms is more guns everywhere: in offices, shops, schools, colleges, and churches. The result: Americans now skim headlines of another day's mass shootings before flipping through the sports section. They have now so habituated themselves to violence that they have normalized derangement. Beside Wayne LaPierre, citizens of the United States point the finger of mental illness at everyone else—but never at themselves. Americans, of course, are the good guys, clothed in an innocence untainted by evil. Means and ends are one, and ours are impeccably justifiable.

Referring to child sacrifice on the fires of Molech's (or Moloch's) altar (Lev. 18:21; 20:1–5)—obscene even to ancient Romans, not remembered for their tenderheartedness—Garry Wills has argued that the gun has become more than an object of American reverence:

> That horror [at Sandy Hook] cannot be blamed just on one unhinged person. It was the sacrifice we as a culture made, and continually make, to our demonic god. We guarantee that crazed man after crazed man will have a flood of killing power readily supplied him. We have to make that offering, out of devotion to our Moloch, our god. The gun is our Moloch. We sacrifice children to him daily—sometimes, as at Sandy Hook, by directly throwing them into the fire-hose of bullets from our protected private killing machines, sometimes by blighting our children's lives by the death of a parent, a schoolmate, a teacher, a protector. Sometimes this is done by mass killings, sometimes by private offerings to the god. ("Our Moloch," 2)

215

Among the evil from which we might pray for deliverance is the first pagan god who, according to Milton, volunteered in Lucifer's war on humanity:

First Moloch, horrid king, besmear'd with blood
Of human sacrifice, and parents' tears,
Though for the noise of Drums and Timbrels loud
Their children's cries unheard, that pass'd through fire
To his grim idol. (*Paradise Lost* 1.392–96; quoted by Wills)

Despair

I've made a long voyage and been to a strange country, and I've
seen the dark man very close. (Thomas Wolfe to Maxwell Perkins
[August 12, 1938], in Perkins, *Editor to Author*, 141)

"Full of" (Luke 4:1), "led up by" (Matt. 4:1), or even "thrown out
by" (Mark 1:12 AT) the Holy Spirit, Jesus spent forty days in the wilderness with nothing to eat. "And afterwards he was hungry" (Matt.
4:2; Luke 4:2): a gem of biblical understatement. After being sent
to hide by the brook Cherith, east of the Jordan, the LORD had sent
ravens, morning and evening, to feed Elijah the prophet (1 Kgs.
17:1–7). Fresh from baptism, acclaimed by God as his Son, Jesus
got nothing. Then the tempter made his move: "If you are the Son
of God, command these stones to become loaves of bread" (Matt.
4:3 = Luke 4:3). Jesus' quotation of Deuteronomy 8:3 explains his
refusal: he will not take orders from the devil; he will live his life
under God's command (Matt. 4:4a = Luke 4:4). In the desert of
God's absence, Jesus held on to "every word that proceeds from
the mouth of God" (Matt. 4:4b RSV). After all his trials, Matthew
(4:11) and Mark (1:13) report that Jesus received angelic ministra-
tions. Luke comments, "When the devil had finished every test, he
departed from him until an opportune time [*akri kairou*]" (4:13).

The climactic opportunity came at Golgotha. After being tortured by crucifixion for nine hours, Jesus' last articulate words in
Matthew (Matt. 27:46) and in Mark (15:34) quoted a psalmist's cry
(22:1) from the bowels of hell: "My God, my God, why have you
forsaken me?" That Jesus' final words differ in Luke (23:46) and in
John (19:30) is true, and those utterances carry their own validity.
For our purpose, however, it is important to confront the paradox
presented by the first two Gospels: at the moment of his death,
Jesus prayed to the God whom he believed had abandoned him,
as had everyone else (Matt. 26:69–75 = Mark 14:66–72 = Luke
22:54b–62; Matt. 27:11–44 = Mark 15:1–32 = Luke 23:1–38). As

in the wilderness, so at Calvary: utterly alone and tempted beyond imagination, Jesus clung to his heavenly Father even when no Hand was visibly there to hold. Jesus' short visit to a strange country led him to see the Dark Man very close.

It's been said that, of all the devil's elixirs, despair is the most toxic. It is the temptation, under unimaginable distress, to resign oneself to the notion that there is no point in going any further; that the well has run dry, never to be replenished; that we have become for ourselves and others a burden no longer worth carrying; that we are alone; that there is no God.

Chronic, harrowing disease is an occasion for the emergence of despair. A physician reflects on the lives of his patients:

> Cancer is not a concentration camp, but it shares [its] quality of annihilation: it negates the possibility of life outside and beyond itself; it subsumes all living. The daily life of a patient becomes so intensely preoccupied with his or her illness that the world fades away. Every last morsel of energy is spent tending the disease. . . . The poet Jason Shinder wrote, "Cancer is a tremendous opportunity to have your face pressed right up against the glass of your mortality." But what patients see through the glass is not a world outside cancer, but a world taken away by it—cancer reflected endlessly around them like a hall of mirrors. (Mukherjee, *Emperor of All Maladies*, 398)

Edna St. Vincent Millay carefully arranged some words on the subject of suffering:

> And must I then, indeed, Pain, live with you
> All through my life?—sharing my fire, my bed,
> Sharing—oh, worst of all things!—the same head?—
> And, when feeding myself, feeding you, too? (*Collected Poems*, 734)

In 1989 two virologists, Harold E. Varmus and J. Michael Bishop, were awarded the Nobel Prize for discovering in the laboratory what Millay had learned from her brain and bones: that cancer genes were no freelance marauders but come *from within* the human genome itself. Genetically we are loaded with potential malignancies, awaiting activation. "We have not slain our enemy, the cancer cell, or figuratively torn the limbs from his body. In our adventures we have only seen our monster more clearly and described his scales and fangs in new ways—ways that reveal a

217

cancer cell to be, like [*Beowulf's*] Grendel, a distorted version of our normal selves" (Varmus, "Banquet Speech"). The mystery of evil will not be dismissed.

Although she did not suffer cancer, Edna Millay did experience severe bouts of depression, "sorrow like a ceaseless rain." Like cancer, depression assaults millions of people around the world; also like cancer, depression is a chute down which many slide into despair. Among them the poor and the elderly are chronically undertreated. Scores of stories are related in Andrew Solomon's semi-autobiographical account, *The Noonday Demon* (2001), which can help those not afflicted by depression to understand something of what it's like. Drawn from a different study is this remarkably articulate expression of a condition that William Styron described as "indescribable" (*Darkness Visible*, 16–17):

> Depression is an insidious vacuum that crawls into your brain and pushes your mind out of the way. It is the complete absence of rational thought. It is freezing cold, with a dangerous, horrifying, terrifying fog wafting through whatever is left in your mind. . . . Depression steals away whoever you were, prevents you from seeing who you might someday be, and replaces your life with a black hole. Like a sweater eaten by moths, nothing is left of the original, only fragments that hinted at greater capacities, greater abilities, greater potentials, now gone. Nothing human beings value matters any more. . . . Suicide sounds terrific, but much too difficult to plan and complete. (Karp, *Speaking of Sadness*, 23–24)

Let's view these testimonies with a wide-focus lens. In the United States alone, 15.5 million people currently living have been treated for cancer. Oncologists expect 1,735,350 new cases to be diagnosed in 2018; during that year 609,640 Americans are expected to die (American Cancer Society, "Cancer Facts," 1). During 2010–16, some 40 million adults were diagnosed with major depressive or generalized anxiety disorders (ADAA, "Facts and Statistics," 1). Of known cases, therefore, about 17.5% of the American population suffers from two chronic illnesses whose principal by-product in many cases is despair. If one reckons with other factors in what de Caussade (*Abandonment*, 11.7) presciently called "that deep abyss of perversity"—other disease, unemployment, poverty, drug addiction, violent crime, environmental destruction, and the submerged,

218

ever-lurking terror of nuclear holocaust—the despair quotient is incalculably higher. Tightening the screws, Satan, Screwtape, & Co. is realizing record profits.

Why pray for rescue from evil? I close with two answers. The first is from Maggie Robbins, who suffered manic depression for decades and a psychotic mental breakdown:

> You can exorcise the demons of schizophrenics who perceive that there's something foreign inside of them. But it's much harder with depressed people because we believe we are seeing the truth. But the truth lies. . . . According to Christian doctrine, you're not allowed to commit suicide because your life is not your own. You are the steward of your life and your body, but they are not yours to destroy. You don't end up battling everything out inside yourself; . . . you're battling it out with these other characters, with Jesus Christ and God the Father and the Holy Spirit. . . . For me, Christianity is the study of what real love, useful love, consists of—and of what constitutes attention. People think that Christianity is against pleasure, as it sometimes is; but it's very, very pro-joy. You're aiming for joy that will never go away, no matter what kind of pain you're in. (Solomon, *Noonday Demon*, 129, 132)

The second response is from one who knew much about evil, death, and the persistence of a life that will finally vanquish the unholy marriage of Satan and death:

> Who will separate us from the love of Christ? Will hardship, or distress, or persecution, or famine, or nakedness, or peril, or sword? As it is written,
> > "For your sake we are being killed all day long;
> > we are accounted as sheep to be slaughtered."
> No, in all these things we are more than conquerors through him who loved us. For I am convinced that neither death, nor life, nor angels, nor rulers, nor things present, nor things to come, nor powers, nor height, nor depth, nor anything else in all creation, will be able to separate us from the love of God in Christ Jesus our Lord. (Rom. 8:35–39)

Joy that will never fade but only swell is the purification of our heart's deepest desire. And indissoluble union with God is the supreme education of our human wanting.

219

Works Cited in Chapter 8

ADAA = Anxiety and Depression Association of America. "Facts and Statistics." ADAA: Silver Spring, MD, 2010–2016. https://adaa.org/about-adaa/press-room/facts-statistics#.

American Cancer Society. "Cancer Facts & Figures 2018." Atlanta: American Cancer Society, 2018. https://www.cancer.org/research/cancer-facts-statistics/all-cancer-facts-figures/cancer-facts-figures-2018.html.

Barth, Karl. *Prayer: Fiftieth Anniversary Edition.* Edited by Don E. Saliers, from the translation by Sara F. Terrien. Louisville, KY: Westminster John Knox, 2002.

BBC News. "Lord's Prayer: Pope Francis Calls for Change." December 8, 2017. http://www.bbc.com/news/world-europe-42279427.

Black, Matthew. "The Doxology to the *Pater Noster* with a Note on Matthew 6.13b." In *A Tribute to Géza Vermès: Essays on Jewish and Christian Literature and History*, edited by Philip R. Davies and Richard T. White, 327–38. Journal for the Study of the Old Testament Supplement Series 100. Sheffield: Sheffield Academic Press, 1990.

Boff, Leonardo. *The Lord's Prayer: The Prayer of Integral Liberation.* Translated by Theodore Morrow. Maryknoll, NY: Orbis Books, 1983.

Brown, Raymond E. "The Pater Noster as an Eschatological Prayer." In *New Testament Essays*, 217–53. New York: Paulist Press, 1965.

Calvin, John. *Institutes of the Christian Religion.* Vol. 2. Edited by John T. McNeill. Translated by Ford Lewis Battles. Library of Christian Classics 21. Philadelphia: Westminster Press, 1960.

Carmignac, Jean. *Recherches sur le "Notre Père."* Paris: Letouzey & Ané, 1969.

Conférence des évêques de France, ed. "Notre Père." Église catholique en France, December 12, 2017. http://eglise.catholique.fr/approfondir-sa-foi/prier/prieres/372214-notre-pere/.

Davies, W. D., and Dale C. Allison Jr. *The Gospel according to Saint Matthew.* Vol. 1. Edinburgh: T&T Clark, 1988.

De Caussade, Jean-Pierre. *Abandonment, or, Absolute Surrender to Divine Providence.* New York: Benziger Brothers, 1887.

Fitzmyer, Joseph A. "And Lead Us Not into Temptation." *Biblica* 84 (2003): 259–73.

Grayston, Kenneth. "The Decline of Temptation—and the Lord's Prayer." *Scottish Journal of Theology* 46 (1993): 279–95.

Harder, Günther. "*ponēros, ponēria.*" *TDNT* 6 (1968): 546–66.

Heneghan, Tom. "Does God Lead Us into Sin? New French 'Our Father' Says No." *National Catholic Reporter*, December 6, 2017. https://www.ncronline.org/news/theology/does-god-lead -us-sin-new-french-our-father-says-no.

Karp, David A. *Speaking of Sadness: Depression, Disconnection, and the Meanings of Illness.* New York: Oxford University Press, 1996.

Knowles, Michael P. "Once More 'Lead Us Not *Eis Peirasmon.*'" *Expository Times* 115 (2004): 191–94.

Kuhn, Karl Georg. "New Light on Temptation, Sin, and Flesh in the New Testament." In *The Scrolls and the New Testament*, edited by Krister Stendahl, 94–113. London: SCM; New York: Harper & Brothers, 1958.

LaPierre, Wayne. "NRA Press Conference, December 21, 2012." https://archive.nytimes.com/www.nytimes.com/interactive /2012/12/21/us/nra-news-conference-transcript.html.

Lewis, C. S. *The Screwtape Letters and Screwtape Proposes a Toast.* New York: Macmillan, 1959, 1961.

Lohmeyer, Ernst. *"Our Father": An Introduction to the Lord's Prayer.* Translated by John Bowden. London: Collins; New York: Harper & Row, 1965.

Lüthi, Walter. *The Lord's Prayer: An Exposition.* Translated by Kurt Schoenberger. Edinburgh: Oliver & Boyd; Richmond: John Knox Press, 1961.

Luz, Ulrich. *Matthew 1–7: A Commentary.* Translated by W. C. Linss. Continental Commentaries. Minneapolis: Fortress Press, 1989.

Millay, Edna St. Vincent. *Collected Poems.* Edited by Norma Millay. New York: Harper & Row, 1956.

Minear, Paul Sevier. "But Whose Prayer Is It?" *Worship* 76 (2002): 324–38.

———. "The Home of the *Our Father.*" *Worship* 74 (2000): 212–22.

———. *The Kingdom and the Power: An Exposition of the New Testament Gospel.* Philadelphia: Westminster Press, 1950.

Montefiore, Claude G., and Herbert Loewe. *A Rabbinic Anthology.* New York: Schocken Books, 1974.

Moule, C. F. D. "An Unresolved Problem in the Temptation-Clause in the Lord's Prayer." *Reformed Theological Review* 33 (1974): 65–75.

Mukherjee, Siddhartha. *The Emperor of All Maladies: A Biography of Cancer.* New York: Scribner, 2010.

Niebuhr, Reinhold. *The Children of Light and the Children of Darkness: A Vindication of Democracy and a Critique of Its Traditional Defenders.* New York: Charles Scribner's Sons, 1945.

Perkins, Maxwell E. *Editor to Author: The Letters of Maxwell Perkins.* Selected and edited by John Hall Wheelock. New York: Charles Scribner's Sons, 1950.

Rutledge, Fleming. *The Crucifixion: Understanding the Death of Jesus Christ.* Grand Rapids: Wm. B. Eerdmans Publishing Co., 2015.

Schechter, Solomon. *Aspects of Rabbinic Theology.* New York: Schocken Books, 1961.

Solomon, Andrew. *The Noonday Demon: An Atlas of Depression.* New York: Scribner, 2001.

Styron, William. *Darkness Visible: A Memoir of Madness.* New York: Random House, 1990.

Varmus, Harold E. "Nobel Banquet Speech." December 10, 1989. https://www.nobelprize.org/nobel_prizes/medicine/laureates /1989/varmus-speech.html.

Vokes, F. E. "The Lord's Prayer in the First Three Centuries." *Studia Patristica* 10. Part 1: 253–60. Texte und Untersuchungen zur Geschichte der altchristlichen Literatur 107. Berlin: Akademie-Verlag, 1970.

Wamsley, Laurel. "Pope Francis Suggests Changing the Words to the 'Lord's Prayer.'" *National Public Radio*, December 8, 2017. https://www.npr.org/sections/thetwo-way/2017/12/08/5693857 69/pope-francis-suggests-changing-the-words-to-lord-s-prayer.

Willis, Geoffrey G. "Lead Us Not into Temptation." *Downside Review* 93 (1975): 281–88.

Wills, Garry. "Our Moloch." *New York Review of Books Daily*, December 15, 2012. http://www.nybooks.com/daily/2012/12/15 /our-moloch/.

PART FOUR

Doxology and Conclusion

For yours is the kingdom and the power and the glory forever. Amen.

Kingdom, Power, and Glory
A Pastoral Coda

CHAPTER 9

Kingdom, Power, and Glory

Stand by for the big show. Life is only the overture.

—Fred Allen

Among others, Tertullian, Augustine, and Thomas Aquinas believed that the Lord's Prayer is the most perfect of prayers. (See appendix C.) If so, its traditional conclusion may be its perfect capstone.

A Brief Tradition History

At several points in this commentary we have become ensnarled in controversial interpretive matters. The reader may be relieved to know that no dispute—text-critically, anyway—is attached to the Prayer's final petition, as prayed in most Protestant and Orthodox churches. Virtually all biblical scholars concur that "Yours is the kingdom and the power and the glory forever. Amen" is a later addition to the text of Matthew 6:9–13. Manuscripts of Luke 11:2–4, even those tending to draw Luke's phraseology into conformity with Matthew's, do not include this clause. Two of our earliest manuscripts of Matthew, Codices Sinaiticus and Vaticanus, witnesses of superior scribal quality that date back to the fourth century, end the prayer at 6:13, *apo tou ponērou* (from evil). Codex Bezae, a fifth-century manuscript whose scribal family tends to take more liberties in

225

transmission, also omits these words. The majority of patristic commentators—among others, Tertullian, Origen, Cyprian, Gregory of Nyssa, Augustine, and Maximus the Confessor—offer no exegesis of this clause. The Latin Vulgate, the great Bible of the medieval West whose authority was confirmed at the Catholic Council of Trent (1545–63), does not contain it; to this day modern Roman Catholic commentaries on the Prayer usually do not interpret it (for instance, Maritain; Weil; Boff; Ayo; Catholic Church, *Catechism*), probably because it is missing from most Roman Missals.

Repetition of the doxology varies in other church liturgies and vernacular versions of the New Testament. In the Greek Orthodox *Divine Liturgy of Saint John Chrysostom* (ca. 400), the doxology is offered by the priest before the celebration of Holy Communion: "For Yours is the kingdom and the power and the glory of the Father and the Son, and the Holy Spirit, now and forever and to the ages of ages" (to which the people reply, "Amen"; *Divine Liturgy*, 27). Luther's estimable translation of the New Testament into German (1522) included the doxology, as did William Tyndale's version (1534), Miles Coverdale's (1535), and the King James Version (1611). Although absent from John Wycliffe's English Bible (1382–95), a brief insertion appears in the text: "Amen, let it be so."

The ancient manuscript tradition of Matthew 6:13 is mildly chaotic. Different churches in different regions added different endings to the Lord's Prayer, following the petition for deliverance from evil.

1. *A no-member clause, with liturgical emphasis*, can be traced as far back as Cyril of Jerusalem (ca. 313–386): a simple "Amen." As we shall see, 'āmēn (Heb.) carries the force of a congregational ratification. So ends a series of twelve curses in Deuteronomy 27:

> The Levites shall declare in a loud voice to all the Israelites: . . . "Cursed be anyone who does not uphold the words of this law by observing them." All the people shall say, "Amen!" (Deut. 27:14, 26)

Likewise in congregational blessings:

> Say also: . . . "Blessed be the LORD, the God of Israel, from everlasting to everlasting." Then all the people said "Amen!" and praised the LORD. (1 Chr. 16:35–36)

> Blessed be the LORD forever. Amen and Amen. (Ps. 89:52)

2. *A one-member clause, followed by an adverb*, is found in a fourth-century Old Latin manuscript: "For yours is the power unto ages of ages." An alternative one-member clause, complemented by a Trinitarian appositive, appears in a fifteenth-century text (no. 1253): "For yours is the kingdom of the Father and of the Son and of the Holy Spirit unto the ages. Amen."

3. *A two-member clause, with adverb*, is the earliest additional ending we can trace. It occurs in the *Didache* (8.2) of the early second century (see appendix B): "For yours is the power and the glory unto the ages." A century or so later, some Egyptian manuscripts added *Amen* to this wording.

"Power and glory" are commonly collocated as divine attributes in ancient Jewish and Christian literature. "I have looked upon you [the LORD] in the sanctuary, beholding your power and glory" (Ps. 63:2). The earth and seas are agitated by "the presence of the Lord and the glory of his power" (2 Esd. 16:12). The apocalyptic coming of the heavenly Son of Man will be attended by "great power and great glory" (cf. Matt. 24:30 = Mark 13:26 = Luke 21:27). The following blessings doubtless reflect the language of early Christian worship:

> To [God] belong the glory and the power forever and ever. Amen. (1 Pet. 4:11)

> To the only God our Savior, through Jesus Christ our Lord, be glory, majesty, power, and authority, before all time and now and forever. Amen. (Jude 25)

> "Hallelujah! Salvation and glory and power belong to our God." (Rev. 19:1 RSV; cf. 4:11; 15:8)

4. *An alternative two-member clause, with adverb*, crops up in a fifth-century Syriac text: "For yours is the kingdom and the glory unto the ages. Amen." There are a few biblical precedents for this pairing. It recurs in Daniel, once to depict the coming of "one like a son of man, . . . to [whom] was given dominion and glory and kingdom" (Dan. 7:13–14 RSV), at other points to typify mortal sovereigns (2:37; 4:36; 11:20). Paul encourages the Thessalonians to "lead a life worthy of God, who calls you into his own kingdom and glory" (1 Thess. 2:12; cf. 2 Tim. 4:18).

The coupling of "kingdom" and "power" seems to have been a neglected option in traditional endings of the Lord's Prayer. These

227

paired appositives are rare in the Bible. The God of heaven bestows on Nebuchadnezzar "the kingdom, the power, the might, and the glory" (Dan. 2:37). After a pitched battle between Michael and his angels against the great dragon (Satan), John says, "I heard a loud voice in heaven, saying, 'Now the salvation and the power and the kingdom of our God and the authority of his Christ have come'" (Rev. 12:10 RSV). Usually "power" is not so much a synonym for God's "kingdom" as a characteristic of it (see Jdt. 2:12; 2 Esd. 12:18; Mark 9:1; 1 Cor. 4:20).

5. After it enters the manuscript tradition of Matthew 6:13, *a three-member clause, with adverb*, becomes the most widely attested conclusion to the Lord's Prayer: "For yours is the kingdom and the power and the glory unto the ages. Amen" (AT). Its earliest appearance may have been in Tatian's *Diatessaron*, a second-century harmony of the four Gospels that was quoted by early patristic sources but has not survived in toto.

The juxtaposition of kingdom, power, and glory is sparse in Scripture. It occurs once with reference to a human potentate, in Daniel's interpretation of Nebuchadnezzar's dream: "[To] you, O king, the king of kings, . . . the God of heaven has given the kingdom, the power, the might, and the glory" (Dan. 2:37). This triplet's only other occurrences in the Old Testament refer to God, in contexts approximating the doxology of the Lord's Prayer.

> Blessed are you, O LORD, the God of our ancestor Israel, forever and ever. Yours, O LORD, are the greatness, the power, the glory, the victory, and the majesty; for all that is in the heavens and on the earth is yours; yours is the kingdom, O LORD, and you are exalted as head above all. (1 Chr. 29:10b–11)

> All your works shall give thanks to you, O LORD,
>   and all your faithful shall bless you.
> They shall speak of the glory of your kingdom,
>   and tell of your power,
> to make known to all people your mighty deeds,
>   and the glorious splendor of your kingdom.
> Your kingdom is an everlasting kingdom,
>   and your dominion endures throughout all generations.
>   (Ps. 145:10–13)

Why did this threefold ascription to God become the favored ending to the Lord's Prayer? We don't know. In liturgy as in story-telling, many worshipers may have observed a rule of three, such as one finds in the seraphic Trisagioi ("three [acclamations of the] holy"):

"Holy, holy, holy is the LORD of hosts;
    the whole earth is full of his glory." (Isa. 6:3)

"Holy, holy, holy,
    the Lord God the Almighty,
    who was and is and is to come." (Rev. 4:8)

The Need for Doxology

We haven't asked the prior question: why did early Christian worshipers think a concluding doxology was necessary for the Lord's Prayer? We can only speculate. Some may have regarded ending the prayer on petitions for deliverance from temptation and evil as too downbeat. That, however, seems not to trouble modern Christians who end their recitation of the Prayer at that point. The likelier reason is liturgical inclination, influenced by Jewish prayers that customarily ended with a sentence of praise or a "seal," often extemporized (Jeremias, *Lord's Prayer*, 3–4, 32; Black, "Doxology"). Once early Christians made the step from offering a prayer "like this" (Matt. 6:9a RSV) to saying *this* prayer, using *these* words (Luke 11:2a), a formulaic ending may have seemed appropriate in congregational worship (see appendix B). But not just any formula would do. Some form of blessing, praising, or thanking God was in order, whether expressed in the subjunctive, imperative, or indicative mood. Scriptural precedents were abundant.

Blessed be the LORD, the God of Israel,
    from everlasting to everlasting.
And let all the people say, "Amen."
    Praise the LORD! (Ps. 106:48)

O give thanks to the LORD, for he is good;
    for his steadfast love endures forever. (Ps. 107:1)

Sing to the LORD, all the earth.
    Tell of his salvation from day to day.
Declare his glory among the nations,
    his marvelous works among all the peoples.

229

> For great is the LORD, and greatly to be praised;
>   he is to be revered above all gods.
> For all the gods of the peoples are idols,
>   but the LORD made the heavens.
> Honor and majesty are before him;
>   strength and joy are in his place. (1 Chr. 16:23–27)

Common to all these hymnic digests are salient synonyms describing the LORD God's majesty, a call for its public acknowledgment, and unimpeachable reasons for doing so.

Jewish prayers in the rabbinic age followed suit. (See appendix A.) Each of the Amidah's Eighteen Benedictions includes an acclamation of praise, either at its beginning or end. In essence the funerary Kaddish is an extended doxology. To this day the Modeh Ani, an ancient morning prayer offered by observant Jews upon waking, comprises thanksgiving for God's sovereign, dependable compassion:

> I thank You, living and eternal King, for giving me back my soul in mercy. Great is your faithfulness. (Sacks, *Authorised Daily Prayer Book*, 5; cf. Lam. 3:22–23)

Likewise are the words of an old Jewish prayer before retiring for sleep:

> Blessed are You, LORD our God, King of the Universe, who makes the bonds of sleep fall on my eyes, and slumber on my eyelids. . . . Blessed are You, LORD, who gives light to the whole world in His glory. (Sacks, *Authorised Daily Prayer Book*, 245; cf. Ps. 3:5)

None of these prayers exactly duplicates the wording of the Lord's Prayer's conclusion, but their affirmations rhyme.

Closer to the textual variants of Matthew 6:13 are doxologies that replicate its formal structure: (1) a nominal or pronominal reference to God, followed by (2) the reason(s) for praise (3) and a temporal indication, to which (4) a closing *amen* is sometimes added (see Chase, *Lord's Prayer*, 169–70).

> [1] To [God] [2] be glory [3] forever. [4] Amen. (Rom. 11:36b RSV)

> Seeing, therefore, that we have all these things from him, we ought in every respect to give thanks to him, [1] to whom [2] be the glory [3] forever and ever. [4] Amen. (*1 Clem.* 38.4)

Although Origen offered no commentary on the doxology in Matthew 6:13, he aims toward its inclusion by paraphrasing its structure: "It is right that we should begin with glorifying and leave off our prayer with glorifying, hymning, and giving glory to the Father of all, through Jesus Christ in the Holy Spirit, to whom be glory forever and ever" (*Prayer* 33.6, trans. Stewart-Sykes).

The Elements of the Matthean Doxology

For (Because)

Unless it is intended as the simplest means of connecting a later addition to the Prayer, the conjunction "for" (*hoti*, in Greek) may seem logically disconcerting. "Does not a doxology need to be *given* an explanation, rather than *to give one*?" (Lohmeyer, *Lord's Prayer*, 236). Not necessarily. Helmut Thielicke's suggestion seems to me closer to the mark: "The closing words of the Lord's Prayer are not an *assumption* which we must have accepted in order to be able to pray, but rather the *final conclusion* to which our repeated use of the Prayer has driven us" (*The Prayer*, 154). With that, Lohmeyer seems to agree: "Everything that has been prayed for [in the Prayer] lies in God's hand, and he has the power to accomplish it, for 'thine is the kingdom'" (*Lord's Prayer*, 236). That makes sense. It is supported by John Chrysostom's reasoning that the Prayer's doxology is joined with the preceding petition: we give thanks that power and glory reside, not in the evil one, but in God. "If the kingdom is his, no one need fear, for the adversary is nothing though he presume the glory for himself" (*Homily on Matthew* 19.10, trans. George Prevost). Adopting a compatible theological construction, Paul is driving at the same idea in Galatians 1:3–5: "Grace to you and peace from God our Father and the Lord Jesus Christ, who gave himself for our sins to set us free from the present evil age, according to the will of our God and Father, to whom be the glory forever and ever. Amen." Despite evil's attacks, God's rule is unconquerable.

The assertion "Thine is the kingdom, the power, and the glory" comprises multiple attitudes. We *praise* God that all these properties belong to him. At the same time we express *gratitude* that we may pray to God in the way the Prayer guides us. We assert *trust* that God hears and binds himself to us as we knit ourselves to God by so praying. We affirm *hope* that all of this Prayer's petitions may be fulfilled, both now and in the age to come. Exaltation,

231

thanksgiving, faith, and hope blend and resolve themselves into adoration: "All we truly want to ask for ourselves from God is God and the grace to do his will. There is certainly nothing else worth asking for. He has nothing else to give" (Ward, *Use of Praying*, 56).

Thine (To You, Yours)

Placing a prepositional phrase at the front of a Greek sentence lends it emphasis (Moule, *Idiom-Book*, 166). *Sou* is a second-person singular pronoun, in the genitive case, here indicating simple possession: "To you [our Father] belong the kingdom and the power and the glory." Conjoined with these particular nouns, the pronoun directs the supplicant's attention back to the addressee of all the Prayer's petitions, especially its first three: for the sanctity of the Holy Name, the advent of God's kingdom, and the finalization of divine will. After the second table of petitions, which have conceded varied dimensions of human need, the small but crucial pronoun *sou* refocuses the petitioners' attention *on God*.

That theocentricity has become this commentary's constant refrain: the Lord's Prayer is seriously yet secondarily concerned with its petitioners and primarily concentrated on the heavenly Father, whom they address. Lest my readers' patience be taxed by harping on this matter, I direct them to a caution issued by a spiritual master of our age, the Dalai Lama:

> Especially today . . . there is not much focus on inner values in education. Then, instead of inner values, we become self-centered—always thinking: *I, I, I.* A self-centered attitude brings a sense of insecurity and fear. Distrust. Too much fear brings frustration. Too much frustration brings anger. So that's the psychology, the system of mind, of emotion, which creates a chain reaction. With a self-centered attitude, you become distanced from others, then distrust, then feel insecure, then fear, anxiety, then fear, then anger, then violence. (Gyatso and Tutu, *Book of Joy*, 77)

Surveying the world around me, I accept this grim diagnosis, convinced that the Lord's Prayer is an antidote for the disease identified. The deeper reason for escape from our egotism is its futility: we cannot save ourselves. That, indirectly, is what we have confessed before God when praying that divine holiness will sanctify

232

this broken world, that divine sovereignty will commandeer all human authorities, and that God's will shall prevail. The Prayer's doxology returns its petitioners to a healthy theocentricity that strengthens their faith (Lohse, *Das Vaterunser*, 50–52). That is the paradox of all faithful prayer: it is an act whose highest responsibility is self-surrender.

Is

The simple verb *eimi*, conjugated in the third-person present tense (*estin*), is one of the first constructions learned by any student of Greek. In that language's classical and later patristic forms, *estin* could be deleted from the doxology in variants of Matt. 6:13 without confusing the reader, who would mentally supply the word. Because Koine Greek of the New Testament tends to spell things out, it's no surprise that it should appear here. It is interesting, however, that the linking verb *always* appears in the textual variants, no matter what property is ascribed to God (sovereignty, power, glory, or some combination thereof). Its recurrence may amount to a kind of liturgical insistence. In variants that attribute to God more than one hallmark, the singular form of the verb always appears: "Yours *is* [not "are," *eisin*] the kingdom and the power and the glory." Such phraseology is grammatically acceptable in Koine Greek, as in its English translation, though again a subtle point of emphasis may be conveyed: "To you belongs ultimate governorship; to you belongs the power to wield it; to you belongs the glory for the manner in which your sovereignty is executed." The singular verb controls all of the sentence's subjects, which denote properties exclusive to God.

The Kingdom

The Greek term *hē basileia* is identical to that which we studied in chapter 5. In view is God's royal dominion. Many commentators detect a shift in meaning of "the kingdom" in the doxology: away from Jesus' own eschatologically charged vision of God's in-breaking reign (Mark 1:15 = Matt. 4:17; Luke 6:20 = Matt. 5:3) toward the church's concurrence with Israel's historic confession that "the LORD is king!" (*yhwh malak*: e.g., 1 Chr. 16:31; Ps. 10:16; see Lohmeyer, *Lord's Prayer*, 238–40; Jeremias, *Lord's Prayer*, 32; Harner,

233

Lord's Prayer, 116). I am not certain that such a turn occurred. As we saw in chapter 5, ancient Israel had already begun to anticipate Jesus' apocalyptically tinged view of the kingdom (Dan. 7:1–28; *Pss. Sol.* 17:3–4; 1QM 6:6; *T. Mos.* 10:1); early Christianity, even into the patristic era, continued to interpret its faith through an apocalyptic lens. There's no good reason to suppose that the churches that supplied the doxology for the Lord's Prayer were incapable of holding together different dimensions of God's kingdom: the one for whose realization they prayed, the same in which they believed themselves already to be living. In any event, "kingdom," referring to God's redemptive reality, is the only key term that appears in the Prayer more than once. "Yours is the kingdom"—at present and in future. God's authority outstrips every power and principality, now and to come.

So far, all this could be claimed by any orthodox Jew, as many of Jesus' first followers considered themselves (Acts 2:14–42; 3:14–37; Phil. 3:4–7; cf. Heb. 1:1–2:18). And yet the same churches that gave us a doxology for the Lord's Prayer believed in and hoped for, not only the kingdom of God, but also the identification of that *basileia* with Christ's own (see Cullmann, "Kingship of Christ"; Hurtado, *Lord Jesus Christ*). Interpreting him as the messianic fulfillment of Psalm 110 (Matt. 22:44; Acts 2:34; 1 Cor. 15:25; Eph. 1:20; Heb. 1:1, 13), Jesus' earliest disciples claimed that God had conferred on him the title "Lord" (Heb., *'adōnai*; Gk., *kyrios*), and had bestowed on Jesus sovereignty over the invisible powers in heaven and visible powers on earth. The earliest attestation of that credo lies in a hymn quoted by Paul in Philippians. Belief in Jesus' royal dominion has left traces throughout the New Testament.

> Therefore God also highly exalted him
> and gave him the name
> that is above every name,
> so that at the name of Jesus
> every knee should bend,
> in heaven and on earth and under the earth,
> and every tongue should confess
> that Jesus Christ is Lord,
> to the glory of God the Father. (Phil. 2:9–11)

> [Jesus Christ] has gone into heaven and is at the right hand of God, with angels, authorities, and powers made subject to him. (1 Pet. 3:22; cf. Matt. 28:18; Col. 1:15–17; Heb. 1:1–4)

234

Kingdom, Power, and Glory

The first Christians were no fools. They realized that, in Christ, the kingdom had not been consummated on earth as in heaven: "As it is, we do not yet see everything in subjection to him. But we see Jesus, who for a little while was made lower than the angels, crowned with glory and honor because of the suffering of death, so that by the grace of God he might taste death for every one" (Heb. 2:8c–9 RSV). At Good Friday and Easter, time was telescoped for all time; by God's conquest of death through Jesus Christ, a down payment was made on the reclamation of all creation, until its groaning in degradation ceases and its hope for restoration is fulfilled (Rom. 5:18–21; 8:18–39; 1 Cor. 15:20–58; Eph. 1:3–22; Rev. 1:12–18). In the meantime discipleship is accountable to Christ's current dominion: "I charge you to keep the commandment unstained and free from reproach until the appearing of our Lord Jesus Christ; and this will be made manifest at the proper time by the blessed and only Sovereign, the King of kings and Lord of lords" (1 Tim. 6:14–15 RSV).

By God's own decree Jesus, the Christ, has been made, not merely King of the Jews (Matt. 2:2; Matt. 27:11 = Mark 15:2 = Luke 23:3; John 18:37) or of Israel (Matt. 27:42 = Mark 15:32; John 1:49; 12:13). Ultimately Christ is Lord of all creation (Rom. 10:9–13; Acts 10:36), yet immediately also the Lord of the church (1 Cor. 1:2; Eph. 1:22; 5:23; Col. 1:18; 1 Thess. 1:1; 2 Thess. 2:1). In praising and beseeching God's kingdom, we do so with the confident responsibility of God's children. When we grow confused or forgetful, Jesus reminds us what that kingdom looks like.

In 1946, amid the smoldering rubble of the Second World War, which came to horrendous climax with "the dropping of that new bomb on a far eastern empire," Walter Lüthi (1901–82; *Lord's Prayer*, 1) courageously confronted his German parishioners with a bitter truth that Christians in every generation must face:

A few years ago another false message about a false kingdom became widespread. The word "Reich" began to grip the imagination of millions of people. Hundreds of thousands of mothers sacrificed their sons and daughters for this "Reich"; hundreds of thousands gave up all they had for it. . . . They believed with near-religious fervour in the "Reich" for which they died. And this terrible thing was bound to happen to a generation that had lost sight of the message of the true Kingdom, a generation that knew only its own Godless or zealous soul. An almost demonic

235

hunger to "participate," to stand and fall for a cause, to join in the building of a kingdom, got a frenzied hold on people. But was not the reason for this fearful going astray primarily the fact that the true message of the true Kingdom had been largely withheld from this generation? And what will cure us of false and destructive dreams of kingdoms in the future? Certainly not a purely personal piety, however profound and sincere it may be, but faith in the Kingdom of Christ, acknowledgment of the Kingdom of Christ, willingness to suffer and die in the service of the Kingdom of Christ. Children of God, it is time to become citizens of God. (Lüthi, *Lord's Prayer*, 78)

The next time you hear an easy identification of your nation, of any nation, with God's own purposes and with "manifest destiny," remember that God's kingdom, whose regent is Jesus Christ, "is *not* of this world" (John 18:36 NIV, emphasis added). The Christian's ultimate allegiance is to no party, no flag, and no country. Our certificates of birth and passports are issued by a transcendent commonwealth. It is time for us to act like the citizens of God's kingdom that we are (cf. Phil. 3:20).

The Power

In the Old Testament God's power is revealed in two ways (see Grundmann, "*dynamai*," *TDNT* 2 [1964]: 290–99). One is the creation of Israel as people of his covenant:

> "For the LORD your God dried up the waters of the Jordan for you until you crossed over, as the LORD your God did to the Red Sea, which he dried up for us until we crossed over, so that all the peoples of the earth may know that the hand of the LORD is mighty, and so that you may fear the LORD your God forever." (Josh. 4:23–24; see also Ps. 77:14–15)

The second evidence of God's power is the world's creation and sustenance:

> Lift up your eyes on high and see:
> Who created these?
> He who brings out their host and numbers them,
> calling them all by name;
> because he is great in strength,
> mighty in power,
> not one is missing. (Isa. 40:26; see also Jer. 27:4b–5; 32:17)

236

The same demonstrations of God's power are affirmed in the New Testament. First, the power of creation:

> You are worthy, our Lord and God,
>   to receive glory and honor and power,
> for you created all things,
>   and by your will they existed and were created. (Rev. 4:11;
>   cf. Acts 4:24–25; Heb. 1:10)

Second, God's power is manifest in generating the church and maintaining its life:

> Blessed be the God and Father of our Lord Jesus Christ! By his great mercy he has given us a new birth into a living hope through the resurrection of Jesus Christ from the dead, and into an inheritance that is imperishable, undefiled, and unfading, kept in heaven for you, who are being protected by the power of God through faith for a salvation ready to be revealed in the last time. (1 Pet. 1:3–5; see also Rom. 1:16; Eph. 3:20–21)

First Peter's linkage of "the power of God" with "the resurrection of Jesus Christ from the dead" points in a new direction that pervades the New Testament, epitomized in the Epistle to the Hebrews as "the power of an indestructible life" (7:16). In Easter's light the first Christians perceived God's power particularly in his raising of the crucified Jesus—"a new creation" (2 Cor. 5:17)—and its envelopment of the lives of those who believe in Christ. "And God raised the Lord and will also raise us by his power" (1 Cor. 6:14; cf. Eph. 1:20–21). Furthermore, the power of human re-creation and governance is attributed to Christ himself, whose power was conferred on him by the God of his resurrection: "But our citizenship is in heaven, and it is from there that we are expecting a Savior, the Lord Jesus Christ. He will transform the body of our humiliation that it may be conformed to the body of his glory, by the power that also enables him to make all things subject to himself" (Phil. 3:20–21).

Especially in Luke-Acts the power of God at work among Jesus' disciples is exhibited by mighty deeds of witness and healing, propelled by the same Holy Spirit who was operative in their master's ministry (Luke 5:17; 10:19; 24:49; Acts 1:8; 2:22; 4:33). After the healing of a lame man at Jerusalem's Beautiful Gate, Peter refocuses onlookers' astonishment onto its proper origin, "the Author of life, whom God raised from the dead, to [which] we are witnesses"

237

(Acts 3:15). "You Israelites, why do you wonder at this, or why do you stare at us, as though by our own power or piety we had made him walk?" (3:12).

Paul insists on the fundamental Christian paradox: "the word of the cross"—shorthand for God's resurrection of the crucified Messiah—is the prism through which God's power must be viewed: "For the message about the cross is foolishness to those who are perishing, but to us who are being saved it is the power of God. . . . We proclaim Christ crucified, a stumbling block to Jews and foolishness to Gentiles, but to those who are called, both Jews and Greeks, Christ the power of God and the wisdom of God" (1 Cor. 1:18, 23–24). Power has been radically redefined. It "is made perfect in *weakness*" (2 Cor. 12:9, emphasis added). What is true of Christ, who "was crucified in weakness, but lives by the power of God" (13:4), holds true for those who live *in* Christ: our own weakness, evacuated of self-reliant strength, allows "the power of Christ [to] dwell in [us]" (12:9).

In Christian perspective, therefore, to ascribe to God power is a revolutionary claim inevitably misconstrued by a world whose redemption is unfinished. God's power is not wielded as a tyrant's indiscriminate dominance and destruction. Its ethos is stamped by the freedom of God's kingdom, which is unlike any realm or empire this world knows. The only thing that God's power destroys is sin, itself a power whose chief instrument is death (Rom. 3:9–26; 1 Cor. 15:51–58; Gal. 3:22–29). To those who deride Christian faith as utopian prattle, let the question be posed without flinching: to what degree are they addicted to their own meager, transitory control and their own fear of death? As we asked in chapter 8 (above), just who is our God? Is it the God of Jesus Christ, who gives life (John 3:16; 5:24; 10:10; Rom. 6:15–23), or is it our Moloch, the great god Gun (cf. Lev. 18:21; 20:1–5), who generates nothing but fear and demands the sacrifice of our reason, our will, and the lives of so many mothers' children? When we acknowledge the power of the true God, pleading for its fulfillment, are we fully aware of what we are asking for?

The Glory

238

If the doxology's first nominative specifies God's realm and the second names the requisite of its maintenance, the third denotes that monarchy's special quality. All three are interconnected:

Who is the King of glory?—
   the LORD, mighty and valiant,
   the LORD, valiant in battle.
O gates, lift up your heads!
   Lift them up, you everlasting doors,
so the King of glory may come in!
Who is the King of glory?—
   the LORD of hosts,
   He is the King of glory! (Ps. 24:8–10 NJPS)

Both Testaments closely associate God's power (Heb., *'ĕzûz*; Gk., *hē dynamis*) and glory (Heb., *kābôd*; Gk., *hē doxa*). These terms are nearly interchangeable. Like "holiness," "glory," which we considered in chapter 4 (above), is God's own "Godness," God's radiant essence, which is inherently powerful (Exod. 16:10; 40:34) and intrinsically beautiful: "O LORD my God, you are very great. You are clothed with honor and majesty, wrapped in light as with a garment" (Ps. 104:1b–2a; cf. 1 John 1:5). In the temple, God's self-revelation is that of "power and glory" (Ps. 63:2); "the temple was filled with smoke from the glory of God and from his power" (Rev. 15:8; cf. Isa. 6:4). To tell of God's power is to speak of the splendor of LORD's dominion:

> [All thy saints] shall speak of the glory of thy kingdom,
>   and tell of thy power,
> to make known to the sons of men thy mighty deeds,
>   and the glorious splendor of thy kingdom. (Ps. 145:11–12 RSV)

> He . . . is the blessed and only Sovereign, the King of kings and Lord of lords. It is he alone who has immortality and dwells in unapproachable light, whom no one has ever seen or can see; to him be honor and eternal dominion. Amen. (1 Tim. 6:15b–16)

God's intrinsic nature is light. Its wattage, so to speak, is divine power. Paul captures these concepts' confluence when referring to "an eternal *weight* of glory beyond all measure" for which God is preparing believers through "slight momentary affliction" (2 Cor. 4:17, emphasis added). Candlelight at a dinner table is "soft"; a klieg light at a grand opening is "heavy." Thus one metaphor slides into another: God's glory is weighty (Pss. 24:8; 138:5); to give glory (*doxazein*) to God is to honor God's importance (Jer. 13:16; Pss. 29:1–2; 96:7–8; 115:1).

239

Like power, God's glory is revealed by creation. "Ever since the creation of the world his eternal power and divine nature, invisible though they are, have been understood and seen through the things he has made," which are evidence of "the glory of the immortal God" (Rom. 1:20, 23; cf. Wis. 13:4–5). Like power, God's glory is bequeathed to his chosen people: "the riches of his glorious inheritance among the saints, and . . . the immeasurable greatness of his power for us who believe" (Eph. 1:18b–19; cf. Isa. 43:7, 21).

For strength the church may pray. But the source of that power must be correctly identified, its discharge compatible with its origin, and all must be oriented to God's honor.

> I pray that, according to the riches of [God's] glory, he may grant that you may be strengthened in your inner being with power through his Spirit, and that Christ may dwell in your hearts through faith, as you are being rooted and grounded in love. I pray that you may have the power to comprehend, with all the saints, what is the breadth and length and height and depth, and to know the love of Christ that surpasses knowledge, so that you may be filled with all the fullness of God. Now to him who by the power at work within us is able to accomplish abundantly far more than all we can ask or imagine, to him be glory in the church and in Christ Jesus to all generations, forever and ever. Amen. (Eph. 3:16–21)

This prayer from Ephesians is an apt exegesis of God's glorification in the doxology of the Lord's Prayer. One prays for the fortification of the church's inmost being by God, in accordance with God's own glory and glorification. Such grandeur resists confusion with any spirit of worldly triumphalism: its character, like that of God's power and God's kingdom, is manifest in Jesus Christ, who "received honor and glory from God the Father when that voice was conveyed to him by the Majestic Glory, saying, 'This is my Son, my Beloved, with whom I am well pleased'" (2 Pet. 1:17). In Christ we have beheld the Father's glory (John 1:14; 17:5, 24), which is registered most intensely at the hour of Jesus' death for the world's sin (1:29; 17:1; Rom. 5:8; 1 John 4:9–10). Here we touch on another cardinal paradox of Christian faith: divine glory, visible to mortal eye, condescends to the deepest pit of human suffering and death, to the shaft of hell itself (1 Pet. 3:18–19). Moses' request to behold the LORD face-to-face was denied; he was permitted to see only the

240

LORD's backside (Exod. 33:17–23: famously explicated by Luther, *Heidelberg Disputations* 20 [1518], in *Selections*, 502). So, too, at Bethlehem and at Golgotha: in Christ, God enters through the back door, descends into the fathoms of human misery in order to redeem it. Patristic, medieval, and modern theologians have pondered this mystery in many ways (see Hylen, "Glory," 408–12).

The motive for Christ's self-sacrifice is a love "that surpasses knowledge" (see also John 3:16; 15:9–13, 17; 17:26; 1 Cor. 2:9; Col. 2:2; 1 John 3:16), is poured by the Holy Spirit into believers' hearts (Rom. 5:5; cf. Gal. 5:22; Phil. 2:1; Col. 1:8), "binds everything together in perfect harmony" (Col. 3:14; cf. Heb. 13:1; 1 Pet. 1:22; 3:8; 2 Pet. 1:7; 1 John 3:11; 4:21), transcends every gift (1 Cor. 13:13), and is undefeatable (Rom. 8:35–39). Like God's glory, "love never ends" (1 Cor. 13:8)—which brings us to the doxology's adverb.

Unto the Ages (Forever)

With reference to God, "the ages" (*hoi aiōnes*) is a biblical term that moves in manifold directions. It may refer backward:

> From ages past no one has heard,
>   no ear has perceived,
> no eye has seen any God besides you,
>   who works for those who wait for him. (Isa. 64:4; cf. Deut. 4:32;
>   Sir. 36:22)

The Lord God of Israel "spoke through the mouth of his holy prophets from of old [*ap' aiōnos*]" (Luke 1:70). "God's wisdom, secret and hidden, [was] decreed [by] God before the ages for our glory" (1 Cor. 2:7). "Everyone [is to] see what is the plan of the mystery hidden for ages in God who created all things" (Eph. 3:9). "The ages" also occupy the present, regard the past, and point to the future: "before all time and now and forever" (Jude 25).

> Blessed be God who lives forever,
>   because his kingdom lasts throughout all ages. (Tob. 13:1bc; cf.
>   1 Tim. 1:17)

Language carries theology along. Depending on context, *ho aiōn* can mean "an age," "a very long time," or even "eternity." *Hoi aiōnes*, which means the same, appears to have been a way to convey

241

the concept of eternity by stretching the singular term into its plural form (Sasse, *"aiōn, aiōnos"*). To extend the sense yet another degree, some texts of Hebrews 13:21b ("to [Christ] be the glory forever" add "and ever," just as many Christian worshipers end their recitation of the Lord's Prayer with such a redundancy. Thus we may paraphrase: "May God's kingdom and power and glory endure unto the ages, and the ages after the ages, into infinity, beyond all human imagining." We pray there shall be no end to God's goodness, with the confidence that such an end shall never come to pass. God will be God.

Amen

"Amen" is a direct carryover into English from the Greek, *amēn*, which is a direct carryover from Hebrew, *'amēn*. As an assertive particle, its primary meaning is "truly": a characteristic emphasis in Jesus' discourse, "[For] truly I tell you" (Matt. 5:18, 26; Mark 3:28; 8:12; Luke 4:24; 9:27, plus another 52× in the Synoptics). A quirk of the Johannine Jesus' phraseology is a doubled *amēn*: "Truly, truly, I say to you" (1:51 RSV, plus 26 other instances; the NRSV obscures that duplication by translating the first *amēn* as "very"). Again drawing from Israelite and Jewish precedents (see appendix A), Christian liturgy appropriated "Amen" as a verbal ratification of the congregants' endorsement of what the cantor or preacher had said. Moreover, to say "Amen" is to bind oneself to that confession's truth and its fulfillment (Jer. 28:6).

> "Blessed be the LORD, the God of Israel,
>   from everlasting to everlasting."
>
> Then all the people said "Amen!" and praised the LORD. (1 Chr. 16:36; cf. Pss. 41:13; 72:19; 89:52; 106:48; Gal. 6:18; Rev. 1:6–7; 5:14; 7:12; 19:4; 22:20–21)
>
> To him belong the glory and the power forever and ever. Amen. (1 Pet. 4:11; cf. 5:11; Rom. 11:36; Gal. 1:5; Eph. 3:21; Phil. 4:20; 1 Tim. 1:17; 6:16; 2 Tim. 4:18; Heb. 13:21; 2 Pet. 3:18)

242

To utter "Amen" is no empty piety. By saying it we affix our personal signature to every petition we have made—not only in the doxology but also in the Prayer as a whole.

In the little word "Amen" lies remarkable profundity: our acclamation of "Yes" to God is elicited by God's prior affirmation of "Yes" to us. Paul is the first on record for having tied the customary liturgical endorsement of congregants at worship to their perception of Jesus.

> Do I make my plans according to ordinary human standards, ready to say "Yes, yes" and "No, no" at the same time? As surely as God is faithful, our word to you has not been "Yes and No." For the Son of God, Jesus Christ, whom we proclaimed among you, Silvanus and Timothy and I, was not "Yes and No"; but in him it is always "Yes." For in him every one of God's promises is a "Yes." For this reason it is through him that we say the "Amen," to the glory of God. But it is God who establishes us with you in Christ and has anointed us, by putting his seal on us and giving us his Spirit in our hearts as a first installment. (2 Cor. 1:17b–22)

That is a remarkable statement. To begin with, Paul hasn't set out to give his listeners in Corinth a lecture in Christology; he's offering a simple explanation of a change in his travel plans (2 Cor. 1:15–16). Yet Paul seems defensive of his reconsidered itinerary (cf. 10:1–18). He's on the spot, having been accused of vacillating double-talk (1:17a). He turns a swift apologia of his own steadfast fidelity toward God's own: "As surely as God is faithful," so am I— and my words have never deviated from my consistent position (1:18). Then comes a stunning, christological twist: Jesus, the Son of God, whom my colleagues and I have preached among you, is no shillyshally. "In [Jesus Christ] it is always Yes. For all the promises of God find their Yes in him" (2 Cor. 1:19b–20a RSV). And *then* there's an ecclesiological pivot: "That is why we utter the Amen through him, to the glory of God" (1:20b). Notice Paul's implied argument: we do not utter "Amen" at the end of prayers out of conventional expectation, handed down from temple and synagogue. Our prayers assert the Amen—our "yes," "indeed, that's the truth, and we're not backing off it"—because God has determined that his Son Jesus, the Christ, is *himself* the Yes to "all the promises of God" from the dawn of the Sinaitic covenant until now. Our Yes ("Amen") is a response to God's Yes (Christ). To make absolutely clear that every initiative rests with God, neither with Paul nor with the church, the apostle insists that God alone (1) has established

243

the apostolic delegation with the Corinthian congregation, (2) has commissioned their mission, (3) has sealed believers to himself, and (4) has infused the hearts of all with the Holy Spirit as a guarantee of that seal (1:21–22). Some worshipers in Corinth may have thought that, by uttering "Amen" at their prayers' end, they were sealing their commitment to the Subject of their prayer. Without denying that, Paul turns their assumption inside out: *through Jesus, God's irrevocable Yes, God's Amen is actually sealing us to himself.* Nor is Paul the only New Testament witness to make this theological move. Without explaining its rationale but on direct orders from the celestial "one like a son of man" (Rev. 1:13, 19 RSV), John of Patmos writes to the Laodicean church, "The words of the Amen, the faithful and true witness, the origin of God's creation" (3:14).

Summing Up

"For Yours is the kingdom and the power and the glory forever. Amen." Examining each word of this doxology, I have attempted three things. First, as ever, I have indicated these terms' rootedness in their indigenous Jewish soil. Second, I have endeavored to remind readers of connections between the doxology's components and the Prayer they intend to conclude. Third, I have suggested that the church's closure to the Lord's Prayer evokes explicitly Christian confessions to which those who gave us the doxology surely clung. The Son never displaces the Father. "Jesus answered, 'If I glorify myself, my glory is nothing. . . . Father, glorify your name.' Then a voice came from heaven, 'I have glorified it, and I will glorify it again'" (John 8:54; 12:28). Through the doxology we live into the mystery of praying with the incarnate Word, who has revealed and is revealing the God whose kingdom, power, and glory summon us, while embracing us with a love that can never be severed.

A Perfect Conclusion to a Perfect Prayer

The doxology is more than "a final polite formula," even less a hodgepodge of "apparently pompous ecclesiastical declarations" (Ellul, "Notre Père," 27). The Prayer's final assertion sutures the Prayer's two tables—our entreaties for God, our pleas for ourselves—and recapitulates, by sublime compression, the comprehensive faith we express by these petitions.

244

And what is the structure of that faith? An adequate answer to that question demands another book. Let this suffice: the Lord's Prayer offers every follower of Jesus—whether they believe, whether they doubt (Matt. 28:17; Mark 9:24)—an entrée into God's kingdom from which their Lord took his bearings and measured earthly appearances, while his followers calculated heavenly hopes by what they believed to be earthly realities. We can, and at our weakest moments do, resist eternal life. We may repudiate God's parental love. We may refuse to sanctify God's holy name. We may insist that our will, not God's, be fulfilled. We may delude ourselves that we need no providence beyond what we provide for ourselves. We may deny mercy to others; we may refuse theirs. We may wallow in the despair of seemingly irresistible temptations and an evil beyond our capacity to overcome. The gospel is clear as crystal that the heavenly Father wants none of that for his children; instead, God gives us the freedom to cling to death in a dying world.

Our alternative is to yield to the truth of the gospel encapsulated in the Lord's Prayer. We have lived in night so long that it hurts to step into sunshine. To do that, we say Amen to all the Prayer's petitions—and mean it, without reservation. Repeatedly we stumble, fall, and again stand upright. No heroism is demanded of us. We need only pray the Prayer. In so doing we confess that our bondage to life on our own terms and this world's bogus promises are a hopeless mess from which we cannot free ourselves. We have tried to do so and have failed. And there's no point in so continuing. *Already we have been liberated. In praying the Prayer, God is realigning our desires to God's own.* We need only to step out of prisons being unlocked into a new life that, through Christ, God has already begun to create.

> The final conflict is that which proceeds between God and the devil, between Christ and "the rulers of this present darkness" (Eph. 6:12). This conflict proceeds in three interlocking realms which the cross has revealed to be *one* realm: it is precipitated in the invisible realm where Jesus met and overcame, during his brief ministry, all the powers of the adversary; it begins and continues in the heart of each [one] who hears the call of God as proclaimed by the Crucified; it proceeds in that heavenly realm where Christ is arrayed against all the spiritual authorities that rule the present evil age. Victory in any one of these realms carries with it a victory in all. . . . The age of bondage is thus in [God's] plan the age of promise, the age of hope, the age of preparation.

245

> Where enslavement is greatest, there the word of liberty is most
> vigorously proclaimed. (Minear, *Kingdom*, 85, 99)

The Lord's Prayer both humbles and encourages. Its petitions expose us to God and to ourselves. Until our lives are purified, that reality is fearsome: we want God in the same moment when we are frightened by what God's claims on us entail. We fear finding ourselves because, as Jesus taught us, that means losing ourselves (Matt. 16:24–26 = Mark 8:34–37 = Luke 9:23–25). Servants are not greater than their master (John 13:16; 15:20); if our Lord was crucified, then our selves must be crucified as well. The Prayer Jesus taught his disciples makes that plain. Equally clear in that prayer, however, is hope: the promise of resurrection by God, who remains the only true Lord over this world, who loves his children supremely, and whose purpose holds fast and cannot fail. Those who pray the Lord's Prayer, who embrace and live into its petitions, come to understand what Paul meant when he said, "I have been crucified with Christ; and it is no longer I who live, but it is Christ who lives in me. And the life I now live in the flesh I live by faith in the Son of God, who loved me and gave himself for me" (Gal. 2:19b–20). Embedded in that confession is an "inheritance . . . imperishable" (1 Pet. 1:4): that "all of us [may] come to the unity of the faith and of the knowledge of the Son of God, to maturity, to the measure of the full stature of Christ" (Eph. 4:13). That is the destination to which the Lord's Prayer drives us in the unending education of our wants and wishes.

Works Cited in Chapter 9

Allen, Fred. *"all the sincerity in hollywood . . .": Selections from the Writings of Radio's Legendary Comedian*. Compiled by Stuart Hample. Golden, CO: Fulcrum, 2001.

Ayo, Nicholas. *The Lord's Prayer: A Survey Theological and Literary*. Lanham, MD: Rowman & Littlefield, 1992.

Black, Matthew. "The Doxology to the Pater Noster with a Note on Matthew 6.13b." In *A Tribute to Géza Vermès: Essays on Jewish and Christian Literature and History*, edited by Philip R. Davies and Richard T. White, 327–38. Journal for the Study of the Old Testament Supplement Series 100. Sheffield: Sheffield Academic Press, 1990.

Boff, Leonardo. *The Lord's Prayer: The Prayer of Integral Liberation.* Translated by Theodore Morrow. Melbourne: Dove; Maryknoll, NY: Orbis Books, 1983.

Catholic Church. *Catechism of the Catholic Church.* Liguori, MO: Liguori Publications, 1994.

Chase, Frederick Henry. *The Lord's Prayer in the Early Church.* Cambridge: Cambridge University Press, 1891.

Cullmann, Oscar. "The Kingship of Christ and the Church in the New Testament." In *The Early Church: Studies in Early Christian History and Theology*, edited by A. J. B. Higgins, 105–39. Translated by S. Godman. Philadelphia: Westminster Press, 1956.

Ellul, Jacques. "Notre Père." *Foi et Vie* 77 (1978): 24–29.

The Greek Orthodox Diocese of North and South America, eds. *The Divine Liturgy of Saint John Chrysostom.* A new translation by members of the Faculty of Hellenic College, Holy Cross Greek Orthodox School of Theology. 3rd ed. Brookline, MA: Holy Cross Orthodox Press, 1985.

Grundmann, Walter. "*dynamai, dynatos.*" *TDNT* 2 (1964): 284–317.

Gyatso, Tenzin (His Holiness the Fourteenth Dalai Lama) and Desmond Mpilo Tutu, with Douglas Abrams. *The Book of Joy: Happiness in a Changing World.* New York: Avery, 2016.

Harner, Philip. B. *Understanding the Lord's Prayer.* Philadelphia: Fortress Press, 1975.

Hurtado, Larry W. *Lord Jesus Christ: Devotion to Jesus in Earliest Christianity.* Grand Rapids: Wm. B. Eerdmans Publishing Co., 2005

Hylen, Susan E. "Glory." *OEBT* 1 (2015): 405–12.

Jeremias, Joachim. *The Lord's Prayer.* Translated by John Reumann. Facet Books. Philadelphia: Fortress Press, 1964.

Lohmeyer, Ernst. *"Our Father": An Introduction to the Lord's Prayer.* Translated by John Bowden. New York: Harper & Row, 1965.

Lohse, Eduard. *Das Vaterunser im Licht seiner jüdischen Voraussetzungen.* Lucas-Preis. Tübingen: Mohr Siebeck, 2008.

Luther, Martin. *Selections from His Writings.* Edited by John Dillenberger. Anchor Books. Garden City, NY: Doubleday, 1961.

Lüthi, Walter. *The Lord's Prayer: An Exposition*. Translated by Kurt Schoenberger. Edinburgh: Oliver & Boyd; Richmond, VA: John Knox Press, 1961.

Maritain, Raïssa. *Notes on the Lord's Prayer*. Translated by Thomas Merton. New York: P. J. Kennedy & Sons, 1964.

Minear, Paul S. *The Kingdom and the Power: An Exposition of the New Testament Gospel*. Philadelphia: Westminster Press, 1950.

Moule, C. F. D. *An Idiom-Book of New Testament Greek*. 2nd ed. Cambridge: Cambridge University Press, 1959.

Sacks, Jonathan, ed. *The Authorised Daily Prayer Book of the United Hebrew Congregations of the Commonwealth*. Translated by Simeon Singer. 4th ed. London: Collins, 2007.

Sasse, Hermann. *"aiōn, aiōnos."* *TDNT* 1 (1964): 197–209.

Thielicke, Helmut. *The Prayer That Spans the World: Sermons on the Lord's Prayer*. Translated by John W. Doberstein. London: James Clarke, 1960.

Ward, J. Neville. *The Use of Praying*. London: Epworth, 1967.

Weil, Simone. "Concerning the Our Father." In *Waiting for God*, translated by Emma Craufurd, 216–27. New York: G. P. Putnam's Sons, 1952.

CHAPTER 10

A Pastoral Coda

I wash everything on the gentle cycle. It's much more humane.
—Anonymous

Consistent with the aims of the Interpretation series, this commentary's focus has been on the church's preaching and teaching. Every pastor knows that these endeavors, indisputably important, do not exhaust clerical responsibilities. For that reason I conclude by amplifying some implications of the Lord's Prayer for other, significant aspects of ministry. All three of these areas—worship, ecumenism, and pastoral care—are vital spheres in which the Prayer continues to purify desire and to educate human wanting.

The Lord's Prayer as Liturgical Catechesis

As appendixes B and C attest, the Lord's Prayer was integrated into the rites of the church from its beginnings, throughout the Middle Ages, and well into the Reformation era. The ways in which the Prayer was incorporated into sacramental observance varied across time and region. From the late second until the early sixth century it was used in educating adult converts to the faith; overlapping that practice, from the fourth century onward, the Prayer also formed a curriculum for neophytes (*competentes*, "seekers"; *illuminandi*,

249

"those to be enlightened") before their baptisms (Hammerling, "Lord's Prayer"). Such catechesis has often been conveyed homiletically, in sermons designed to explain intricate christological and Trinitarian concepts by way of the Prayer's petitions (see Stevenson, "Christology and Trinity"). These pedagogical and homiletical practices continue, worthy of thoughtful theological endorsements (Jacobson, "Word in Season"; Westhelle, "Displacing Words"; Vallee, "Lord's Prayer").

Following the leads of two liturgical scholars, Debra Dean Murphy and Don E. Saliers, here I suggest a more theologically precise approach to the place of the Lord's Prayer in liturgy and catechesis. It is so fundamental that it is easily overlooked. Drawing upon Augustine's theology, particularly that expressed in his *Confessions* (ca. AD 400), Murphy argues that, since Descartes, we have confused ourselves by assuming that knowledge is objective, free of self and context, whose validity may be tested by neutral criteria. To the contrary, Murphy argues:

> Knowledge is . . . *participation*, not mere contemplation; it is *ontos*, not simply *epistēmē*. As participation it is enacted in and through time by the sharing of Christ's body and blood in the fellowship of believers in Christian community. . . . To know rightly is to desire God; to desire God is to have the knowledge that human beings need. . . . This means that the knowledge that comes through the worship of the triune God is ultimately a kind of counterknowledge to the ways in which the real and the good are instantiated in the wider culture, thus affording the possibility of resistance to what Christians might take to be false and harmful construals of what is real and what is good. ("Worship as Catechesis," 329–31)

Saliers identifies the intersection of worship and ethics as the point at which "certain affections and virtues are formed and expressed in the modalities of communal prayer and ritual action. These modalities of prayer enter into the formation of the self in community" ("Liturgy and Ethics," 17 [originally in italics]). In other words, the Christian moral life depends on a vision of the world that is formed, sustained, and activated by communal prayer. When our actions betray or fail to reach the virtues peculiar to that vision, we recognize that gap, and our affections are expressed as repentance.

250

The positions of Saliers and Murphy share at least five important convictions. (1) What we know, what we do, and how we pray are grounded in the life of God; they are co-inherent and mutually reciprocal. (2) Such knowledge, decisions, and affections are never projects of the solitary self; rather, they are molded within a particular community that, through formation by the gospel, *knows differently and acts accordingly.* (3) Neither liturgy nor catechesis nor ethical reflection is a utilitarian tool by which we dutifully talk ourselves into being "better people." Worship is first and foremost grateful service to God, needing no other justification, whose *by-product* is the transformation of worshipers who come to realize their life before God and in God. "In fact, we are not apt to be changed by worship if we come to it primarily to be changed, for then we will be back to concentrating on ourselves" (Webber and Clapp, *People of the Truth*, 69–70). (4) When in corporate worship we pray for others and share Christ's peace, we are not merely saying or doing symbolic things. We disclose and embody something real about God, which reminds us of who we are: creatures made in God's image. (5) Because, by their worship, Christians are constituted differently from others, they enact "a counter-community, a different polis, another way of being" (Murphy, "Worship," 327). They bear witness to the living God, of whom the world is largely ignorant and onto whom that world projects distorted and unworthy ideas. Karl Barth made the same point aphoristically: "To fold one's hands in prayer is the beginning of an uprising against the disorder of the world" (quoted by Lochman, "Lord's Prayer," 18–19). To confuse doxology with either pragmatic consumerism or atheistic social justice invites calamity: as the old saying goes, when the church marries the spirit of the age, she will be left a widow in the next generation.

We seem to have strayed from the Lord's Prayer; yet its bearing on our worship, catechesis, and conduct has been implicit throughout. To honor God as the heavenly Father, whose Name is ever to be sanctified and praised, lies at liturgy's core. Our hearts desire this God, rightly known, and dispose us in wonder and gratitude toward the world and humanity's place in the orders of God's creation. To beg for bread simultaneously confesses our need and recalls (*anamnēsis*) God's feeding of Israel's children in the wilderness and Christ's feeding of the multitudes and then his disciples "on the night when he was betrayed" (1 Cor. 11:23). Similarly, the cry for

251

rescue from temptation is not a disquisition on the problem of evil; instead, we kneel with Christ in Gethsemane, pitching ourselves into the mysterious face-off between human will and divine will. To ask forgiveness while interceding for others by canceling their indebtedness to us holds a mirror to our spiritual bankruptcy while restructuring our affections toward pity and compassion. Uttering these words is more than an expression of pious intent and need for God's clemency: *in the saying is the action itself.* "For we forgive our debtors": we *do* it when we *say* it, just as we know that God in that moment is doing the same for us (Hultgren, "Forgive Us"). Unreservedly acknowledging God's eternal kingdom, power, and glory—"the in-streaming power of the future world" (Moltmann, *The Coming God*, 138)—shapes our hope in alignment with central symbols of scriptural faith, but "it must be accountable to the way we make actual decisions" in a world yet to be fully redeemed (Bloom, *Living Prayer*, 123).

In a word, the Lord's Prayer instantiates what is true of Christian worship overall. Catechesis cannot be separated from liturgy, any more than liturgy can be divorced from ethics. Praying as Jesus taught his disciples realigns the church's vision and virtues toward knowing God as God wishes to be known and restructuring the affections of the body of Christ to give itself for the world as did Christ himself. If all this sounds too heady, the case of Ruby Bridges in chapter 7 (above) brings things down to earth. By her own testimony, Miss Bridges learned how and why to forgive brutal assailants nine times her age by praying in church.

The Prayer of Jesus as Invitation to Interreligious Communion

It is interesting to observe the degree to which the Lord's Prayer, so characteristic of Christian piety and practice, intersects with the aspirations of other religions. To be clear: I am not advocating that the Prayer Jesus taught his disciples be reduced to a facile instrument of interreligious dialogue. Communion with God for God's own sake is the genuine purpose of the Prayer Jesus taught his disciples. Yet in this prayer lies a paradox: the more intense its focus on God, the greater its capacity to construct the one who prays it into a being more fully human, a creature more compassionate toward

252

fellow creatures of disparate beliefs. In the comments that follow I shall restrict myself to the Abrahamic religious traditions.

Judaism

Repeatedly throughout this study we have noted the resemblance of Jesus' petitions with those of the synagogue. Abundant evidence of this similarity is also manifest in the prayers reproduced in appendix A. "Father, may your kingdom come" rhymes with the opening of the Abhinu Malkenu ("Our Father, Our King"), the great litany of the Jewish High Holidays whose germinal form can be traced to Rabbi Akiba (ca. 40–137):

> Our Father, our King, we have no King but You.
> Our Father, our King, for Your sake have mercy upon us. (*b. Ta'anit* 25b)

The Kaddish, a mainstay of synagogue liturgy, "exalt[s] and hallow[s] [the LORD's] great Name" and prays that "He may establish His kingdom." An ancient form of the third among the Eighteen Benedictions acclaims, "Holy are You, and awe-inspiring is Your Name." Among "The Substance [or Abstract] of the Eighteen" (*b. Berakhot* 29a) are other petitions reminiscent of Jesus' prayer:

> Forgive us, so that we may be redeemed.
> Keep us far from sorrow,
>   and feed us from the pastures of Your land. (*m. Berakhot* 4.3)

> In every time of crisis let [the] needs [of Your people] come before you. (*m. Berakhot* 4.4)

Some elements pervasive in synagogue liturgy are conspicuously absent from the Lord's Prayer. Unlike the twelfth of the Eighteen Benedictions, it invokes no imprecations against the unrighteous. Absent, too, is thanksgiving for the Torah (cf. *b. Berakhot* 17a: "Open my heart to Thy Torah"). Also missing are prayers for Zion, Jerusalem, and the temple (cf. the Amidah's seventeenth benediction: *b. Berakhot* 29b). It is curious that these ingredients, all of which highlight Israel's distinctiveness, are muted in a Jewish prayer that was rapidly adopted by a religious movement populated chiefly by Gentiles. Even more striking is the lack of any direct petition for the people and land of Israel, a stable fixture in Jewish

253

liturgical texts of the rabbinic era (Petuchowski and Brocke, *Lord's Prayer*, 26, 29):

O Rock of Israel,
Arise to the help of Israel.
Deliver, as you have promised, Judah and Israel.

Have compassion, O Lord, in Your abundant mercies,
Upon Israel, Your People,
Upon Jerusalem Your city,
Upon Zion, Your glorious dwelling-place.

Be that as it may, many Jewish scholars recognize in the prayer Jesus taught his disciples many characteristics of Jewish private prayer: address to God in the second person, brevity, and simplicity of style. This Prayer epitomizes what Abraham Heschel wrote of Jewish prayer in general: "In prayer we shift the center of living from self-consciousness to self-surrender. God is the center toward which all forces tend. Prayer . . . enables us to see the world in the mirror of the holy" (*Between God and Man*, 198). For that reason Baruch Graubard's poignant memoir of the Shoah may be less surprising than one might expect:

I was at that time an outlaw escaped abroad to Slovakia after many difficult experiences. I had surrendered and forgotten my identity. In 1944 I slid into an identity borrowed from a Franciscan monastery in Prescov. It hardly fitted me but fitted more than any other. Then I discovered a token of this identity in the Lord's Prayer. That was like a Jewish prayer, like an abbreviation of the Eighteen Benedictions. A calm prayer, only I missed the petition for peace. The Father was addressed only indirectly as King, and it seemed to me at that time that the Father, too, was in need of help just like me. Perhaps he was calmer, more certain of his goal and knew the future. The prayer opened an inner relationship to hope for me, and conquered fear. ("The *Kaddish* Prayer," 61)

Islam

For those who honor the Prophet (570–632), prayer (*tsalāt*) is one of five pillars on which Islam rests. Especially impressive is *Sūrat al-fāti'a*, the Opening of the Qur'an's first chapter, considered by

254

one Muslim commentator "the heart of the Quran, [which] contains the message pertaining to the dimensions of the ultimate relation between human beings and God" (Nasr, *Heart of Islam*, 131):

> In the name of Allah, most merciful, most compassionate.
> Praise to Allah, Lord of the universe, most merciful, most
> compassionate.
> Master of the day of judgment.
> You alone do we worship, and from You do we seek help.
> Guide us along the straight path:
> The path of those whom You have blessed,
> Not the path of those on whom is Your anger,
> Nor the path of those who are astray. (*Sūra* 1.1–7; *The Holy Qur'an*,
> 14–15)

Although these words of the *Sūrat al-fāti'a* and those of the Lord's Prayer are not interchangeable, in several respects they are mutually resonant. Both are exquisitely terse yet comprehensive. Structurally, both are bipartite: the petitioner begins with direct address to God before petitioning God for help. That would be expected of Islam, whose very meaning is "perfect submission." The adjectives *rachmān* and *rachīm* (peerlessly merciful, incomparably compassionate) dovetail with Jesus' teaching about God in the Gospels. "Lord and Master [of all worlds]" acknowledges what Jesus implies with reference to God's "kingship" or "dominion," which in the Gospels embraces both nurturance and judgment. "Praise in the name of Allah" is akin to the expression of hope "Let your name be hallowed." The register of "give," "forgive," and "prevent [from temptation]" in the Lord's Prayer is without precise equivalent in the Qur'an's "Opening"; however, *Sūrat al-fāti'a* sums up humanity's inherent want and satisfaction in God alone. "You alone do we ask for help. Show us the straight way." Elsewhere the Qur'an encourages Muslims to pray to God for sustenance and forgiveness. In private correspondence (April 5, 2013) Professor Maria Massi Dakake informs me, "The virtue of human forgiveness of others [is extolled] as the highest moral response to having been wronged in any way." Notice, too, that the Lord's Prayer and the Qur'an's "Opening" employ first-plural pronouns: to offer either prayer is to locate oneself among all who praise God and are strengthened by a fellowship of faith.

255

The Lord's Prayer reveals both the limits and the prospects for interreligious conversation. Though "Father" is an acceptable metaphor for God in Judaism, it is objectionable to Muslims, whose Qur'an repeatedly asserts that Allah has no offspring (e.g., *Sūra* 112.1–4). However sympathetic in general character the Lord's Prayer may be with the prayers of either Islam or Judaism, Muslims and Jews do not recognize Jesus as Lord: the final "Seal of the Prophets," the position occupied by Muhammad (*Sūra* 33.40), or the Messiah greater than whom none may be expected (*b. Sanhedrin* 98a–99a; Maimonides, *Mishneh Torah: Hilchot Melachim* 11–12). The divinity, as well as humanity, that orthodox Christianity accords to Jesus is deeply problematic and indeed offensive to most Jews and Muslims, who understandably cannot accept such a claim as anything other than a violation of the radical monotheism that Christians also affirm (John 5:18; 8:58–59; *Sūra* 5.17: "They have disbelieved who say, 'Truly, Allah is the Messiah, the son of Mary'"). Precisely because Jesus occupies a place of nonnegotiable importance for orthodox Christians, the prayer he taught his disciples is, for them, the bedrock of all other prayers. It is Christianity's "default setting" in prayer, because the one whom they revere as Lord and Christ taught them to pray like this.

Yet Christians do well to bear in mind that nowhere in their Lord's Prayer does Jesus point to himself or his own significance. Instead, Jesus concentrates his disciples' attention on the God of Abraham, Isaac, and Jacob: the one God to whom Jews and Muslims also pray, with devotion no less sincere. "Truly your God is one [*tawchīd*]" (*Sūra* 37.4; cf. Deut. 6:4–5; Matt. 22:37 = Mark 12:29–30 = Luke 10:27). With the possible exception of the church's appended doxology (see chap. 9 above), the christological significance of the Lord's Prayer is implicit and contextual, neither explicit in nor constituent of the Prayer itself. The prayer of Jesus underlines the limits of human ability—including the contingent finitude of all religious understanding—and beseeches a merciful, just God to restore, in perfect peace, a diseased and tormented world. That is an essential hope in which Jews, Christians, Muslims, and all human beings of goodwill share alike. The day may yet come when, in praying most fervently the prayers native to their traditions, religious peoples may recognize more clearly the face of God in those other than themselves. And as that day

dawns—as the shadows of fear are burned away by love's light—
God's name may be more truly sanctified and God's kingdom may
more quickly come.

The Lord's Prayer in Care with the Aged

Among Protestant Christians the Lord's Prayer and the Twenty-
Third Psalm are the prayers most frequently offered by and for the
elderly. They are brief and, after years of repetition, easier to recall
than other things inaccessible by failing memories. Furthermore,
their themes intersect in ways that speak with significance to those
nearing life's end. We shall touch on six issues, common to the aged
and others nearing death, to which both Psalm 23 and the Lord's
Prayer speak: dependence, deterioration, release, simplicity, loyalty, and hope.

Dependence

The LORD is my shepherd . . . (Ps. 23:1)

Our Father which art in heaven . . . (Matt. 6:9b KJV)

Many are the paths to the grave. Some of us are taken out by an
accident or drop dead. Some go their customary ways until "a
major event" precipitates a nosedive. Others suffer bumpy declines
that grow steeper. Advanced techniques of medical maintenance,
patching, and replacement produce long, slow fades. As we age, we
return to a dimension of childhood we thought was forever behind
us: dependence on others—spouses, partners, children, nurses, and
doctors. Others do for us what we can no longer do for ourselves:
move us, house us, bathe us, groom us, dress us, and feed us. To all
this we may respond with irritability or resignation, but the course
is as inevitable as the sun's setting.

One advantage over infants that the elderly enjoy is a depth of
perspective. With that may come the realization of God's continued
engagement with us as a devoted shepherd or a tender Parent. God
is not God-centered; God remains indissolubly committed to us.
Friends precede us in death; stretches between visits by children or
grandchildren may grow longer. Bereavement and loneliness take

257

their toll. To address God as "Father" is a reminder that we matter to God now and forever, that our identity as God's children is unbreakable, that our kinship with all who pray the Lord's Prayer is permanent even when invisible.

Deterioration

> Yea, though I walk through the valley of the shadow of death,
> I will fear no evil:
> for thou art with me;
>   thy rod and thy staff they comfort me. (Ps. 23:4 KJV)

> And lead us not into temptation, but deliver us from evil,
>   (Matt. 6:13a KJV)

With age may come wisdom (Job 12:12), and even youths may fall faint (Isa. 40:30), but the Preacher of Ecclesiastes receives full marks for an honest diagnosis. Our bodies are houses that dilapidate: arms and legs give way, teeth rot, eyes dim, ears go deaf, the voice softens, hair turns gray, "and the dust returns to the ground as it was, and the lifebreath returns to God Who bestowed it" (Eccl. 12:1–7 NJPS). This is a bitter pill for cultures, terrified by death, which huckster youthful vitality on the covers of glossy supermarket tabloids ("Super Sex in Your Seventies!"). The body is wiser; the genetic process is relentless. Given enough time, we just fall apart, scheduling more appointments in "the body shop" to replace this hip, that knee, or a mitral valve.

Because death overshadows before catching up with us, temptations to depression are understandable. They can also be resisted. We cannot defy mortality, but we can face it squarely and ask God's deliverance from the evil, yawning maw of despair. In less stressful moments the Lord's Prayer reminds those who give and receive care that the task of dying well depends, not on a Stoic apathy grounded in self-reliant human pride, but instead on our mutual interdependence of faith in a God whose providence suffers no degradation (Vogt, *Patience, Compassion*, 97–139).

258 Letting Go

> Surely goodness and mercy shall follow me
> all the days of my life. . . . (Ps. 23:6a)

And forgive us our debts,
    as we forgive our debtors. (Matt. 6:12 KJV)

Debilitation isn't what it used to be. The momentum of medical treatment has become a juggernaut no one wants to steer.

> When there is no way of knowing exactly how long our skeins will run—and when we imagine ourselves to have much more time than we do—our every impulse is to fight, to die with chemo in our veins or a tube in our throats or fresh sutures in our flesh. The fact that we may be shortening or worsening the time we have left hardly seems to register. We imagine that we can wait until the doctors tell us that there is nothing more they can do. But rarely is there nothing more that doctors can do. They can give toxic drugs of unknown efficacy, operate to try to remove part of the tumor, put in a feeding tube if a person can't eat: there's always something. We want these choices. But that doesn't mean we are eager to make the choices ourselves. Instead, most often, we make no choice at all. We fall back on the default, and the default is: Do something. Fix something. Is there any way out of this? (Gawande, *Being Mortal*, 173–74)

Ultimately none of us is getting out of here alive. Before we leave, always there is unfinished business. Some of it is bound up with debt and forgiveness: a weight lugged for untold years, a pardon we have withheld, our own absolution whose receipt we have refused. But the debt whose forgiveness we may most resist, the loan whose cancellation is refused with greatest vehemence, is God's gift of life itself. We do not want to relinquish it. We have no choice: we must let go. Our wants must be trained and our desires cleansed. Thoughtful offering of the Lord's Prayer may lead the elderly and dying to expressions of serene, even joyful release.

Simply Being

He maketh me to lie down in green pastures:
He leadeth me beside the still waters.
He restoreth my soul. (Ps. 23:2–3a KJV)

Thy will be done, on earth as it is in heaven. (Matt. 6:10 RSV)   259

As young adults we are focused on sorting options and refining ambitions. The future is limitless; we are going to live forever. In middle age we struggle to realize our goals and establish ourselves while providing for loved ones. With old age our focus changes. The horizon is foreshortened; the road behind us, longer than that which lies ahead. The truth of a parable recounted by Jesus in Luke 12:16–21 rings more clearly than ever:

> The land of a rich man produced abundantly. And he thought to himself, "What should I do, for I have no place to store my crops?" Then he said, "I will do this: I will pull down my barns and build larger ones, and there I will store all my grain and my goods. And I will say to my soul, Soul, you have ample goods laid up for many years; relax, eat, drink, be merry." But God said to him, "You fool! This very night your life is being demanded of you. And the things you have prepared, whose will they be?" So it is with those who store up treasures for themselves but are not rich toward God.

With advanced age our desires diminish, our needs become fewer. When confronted by our finitude, striving for more wealth and more power becomes less important. If we have daily bread, we are not in genuine want (Matt. 6:11; Ps. 23:1). Everyday pleasures like sitting in sunshine or going to the bathroom unassisted become gifts for which we are most grateful. Allowing for occasional bursts of obstinate frustration, we have outfoxed ourselves often enough to have learned that yielding to God's will may no longer be the struggle that once it was. We have lived long enough to see the alternatives, which haven't turned out very well.

A Difficult Loyalty

> He leadeth me in the paths of righteousness
> for his name's sake. (Ps. 23:3 KJV)

> Hallowed be thy name. (Matt. 6:9b KJV)

In *The Philosophy of Loyalty* (1908), Josiah Royce (1855–1916) defended the proposition that self-interest, finally, is "chaos of conflicting passions." "Left to myself alone, I can never find out what my will is" (28). Human beings, he contended, are not only entitled but actually compelled to a devotion to something greater than

260

themselves. The light outside us may lead to painful consequences, but even they are preferable to an inner light that only flickers before evanescing. "Loyalty . . . solves the paradox of our ordinary existence by showing us outside of ourselves the cause which is to be served, and inside of ourselves the will which delights to do this service, and which is not thwarted but enriched and expressed in such service" (42).

The Jewish and Christian definition of Royce's "outer light" is the sacredness of God's name and rededication to God's righteousness, on earth as in heaven. Without that, mortality shrivels into a vacuous terror, a refrain posed by Peggy Lee's wistful question, "Is that all there is?" To pledge one's self to the kingdom's cause in daily, small acts of kindness and justice does not guarantee ease near life's end, but such loyalty to God's cause brings to fulfillment the meaning of a faithful and happy life.

A Courageous Hope

I will dwell in the house of the LORD for ever. (Ps. 23:6 KJV)

Thy kingdom come. . . .
For thine is the kingdom, and the power,
    and the glory, for ever. Amen. (Matt. 6:10, 13 KJV)

The Lord's Prayer distinguishes genuine hope from bogus optimism. Contingent on the circumstances—an important qualification—the latter may be inappropriately articulated. "We're going to beat this." "You'll be back on the golf course in no time." "You're not going to die." Christian faith offers a different response. Sickness and death are inescapable. Christ suffers with all who die, walking with us through the valleys of death's shadow. God can be trusted to bring good out of evil.

On his deathbed actor Edmund Gwenn (1877–1959), who played Kris Kringle in *Miracle on 34th Street* (1947), is said to have quipped, "Dying is easy. Comedy is hard." Our own deaths may turn out to be easy, or they may not. The *prospect* of our death will be harder to bear if it is bound by fear, much lighter to approach if borne by hope. The Christian vision of God's kingdom is comedic in the literal sense of the term's Greek roots: *kōmos* (revel) + *aoidos*

261

(singer). The news is good, joyous enough to sing, because our hope is anchored in the authority of a God whose love for us and for all is as invincible as it is pure.

Works Cited in Chapter 10

Bloom, Anthony. (Anthony, Metropolitan of Sourozh). *Living Prayer.* Springfield, IL: Templegate, 1966.

Gawande, Atul. *Being Mortal: Medicine and What Matters in the End.* Metropolitan Books. New York: Henry Holt, 2014.

Graubard, Baruch. "The *Kaddish* Prayer." In *The Lord's Prayer and Jewish Liturgy*, edited by Jakob J. Petuchowski and Michael Brocke, 59–72. London: Burns & Oates, 1978.

Hammerling, Roy. "The Lord's Prayer: A Cornerstone of Early Baptismal Education." In *A History of Prayer: The First to the Fifteenth Century*, edited by Roy Hammerling, 167–82. Brill's Companions to the Christian Tradition 13. Leiden: E. J. Brill, 2008.

Heschel, Abraham J. *Between God and Man: An Interpretation of Judaism.* Edited by F. A. Rothschild. New York: Free Press, 1959.

The Holy Qur'an: Text, Translation and Commentary. Edited by Abdullah Yasuf Ali. Elmhurst, NY: Tahrike Tarsile Qur'an, 2011.

Hultgren, Arland J. "Forgive Us, as We Forgive (Matthew 6:12)." *Word & World* 16 (1996): 284–90.

Jacobson, Karl N. "A Word in Season: Preaching the Lord's Prayer." *Word & World* 22 (2002): 88–93.

Lochman, Jan Milač. "The Lord's Prayer in Our Time: Praying and Drumming." *Princeton Seminary Bulletin*, Supplementary Issue 2 (1992): 5–19.

Moltmann, Jürgen. *The Coming God: Christian Eschatology.* Minneapolis: Fortress Press, 1996.

Murphy, Debra Dean. "Worship as Catechesis: Knowledge, Desire, and Christian Formation." *Theology Today* 58 (2001): 321–32.

Nasr, Seyyed Hossein. *The Heart of Islam: Enduring Values for Humanity.* New York: Harper One, 2002.

Petuchowski, Jakob J., and Michael Brocke. *The Lord's Prayer and Jewish Liturgy.* London: Burns & Oates, 1978.

Royce, Josiah. *The Philosophy of Loyalty*. New York: Macmillan, 1908.

Saliers, Don E. "Liturgy and Ethics: Some New Beginnings." In *Liturgy and the Moral Self: Humanity at Full Stretch before God: Essays in Honor of Don E. Saliers*, edited by E. Byron Anderson and Bruce T. Morrill, 15–35. A Pueblo Book. Collegeville, MN: Liturgical Press, 1998.

Stevenson, Kenneth. "Christology and Trinity: Interpreting the Lord's Prayer." In *The Place of Christ in Liturgical Prayer: Trinity, Christology, and Liturgical Prayer*, edited by Bryan D. Spinks, 222–42. Collegeville, MN: Liturgical Press, 2008.

Vallee, Sherri L. "The Lord's Prayer as Preparation for Communion." *Theoforum* 35 (2004): 279–300.

Vogt, Christopher P. *Patience, Compassion, Hope, and the Christian Art of Dying Well*. Lanham, MD: Rowman & Littlefield, 2004.

Webber, Robert, and Rodney Clapp. *People of the Truth*. Harrisburg, PA: Morehouse, 1988.

Westhelle, Vítor. "On Displacing Words: The Lord's Prayer and the New Definition of Justice." *Word & World* 22 (2002): 27–35.

Appendixes

*Prayers of the Synagogue
in the Postbiblical Era
The Version of the Lord's Prayer
in the* Didache
*A Conspectus of Interpretation:
The Lord's Prayer in Christian
Thought*

Prayers of the Synagogue in the Postbiblical Era

Apparently anchored in the *Shema Yisrael* ("Hear, O Israel": Deut. 6:4) and the priestly blessing ("May the LORD bless you and keep you": Num. 6:24–26), Jewish prayer books, or *siddurîm* (from a Hebrew root meaning "to arrange"), were formalized over many centuries and continue to evolve. According to the Talmud (*b. Megillah* 18a; *b. Berakhot* 33a) a version of the Amidah (see below) is believed to have been formulated under the auspices of Gamaliel II at a rabbinical council at Jamnia, in central Israel, in the late first century AD, following the Second Temple's destruction. Liturgical wording was fluid across many centuries. The earliest known codification of Jewish prayers, the mid-ninth-century Siddur Rab Amram, was that of Amram Gaon (d. 875), head of the Jewish Talmud Academy in Sura, southern Babylon; the first printed *siddur* was issued from Soncino, Italy, in 1486. To the present day different versions of synagogue prayers reflect different nations, variant sects of Judaism (Ashkenazi Orthodox, Conservative, Reform), and diverse groups (feminist and humanistic) within progressive (Reform) Judaism. Some factors have remained constant: "Fixed prayer is first and foremost . . . communal; . . . it cannot be wholly or perfectly fulfilled by the solitary individual" (Heinemann, *Prayer in the Talmud*, 15). These corporate prayers also reach for a harmony of human with the divine: "A praying man, as the Pharisees said, is

267

in the Divine Presence" (Abrahams, "Rabbinic Ideas," 90, citing *b. Sanhedrin* 22a; *b. Yoma* 53b).

At least three prayers have attained historic, pervasive importance in the synagogue: the Amidah, the Kaddish, and the Abhinu Malkenu. Versions of each of these are reprinted here, for the benefit of Christians who can detect in each of them both similarities and differences from the prayer that Jesus taught his disciples. The piety of today's church may be reinforced by so much praise, petition, and gratitude shared in common with the synagogue.

The Amidah (Standing [Prayer]), or Shemoneh Esrei (Eighteen Benedictions)

Considered by some *"the* prayer [*ha-tefillah*] of Judaism," the Amidah occupies a crucial place in synagogue prayer both ancient and modern. Its earliest Palestinian form contains eighteen benedictions, which may be formally divided into three sections: praise (the first three blessings), petitions (the middle thirteen benedictions), and thanksgiving (the last two blessings). In talmudic tradition Gamaliel II urged the addition of what is now the Twelfth Benediction (actually a curse against heretics), for a total of nineteen in all (*m. Berakhot* 4.3). Conflations in what may originally have been correlative petitions, such as the Fourteenth, were made to retain the sobriquet, "The Eighteen." Some rabbis suggested condensed versions of the Amidah for personal prayer or in times of emergency (*m. Berakhot* 4.3–4; *b. Berakhot* 29b; see Petuchowski, "Liturgy of the Synagogue").

[1]You are praised, O Lord our God and God of our fathers,
God of Abraham, God of Isaac, and God of Jacob,
The great, mighty, and awe-inspiring God,
God Supreme, Creator of heaven and earth,
Our Shield and Shield of our fathers,
Our trust in every generation.
You are praised, O Lord, Shield of Abraham.
[2]You are mighty, bringing low the proud,
powerful, judging the arrogant,
ever-living, raising up the dead;
causing the wind to blow and the dew to descend;
sustaining the living, quickening the dead,

268

O cause our salvation to sprout as in the twinkling of an eye.
You are praised, O Lord, who quickens the dead.
[3]Holy are You,
and awe-inspiring is Your Name;
and beside You there is no God.
You are praised, O Lord, the holy God.
[4]Our Father, favor us with knowledge from You,
and with discernment and insight from Your Torah.
You are praised, O Lord, gracious Giver of knowledge.
[5]Turn us back to you, O Lord, and we shall return;
renew our days as of old.
You are praised, O Lord, who delights in repentance.
[6]Forgive us, our Father, for we have sinned against You.
Blot out and remove our transgressions from before Your sight,
For Your mercies are manifold.
You are praised, O Lord, who abundantly pardons.
[7]Look at our affliction, and champion our cause,
and redeem us for the sake of Your Name.
You are praised, O Lord, Redeemer of Israel.
[8]Heal us, O Lord our God, of the pain of our hearts.
Remove us from grief and sighing,
and bring healing for our wounds.
You are praised, O Lord, who heals the sick of His people Israel.
[9]Bless, O Lord our God, this year for us,
and let it be good in all the varieties of its produce.
Hasten the year of our redemptive End.
Grant dew and rain upon the face of the earth,
and satiate the world out of the treasuries of Your goodness;
and grant a blessing to the work of our hands.
You are praised, O Lord, who blesses the years.
[10]Sound the great horn for our freedom,
and lift up a banner to gather in our exiles.
You are praised, O Lord, who gathers in the outcasts of His people
   Israel.
[11]Restore our judges as at first,
and our counselors as at the beginning;
and reign over us—You alone.
You are praised, O Lord, who loves justice.
[12]For the apostates let there be no hope,
and uproot the kingdom of arrogance, speedily and in our days.
May the Nazarenes and the sectarians perish as in a moment.
Let them be blotted out of the book of life,
and not be written together with the righteous.

269

You are praised, O Lord, who subdues the arrogant.
[13]May Your compassion be aroused towards the true proselytes;
and grant us a good reward together with those who do Your will.
You are praised, O Lord, the trust of the Righteous.
[14]Have compassion, O Lord, in Your abundant mercies,
upon Israel, Your people,
upon Jerusalem, Your city,
upon Zion, Your glorious dwelling-place,
upon Your temple and upon Your abode,
and upon the kingdom of your house of David, Your righteous
    anointed.
You are praised, O Lord, God of David, Builder of Jerusalem.
[15]Hear, O Lord our God, our prayerful voice,
and have mercy upon us,
for You are a gracious and merciful God.
You are praised, O Lord, who hears prayer.
[16]Be pleased, O Lord our God, to dwell in Zion;
and may your servants worship You in Jerusalem.
You are praised, O Lord, whom we worship with reverence.
[17]We acknowledge to You
that You are the Lord our God and the God of our fathers;
and we thank you
for all the goodness, the loving-kindness and the mercies
which You have bestowed upon us,
and which You have wrought for our fathers before us.
And were we to say, "Our foot is slipping,"
Your loving-kindness, O Lord, would sustain us.
You are praised, O Lord, to whom it is good to give thanks.
[18]Grant Your peace
upon Israel, Your people,
upon Your city,
and upon Your inheritance.
and bless us—all of us together.
You are praised, O Lord, the Maker of peace.
    (trans. Petuchowski and Brocke, *Lord's Prayer*, 27–30)

The Kaddish (Holy → Magnification and Sanctification of God's Holy Name)

Like the Amidah, the Kaddish (cf. Ezek. 38:23) evolved in various forms (see Graubard, "The *Kaddish* Prayer"). Its most primitive version may also be traced to the Siddur Rab Amram (see above).

Presented here is the so-called Complete Kaddish, including a bracketed portion appearing in some rites, whose fourth and fifth petitions extend the so-called Half Kaddish.

[1]Exalted and hallowed be His great Name
in the world that He created
according to his will.
May He establish His kingdom [and cause His salvation to sprout,
and hasten the coming of His messiah,]
in your lifetime and in your days,
and in the lifetime of the whole household of Israel,
speedily and at a near time.
And say: Amen.
[2]May his great Name be praised forever
and unto all eternity.
[3]Blessed and praised,
glorified and exalted,
extolled and honored,
magnified and lauded
be the Name of the Holy One, praised be He—
although He is beyond all blessings and hymns,
praises and consolations
that may be uttered in the world.
And say: Amen.
[4]May the prayers and supplications
of the whole household of Israel
be acceptable before their Father in heaven.
And say: Amen.
[5]May He who makes peace in His high heavens
make peace for us and for all Israel.
And say: Amen.

The Kaddish came to be associated especially with Jewish funeral rites. Accordingly, a "Burial" or "Mourner's" petition like the following is normally attached to the preceding:

Exalted and hallowed be His great Name
In the world that He will renew,
Resurrecting the dead,
And raising them up to eternal life.
He will rebuild the city of Jerusalem
And establish His temple in its midst.
He will uproot idolatry from the earth
And restore the worship of God to its place.

271

The Holy One, praised be He, will reign
In His sovereignty and in His glory.
May this be in your lifetime and in your days,
And in the lifetime of the whole household of Israel,
Speedily and at a near time.
And say: Amen.
(trans. Petuchowski and Brocke, *Lord's Prayer*, 37–39)

Some scholars (e.g., Ullendorff, "Relationship") regard the Lord's Prayer as dependent on the Kaddish; others think the influence is vice versa. The evidence is inconclusive. It is safer and sufficient to say that between the two prayers lies a great affinity.

The Abhinu Malkenu (Our Father, Our King)

According to the Talmud (*b. Ta'anit* 25b) a brief confession and petition were ascribed to Akiba, the second-century rabbi:

Our Father, our King, we have no King but You.
Our Father, our King, for Your sake have mercy upon us.

By the ninth century (Siddur Rab Amram) an expanded version of this prayer is recorded, variations on which have since been incorporated in synagogue liturgies at Rosh Hashanah (the Jewish New Year) and on the Ten Days of Repentance, extending from Rosh Hashanah through Yom Kippur (the Day of Atonement). "The *Abhinu Malkenu* prayer is among the high points of the service on the High Holidays, and has deeply penetrated into [Israel's] consciousness" (Lauer, "*Abhinu Malkenu*," 73).

Our Father, Our King, we have sinned before You.
Our Father, Our King, we have no King but You.
Our Father, Our King, deal with us for the sake of Your Name.
Our Father, Our King, nullify evil decrees from us.
Our Father, Our King, renew for us good decrees.
Our Father, Our King, nullify from us the designs of those who hate us.
Our Father, Our King, confound the counsel of our enemies.
Our Father, Our King, send perfect healing to the sick of Your people.

272

Our Father, Our King, prevent the plague from Your people.

Our Father, Our King, of pestilence, sword, famine, and destruction rid the partners of Your covenant.

Our Father, Our King, remember that we are but dust.

Our Father, Our King, do it for Your sake, and not for ours.

Our Father, Our King, rend from us the evil judgment decreed against us.

Our Father, Our King, erase the records of our guilt.

Our Father, Our King, pardon and forgive our iniquities.

Our Father, Our King, blot out our transgressions, and make them pass away from Your sight.

Our Father, Our King, let us return in perfect repentance before You.

Our Father, Our King, inscribe us in the book of life.

Our Father, Our King, inscribe us in the book of remembrance.

Our Father, Our King, inscribe us in the book of merits.

Our Father, Our King, inscribe us in the book of maintenance and sustenance.

Our Father, Our King, let salvation sprout for us soon.

Our Father, Our King, hear our voice, pity us, and have mercy upon us.

Our Father, Our King, accept our prayer in mercy and in favor.

Our Father, Our King, do it for the sake of Your great Name.

Our Father, Our King, do it for the sake of Your abundant mercies; and have compassion upon us.

Our Father, Our King, be gracious unto us and answer us, for we have no good works to show.

Deal charitably and kindly with us, and save us.

(Petuchowski and Brocke, *Lord's Prayer*, 39–40)

For Rabbi Yohanan (180–279), "A benediction in which God's kingship is not mentioned is no benediction at all" (*b. Berakhot* 40b). The Abhinu Malkenu leaves no possible doubt that this is a true benediction.

Works Cited in Appendix A

Abrahams, Isaac. "Some Rabbinic Ideas on Prayer." In *Studies in Pharisaism and the Gospels*, 72–93. First Series. New York: Ktav, 1967.

Graubard, Baruch. "The *Kaddish* Prayer." In *The Lord's Prayer and Jewish Liturgy*, edited by Jakob J. Petuchowski and Michael Brocke, 59–72. London: Burns & Oates, 1978.

Heinemann, Joseph. *Prayer in the Talmud: Forms and Patterns.* Studia Judaica 9. Berlin: de Gruyter, 1977.

Lauer, Simon. "*Abhinu Malkenu*: Our Father, Our King." In *The Lord's Prayer and Jewish Liturgy*, edited by Jakob J. Petuchowski and Michael Brocke, 73–80. London: Burns & Oates, 1978.

Petuchowski, Jakob J. "The Liturgy of the Synagogue." In *The Lord's Prayer and Jewish Liturgy*, edited by Jakob J. Petuchowski and Michael Brocke, 45–57. London: Burns & Oates, 1978.

Petuchowski, Jakob J., and Michael Brocke, eds. *The Lord's Prayer and Jewish Liturgy*. London: Burns & Oates, 1978.

Ullendorff, Edward. "Some Notes on the Relationship of the Paternoster to the Qaddish." *Journal of Jewish Studies* 54 (2003): 122–24.

The Version of the Lord's Prayer in the *Didache*

The Teaching [= *Didache*] *of the Lord through the Twelve Apostles* is a composite document of unknown authorship, offering snapshots of primitive Christian catechesis (1.1–6.3), liturgy (7.1–10.7), church order (11.1–15.4), and apocalypticism (16.1–8). On its dating and provenance we are in the dark. Some scholars assign to it a date as early as AD 60; others, as late as the third century. At present many experts reckon a date of around AD 100–120 as likely; certainly the book or its primary constituents were known by the fourth century. Most scholars consider Syria or Syro-Palestine to have been a credible place of origin (van de Sandt and Flusser, *The Didache*, 48–52). Nowadays the *Didache* (pronounced *di-dah-KAY*) is included in a corpus of early Christian literature known as the Apostolic Fathers (see Gregory and Tuckett, *Reception* and *Trajectories*).

For our purposes this manual of discipline is important because it contains the earliest written attestation of the Lord's Prayer outside the New Testament, perhaps not much later than two or three decades after Matthew's and Luke's compositions. The Prayer is located in a section of the *Didache* that prescribes a regular order of Christian baptism (7.1–4), fasting and prayer (8.1–3), and Eucharist (9.1–10.7). Unspecified "hypocrites" are said to have fasted on Mondays and Thursdays; this manual's adherents are directed to fast on Wednesdays and Fridays (8.1). Likewise, this book's

275

Christian readers are dissuaded from praying as "the hypocrites" do; "instead, [pray] in this way, as the Lord directed in his gospel" (8.2). The identity of those opposed is not specified; although some commentators (van de Sandt and Flusser, *The Didache*, 32–33, 291–94; Niederwimmer, *The Didache*, 131–34) believe they were pious Jews from whom Christians were encouraged to separate themselves, nothing in the text itself verifies that identification. (On the convoluted religious history underlying the *Didache*, see Jefford, "Social Locators.") Equally obscure is "the gospel" (*euangelion*) in which the Lord instructed his disciples to pray: it could refer to one of the New Testament Gospels, yet neither here nor elsewhere in the *Didache* (11.3; 15.3, 4) does the term clearly refer to a literary source. "The gospel" may simply refer to remembered words of Jesus, "our Lord's good news" (15.4). If one concludes that the *Didache* depended directly on no written Gospels—whose own manuscripts were probably in flux at the time of the *Didache*'s compilation—that in itself would be telling. As late as the early second century, by which time all the New Testament Gospels had been composed and were in circulation, early Christians maintained a lively remembrance of Jesus' words and deeds, disseminated by word of mouth. That deduction tallies with a comment of Papias of Hierapolis (ca. 60–155), who exemplifies his generation's bias for information that was oral, not written:

> For unlike the many, I did not delight in those who have much to say, but in those who teach the truth, nor in those who relate the commandments of others, but in those who repeated [the commandments] given in faith by the Lord and derived from truth itself. And if ever anyone came who had been a follower of the elders, I inquired into the words of the elders—what Andrew or what Peter had said, or what Philip, or what Thomas or James, or what John or Matthew, or any other of the Lord's disciples . . . were saying. For I was of the opinion that things out of books do not profit me so much as what comes from a living and abiding voice. . . . I listened earnestly to these things, making notes of them not on paper but in my heart; and ever since by the grace of God I ruminate on them. (Eusebius, *Church History* 3.39.4; 5.20.7 AT)

276

One may easily compare the *Didache*'s version of the Lord's Prayer with that in Luke and in Matthew by arranging them in parallel columns. Words underlined in the third column differ from, or lack attestation in, those in the first and second columns. Variations include Greek articles and prepositions that, when carried over into English, appear identical in form.

When one compares the *Didache*'s version with those in Luke and in Matthew, four things stand out.

1. In all three cases the substance of the Prayer itself—from the address to the "Father" up to the petition of deliverance from evil— is the same, its petitions presented in identical sequence. Most of the *Didache*'s alterations in wording are minor and correspond to modifications already evident within the New Testament. From Luke's simple address to "Father," Matthew predicates the Father "who is in the heavens," which the *Didache* adjusts to "the [singular] heaven." Similarly, release from "debts" (Matthew) is shifted to a singular, representative "debt" (*Didache*). It's reasonable to conclude that, after Jesus was remembered to have taught disciples to pray in a particular way, his words stuck in their memory and were repeated almost verbatim.

2. The Lord's Prayer in the *Didache* is closer to Matthew's form than that of Luke. The *Didache* remembers the Prayer in its longer version: address to the heavenly Father, the entreaty that God's will be realized on earth as in heaven, petition for deliverance from evil (or the evil one). Yet small differences from Matthew are also evident: a shift in a verb's tense from the perfect ("we also have forgiven") to the present ("we also forgive," as in Luke); the singular "heaven"; a singular "debt." The simplest explanation for these changes is that the *Didache* slavishly followed *neither* Matthew *nor* Luke but drew from an oral tradition in which such alterations would be expected (thus Koester, *Ancient Christian Gospels*, 16–17, 141–42; for a cautious claim that the *Didache* was "significantly informed by the text of the gospel of Matthew," see Tuckett, "The *Didache* and the Writings," 105–6).

3. The longest expansion in the *Didache*'s version of the Prayer comes at the end: a strophic doxology absent from the earliest manuscripts of both Luke and Matthew: "For yours is the power and the glory forever." A doxological conclusion of the Lord's Prayer appears for the first time in the *Didache*; it is absent even from the late second-century and early third-century commentaries of Tertullian, Cyprian, and Origen. Given the context of the *Didache*'s recital of the prayer—a large section on the practice of public worship (7.1–10.7)—one may infer that these words were added to close the prayer liturgically. As noted in chapter 9 (above), they are

277

Table 4: Three Ancient Versions of the Lord's Prayer (AT)

Luke 11:2–4	Matthew 6:9–13	Didache 8.2–3
[2]And [Jesus] said to them, "When you pray, say:	[9]"Pray then like this:	[2]Neither pray as [do] the hypocrites; but rather, as the Lord commanded in his good news, pray like this:
Father,	Our Father who is in the heavens,	"Our Father who is in heaven,
May your name be hallowed. May your kingdom come.	May your name be hallowed. [10]May your kingdom come, may your will come to pass, as in heaven, so also on earth.	May your name be hallowed. May your kingdom come, may your will come to pass, as in heaven, so also on earth.
[3]Keep giving us each day the bread we need, [4]and cancel our sins, for we also forgive* everyone indebted to us. And do not bring us into temptation."	[11]Give us today the bread we need, [12]and cancel our debts, as we also have forgiven those indebted to us. [13]And do not bring us into temptation, but rescue us from the evil one."	Give us today the bread we need. And cancel our debt, as we also forgive* those indebted to us. And do not bring us into temptation, but rescue us from the evil one. For yours is the power and the glory unto the ages [= "forever"]." [3]Pray this way three times a day.

*Luke and the *Didache* preserve minor, dialectical variations on the spelling of the present indicative active form of the Greek verb *aphiēmi*, "forgive": *aphiomen* (Luke), *aphiemen* (*Didache*, a variant spelling that appears in a few late Lukan manuscripts).

reminiscent of, albeit simpler than, 1 Chronicles 29:11: "Thine, O LORD, is the greatness, and the power, and the glory, and the victory, and the majesty; for all that is in the heavens and in the earth is thine; thine is the kingdom, O LORD, and thou art exalted as head above all" (RSV). Concluding doxologies tally with later Jewish liturgical custom: thus, each of the Amidah's Eighteen Benedictions ends, "You are praised, O Lord" (see appendix A above). Beginning in the eighth and ninth centuries, manuscripts of Matthew's version of the Prayer append concluding doxologies with abundant variations in phraseology: "for yours is the kingdom and [the power and] the glory [forever {and ever}]. Amen"; "for yours is the power [and the glory] forever and ever. [Amen.]"; "of the Father and of the Son and of the Holy Spirit" (Metzger, *Textual Commentary*, 14). These variants likely betoken regional differences: manuscripts of Matthew, though usually not of Luke, were adjusted to reflect the liturgies of worshipers in different locales.

An interesting feature of the *Didache's* earliest doxology is its repetition in that manual's presentation of liturgy for the Eucharist:

- As for thanksgiving, give thanks in this way. First, as regards the cup: We thank you, our Father. . . . To you be glory forever. (9.1, 2a, 2e)
- And with regard to the bread: We thank you, our Father. . . . To you be glory forever. (9.3ab, 3f)
- . . . For glory and power are yours through Jesus Christ forever. (9.4d)
- When you have had your fill, give thanks in this way. We thank you, holy Father. . . . To you be glory forever. (10.1, 2a, 2g)
- For all things we thank you, Lord, because you are powerful. To you be glory forever. (10.4)
- . . . For power and glory are yours forever. (10.5–6)

As prescribed in the *Didache*, the doxology of the Lord's Prayer matches a repeated, two-part formula in the Lord's Supper that consistently omits reference to "the kingdom." We should forgo cudgeling our brains over that anomaly while oblivious to the obvious: perhaps as early as the second century the Lord's Prayer was coalescing with Eucharistic liturgy (Chase, *Lord's Prayer*, 12–13, 172–73; Dodd, "Sacrament of the Lord's Supper").

4. The greatest variance from the Gospels in the *Didache's* presentation of the Lord's Prayer lies in its framing context of prohibition and exhortation. "Neither pray as [do] the hypocrites" (8.2) recalls a word from Matthew (*hypokritai*: 6:2, 5, 16) that is applied to pious showboats; in the *Didache*, by contrast, the term refers to those who pray in a manner that veers away from "the Lord's directions." Nor is there anything in Matthew or Luke like that found in *Didache* 8.3: "Pray this way three times a day." That instruction echoes an ancient Jewish custom of offering prayer thrice daily at a fixed time (Dan. 6:9–12). While not touching the essence of the Lord's Prayer itself, both of these differences in the *Didache* may have exerted tremendous impact on Christian worship from its beginnings to the present day. With the prescription to offer this prayer three times a day, we may be witnessing a precedent for third (*terce*), sixth (*sext*), and ninth (*none*) hours of Christian prayer, which were apparently conventional by the time of Tertullian (*Prayer* 25) and Clement of Alexandria (*Miscellanies* 7.7; 40.3) and were later amplified in monastic orders like that of Benedict of Nursia (*Rule* 8–19). Arguably, with the *Didache* another threshold is crossed: while Luke 11:2 may be interpreted more prescriptively ("When you pray, say"), Matthew 6:9 connotes something looser ("Pray then like this" [RSV]). The *Didache* is clearest and firmest of all: "Pray as the Lord commanded in his gospel." Jesus is regarded as having established a regulatory prayer that his disciples are obligated to pray. They did so and have ever since.

Works Cited in Appendix B

Chase, Frederick Henry. *The Lord's Prayer in the Early Church*. Cambridge: Cambridge University Press, 1891.

Dodd, C. H. "The Sacrament of the Lord's Supper in the New Testament. "In *Christian Worship: Studies in Its History and Meaning by Members of Mansfield College*, edited by Nathaniel Micklem, 68–82. Oxford: Oxford University Press, 1936.

Gregory, Andrew F., and Christopher M. Tuckett, eds. *The Reception of the New Testament in the Apostolic Fathers*. The New Testament and the Apostolic Fathers. Oxford: Oxford University Press, 2005.

————, eds. *Trajectories through the New Testament and the Apostolic Fathers.* The New Testament and the Apostolic Fathers. Oxford: Oxford University Press, 2005.

Jefford, Clayton N. "Social Locators as a Bridge between the *Didache* and Matthew." In Gregory and Tuckett, *Trajectories,* 245–64.

Koester, Helmut. *Ancient Christian Gospels: Their History and Development.* London: SCM; Philadelphia: Trinity Press International, 1990.

Metzger, Bruce M. *A Textual Commentary on the Greek New Testament.* 2nd ed. Stuttgart: Deutsche Bibelgesellschaft; New York: United Bible Societies, 1994.

Micklem, Nathaniel, ed. *Christian Worship: Studies in Its History and Meaning by Members of Mansfield College.* Oxford: Oxford University Press, 1936.

Niederwimmer, Kurt. *The Didache: A Commentary.* Hermeneia. Translated by Linda M. Maloney. Edited by Harold W. Attridge. Minneapolis: Fortress Press, 1998.

Tuckett, Christopher M. "The *Didache* and the Writings That Later Formed the New Testament." In Gregory and Tuckett, *Reception,* 83–127.

van de Sandt, Hub, and David Flusser. *The Didache: Its Jewish Sources and Its Place in Early Judaism and Christianity.* Compendia Rerum Iudaicarum ad Novum Testamentum 3.5. Assen: Royal Van Gorcum; Minneapolis: Fortress Press, 2002.

A Conspectus of Interpretation

The Lord's Prayer in Christian Thought

Thoughtful exegesis of the prayer Jesus taught his disciples did not need to wait until the dawn of modern biblical criticism. The present commentary has drawn on the insights of many throughout the ages who immersed themselves in Scripture. A lot of such expositions, often delivered as sermons for Christian congregations, are scattered and hard to retrieve. The following overview—selective, not exhaustive—offers an appreciation of attitudes toward the Lord's Prayer and trends in its interpretation across the centuries. For both practicality and historical perspective, all the interpreters considered here were born before 1900.

Most of the extant patristic interpretations of the Lord's Prayer are located in liturgical frameworks (Froehlich, "Lord's Prayer"; Taft, *Liturgy of the Hours*). In appendix B (above) we noted that the *Didache* prescribed offering the Lord's Prayer "three times each day" (8.3). Whether that prescription refers to individual or corporate prayer is uncertain; what is certain is that the *Didache's* presentation of this Prayer (8.2–3) is situated among a "liturgical agenda" that includes directions for baptism (7.1–4), fasting (8.1), and the Eucharist (9.1–10.7; Niederwimmer, *Didache*, 125). The *Didache* locates the Lord's Prayer in the catechesis of novice Christians, as does, apparently, Tertullian, Cyprian, Cyril, Augustine, and others (Bouhot, "La tradition catéchétique"). In some traditions the Lord's Prayer may have been recited as the first prayer following a catechumenate's baptism (Cyprian, *Lord's Prayer* 9–10;

283

Apostolic Constitutions [ca. 380] 7.45.1; see Hammerling, "Lord's Prayer"). Association of God's kingdom with a banquet, the petition for bread, and the need for communal forgiveness seem naturally to have positioned the Lord's Prayer before celebration of the Lord's Supper, or Eucharist (*Did.* 14.1–2; Tertullian, *Prayer* 6.2; Cyprian, *Lord's Prayer* 18; see Rordorf, "Lord's Prayer"). In the Western church of the late Middle Ages, sermons on the Lord's Prayer were commonly preached on Rogation Days, the three days of prayer and fasting before the Feast of the Ascension (Robinson, "Sermons on the Lord's Prayer"). Surveying the contributions of the following commentators, we are well reminded that most of them were firmly situated in the liturgical life of Christian worshipers (Chase, *Lord's Prayer*).

Tertullian (ca. 160–ca. 240)

A founder of Christian theology in West, specifically Roman Carthage in North Africa, Tertullian offered the earliest, full-scale commentary on the Lord's Prayer in a twenty-nine-chapter discourse on *Prayer* (ca. 205). Famously, he suggested that this prayer includes the whole of Jesus' teaching, "a summary of the whole gospel" (chap. 1, trans. Stewart-Sykes, here and throughout). The prayer's address to the "Father" is a reminder both that Christians are privileged as children (John 1:12) to speak of God in this way and that "Mother Church" should likewise be honored (chap. 2). To Moses, God gave a different name (Exod. 3:14–15); "Now [we Christians] know that Son is the new name of the Father" (chap. 3, quoting John 17:6).

Departing from the order evidenced in the fluid Latin New Testament of his era, Tertullian inverts the third and second petitions. "Let your will be done in the heavens and on the earth" (chap. 4) is understood by appeal to Christ's subordination of himself to God's will (Matt. 26:39 pars.; John 5:30; 6:38). The similar petition, "May your kingdom come," is a prayer that God may realize among ourselves what we need and desire amid "the consummation of this world" (chap. 5). "When we ask for our daily bread, we are asking that we should perpetually be in Christ and that we should not be separated from his body" (chap. 6; Matt. 26:26 pars.; John 6:48; 1 Cor. 11:24). Remission of debts is correlated with the practice of confession before the church (chap. 7). "Far be it that the Lord

284

should seem to tempt, as though he were either ignorant of the faith of each of us, or sought to dethrone it, for weakness and malice are of the devil" (chap. 8; cf. Gen. 22:1–19; Matt. 10:37; Luke 22:40).

The rest of Tertullian's treatise takes up the conditions under which prayer should be offered (chaps. 11–27). While other petitions are efficacious (chap. 10), by this prayer the Lord Jesus perfected prayer (chap. 1): "God alone could teach us the manner in which he would have us pray" (chap. 9). Prayer is intended to calm our restless souls (chap. 12) by channeling God's peace (chap. 11). Tertullian ends in praise of prayer as "the buttress of our faith, our armor and weaponry against the enemy that watches us from every side" (chap. 29).

Cyprian (ca. 200–258)

Rhetorically exquisite, Cyprian's essay *The Lord's Prayer* (ca. 272) opens with an introduction (chaps. 1–9a), proceeds with verse-by-verse explanation (chaps. 9b–28), and concludes in exhortation (chaps. 29–36). Befitting a bishop of Carthage, Cyprian's exposition has a more vividly ecclesial, even baptismal, coloring than that of Tertullian, on which Cyprian was dependent (see chaps. 1–3). "When we gather together with our brothers to celebrate the divine sacrifices with God's priest [*sacerdos*, understood here as a bishop], we should be mindful of reverence and order. . . . Our prayer is common and collective, and when we pray we pray not for one but for all people, because we are all one people together" (chaps. 4, 8).

Cyprian's procedure is catechetical: "There is nothing whatever omitted [in the Lord's Prayer] with regard to our pleading, . . . nothing not contained in this summary of heavenly doctrine" (chap. 9). The hallowing of God's name is a way of asking "that his name should be hallowed in us": first in baptism, then in daily sanctification, that "we may have the ability to persist in the way we have begun" (chap. 12). "It is indeed possible, beloved brothers, that Christ himself is that Kingdom whose coming we daily desire" (chap. 13); Christ's activity and teaching is the indicator of God's will, for whose fulfillment catechumenates pray (chaps. 14–15). "We are ourselves both earth and heaven; we pray, therefore, that the will of God be done in both, both in our body and in our spirit" (chap. 16). Accordingly, prayer for daily bread is both literal ("sustenance for that one day," chap. 19) and spiritual (daily Eucharist,

285

"the food of salvation," chap. 18). The law of forgiveness is binding on all by dominical precept (Matt. 5:23–24; 7:2; 18:34; Mark 11:25); "the greater sacrifice to God is our peace and brotherly concord, as a people unified in the unity of the Father and the Son and the Holy Spirit" (chap. 23).

Staining Cyprian's homily is a deplorable polemic against Jews, whose desertion of God has revoked their eligibility to address God as "our Father" (chap. 10). Also characteristic of Cyprian is his sensitivity to political persecution of Christians: "The Lord commands and counsels us to love even our enemies and also to pray for those who persecute us" (chap. 17; cf. Matt. 5:44). "The lions [in Dan. 6:16–17, 22] were merciful, the birds brought food [to Elijah: 1 Kgs. 17:6]—and men lay snares and savagely attack. How detestable the cruelty of human evil!" (chap. 21). Abel, "peaceable and just, . . . was the first to show us martyrdom and to inaugurate the Lord's passion through the glory of his blood" (chap. 24; cf. Gen. 4:3–5). "Who can be afraid of the present world when God in the present world is his protector?" (chap. 27). In 258 Cyprian was beheaded by Emperor Valerian.

Origen (ca. 185–ca. 254)

Like Tertullian, aspects of Origen's theology came to be regarded with suspicion. On his own terms, however, Alexandria's most accomplished exegete intended to commend orthodox faith to his contemporaries, leading them into the mysteries of prayer while insisting on "an intimate connection between our lived life and our life of prayer" (Cunningham, "Origen's 'On Prayer,'" 338). Origen veers away from both Tertullian and Cyprian: the accents of Origen's *Prayer* (ca. 235) seem less upon catechetical instruction, more on the contemplation of God in Platonist terms, the soul's ascent from earth to heaven (chaps. 1–17). "Communion with God" is this prayer's overarching aim (19.2); the kingdom for which we pray is that to be perfected in us. While "on a pilgrimage toward perfection in knowledge, wisdom, and other virtues" (25.2), the Lord's Prayer rightly directs our dispositions, manner, and pleas (chaps. 18–34). Origen wrestles with the hapax legomenon of bread that is *epiousios*: "the word . . . is not employed by any of the Greek writers, nor by philosophers, nor by individuals in common usage, but seems to

286

have been formed by the evangelists; at least Matthew and Luke concur in employing the term in an identical manner" (27.7). After considering various alternatives, Origen anticipates Jerome (347–420; see the latter's *Commentary on Matthew* 1.6.10) in deciding that the preferred interpretation of *epiousios* is "supersubstantial" bread: being immortal, the word of God most closely corresponds to the soul's rational nature, conferring health, strength, and immortality to all who ingest it (Origen, *Prayer* 27.9). Unlike Tertullian, startled by the prospect that God might tempt, Origen regards "the whole of human life [as] a time of testing" (29.1): "God tests everyone in some way" (29.3). A review of Scripture suggests not that "we should pray not to be tested, for this is impossible, but that we should not be engulfed by testing, for those who are in its midst are so overcome" (29.11). Rescue from evil is assured "when we make a brave stand against [enemy assaults] and are victorious" (30.1).

Origen's approach was adapted and popularized by Cyril of Jerusalem (ca. 313–386), whose *Mystagogic Catecheses* (ca. 375 or later) is concentrated on the Lord's Prayer. The authorship of these brief instructions is disputed; some scholars ascribe them to John of Jerusalem, Cyril's episcopal successor. At any rate these *Catecheses* were designed to train those newly baptized in the Christian mysteries of faith and the sacraments, in preparation for proper receipt of the Eucharist.

Gregory of Nyssa (ca. 335–ca. 394)

Beside his elder brother Basil of Caesarea (ca. 330–379) and his friend Gregory Nazianzus (ca. 329–390), Gregory of Nyssa is best remembered as a Cappadocian Father who moved the Great Church into the Trinitarian doctrine espoused by the Nicene Creed of 325. Influenced by Origen's Platonism, Gregory's five sermons on prayer, designed for all faithful Christians, are preoccupied by the restoration within us of God's occluded image. While often dismissed in the workaday world, prayer is utterly necessary. Because "all things indeed depend on the Divine Will, and life here below is ordered from above," prayer offers intimacy with God that satisfies our truest yearnings (*Lord's Prayer* 1.23, trans. Hilda Graef). When, prodigal children all (cf. Luke 15:11–32), we pray, "Our Father in heaven," we remember "the fatherland from which we have fallen

287

and the noble birthright that we have lost. . . . [God] sets you on the way that will lead you back to your original country" (2.9).

Prayers for the hallowing of God's name and the kingdom's coming are pleas for our conformation to God's own character, "that the passions which still rule me mercilessly may depart from me, or rather [be] altogether annihilated" (3.13). If I glorify God, then I beseech divine help to become "blameless, just and pious, [that I may] abstain from every evil, speak the truth, do justice, [and] walk in the straight path" with temperance, wisdom, and prudence (3.10). Paraphrasing a rare variant of Luke 11:2—"May your Holy Spirit come upon us and cleanse us," which may or may not be traceable to Marcion's second-century version of the Gospel of Luke (see Roth, "Text of the Lord's Prayer," 49–59)—Gregory implores the coming of God's Holy Spirit to purify our lingering sin (3.15–19).

We pray for the fulfillment of God's will on earth as in heaven, even as the sick yearn for a cure restoring balance to a body that has been violently disturbed (4.1–6). As we are unstable amalgams of angelhood and creatureliness (4.7–10), we ask God for basic bread "because our life needs it; [we] owe it to the body because of [our] nature" (4.13). "Bread is for our use today; the Kingdom belongs to the beatitude for which we hope" (4.21). In the prayer for forgiveness Gregory ventures a "holy audacity" (5.4): "Just as in us the good is accomplished by imitating the Divine goodness, so we dare hope that God will also imitate us when we accomplish anything good" (5.6). Petition for deliverance from evil reiterates that for diversion from temptation: both amount to a plea for rescue from materialistic greed (5.18)—a constant warning throughout these homilies (1.1–2, 10–11, 20, 22, 25; 3.2, 8; 4.5, 12–15; 5.13, 21; see Brown, "Piety and Proclamation"). Though not without blemish (Hammerling, "Gregory of Nyssa's Sermons," 69–70), it is hard to deny that Gregory's treatment is "the most extensive and the most profound of the patristic expositions of the Lord's Prayer" (Lampe, "'Our Father' in the Fathers," 23).

John Chrysostom (ca. 347–407)

288   The aspect of John Chrysostom's exposition of the Lord's Prayer that attracts many moderns is his view on *epiousios* bread: it is daily bread, sufficient for a single day (*Homilies on Matthew* 19.8).

But the most salient characteristic of this commentary is its social urgency. Jesus calls disciples to pray, not to "my Father," but rather to "'our Father,' offering up supplications for the body in common; nowhere looking to his own, but everywhere to his neighbor's good" (19.4, trans. Prevost): "By this [Christ] at once takes away hatred and quells pride and casts out envy and brings in the mother of all good things, even love, and exterminates the inequality of human things and shows how far the equality reaches between the king and the beggar: for in those things that are greatest and most indispensable, we are all of us kindred" (19.6).

Our common Father has drawn us out of earthly divisions, fixed us in heaven's merciful love, and restored our equality with all brothers and sisters (19.7). God's name is glorified when our life is so beyond reproach that all who behold it offer to the Lord the praise that is due him (Matt. 5:16). If we pray for the kingdom's coming, we commit ourselves to God's cause in restoring earth along heavenly contours—"not *in me*, or *in us*, but everywhere" (19.7).

Debt forgiveness is tied to the Lord's warning in Matthew 6:14: even though all offenses might be forgiven tout court, God wills "countless occasions of gentleness and love among human creatures, casting out what is brutish in you, quenching your wrath, and in every way cementing you to one who is your own member" (19.9). We ask for deliverance, not from "wicked ones," neighbors at whose hands we might suffer, but instead from "the Wicked One," the real cause of all that is wrong, the target of our enmity (19.10). "The kingdom, the power, and the glory" all fasten our attention on the One whose glory is unutterable, whose power is unconquerable, whose kingdom embraces "even those warring against us" (19.10).

Augustine of Hippo (354–430)

"Prayer," said Augustine, "is the affectionate reaching out of the mind for God" (*Sermon* 9.3; trans. Thomas Hand, *Augustine on Prayer*). Although he dedicated no complete treatise to prayer, Augustine commented on the Lord's Prayer while preaching on the Lord's *Sermon on the Mount* (ca. 393), in his *Handbook on Faith, Hope, and Love* (ca. 422), in four sermons (56–59) for catechumens (see Harmless, *Augustine and the Catechumenate*), and in three letters to the aristocratic ladies Proba (412), Juliana (ca. 413), and

289

Demetrias (414). He was fond of stressing that praying the Lord's Prayer is a "daily cleansing" or a "daily baptism" (*Sermons* 56.12; 59.7; 213.8), its petitions milestones in the Christian's pilgrimage toward eternal life (*Sermon on the Mount* 2.10.36–37, trans. John Epson; see Jackson, "Lord's Prayer").

Following an awful precedent set by Cyprian (*Lord's Prayer* 10) and Gregory of Nyssa (*Lord's Prayer* 3.18), Augustine claims that disobedient Jews could address God only as "Master," never as "Father." Realizing their own unworthiness, Christians have no right to address God so affectionately and may do so only by Christ's merciful gift (*Sermon* 213.1). Appeal to God as Father and to the church as Mother affiliates supplicants with a new race that levels hierarchies: masters and slaves become siblings, as do rich and poor, commanders and common soldiers (*Sermon* 59.2). "'You, Reverend Bishop—you, a debtor?' 'Yes, me, too'" (*Sermon* 56.11, AT). "Let us, then, consider whose children we have begun to be, and let us live as becomes those who have such a Father" (*Sermon* 57.2, trans. Hand).

For Augustine, "hallowing the name" of God takes a curiously anthropological twist: "It is for ourselves and not for God that we [so] pray. We do not wish well for God, to whom no evil can ever happen; rather, we desire what is good for ourselves, that his holy name may be hallowed in us, that that which is always holy may be hallowed in us" (*Sermon* 58.3, trans. Hand). Likewise is prayer for the coming kingdom: "Just as light that is present is absent to the blind or to those who shut their eyes, so the kingdom of God, though it never departs from the earth, yet is absent to those who know nothing about it" (*Sermon on the Mount* 2.6.20, trans. Epson). "The kingdom . . . shall come whether you ask for it or not. Why, then, make this petition unless it be . . . that God will include you in the number of his elect to whom his kingdom will come?" (*Sermon* 59.4, trans. Hand). To pray for God's kingdom is nothing other than the desire that we may prove worthy to be received into it (*Sermon* 58.3). To ask that God's will be done is to pray that it be done in me (*Sermon* 56.7). To plead for its accomplishment on earth as in heaven is to hope for the fulfillment of God's purposes in our risen, transformed bodies, no longer frustrated by the flesh's weakness and bad habits (*Sermon* 57.6; *Sermon on the Mount* 2.6.23).

290 Prayer for daily bread combines several things: everyday sustenance, the Eucharist, and the word of God (*Sermon on the Mount* 2.7.27). Forgiveness of wrongs done to us, beset by anger

and hatred, is possible only by God's grace (*Sermons* 56.14; 58.7); if following the crucified Christ's example (Luke 23:34) is beyond our capacity, still we must forgive if our enemy asks our pardon (*Sermons* 56.16; 59.7). While God does test the virtue of the faithful (Deut. 13:4; John 6:6), we rightly pray not to be led into trials beyond our endurance (*Sermon on the Mount* 2.9.30–31, 34; *Sermon* 57.9): "A person who must undergo a trial by fire would not pray that he might not be touched by the fire, but that he might not be consumed by it" (*Sermon on the Mount* 2.9.32, trans. Epson). To beseech deliverance from evil looks backward, toward escape from that lust for vengeance which depends on the mercy we show those who have wronged us (*Sermon* 57.11), as well as forward: a perception of evil kindles hope for that realm in which evil will no longer harass us (*Letter* 130.21).

Timothy Maschke suggests that "gracious conformation" lies at the heart of Augustine's theology of prayer: "The humble restructuring or reforming of the Christian's life to the divine will as empowered by the assurance of God's grace" ("St. Augustine's Theology," 431). The point of praying is neither to instruct nor to cajole God but to surrender our desires to holy reconstruction. "[The meaning of the Lord's Prayer] may be said to abide in us, when we do what he has commanded us and love what he has promised us" (*Gospel of John* 81.4, trans. Hand)

John Cassian (ca. 365–ca. 435)

A contemporary of Augustine, John Cassian studied with masters of Egyptian spirituality before relocating himself in Western Europe, founding monasteries for both monks and nuns in Marseilles. Like Benedict of Nursia (480–547), whose monastic rule he heavily influenced, Cassian advocated a moderate, practical spirituality: "There are plenty of roads to God" (*Conferences* 14.6, trans. Luibheid, here and throughout). The core of his approach is summarized in two published *Conferences* (9 and 10) on prayer. "The monk's whole purpose . . . is total and uninterrupted dedication to prayer" (9.2), which fundamentally consists of resolution, penitence, petition, and thanksgiving (9.12–14; cf. 1 Tim. 2:1). On this basis Cassian modulates to simple, pointed musings on the Lord's Prayer. To address God as Father is an assertion that the Lord of the universe has

291

transferred us from slavery to adoption as children (9.18; cf. Gal. 4:7). To acknowledge this Father as heavenly reminds us that our life on earth is "a kind of exile" from the domain that God has prepared for us to inhabit (9.18). "When we say, 'Hallowed be your name,' what we are really saying is, 'Father, make us such as to deserve knowledge and understanding of how holy you are, or at least let your holiness shine forth in the spiritual lives we lead'" (9.18).

To pray for the kingdom's coming is to accept Christ's promise that God's reign is made ready for all of God's children, a realm in which "anger [is] overcome, peace is king, [and] humility is sovereign" (9.19). "No greater prayer can be offered than that the things of earth should be put on a level with those of heaven" (9.20). "With 'daily' the evangelist shows that without this bread we cannot live a spiritual life for even a day" (9.21). The petition for debt forgiveness models and disciplines acceptable prayer: God is unspeakably merciful, yet "we shall be forgiven proportionately with the forgiveness we display to those who, whatever their malice, have injured us" (9.22). Temptation, or testing, fortifies our character (cf. Jas. 1:12): Abraham, Joseph, and Job were tempted; none was actually led into temptation, for none capitulated to the tempter (9.23). To beg for deliverance from evil reiterates Paul's assurance (1 Cor. 10:13) that we shall not be tempted beyond endurance: "With every temptation there is a way out" (9.23).

In sum: the Lord's Prayer both contains the fullness of Christian perfection and lays a yardstick alongside our poor petitions. "There is no request for riches, no reminder of honors, no plea for power or bravery, no reference to bodily well-being or to this present life" (9.24). For Cassian, the Lord who gave us this Prayer knew our own human condition. "He withdrew to the solitude of the mountain, and in the silent prayer of his agony he gave with his bloody sweat an inimitable example of ardor [for God; cf. Luke 22:44]" (9.25).

Maximus the Confessor (ca. 580–662)

292

From its opening sentences, Maximus's *Commentary on the Our Father* (ca. 630) stands apart: he speaks not to his fellow monks or catechumenates but directly addresses the Lord with love (Prologue 1–3). "The full import of the Lord's Prayer" is "the deification [*theōsis*] of our nature" (1, trans. Berthold, here and throughout; see Nodes, "Witness to Theosis"). What we ask for in this life is nothing other than "whatever the Word of God himself wrought through the flesh in his self-abasement" without sin (1).

In scope the prayer consists of seven mysteries: (1) knowledge of God (*theologia*), (2) our adoption in grace, (3) the gift of an honor equal to that of the angels, (4) participation in eternal life, (5) the restoration of human nature toward holy tranquillity, (6) abolition of the law of sin, and (7) the overthrow of evil's tyranny through deceit. The prayer's petitions demonstrate both what Christ has achieved and the point of that victory for every Christian who learns to pray this prayer properly. The incarnate Word, God's own dynamic power, generates that *dynamis* through sacrament, Scripture, and the Lord's own prayer (Madden, "Maximus Confessor," 129–31).

On this basis Maximus contemplates the prayer's clauses. Address to "our Father," "the creative Cause of our coming into being," initiates those who pray into the mystery of "the Father, the Father's name, and the Father's kingdom, to help us learn from the source himself to honor, to invoke, and to adore the one Trinity" (4). Adam's abuse of free choice defaced the image of God in those begotten of him in the flesh, but the *imago Dei* was not obliterated: "a union of relation" is forged by "the will of the one who supplies the grace" of such a prayer with "the free will of those who make its requests" (4). Therefore, to say "our Father" entails a free choice of will, exercised by a child of God through the mediation of that Word in whom divinity and humanity are united. By sanctifying the Name we are purified of "corrupting passions . . . and the indecent howling of anger" (4). Prayer for the kingdom's coming exercises the soul's self-transformation, guided by the divine image, into God's likeness (4.5). To ask that God's will be comprehensively accomplished amounts to "giving God worship in every way in imitation of the angels in heaven, [that] we shall exhibit in earth the same manner of the angels in having, as they do, the mind totally moved in the direction of nothing less than God" (4.9).

Sharing in eternal life is the outcome of the Eucharist: Christ, the bread of life (John 6:35, 48), "mixes a divine quality for the deification of those who eat" (4). The act of forgiveness is a transparent sign of *theōsis*: reconciliation with others imitates Christ's reunification of body and spirit in new creation (4; cf. Col. 1:15–20). Implied

293

in this restoration is purification from sin and release from evil's tyranny: God will protect from the devil and all other impediments those who dedicate themselves to extinguishing restless passions and reckless fury (5). "Let us love more intensely the one who so wisely prepared for us such a salvation [from the weight of sin that once pushed us down]. By what we do let us show that the prayer is being fulfilled and let us manifest and proclaim that God is truly our Father through grace" (6).

As a devotional yet practical contemplation of the Lord's Prayer, that of Maximus leaves all its predecessors and many of its successors in the shade. While theologically congruent with Origen and Gregory, Maximus neither parrots nor polemicizes. Though the approach could hardly be more mystical—Christ's leading of the supplicant into the life of the triune God—the presentation is extraordinarily clear, even moving. Here, in truth, we are in the hands of a commentator who loves God with his mind. "Maximus penetrates the internal coherence of the prayer in a way we have not so far seen, and among Eastern writers he emerges as the spiritual giant" (Stevenson, *Lord's Prayer*, 61)—arguably, among Western authors as well. One measure of Maximus's continuing influence is his impression on the nineteenth-century Russian classic *The Way of a Pilgrim* (also known as *The Pilgrim's Tale*), which, while spotlighting the Jesus Prayer ("Lord Jesus Christ, Son of God, have mercy on me, a sinner"; cf. Luke 18:13), commends the Lord's Prayer, especially as Maximus interpreted it (54):

> The *Our Father* is the loftiest and most precious of all the written prayers that we Christians have, for the Lord Jesus Christ himself taught it to us. . . . Everything necessary and useful for our soul and our life is wisely brought into one here. . . . If you get up and say the *Our Father* as Christ taught us, then you're right for the whole day, instead of rhyming off the same thing over and over again. That is how you'll go crazy, if you'll pardon me—and besides, it's bad for your heart. (*Pilgrim's Tale*, 54, 107, 40, trans. Smith)

Thomas Aquinas (ca. 1225–74)

294   Over a span of two decades (1252–73) Thomas composed at least seven works that took up the Lord's Prayer (Murray, *Praying with Confidence*, 101–5). The most extended explorations were his

Lectures on St. Matthew (ca. 1260) and his probing of prayer in the *Summa theologiae* (II-II.83; ca. 1270). Their premises, procedure, and conclusions are complementary. Many of the questions that exercise Thomas are Aristotelian: What is the good? How may evil be avoided? What shape do human desires for the good assume? What are the effective means by which those desires are realized? "Reason entreats us toward what is best" (Aristotle, *Nicomachean Ethics* 1.13; cited in *Summa theologiae* II-II.83.1, AT). "The Lord's Prayer is the most perfect prayer of all because, as Augustine says, if we pray rightly and properly we cannot say anything except what is contained in this prayer the Lord gave us" (II-III.83.9, trans. Murray; cf. Augustine, *Letter to Proba* 10.12.22). Why is this so?

> Prayer is a kind of presentation of our desire before God. . . . Obviously the first thing our desire lights on is our goal, and then the things that lead to the goal. And our goal is God. . . . We do not proffer our prayers to God in order to make him change his mind, but in order to stimulate our own confidence in pleading; and this confidence is particularly aroused by the consideration of his love for us, which wills our good (and this is why we say, "Our Father"), and by the consideration of his supremacy, which means that he has the power to do good to us (and this is why we say, "Who art in heaven"). (*Summa theologiae* II-II.83.9, trans. Murray)

Because God is the ultimate goal of everything, the first thing to be desired is God's honor. "So this is what we ask for first: 'Hallowed be thy name'" (*Lectures on Matthew* 6:9–15, trans. Tugwell).

Characteristically Thomas discerns multiple senses in the petition for the kingdom's coming. Its literal interpretation is for eternal life: "Make us come to and share in eternal beatitude" (*Lectures on Matthew* 6:9–15, citing Matt. 25:34; Luke 22:29). The prayer also leans toward eschatological fulfillment, when Christ puts God's enemies under his feet (1 Cor. 15:25). Alternatively, prayer for the kingdom's coming has a moral coloring: "May the reign of sin be destroyed and you, Lord, reign over us" (Rom. 6:12). The petition thus merges into the plea that the divine will be done: we pray that our image may be restored into that of the man of heaven, Jesus Christ (1 Cor. 15:49). Similarly, Thomas expresses no need to resolve all the nuances of bread into one. We pray, at once, for Christ the bread of life (John 6:48), particularly in the sacrament, for God's commandments (Prov. 9:5; John 4:34), and for bread that

295

nourishes the body (Gen. 28:20; 1 Tim. 6:8). The last three petitions have as their aim their supplicants' removal from evil. To ask forgiveness is to plead that "the single most important ill is taken away, namely guilt"—and, if all are counseled by the Lord to pray this, then in this life there are no perfect people (versus Pelagius). "'Lead us not [into temptation]': that is, do not permit us to succumb" (1 Cor. 10:13). The final request is comprehensive: "'Deliver us' from past, present, and future evil, from the evil of guilt, of punishment, and of all ill" (Ps. 58:2; Isa. 51:12).

For Thomas, as for Augustine, good and evil are in constant contest within mortal flesh. The point of praying in this way is to cultivate the virtues that resist what is harmful, allowing good health to prevail. "[The Lord's Prayer] not only instructs our pleading; it also gives shape to all our affections" (*informativa totius nostri affectus*; *Summa theologiae* II-II.83.8, trans. Murray). Christ is himself the model, the *exemplum*, of prayer, drawing from the believer that hope for eternal happiness built into every human being (Barnes, "On Christ's Prayer"). "The Lord's Prayer is the most perfect of prayers. . . . In it we ask, not only for all the things we can rightly desire, but also in the sequence that they should be desired" (*Summa theologiae* II-II.83.9).

Margaret Ebner (1291–1351)

In the ruminations of this Dominican nun converge the streams of Thomist theology and the German mysticism of Meister Eckhart (ca. 1260–1327), Johannes Tauler (ca. 1300–1361), and Henry Suso (ca. 1300–1366). From about the age of nineteen she began to suffer a mysterious illness that buffeted her for thirteen years, repeatedly bringing her to the verge of death and leaving her bedridden for long stretches (*Revelations*, in *Major Works*, 86). During these years

> I took great delight and joy in my prayer, . . . especially in my *Pater Noster*. Often I could not sleep at night because of the anticipation of the delight I would have from praying it in the morning. I desired nothing more from God than a simple, plain life. . . . On our Lady's Day I was stricken by a sickness about which I cannot speak. . . . Especially during my *Pater Noster* [a feeling of

sweetest grace with great power] often becomes more forceful by strong, mysterious grace that is beyond my human senses. I thought I could not finish my *Pater Noster* alive due to the overflow of grace. It is so well with me then that I think, "Can heaven be better than this?" . . . Frequently when I began my *Pater Noster* my heart was captured by such a mysterious grace that I did not know what should come of it. (*Major Works* 89, 108, 111, trans. Hindsley, here and throughout)

On other occasions Ebner felt as though her *Pater Noster* had been taken from her—"I had forgotten all the petitions and could remember nothing"—only for it to be restored to her in increments (121–23, 137–38). In moments of ecstasy she "experienced the strongest, sweetest, and most mysterious grace during the *Pater Noster* and all my petitions. I cannot write about [this sweet joy], and any heart that itself has not felt the grace cannot understand it" (125).

One cannot always be sure what Saint Margaret means by "her *Pater Noster*." At times it may simply refer to the Lord's Prayer. We know for a fact, however, that she created her own paraphrase of the Prayer, one that is truly "her" *Pater Noster*, because its text has survived (*Major Works*, 173–78). It is a stunning liturgical rhapsody. While grounded in concepts native to the biblical prayer ("guided by your will"; "purified from all our sins"; "deliver us from all evil"; "your honor is our eternal food and your power our eternal joy"), it is preeminently an offering of praise for Christ's pure love, with varied petitions for "a real union with the innermost good which is yourself, O God" (175). Its basic plan may be roughly outlined:

An opening Commendation to the Lord of the supplicant's truthful, sincere intentions (¶1)

Extended Prayers for
- The supplicant's heartfelt love for God (¶¶2–3)
- Providential direction, "be good or ill done to us" (¶4)
- A piercing by Christ's loving passion (¶5)
- Grace conveyed through the Eucharist (¶¶6–7)
- God's merciful attention to all human desires (¶8)
- God's deliverance of us from evil, "all that is not you" (¶9)
- Eternal peace (¶10)
- Enlightenment to recognize in Christ "the real and only truth" (¶11)

297

- Assurance of salvation (¶12)
- Mary's motherly help (¶13), which leads to

A concluding Doxology: "And give us, my Lord, a true increase in all your graces until we come to the point where your divine grace will be our eternal joy and our everlasting reward. Amen. *Deo gratias!*" (¶14)

Ebner's interpretation of the Lord's Prayer is encomiastic in style, Thomist in form, and soteriological in substance. From the eternal Godhead, the source of all truth, flows (*exitus*) eternal love. Through the grace of Christ, humanity is made sacred and we are transformed: strengthened to perceive and repent of our sin, to recognize genuine joy, to love with purity, and to be assured of union with the God who saves. This is *reditus*: humanity's reciprocation of love that originates in God. Saint Margaret's *Pater Noster* is not an exposition but an explosion. The Lord's Prayer has become the ecstatic exegesis of a life immersed in God.

Nicholas of Cusa (1401–64)

Born in southwestern Germany, Nicholas was a brilliant polymath: prince-bishop, political theorist, theologian, and mathematician. Best remembered for his notion of the "coincidence of opposites" (*coincidentia oppositorum*), expressed in *On Learned Ignorance* (1440), Nicholas stood at the threshold from Renaissance humanism into modern philosophy, influencing thinkers as diverse as Ernst Cassirer (1874–1945), Martin Buber (1878–1965), Karl Jaspers (1883–1969), Paul Tillich (1886–1965), C. S. Lewis (1898–1963), Hans-Georg Gadamer (1900–2002), Thomas Merton (1915–68), and Wolfhart Pannenberg (1928–2014; see Bond in *Nicholas of Cusa*, 16–17). Less well known is a sermon on the Lord's Prayer, which Nicholas preached in Augsburg on January 1, 1441 (see Hudson and Tobin, "Sermon on the *Pater Noster*"). On first reading it may seem a heady, philosophical paraphrase, but from Nicholas's standpoint the simplicity of this prayer "embraces the highest teaching and wisdom. For just as divinity lay hidden in the humanity of Christ, so also all intelligible wisdom is hidden in the simple words of Christ's teaching, which no one in this world can completely understand" (*Pater Noster* 1, trans. Hudson, here and throughout).

298

Nicholas's central, deliberately circular point is that God is the source from which all things flow out and the final end to which all things return. Every element in the Lord's Prayer expresses the truth of divine immanence (3). "Our Father, who art in heaven" reminds us that we all, however many we may be, derive from one. We are nothing from ourselves; all creatures are from one Father, who is in all things, from highest to lowest (7–10). We hope that God's name, "the highest word like unto the Father's intellectual nature" (11), may finally be sanctified through us "above everything that is holy, true, and just" (12).

To pray for God's kingdom is to understand that the highest conceivable union, both now and to come, is that of the Father, the Son, and the Spirit; it is also to confess that this peaceful, eternal kingdom of joy comes to us and ultimately will be realized by us only through God's gracious self-expression (14–17). The words "Thy will be done" indicate the outflow of all things in the Holy Trinity: "Thy" refers to the Father; "be done," to the Son; "will," to the Holy Spirit. "Each and every thing that exists has an image of God and the Holy Trinity in it, through which image the thing exists" (19). "On earth, as in heaven" concedes our fleshly feebleness, which depends on God's grace for union with his obedience and a share in divine eternity (23).

The prayer for daily bread is multifaceted: we ask for Christ, the bread of life (24–28); we seek this nourishment "united with the congregation" among "the body of the faithful" (29); we share our surplus with the poor and needy (33). "We ask for this bread and should receive it with total faith, the greatest possible hope, and the greatest amount of love" (32).

Our guilt's forgiveness depends on the bread we are daily given: only in union with Christ, in the Christian assembly, can we beseech forgiveness and hope for redemption (36–38). "Your 'debtor' is God's creature, just as you are. And God wants him to be freed by you" (39). Because we fall away from God, the highest good, into seductive and illusory good, we pray for divine preservation and protection (41), "ask[ing] for deliverance from this frail, transitory life so that [we] can be with [our] most beloved good" (44). To summarize: "In the teaching of the master lies the performing of the skill; and so we find Christ in his teaching. And the teachings of the holy *Pater Noster* in which Christ dwells prove this to us": teachings "full of all wisdom, full of all virtue, and, just like its master, cannot be improved upon" (32).

299

Martin Luther (1483–1546)

The Lord's Prayer was a favorite text for Luther's exegesis: by one estimate he preached or commented on it at least twenty-one times during 1516–35 (Carmignac, *Recherches*, 166–70). Across that nearly two-decade span his interpretation underwent modifications: by 1529 he broadened the prayer for daily bread beyond spiritual concerns, taking more seriously material needs: "food, drink, clothing, shoes, house, home, field, cattle, money, goods, a pious spouse, pious children, pious servants, pious and faithful rulers, good government, good weather, peace, health, discipline, honor, good friends, faithful neighbors, and the like" (Small Catechism 3.6, trans. Krey and Krey; cf. Exposition of the Apostles' Creed 2.17.53–54). Nevertheless, Luther's exegesis of the Prayer is impressive in its consistency across six major presentations: "An Exposition of the Lord's Prayer for Simple Laymen" (1519), the Large Catechism (April 1529) and Small Catechism (May 1529; still widely used in Lutheran churches for educating youth prior to Confirmation), his sermons on *The Sermon on the Mount* (ca. 1532–33), "A Simple Way to Pray, for Peter the Master Barber" (1535), and a nine-stanza musical paraphrase, "Our Father in the Heavenly Kingdom" (ca. 1538, still found in Lutheran hymnals; see Leaver, *Luther's Liturgical Music*, 128–34).

With this, as with practically all scriptural texts he interpreted, Luther never withheld his feelings: "The Lord's Prayer is my prayer. This I pray, at times adding a bit from the Psalms. . . . There's nothing like the Lord's Prayer. I prefer it over any psalm" (*Table Talk*, §183, trans. Hazlitt). That's no small praise from one who loved the Psalter as Scripture in miniature, "an entire summary of [the whole Bible], comprised in one little book" ("Preface to the Psalter" [1528], 254, AT), and expounded on the Psalms more than any other portion of Scripture—far more than any New Testament book (Bornkamm, *Luther and the Old Testament*, 9).

It has been said that the distinctive qualities of Luther's exposition of the Lord's Prayer are its soteriological concern and existential engagement (Lienhard, "Luther et Calvin," 86–87). That is both true and perceptive. Yet there is another, intimately related aspect that must not be overlooked: the Prayer's embeddedness in the church's liturgical and creedal confession (see Peters, *On Luther's Catechisms*). In both of Luther's catechisms the Lord's Prayer follows an exposition, first, of the Ten Commandments; second, of the Apostles' Creed. Then comes the Lord's Prayer, which leads to instruction in baptism and the Lord's Supper. Even in the stream-lined teaching on the Lord's Prayer that he prepared for his old friend Peter Beskendorf, Luther concludes with expositions of all Ten Commandments and "a simple exercise" for contemplating the Creed's first three articles on God, Christ, and the Spirit (200–211). Luther explains his reasons for so proceeding:

> [In the Decalogue] we have seen all that God wishes us to do or not to do. The Creed properly follows, setting forth all that we must expect and receive from God; in brief, it teaches us to know him perfectly. . . . We have heard what we are to do and to believe. The best and most blessed life consists of these things. Now follows the third part, how we are to pray. . . . The first thing to know is this; it is our duty to pray because God has commanded it. . . . In the second place, . . . God has promised that our prayer will surely be answered, as he says to you in Ps. 50:15; "Call upon me in the day of trouble and I will deliver you." . . . Furthermore, we should be encouraged and drawn to pray because [though the Lord's Prayer] God takes the initiative and puts into our mouths the very words we are to use. Thus we see how sincerely he is concerned over our needs, and we shall never doubt that our prayer pleases him and will assuredly be heard. (Large Catechism 2.1; 3.1, 4–5, 18–19, 21–22, trans. Fischer)

This context is critical for understanding Luther's interpretation of the Prayer's petitions. In effect it restates the dictum for which he is best remembered: Christian faith lived *simul iustus et peccator*, in the justified sinner's paradoxical relationship to God. The sup-plicant prays this noblest of all earthly prayers quite literally at the crux: the crucified intersection of the law's relentless demands and the gospel's indomitable hope. "The Lord's Prayer is a cry wrung from the crucible, an exposition of the shape of life lived under the sign of the cross in the hope of the resurrection" (Nestingen, "Lord's Prayer," 40). This, for Luther, was no mere idea: throughout his life he suffered *Anfechtungen*, hideous nights of spiritual assault, under a self-reproachful terror of God's abandonment, from which deliverance came only from being driven by Christ away from the devil, back to the medicine of the church: its Scripture, sacraments, and fellowship with other beleaguered yet sanctified souls. This

301

convergence of shriven anthropology, christocentric soteriology, and ecclesiological comfort is what gives Luther's explanation of the Lord's Prayer its peculiar bite. It is a veritable battle hymn of the Christian life (Marty, *Hidden Discipline*, 108), the cry *of* faith that is a cry *for* faith (Arand, "Battle Cry," 45, trans. Fischer).

> For whenever a good Christian prays, "Dear Father, thy will be done," God replies from on high, "Yes, dear child, it shall indeed be done in spite of the devil and all the world." (Large Catechism 3.31–32)

> The kingdom of God comes indeed without our prayer, of itself, but we pray in this petition that it may come to us also . . . [by the gift of] His Holy Spirit, so that by his grace we believe His holy Word and lead a godly life, here in time and hereafter in eternity. (Small Catechism 3.7–8, trans. Krey and Krey)

> The good and gracious will of God is done indeed without our prayer; but we pray . . . that it may be done among us also . . . when God breaks and hinders every evil counsel and will which would not let us hallow God's name nor let His kingdom come, such as the will of the devil, the world, and our flesh; but strengthens and preserves us steadfast in His Word and faith until our end. (Small Catechism 3.10–11)

> Christ tells us to ask for daily bread in order to teach us that [it] is a gracious gift of God and that we may receive it with thanksgiving. (Small Catechism 3.13) . . . Grant us thy blessing also in this temporal and physical life. Grant us blessed peace. Protect us against war and disorder. . . . Defend us against the Destroyer and all his wicked angels who would do harm and mischief in this life. ("Simple Way to Pray," 196–97, trans. Krey and Krey)

> Do not look upon how good or how wicked we have been but only upon the infinite compassion which thou hast bestowed upon us in Christ, thy dear Son. Grant forgiveness also to those who have harmed or wronged us, as we forgive them from our hearts. . . . We are not helped by their ruin; we would much rather that they be saved with us. ("Simple Way to Pray," 97)

> Temptation to evil consists in this, that the devil, the world, and our flesh try to deceive us or seduce us into misbelief, despair, and other great shame and vice. (Small Catechism 3.18)

Amid so much great danger and need, we cannot live the way we should; nor would we be able to stand it for a single day. We ask [God], therefore, to sustain us in the midst of this danger and need so that it does not overcome and destroy us. (*Sermon on the Mount*, 147, trans. Pelikan)

But thou, dear Father, knowest our frailty; therefore help us to pass in safety through so much wickedness and villainy; and, when our last hour comes, in thy mercy grant us a blessed departure from this vale of sorrows so that in the face of death we do not become fearful or despondent but in firm faith commit our souls into thy hands. . . . Finally, mark this: that you must always speak the Amen firmly. Never doubt that God in his mercy will surely hear you and say "yes" to your prayers. . . . All devout Christians are standing there beside you and you are standing among them in a common, united petition which God cannot disdain. ("Simple Way to Pray," 197–98, trans. Krey and Krey)

For Luther the Lord's Prayer cannot be bettered because it dilates the situation of God *pro nobis*, before us. It is "*Oratio Orationum*, the prayer above all prayers, a prayer which the most high Master taught us, wherein are comprehended all spiritual and temporal blessings, and the strongest comforts in all trials, temptations, and troubles, even in the hour of death" (*Table Talk* §267, trans. Hazlitt).

Katharina Schütz Zell (ca. 1498–1562)

As a devout laywoman without formal theological education, Katharina Schütz Zell is hardly a household name, but in this survey she should not be forgotten. According to Elsie Anne McKee, "[Zell's] exposition of the Lord's Prayer . . . presents a careful, conscious thought by a Protestant lay theologian, a mother writing as a pastor for women and children, inviting her hearers to think about the central Biblical prayer and the God Whom it addresses with trust and confidence, and using a combination of scriptural wisdom and homely images to teach and pray with her readers" ("Zell and the 'Our Father,'" 247). Paired with a meditation on Psalm 51, Zell's interpretation of the Lord's Prayer was published in 1558 (McKee, *Zell*, 2.340–66). It is a remarkable combination of biblical and

303

devotional theology, exegesis and Trinitarian reflection, creedal catechesis and pastoral care. A striking aspect is its use of maternal imagery for Christ the Son and, by extension, God the Father. Through his passion "[Christ] so hard and bitterly bore us, nourished us and made us alive, gave us to drink from His breast and side with water and blood [John 19:34], as a mother nurses her child" (trans. McKee, *Zell*, 2.343–44). Blending Isaiah 49:15 (the LORD who can no more forget Zion than a woman her nursling), Philippians 2:6–7, Hebrews 4:15–16, and other scriptural texts, Zell prepares the supplicant of the Lord's Prayer with a deeply familial midrash on Galatians 4:4–7:

> Through the Beloved we are all loved, for through the Son[,] God has borne us again, and borne the Son from eternity. As a grandfather loves the child of his child, and also the father and the child are his heirs because the child is borne of his child, so also is God our Father, yes, our grandfather, and we are his heirs through Jesus Christ his Son, through whom we are borne again by God as new people, and so we dare confidently to cry out and say, "Abba, dear Father," through the adopting Spirit whom we have received from Christ, which Spirit assures us that we are God's children and his fellow heirs with Christ. (trans. McKee, *Zell*, 2.344)

As McKee notes ("Zell and the 'Our Father,'" 246), Zell prepares her audience to pray the Lord's Prayer by combining Chalcedonian Christology, medieval contemplation of Jesus as Mother (Bynum), and a Protestant emphasis on God's saving work in and for us.

John Calvin (1509–64)

Calvin's training in civil law at Orléans and Bourges lent to his *Institutes of the Christian Religion* (1536; revised, 1539–59) a systematic quality reminiscent of Thomas Aquinas's *Summa*. Near the end of the *Institutes'* book 3 (chap. 20), Calvin renders a profound, clause-by-clause analysis of the Lord's Prayer. Although it has been described as "both theocentric and anthropocentric" (Stevenson, *Lord's Prayer*, 165), that characterization seems off-key for a thinker whose sensitivities to divine sovereignty and human depravity are so acute. It is more accurate to say that Calvin maintains

304

a constant tension between two theological poles: God's brilliance irradiates human darkness; God's mercy resets our pervasive perversity toward righteousness. That line of reclamation lies by way of Jesus Christ alone: "We ought to offer all prayer to God only in Christ's name, as it cannot be agreeable to [God] in any other name" (3.20.36, trans. McKee, here and throughout; cf. Acts 4:12).

The point is proved by representative instances of Calvin's exegesis. "With what confidence would anyone address God as 'Father,' who would break forth into such rashness as to claim for himself the honor of a son of God, unless we had been adopted as children of grace in Christ?" (3.20.36). Intriguingly, for a theologian so closely associated with the doctrine of predestination, Calvin urges the Christian to "conform his prayers to this rule [of the divine household], in order that they may be in common and embrace all who are his brothers in Christ, not only those whom he at present sees and recognizes as such, but all people who dwell on earth" (38). To acknowledge God as heavenly Father simultaneously warns us away from applying to God our puny measures and arouses our confidence "that heaven and earth are ruled by his providence and power . . . [and] that we do not come to Him in vain, for He willingly meets us with present help" (40). The need for the hallowing of the divine name "is associated with our great shame. For what is more unworthy than for God's glory to be obscured partly by our ungratefulness, partly by our ill will, and so far as lies in our power, destroyed by our presumption and insane impudence?" Our contempt is curtailed: by the vindication of God's sacred name, the whole human race will be subdued for its proper reverence (41). Petition for the kingdom's coming is an entreaty that God will "shape all our thoughts in obedience to his rule, . . . to bring all people's minds and hearts into voluntary obedience to it" (42). Prayer for the realization of God's will yearns for the destruction of all arrogance and wickedness and pleads for the formation of our selves' denial, "so God may rule us according to His decision" (43). In these first three petitions God's purpose is to draw us wholly to Himself, kindling our zeal for "the honor that is owed [only] to our Lord and Father" (43).

The last three petitions concern our own interests—but with this limitation: "that we seek nothing for ourselves without the intention that whatever benefits [God] confers upon us may show forth His glory, for nothing is more fitting than that we live and die to Him" (44; cf. Rom. 14:8). Throughout his interpretation of the final petitions, Calvin never pussyfoots around human sin;

305

nevertheless, he expresses God's compassion for equally genuine human need. Unimpressed by "philosophizing about 'supersubstantial bread,'" Calvin stresses God's providence, which encourages us "to expect everything from Him, even to a crumb of bread and a drop of water" (44). Forgiveness of our debts "comes of [God's] free mercy, by which He Himself generously wipes [them] out" (45). The clause "as we forgive our debtors" places no condition upon God's pardon and implies no desert for forgiveness. "Rather, by this word the Lord intended partly to comfort the weakness of our faith: . . . a sign to assure us He has granted forgiveness of sins to us just as surely as we are aware of having forgiven others" with hearts purged of hatred and vengeance (45). The petition for diversion from temptation receives a fascinating interpretation:

> God tries in one way; Satan, in another. Satan tempts that he may destroy, condemn, confound, [and] cast down; but God [proves] His own children . . . and establish[es] their strength and courage by exercising it. . . . Satan attacks those who are unarmed and unprepared that he may crush them unaware. God, along with the temptation, makes a way of escape, that His own may be able to patiently bear all that He imposes upon them. (46; cf. 1 Cor. 10:13; 2 Pet. 2:9)

Finally, the prayer's doxology "is firm and tranquil repose for our faith." However miserable we may be, we never want for reason to pray and never lack for assurance. "[Our] confidence of being heard stems solely from God's nature" (47).

The preceding summary obscures the development of Calvin's thinking about the Lord's Prayer across thirteen years (on which, consult McKee, "John Calvin's Teaching"). In general, however, he seems to have held fast to some fixed points: (1) This Prayer models the chief concerns of all prayer. (2) This Prayer is a providential gift from God through Christ, assuring supplicants of God's loving care. (3) This Prayer remains focused on God's glorification.

Teresa of Avila (1515–82)

306   While the Counter-Reformation was promulgating a *List of Prohibited Books* (1559; formally abolished by Pope Paul VI in 1966), the Spanish Carmelite Teresa composed a devotional work, *The Way*

of Perfection (*El Camino de Perfección*, ca. 1567). This, as Rowan Williams notes, is "perhaps Teresa's most consciously mischievous book." Laced with acerbic asides on clerical pomposity, repudiation of her era's misogyny, and even a detached derision of the Spanish Inquisition, Teresa's *Way* is an orthodox, intimate colloquy with her monastic sisters, licensed by her confessor while adopting a sidelong glance "to see if the audience [of censors] is paying attention" (Williams, *Teresa of Avila*, 78–79). Its first eighteen chapters are dedicated to the Carmelite ethos; the next eight, to prayer in general; finally, chapters 27–42, to the Lord's Prayer as a guide for the journey of faith. Many of Teresa's remarks are poised on a knife's edge: being utterly pure, God's love can shock our soul's system (19.1–8); Christ, our companion in suffering, both affirms and challenges our emotions (26.4–6). "O Son of God and my Lord: You give us in the name of your Father all that can be given. . . . If we return to [God] like the prodigal son, he has to pardon us, because your word cannot fail. Indeed, [God] must be better than all the world's fathers, because in him everything must be faultless" (27.2, trans. Peers, here and throughout). God's hallowed name startles us from sleep once we realize how deserving we are of punishment yet how certain we are of being rewarded (30). "Although what [the Lord] gives [in his kingdom, by his will] is better than what we ask, we don't think we'll ever become rich because we're blind to the money in our hand" (30.2).

Teresa's meditation on the prayer for bread (33–35) is both focused (on the Eucharist) and expansive (in exploring Christ's self-donation to the sinner). "I cannot believe that one who has approached so near to the Source of all mercy, which has shown the soul what it really is and all that God has pardoned it, would not instantly and willingly forgive, and be at peace, and remain on good terms with any one who has offended her" (36.10). What matters is not a heroic disregard of slights to one's dignity but, rather, the love of Christ that consolidates his members into souls unpreoccupied by individual rights.

The final petitions—prevention from falling, protection from evil—evoke our need for serene reliance on God when our self-knowledge is so susceptible to corruption (39.1–4). For Teresa, "the devil's work is to make us *interested* in our spiritual state in an obsessive way, whether this takes the form of self-satisfaction or of false humility, paralysing anxiety about one's condition" (Williams,

307

Teresa of Avilla, 100–101). Among classical expositions of the Lord's Prayer, Teresa's is rambling, bracing, and shrewd.

John Wesley (1703–91)

Much of Wesley's interpretation of the prayer is straightforward exegesis, homiletically framed ("Sermon 26"), within a series of sermons on Matthew 5–7. As with expositors of earlier centuries, one is amazed by the erudition Wesley assumed of his listeners when clarifying nuances of Greek and Hebrew terms: among others, *mē battalogēsēte* (26.2.4; "don't jabber," Matt. 6:7 AT), *bārā' 'ĕlōhîm* (3.7; "God created," Gen. 1:1), even a quotation of Homer's *Iliad* (1.544): *Patēr andrōn te theōn te* (3.5, "Father of men and of gods"). Wesley strikes several keynotes. First, following Thomas à Kempis (*Imitation of Christ* 2.6.3 [ca. 1425]), Wesley stresses the disciple's "pure and holy intention" in discharging works of piety, mercy, and prayer (Sermon 26.1.1–2). "Beware not to speak what thou dost not mean. Prayer is the lifting up of the heart to God" (2.1). The Lord's Prayer is important, "first, [because] it contains all we can reasonably or innocently pray for. . . . Secondly, it contains all we can reasonably or innocently desire. . . . Thirdly, it contains all our duty to God and man" (3.2).

Another of Wesley's central themes is the prayer's embrace of all creation. We are counseled to address "'*Our* Father'—not *mine* only . . . but *ours*, in the most extensive sense, . . . the Father of the universe, of all the families both in heaven and earth" (3.5). The petition for the hallowed name expresses the hope that "[God] may be known, such as he is, by all that are capable thereof, by all intelligent beings; . . . that he may be duly honoured and feared and loved by all in heaven above and in the earth beneath [Josh. 2:11]; by all angels and men, whom for that end he has made capable of knowing and loving him to eternity" (3.7). Indeed, the angels in heaven model prayer that God's will be done: they praise God "*willingly*," "*continually*," and "*perfectly*" (3.9, alluding to Rev. 4:8). "In other words, we pray that we, and all mankind, may do the whole will of God in all things" (3.10).

308   The petitions for bread, forgiveness, and deliverance encapsulate a doctrine of grace. "'Give us'; for we claim nothing of right, but only of free mercy. We deserve not the air we breathe, the earth

that bears, or the sun that shines upon us. All our desert, we own, is hell. But God loves us freely. Therefore we ask him to *give* what we can no more *procure* for ourselves than we can *merit* it at his hands" (3.12). The doxology concludes in the same tone: to God belongs "the sovereign right of all things that are or ever were created," the executive power that governs "all things," for which "praise [is] due from every creature" (3.16; see Blevins, "'On Earth'").

True to his and brother Charles's fashion, John ends his sermon with a hymnic paraphrase that underscores a final motif. Although God's love, as such, is not explicit in the Lord's Prayer, Wesley cannot sing of it without giving thanks for that love, as these excerpts indicate:

> Father of all, whose powerful voice
> Called forth this universal frame,
> Whose mercies over all rejoice,
> Through endless ages still the same:
>
> Thou by thy word upholdest all;
> Thy bounteous LOVE to all is showed,
> Thou hear'st thy every creature call,
> And fillest every mouth with good. . . .
>
> Wisdom, and might, and love are thine,
> Prostrate before thy face we fall,
> Confess thine attributes divine,
> And hail the sovereign Lord of all. . . .
>
> Son of thy sire's eternal love,
> Take to thyself thy mighty power;
> Let all earth's sons thy mercy prove,
> Let all thy bleeding grace adore. . . .
>
> Inflame our hearts with perfect love,
> In us the work of faith fulfill;
> So not heaven's hosts shall swifter move
> Than we on earth to do thy will. . . .
>
> To every soul (all praise to thee!)
> Our bowels of compassion move:
> And all mankind by this may see
> God is in us; for God is love.
>   (Sermon 3.16; cf. 1 John 4:7–12)

309

George Bernard Shaw (1856–1950)
versus
Gilbert Keith Chesterton (1874–1936)

The Irish playwright (Shaw) and the English litterateur (Chesterton) were famously friendly adversaries. In a letter to Gilbert Murray (1866–1957), the inspiration for "Adolphus Cusins" in Shaw's *Major Barbara* (1905), Shaw articulates his own religious views as a parody of the Lord's Prayer:

> Our blunderer which art not in heaven, blessed be thy excellent intentions, hurry up with thy kingdom which is so long coming, get thy job done on earth which will then be heaven. Give us this day our daily vitality; and forgive us our trespasses as we forgive yours, knowing that you mean well. Lead us into all sorts of temptations, and never say die; for thine is the impulse and the gumption and the glory, world without end. Amen. (Albert, "Lord's Prayer," 107)

Sidney Albert, a specialist in Shavian criticism, argues that a lot of Shaw's theology is conveyed in that comic travesty, which was imported into *Major Barbara*: the tale of a Salvation Army officer, disillusioned by her shelter's acceptance of a handsome donation from her father, a munitions mogul. In the play's climax Barbara leaves the Army shelter, decides to redirect her preaching away from London's slum dwellers toward its factory workers, and confesses a newfound, Promethean faith in meliorism to her fiancé, Adolphus:

> [*She is transfigured.*] I have got rid of the bribe of bread. I have got rid of the bribe of heaven. Let God's work be done for its own sake: the work he had to create us to do because it cannot be done except by living men and women. When I die, let him be in my debt, not I in his; and let me forgive him as becomes a woman of my rank. (Shaw, *Plays* 3.184)

Newly converted to a courageous socialism, Barbara dedicates herself to humanity's striving for divinity: the life force of the human will to bring a limited, piteous God into realization.

310

Predictably, the themes of *Major Barbara* left G. K. Chesterton discontented. He interpreted Barbara's decision for "materialistic pessimism" as incoherent with Shaw's own aspirations.

The point of this particular drama is that even the noblest enthusiasm of a girl who becomes a Salvation Army officer fails under the brute money power of her father who is a modern capitalist. . . . For [Shaw's] serious faith is in the sanctity of the human will, in the divine capacity for creation and choice rising higher than environment and doom; and so far as that goes, *Major Barbara* is not only apart from his faith but against his faith. *Major Barbara* is an account of environment victorious over heroic will. (Chesterton, *Collected Works* 11.458)

The deeper problem, in Chesterton's diagnosis, is a radical confusion about God that would bestir Shaw to lampoon the Lord's Prayer into such a lightweight farce.

I must frankly say that Bernard Shaw always seems to me to use the word God not only without any idea of what it means, but without one moment's thought about what it could possibly mean. He said to some atheist, "Never believe in a God that you cannot improve on." The atheist (being a sound theologian) naturally replied that one should not believe in a God whom one could improve on; as that would show that he was not God. In the same style in *Major Barbara* the heroine ends by suggesting that she will serve God without personal hope, so that she may owe nothing to God and He may owe everything to her. It does not seem to strike her that if God owes everything to her He is not God. These things affect me as merely tedious perversions of a phrase. It is as if you said, "I will never have a father unless I have begotten him." (Chesterton, *Collected Works* 11.457)

Evelyn Underhill (1875–1941)

A lifelong Anglican, Underhill exercised a capacious mind that in different seasons of her life was informed by atheism, Neoplatonism, modernism, pacifism, and Catholic mysticism of the high Middle Ages. She published verse, short stories, novels, and twenty-two volumes on religious subjects, including *Mysticism* (1911), the work for which she was most celebrated and remains best remembered. Underhill was the first woman invited by Oxford University as an honorary speaker (the Upton Lectures, 1921); was named a fellow of King's College, London (1927); and was widely engaged as a print and radio journalist. Toward her life's end *Abba: Meditations*

311

Based on the Lord's Prayer (1940) originated in a retreat conducted in Essex (1935).

Following paths laid down in *Worship* (1936), while drawing on both Roman and Russian Orthodox liturgy, *Abba* concentrated less on private experience and more on corporate worship, adoring God for his own sake and loving all creatures in God. The seven clauses of the Lord's Prayer become "seven moments in a single act of communion, seven doors opening upon 'the world that is unwalled'" (*Abba*, 5). Addressing "our Father," Christians accede to "the source alike of our hope and our penitence; the standard which confounds us, the essence of religion, the whole of prayer" (13); the living church accepts membership in the whole human family, renouncing all claims to private advantage and every violation of the law of Charity (14–15). The hallowing of God's name is "selfless adoration" (6) that transcends mere aspiration to sacramental expression in all we do: "peaceful suffering, patient and inconspicuous devotion to uncongenial tasks, the steady fight against sin, ugliness, squalor, and disease, the cleansing of national thought and increase of brotherhood among men" (25).

To pray for the kingdom's coming is no empty wish for utopian social justice; it is, rather, our confession that "the world is not saved by evolution, but by incarnation," not by admirable causes but by Eternal Charity transfiguring the natural order (30). "'Thy will be done' means always being ready for God's sudden No over against our eager and well-meaning Yes" (43): a suppleness of the soul, "a deep and disciplined love" that responds "peacefully, joyfully, and perfectly" as Heaven is so governed (47).

The prayer for food draws no distinction between the gifts of daily nourishment and the Bread of Life; on both we depend; in both the mystery of the incarnation is disclosed (52, 58). "Every soul that appeals for God's forgiveness is required to move over to His side, and share the compassionate understanding, the unmeasured pity, with which he looks on human frailty and sin" (65). The cry for prevenient care recognizes everything in our conflicted lives that might "twist [us] away from Holiness," praying that God's energetic grace may strengthen our feeble will and harmonize it with God's own (77).

312   The final acclamation of God's glory acquires poignancy in Underhill's own experience: only months away from her own death, debilitated by illness and anguish over the Second World War, and

"speaking within the agony and bewilderment of life" (86), she knelt beside Elijah on Carmel (1 Kgs. 19:9–12) and Jesus in Gethsemane (Mark 14:32–42):

> Behind every closed door which seems to shut experience from us [God] is standing; and within every experience which reaches us, however disconcerting, His unchanging presence is concealed. . . . The last phase of prayer carries the soul forward to an entire self-oblivion, an upward and outward glance of awestruck worship which is yet entinctured with an utter and childlike trust. (86–87)

Karl Barth (1886–1968)

Although its petitions are interwoven throughout his *Church Dogmatics*, especially in the posthumously published volume (4/4), *The Christian Life*, Barth's most intensive consideration of the Lord's Prayer comes to us in a series of lectures delivered in Neuchâtel during 1947 and 1949. Repeatedly referring to the exegeses of Luther and Calvin, Barth's exposition is lovingly couched in their traditions (*Prayer*, 3–21, trans. Terrien, here and throughout). Barth begins by observing, "Prayer is a grace, an offer of God" (13), specifically God's self-offering through Jesus Christ, who taught us to pray in this particular way:

> God is the Father of Jesus Christ, and that very man Jesus Christ has prayed, and is praying still. . . . It is as if God himself has pledged to answer our request because all our prayers are summed up in Jesus Christ; God cannot fail to answer, since it is Jesus Christ who prays. . . . In the Lord's Prayer . . . God himself teaches us how we are to pray. . . . [And] in order that our act may become true prayer, we must accept the offer that God tenders us. . . . God wishes us to live with him, and we on our side reply, "Yes, Father, I wish to live with thee." And then he says, "Pray [in this way], call me; I am listening to you. I shall live and reign with you." (14, 17, 20–21; see also *CD* 3/3:268)

Beyond its christological grounding, Barth emphasizes other aspects of the Prayer. One is its universality. While the Prayer is obviously one by which Jesus taught his disciples to model their prayers (*Prayer*, 23), the "us" implied in the address to "Our Father"

313

is "the communion of all humanity praying with Jesus Christ, our existence in the fellowship of the children of God" (22; also 44–45; CD 4/4:76). "We are also in communion with those who do not yet pray, perhaps, but for whom Jesus Christ prays, since he prays for humankind as a whole" (*Prayer*, 23). Christians, then, are proxies for those who do not pray, "in the same manner as Jesus Christ has entered into solidarity with sinners, with a lost human race," for Jesus' disciples, too, are "without power, without merit, without proper faith, and empty-handed" (23).

Another element is stressed by Barth: by these petitions we pray for the completion of that which has already been effected (*CD* 3/3:49). Already God's name is hallowed: "This prayer then is answered before we formulate it" (*Prayer*, 32). So also the kingdom, which in Christmas, Good Friday, Easter, and Pentecost has already come. "They are all that has happened and is behind us" (37), yet "the future must bear marks of the past, our past must become our future, and the Lord who has come must come again" (38). The will of the eternal God has been done, will be done, and will unfold itself in time as it is being done ceaselessly in heaven (41–42). So too, the last three petitions: even before we ask, God has already supplied us bread earthly and celestial (47–51), has already granted us his pardon (56), has already snatched us from the devil's jaws, an evil from which we have neither the strength nor the intelligence nor the piety with which to preserve ourselves (59–64).

A third accent lies on the prayer's internal coherence. "All our entreaties presuppose that we ask to participate in God's cause" (27): for the hallowed name, the coming kingdom, the fulfillment of divine will. "We must have ground on which to walk, and in prayer we walk on the ground of these first three petitions" (27). They are like sighs, uttered by those dazzled by God's grandeur (43). The last three petitions—for bread, forgiveness, and rescue—are direct, active, even audacious (45), spoken with the confidence that "God participates in our affairs and in our needs, in our cares and in our distresses, in our expectations, in everything" (29). Compartmentalization of God's cause and our own is illusory, provided that, in Christ, our cause is being united with and comprehended within God's (29–30). Although the closing doxology is textually inauthentic, "these final words encompass the whole prayer" (65).

314

Don E. Saliers perceptively observes that Barth's exposition of the Lord's Prayer comprises "an entire theology oriented toward prayer and worship" ("Prayer and Theology," xix). The evidence for this lies in Barth's own summary of the Lord's Prayer:

> We say: "Our Father, here we are just as thou findest us, exactly as we are, and, it well seems, in the state in which thou desirest to meet us. Here we are, engrossed in thy cause (we presume that our prayer is in earnest), kindled by the ardent desire to see thy name hallowed. We have no other task; this is our care. It is not a question of being able to help ourselves. Any preoccupation of this kind could only be infidelity, disloyalty, disobedience. Therefore, to thee we hand over our existence—to thee, who hast invited and commanded us to pray, to live for thy cause. Here we are. It is now up to thee to concern thyself with our human cause." (45–46; cf. *CD* 4/4:89)

Ernst Lohmeyer (1890–1946)

If anyone may be honored as grandparent of twentieth-century commentary on the Lord's Prayer, it is Ernst Lohmeyer. The format of his presentation is conventional yet logical: after addressing "preliminary questions" of tradition, occasion, and form (*Lord's Prayer*, 13–31), Lohmeyer considers the prayer's address (32–62), its discrete clauses (63–229), and the closing doxology (230–46). Careful comparison of the prayer's alternative Gospel forms is drawn (247–70), the deviations between them attributed to "changes in the eschatological approach in different groups of communities" (258, trans. Bowden, here and throughout). A concluding chapter (271–99) examines the prayer's internal unity and theological basis, the kind of community implied and created by its petitions, the Matthean and Lukan differences as functions of discernible streams within primitive Christianity, and the prayer's anchorage in "the historical work and preaching of Jesus" (299).

With Lohmeyer we cross the threshold into classical historical criticism, of a kind not entirely representative of German scholarship practiced by his contemporaries. Typical of his time, Lohmeyer is overconfident in identifying provenances of the prayer based on subtle linguistic differentiae: thus, Matthew's dialect points to a Galilean milieu, while Luke's "West-Aramaic language" betokens its Jerusalem origin (27–31, 294–95). Slicing the pastrami so fine, such arguments have not been upheld by subsequent investigation. That,   315 however, is a trivial cavil when placed alongside Lohmeyer's undeniable achievements. First, his scholarship is consummate and capacious, steeped in patristic as well as in biblical thought. Second, he was among his era's pioneers in giving the text's eschatological vision its due: "The whole of this prayer is hope and longing for the day of consummation" (277). Nevertheless, Lohmeyer underlined important points at which the prayer's apocalypticism deviates from other species of its time (276–84). Third, in page after page and with bracing clarity, his commentary elucidates the theological implications of a formidable historical criticism. One example of its profundity:

> [The prayer's] first petition begins with God's innermost being, the second moves on to the external kingdom or action of God, and the third ends with the existing world, heaven and earth. As a result, these petitions lie almost like concentric circles round the one point, the address, "Our Father, who art in heaven." The event of eschatological consummation for which all petitions pray shines out over increasingly extensive areas and with ever-increasing strength; the third petition ["Thy will be done"] gives the final and extreme boundary. (131)

Finally, Lohmeyer situates the prayer "on the firm and never repudiated foundation of the Old Testament" (281–82) and its extensions into Pharisaic and rabbinic thought. This decision was historically sound, a welcome relief from centuries of anti-Jewish exposition of the Prayer, and dangerous in Germany of the 1930s and 1940s (Edwards, "Ernst Lohmeyer"). Having written Martin Buber in 1933 that "the Christian faith is Christian only as long as it holds in its heart the Jewish faith" (Köhn, *Ernst Lohmeyer*, 298), Lohmeyer rejected fascist *Nationalsozialismus*. For this he was relieved by the Nazis of the prestigious rectorship of Breslau University and reassigned to the comparative backwaters of Greifswald. On February 15, 1946, the night before that university's official postwar reopening, Lohmeyer was arrested and whisked away by the Soviet military police. For twelve years thereafter his family could confirm no details of his whereabouts. In late 1957 it was confirmed that the KGB had executed Lohmeyer on September 19, 1946 (Köhn, *Ernst Lohmeyer*, 140). Posthumously published (1946), *Das Vater-Unser* was the first of his works to be translated into English (*Lord's Prayer*, 1965). It remains a magnificent specimen of biblical scholarship, the one among hundreds consulted for the present volume that this author wishes he had possessed the wit and the courage to write.

Aldous Huxley (1894–1963)

Best known for his dystopian novel *Brave New World* (1932), Huxley was a prolific essayist who published three "Reflections on the Lord's Prayer" (1945; anthologized in *Huxley and God*, 140–61) that constitute an amalgam of his tempered humanism and religious universalism. These "reflections" are not discursive; they are tightly argued and proceed clause by clause, sometimes word by word. While not averse to either Christianity's figures (Christ and Lucifer: 152, 159) or saints (Bernard of Clairvaux: 141, 143; Catherine of Siena: 150), Huxley writes as a philosopher attempting to plumb the Prayer's religious bearing for all humankind. He regards as "the central truth of all spiritual religion [and] the major premise of the Lord's Prayer" an assertion by Cardinal Pierre de Bérulle (1575–1629): "Man is a nothing surrounded by God, indigent of God, capable of God, and filled with God if he so desires" (159). God "is the universal source and principle, the being of all beings, the life of all that lives, the spirit of every soul" (140–41), whose "fatherhood"—begetting, supportive, educating, loving, punishing—is in itself unknowable "until we have fitted ourselves for the beatific vision of divine reality" (143) that goes by many names: "heaven" (144), "the kingdom of God" (148–50), timeless eternity (148–49), the resolution of Buddhist samsara into nirvana (144, 148).

The hallowing of God's name is an affirmation of God as "the highest, most real good," to whose service alone "we should dedicate our lives" (146). This "living experience of reality" is prerequisite for achieving the Prayer's other aims (147). Thus, doing God's will is "doing what is necessary to fit ourselves for the grace of enlightenment" (149). Asking for daily bread expresses our reliance on God's grace in human space-time, for "the nature of grace is such that it can only come now, to those who are ready to live in the eternal present" (153). Like repentance and humility, forgiveness is a giving up of the egoistic life, thereby to some extent transforming the world around us into a realm less evil and more compassionate (154–58). "[We] modify for the better the destinies unfolding around [us] by inspiring the makers of these destinies

317

with the wish and the power to give" of themselves (158). Deliverance from evil and concession of God's glory are two sides of one coin: because only God may be worshiped and loved beyond all else (160), evil consists "in acting upon the insane and criminal belief" that God's kingdom, power, and glory are ours (158). Until we realize that "God is everything and man, as man, is nothing, . . . so long as we remain average, sensual, unregenerate individuals, we shall constantly be tempted to think God-excluding thoughts and perform God-excluding actions" (158–59).

Huxley's exposition is a curious blend of orthodoxy and heresy. For him the Lord's Prayer exposes modernity's "heretical anthropocentricism or, as we now prefer to call it, 'humanism'" (161), which trumpets heroic individualism (149) and prideful will (150) while disguising the spiritually warped and morally degenerate character of self-preoccupied egoism (142, 150, 152, 156). On the other hand, he remains wedded to a Stoic anthropology: "God . . . is *ours*, immanently in every soul and transcendently as that universal principle in which we love and move and have our being" (141, with original emphasis). Within every human soul lies "the latent and potential seed of reality . . . [that] may become fully actualized" (160). What is the medium of such actualization? For Huxley it is "spiritual religion" (147), an enlightenment (150, 154) of "mystical insight into reality" (143). Who are its mediators? "All the great religious teachers of the world" (155, 160), "all the great spiritual teachers of history" (152), "the contemplative saints" (148, 152): "the mystic"—like Christ, "a supremely enlightened being" (160)—"[who] is able to live uninterruptedly in the presence of God" (144). By their example, "making oneself fit to receive grace, . . . the enlightened person transforms not merely himself, but to some extent the world around him" (158)—just as precursory mystagogues have done for him. Whether Huxley's interpretation finally escapes the solipsism it castigates is a good question. In any event, what is most obviously missing from his reading of the Lord's Prayer is the Lord himself.

Works Cited in Appendix C

318   Albert, Sidney P. "The Lord's Prayer and *Major Barbara*." In *Shaw and Religion*, edited by Charles A. Berst, 107–28. University Park: Pennsylvania State University Press, 1981.

Arand, Charles P. "The Battle Cry of Faith: The Catechisms' Exposition of the Lord's Prayer." *Concordia Journal* 21 (1995): 42–65.

Augustine of Hippo. *The Lord's Sermon on the Mount*. Translated by John J. Epson, SS. Ancient Christian Writers 5. New York: Paulist Press, 1948.

Ayo, Nicholas. *The Lord's Prayer: A Survey Theological and Literary*. Lanham, MD: Rowman & Littlefield, 1992.

Barnes, Corey. "Thomas Aquinas on Christ's Prayer." In *A History of Prayer: The First to the Fifteenth Century*, edited by Roy Hammerling, 319–36. Brill's Companions to the Christian Tradition 13. Leiden: E. J. Brill, 2008.

Barth, Karl. *Church Dogmatics*. Vol. 3/3, *The Doctrine of Creation*. Edited and translated by Geoffrey W. Bromiley, R. J. Ehrlich, and Thomas F. Torrance. Edinburgh: T&T Clark, 1960.

———. *Church Dogmatics*. Vol. 4/4, *The Christian Life (Fragment)*. Edited and translated by Geoffrey W. Bromiley. Edinburgh: T&T Clark, 1960.

———. *Prayer: Fiftieth Anniversary Edition*. Edited by Don E. Saliers, from the translation by Sara F. Terrien. Louisville, KY: Westminster John Knox Press, 2002.

Blevins, Dean G. "'On Earth as (If) It Is in Heaven': Practicing a Liturgical Eschatology." *Wesleyan Theological Journal* 40 (2005): 69–92.

Bornkamm, Heinrich. *Luther and the Old Testament*. Translated by Eric W. and Ruth C. Gritsch. Edited by Victor I. Gruhn. Philadelphia: Fortress Press, 1969.

Bouhot, Jean-Paul. "La tradition catéchétique et exégétique du Pater Noster." *Recherches Augustiniennes* 33 (2003): 3–18.

Brown, Michael Joseph. *The Lord's Prayer through North African Eyes: A Window into Early Christianity*. New York: T&T Clark International, 2004.

———. "Piety and Proclamation: Gregory of Nyssa's Sermons on the Lord's Prayer." In *A History of Prayer: The First to the Fifteenth Century*, edited by Roy Hammerling, 79–116. Brill's Companions to the Christian Tradition 13. Leiden: E. J. Brill, 2008.

Bynum, Caroline Walker. *Jesus as Mother: Studies of Spirituality in the High Middle Ages*. Berkeley: University of California Press, 1982.

Calvin, John. *Institutes of the Christian Religion*. Vol. 2. Edited by John T. McNeill. Translated by Ford Lewis Battles. Library of Christian Classics 21. Philadelphia: Westminster Press, 1960.

Carmignac, Jean. *Recherches sur le "Notre Père."* Paris: Letouzey & Ané, 1969.

Cassian, John. *Conferences*. Translated by Colm Luibheid. Classics of Western Spirituality. New York: Paulist Press, 1985.

Chase, Frederick Henry. *The Lord's Prayer in the Early Church*. Cambridge: Cambridge University Press, 1891.

Chesterton, G. K. *The Collected Works of G. K. Chesterton*. Vol. 11, *Plays, Chesterton on Shaw*. Compiled and introduced by Denis J. Conlon. San Francisco: Ignatius Press, 1989.

Cunningham, Lawrence. "Origen's 'On Prayer': A Reflection and Appreciation." *Worship* 67 (1993): 332–39.

Ebner, Margaret. *Major Works*. Translated and edited by Leonard P. Hindsley. Classics of Western Spirituality. New York: Paulist Press, 1993.

Edwards, James R. "Ernst Lohmeyer—ein Schlußkapitel." *Evangelische Theologie* 56 (1996): 320–42.

Froehlich, Karlfried. "The Lord's Prayer in Patristic Literature." *Princeton Seminary Bulletin*, Supplementary Issue 2 (1992): 71–87.

Gregory of Nyssa. *The Lord's Prayer, The Beatitudes*. Translated and annotated by Hilda C. Graef. Ancient Christian Writers 18. New York: Paulist Press, 1954.

Hammerling, Roy. "Gregory of Nyssa's Sermons on the Lord's Prayer: Lessons from the Classics." *Word & World* 22 (2002): 64–70.

———, ed. *A History of Prayer: The First to the Fifteenth Century*. Brill's Companions to the Christian Tradition 13. Leiden: E. J. Brill, 2008.

———. "The Lord's Prayer: A Cornerstone of Early Baptismal Education." In Hammerling, *A History of Prayer*, 167–82.

Hand, Thomas A. *Augustine on Prayer*. New ed. New York: Catholic Book Publishing, 1986.

Harmless, William, SJ. *Augustine and the Catechumenate*. Collegeville, MN: Liturgical Press, 1995.

Hudson, Nancy, and Frank Tobin. "Nicholas of Cusa's Sermon on the *Pater Noster*." In *Cusanus: The Legacy of Learned Ignorance*, edited by Peter J. Casarella, 1–25. Washington, DC: Catholic University of America Press, 2006.

Huxley, Aldous. "Reflections on the Lord's Prayer: I, II, III." In *Huxley and God: Essays on Religious Experience*, edited by Jacqueline Hazard Bridgeman, 140–61. New York: Crossroad, 2003.

Jackson, M. G. St. A. "The Lord's Prayer in St. Augustine." In *Cappadocian Fathers, Greek Authors after Nicaea, Augustine, Donatism, and Pelagianism*, edited by Elizabeth A. Livingstone, 311–21. Studia Patristica 27. Leuven: Peeters, 1993.

John Chrysostom. "Homily 19 on Matthew 6:1–15." In *Chrysostom: Homilies on the Gospel of Saint Matthew*, in *Nicene and Post-Nicene Fathers*, 10:130–40. Edited by Philip Schaff. First Series. Peabody, MA: Hendrickson Publications, [1888] 1994.

Köhn, Andreas. *Der Neutestamentler Ernst Lohmeyer: Studien zu Biographie und Theologie*. Tübingen: Mohr Siebeck, 2004.

Lampe, Geoffrey. "'Our Father' in the Fathers." In *Christian Spirituality: Essays in Honour of Gordon Rupp*, edited by Peter Brooks, 9–31. London: SCM, 1975.

Leaver, Robin A. *Luther's Liturgical Music: Principles and Implications*. Lutheran Quarterly Books. Minneapolis: Fortress Press, 2017.

Lienhard, Marc. "Luther et Calvin: Commentateurs du Notre Père." *Revue d'Histoire et de Philosophie Religieuses* 72 (1992): 73–88.

Lohmeyer, Ernst. *"Our Father": An Introduction to the Lord's Prayer.* Translated by John Bowden. London: William Collins & Sons; New York: Harper & Row, 1965.

Luther, Martin. "An Exposition of the Lord's Prayer for Simple Laymen." In *Devotional Writings I*, translated by Martin H. Bertram, edited by Gustav K. Wiencke, in *Luther's Works: American Edition*, 42:15–81. Philadelphia: Fortress Press, 1968.

———. *The Large Catechism of Martin Luther*. Translated by Robert H. Fischer. Philadelphia: Fortress Press, 1959.

———. *Luther's Spirituality*. Edited and translated by Philip D. W. Krey and Peter D. S. Krey. Classics of Western Spirituality. New York: Paulist Press, 2007.

———. *Luthers Werke. Tischreden, 1531–46*. Vol. 1. Weimar: Böhlau, 1912.

———. *Luther's Works: American Edition*. Vol. 21, *The Sermon on the Mount (Sermons) and The Magnificat*. Translated and edited by Jarsolav Pelikan. Saint Louis: Concordia, 1956.

321

————. "Preface to the Psalter 1545 (1528)." In *Word and Sacrament I*, edited by E. Thomas Bachmann and Helmut T. Lehmann, in *Luther's Works: American Edition*, 35:253–57. Philadelphia: Muhlenburg Press/Fortress Press, 1960.

————. *A Short Explanation of Dr. Martin Luther's Small Catechism: A Handbook of Christian Doctrine*. Rev. ed. Saint Louis: Concordia, 1965.

————. "A Simple Way to Pray." In *Devotional Writings II*, translated by Carl J. Schindler, edited by Gustav K. Wiencke, in *Luther's Works: American Edition*, 43:187–211. Philadelphia: Fortress Press, 1968.

————. *Table Talk*. Translated by William Hazlitt. Fount Classics: Spiritual Direction. London: HarperCollins, 1995.

Madden, Nicholas. "Maximus Confessor: On the Lord's Prayer." In *Scriptural Interpretation in the Fathers: Letter and Spirit*, edited by Thomas Finan and Vincent Twomey, 119–41. Cambridge: Four Courts, 1995.

Marty, Martin E. *The Hidden Discipline*. St. Louis: Concordia, 1962.

Maschke, Timothy. "St. Augustine's Theology of Prayer: Gracious Conformation." In *Augustine: Presbyter Factus Sum*, edited by Joseph C. Leinhard, Earl C. Muller, and Ronald J. Teske, 431–46. Collectanea Augustiniana. New York: Peter Lang, 1993.

Maximus Confessor. "Commentary on the Our Father." In *Maximus Confessor: Selected Writings*, translated and annotated by George C. Berthold, 99–125. Classics of Western Spirituality. New York: Paulist Press, 1985.

McKee, Elsie Anne. "John Calvin's Teaching on the Lord's Prayer." *Princeton Seminary Bulletin*, Supplementary Issue 2 (1992): 88–106.

————. *Katharina Schütz Zell*. Vol. 2, *The Writings: A Critical Edition*. Studies in Medieval and Reformation Thought 69.2. Leiden: E. J. Brill, 1999.

————. "Katharina Schütz Zell and the 'Our Father.'" In *Oratio: Das Gebet in patrischer und reformatorischer Sicht*, edited by Emidio Campi, Leif Grane, and Adolf Martin Ritter, 239–47. Forschungen zur Kirchen- und Dogmengeschichte 76. Göttingen: Vandenhoeck & Ruprecht, 1999.

Murray, Paul. *Praying with Confidence: Aquinas on the Lord's Prayer*. London: Continuum, 2010.

Nestingen, James Arne. "The Lord's Prayer in Luther's Catechism." *Word & World* 22 (2002): 36–48.

Nicholas of Cusa: Selected Spiritual Writings. Translated and introduced by H. Lawrence Bond. Classics of Western Spirituality. New York: Paulist Press, 1997.

Niederwimmer, Kurt. *The Didache: A Commentary.* Translated by Linda Maloney. Edited by Harold W. Attridge. Minneapolis: Fortress Press, 1998.

Nodes, Daniel J. "A Witness to Theosis Effected: Maximus Confessor on the Lord's Prayer." *St Vladimir's Theological Quarterly* 54 (2010): 69–83.

Peers, E. Allison, ed. *Way of Perfection: Saint Teresa of Avila.* London: Sheed & Ward, 1999.

Peters, Albrecht. *Commentary on Luther's Catechisms: Lord's Prayer.* Translated by Daniel Thies. Saint Louis: Concordia, 2011.

The Pilgrim's Tale. Edited by Aleskei Pentkovsky. Translated by T. Allan Smith. Classics of Western Spirituality. New York: Paulist Press, 1999.

Robinson, Paul W. "Sermons on the Lord's Prayer and the Rogation Days in the Later Middle Ages." In *A History of Prayer: The First to the Fifteenth Century*, edited by Roy Hammerling, 441–62. Brill's Companions to the Christian Tradition 13. Leiden: E. J. Brill, 2008.

Rordorf, Willy. "The Lord's Prayer in the Light of the Liturgical Use in the Early Church." *Studia Liturgica* 14 (1980/81): 1–19.

Roth, Dieter T. "The Text of the Lord's Prayer in Marcion's Gospel." *Zeitschrift für die neutestamentliche Wissenschaft und die Kunde der Älteren Kirche* 103 (2012): 47–63.

Saliers, Don E. "Prayer and Theology in Karl Barth." In *Prayer: Fiftieth Anniversary Edition*, edited by Don E. Saliers, from the translation by Sara F. Terrien, ix–xx. Louisville, KY: Westminster John Knox Press, 2002.

Shaw, George Bernard. *George Bernard Shaw's Plays.* Norton Critical Editions. 2nd ed. Edited by Sandie Byrne. New York: W. W. Norton & Co., 2002.

Stevenson, Kenneth W. *The Lord's Prayer: A Text in Tradition.* London: SCM Press, 2004.

Taft, Robert F., SJ. *The Liturgy of the Hours in East and West: The Origins of the Divine Office and Its Meaning Today.* Collegeville, MN: Liturgical Press, 1986.

Tertullian, Cyprian, and Origen: On the Lord's Prayer. Translated and annotated by Alistair Stewart-Sykes. Popular Patristics Series. Crestwood, NY: St Vladimir's Seminary Press, 2004.

Thomas Aquinas. "From the Lectures on Saint Matthew"; "Prayer: *Summa Theologiae* II-II Question 83." In *Albert and Thomas: Selected Writings*, translated, edited, and introduced by Simon Tugwell, 445–519. Classics of Western Spirituality. New York: Paulist Press, 1988.

Underhill, Evelyn. *Abba: Meditations based on the Lord's Prayer.* London: Longmans, Green & Co., 1940.

Wesley, John. "Sermon 26: Upon our Lord's Sermon on the Mount. Discourse the Sixth: Matthew 6:1–15." In *The Works of John Wesley*, vol. 1, *Sermons I: 1–33*, edited by Albert Outler, 572–91. Nashville: Abingdon Press, 1984.

Williams, Rowan. *Teresa of Avila.* Outstanding Christian Thinkers. London: Geoffrey Chapman; Harrisburg, PA: Morehouse, 1991.

INDEX OF SCRIPTURE AND OTHER ANCIENT SOURCES

336

337

344

INDEX OF SUBJECTS

Italicized page numbers indicate tables.

349

357